# Journal of Narrative and Life History

Volume 7, Numbers 1–4

---

Introductory Note . . . . . . . . . . . . . . . . . . . . . . . . . . . . . . . . . . 1
*Michael G. W. Bamberg*

Narrative Analysis: Oral Versions of Personal Experience . . . . . . . . . . . . . . . 3
*William Labov and Joshua Waletzky*

Narratology and Narratological Analysis . . . . . . . . . . . . . . . . . . . . . . 39
*Gerald Prince*

Labov and Waletzky in Context . . . . . . . . . . . . . . . . . . . . . . . . . . . 45
*Cynthia Bernstein*

From Labov and Waletzky to "Contextualist Narratology": 1967–1997 . . . . . . . . 53
*Joyce Tolliver*

Labov and Waletzky, Thirty Years On . . . . . . . . . . . . . . . . . . . . . . . . 61
*Jerome Bruner*

A Matter of Time: When, Since, After Labov and Waletzky . . . . . . . . . . . . . 69
*Elliot G. Mishler*

Dualisms in the Study of Narrative: A Note on Labov and Waletzky . . . . . . . . . 75
*Paul J. Hopper*

Narrative Authenticity . . . . . . . . . . . . . . . . . . . . . . . . . . . . . . . . 83
*Elinor Ochs and Lisa Capps*

Struggling Beyond Labov and Waletzky . . . . . . . . . . . . . . . . . . . . . . . 91
*Janet Holmes*

"Narrative Analysis" Thirty Years Later . . . . . . . . . . . . . . . . . . . . . . . 97
*Emanuel A. Schegloff*

Toward Families of Stories in Context . . . . . . . . . . . . . . . . . . . . . . . 107
*Marjorie Harness Goodwin*

*(Continued)*

Narrative Structure and Conversational Circumstances . . . . . . . . . . . . . . . . 113
  *Aylin Küntay and Susan Ervin-Tripp*

Were You Ever in a Situation Where You Were in Serious Danger of
Being Killed? Narrator–Listener Interaction in
Labov and Waletzky's Narratives . . . . . . . . . . . . . . . . . . . . . . . . . . . 121
  *Uta M. Quasthoff*

Stories in Answer to Questions in Research Interviews . . . . . . . . . . . . . . . 129
  *Deborah Schiffrin*

Structure and Function in the Analysis of Everyday Narratives . . . . . . . . . . . 139
  *Derek Edwards*

Intertextuality and the Narrative of Personal Experience . . . . . . . . . . . . . . 147
  *Deborah Keller-Cohen and Judy Dyer*

A Short Story About Long Stories . . . . . . . . . . . . . . . . . . . . . . . . . . 155
  *Catherine Kohler Riessman*

The "Labovian Model" Revisited With Special Consideration of
Literary Narrative . . . . . . . . . . . . . . . . . . . . . . . . . . . . . . . . . . . 159
  *Suzanne Fleischman*

Why Narrative? Hermeneutics, Historical Understanding, and the
Significance of Stories . . . . . . . . . . . . . . . . . . . . . . . . . . . . . . . . 169
  *Mark Freeman*

Sequentiality and Temporalization in the Narrative Construction of a
South American Cholera Epidemic . . . . . . . . . . . . . . . . . . . . . . . . . . 177
  *Charles L. Briggs*

Speakers, Listeners, and Speech Events in Issues of Universality . . . . . . . . . . 185
  *Courtney B. Cazden*

Thematized Echoes . . . . . . . . . . . . . . . . . . . . . . . . . . . . . . . . . . 189
  *James Paul Gee*

Beyond Labov and Waletzky: The Antecedents of Narrative Discourse . . . . . . . 197
  *Catherine E. Snow and Alison Imbens-Bailey*

Making Sense of the Sense-Making Function of Narrative Evaluation . . . . . . . . 207
  *Colette Daiute and Katherine Nelson*

*(Continued)*

The Mutual Construction of Narrative by Mothers and Children:
Cross-Cultural Observations . . . . . . . . . . . . . . . . . . . . . . . . . . . . . . 217
*Jean Berko Gleason and Gigliana Melzi*

Frog Stories From Four-Year-Olds: Individual Differences in the
Expression of Referential and Evaluative Content . . . . . . . . . . . . . . . . . . . . 223
*Erika Hoff-Ginsberg*

How to Read the Work of a Child: A Tribute to Labov and Waletzky . . . . . . . . 229
*Susan Engel*

Narrative Theory and Narrative Development: The Labovian Impact . . . . . . . . . 235
*Ruth A. Berman*

Narrative Units and the Temporal Organization of Ordinary Discourse . . . . . . . . 245
*Björn Wiemer*

Extending Labov and Waletzky . . . . . . . . . . . . . . . . . . . . . . . . . . . . . 251
*Carole Peterson and Allyssa McCabe*

Some Observations on Narratives by Aphasics and
Their Contributions to Narrative Theory . . . . . . . . . . . . . . . . . . . . . . . . 259
*Hanna K. Ulatowska and Gloria Streit Olness*

The Role of Narrative in the Study of Language and Aging . . . . . . . . . . . . . 265
*Anne R. Bower*

Micro-Units and Macro-Units in Text Theory and in Investigations of
Left- and Right-Brain-Damaged Patients . . . . . . . . . . . . . . . . . . . . . . . 275
*Wolfgang U. Dressler and Heinz Karl Stark*

Narrative: Experience, Memory, Folklore . . . . . . . . . . . . . . . . . . . . . . . 281
*Charlotte Linde*

Narrative Explanations: Accounting for Past Experiences in Interviews . . . . . . . 291
*Jenny Cook-Gumperz and John J. Gumperz*

Construing Experience: Some Story Genres . . . . . . . . . . . . . . . . . . . . . . 299
*J. R. Martin and G. Plum*

Labov's Model of Narrative Analysis as an
Emerging Study in Discourse . . . . . . . . . . . . . . . . . . . . . . . . . . . . . . 309
*Martha Shiro*

*(Continued)*

Social Characteristics and Self-Expression in Narrative . . . . . . . . . . . . . . . . . 315
    *Barbara Johnstone*

Literary Texts and the Violation of Narrative Norms . . . . . . . . . . . . . . . . . 321
    *Susan Ehrlich*

"He Lived to Tell the Tale" . . . . . . . . . . . . . . . . . . . . . . . . . . . . . . . 331
    *Rom Harré*

Positioning Between Structure and Performance . . . . . . . . . . . . . . . . . . . 335
    *Michael G. W. Bamberg*

When Sentences Are Not Enough: Narrative Data and Cultural Identity . . . . . . . 343
    *Alison Imbens-Bailey*

Everything *Including* Talk and Why You Hafta Listen . . . . . . . . . . . . . . . . 351
    *Richard Ely*

Talking With the Dead: Self-Construction as Dialogue . . . . . . . . . . . . . . . . 359
    *Ingrid E. Josephs*

Labov's Legacy for Narrative Research—and Its Ironies . . . . . . . . . . . . . . . 369
    *Ageliki Nicolopoulou*

Analyzing Stories of Moral Experience: Narrative, Voice, and the
Dialogical Self . . . . . . . . . . . . . . . . . . . . . . . . . . . . . . . . . . . . . 379
    *Mark B. Tappan*

Dialogue Shakes Narrative: From Temporal Storyline to
Spatial Juxtaposition . . . . . . . . . . . . . . . . . . . . . . . . . . . . . . . . . 387
    *Hubert J. M. Hermans*

Some Further Steps in Narrative Analysis . . . . . . . . . . . . . . . . . . . . . . . 395
    *William Labov*

# Introductory Note

## Michael G. W. Bamberg
*Department of Psychology, Clark University*

"Narrative Analysis: Oral Versions of Personal Experience" was originally presented by William Labov and Joshua Waletzky during the spring meeting of the American Ethnological Society in 1966 and published in 1967 in the proceedings, edited by June Helm under the title *Essays on the Verbal and Visual Arts*. We are able to reprint the original paper in this volume,[1] followed by 47 new contributions, which all take the original article by Labov and Waletzky as the springboard to reflect on narrative and narrative analysis. In this sense, the contributions to this volume are, first of all, a retrospective and an appreciation of the originality of the 30-year-old paper and its enormous influence on the emerging field of narrative (out of which this journal was born in 1990).

However, within the last 30 years many new orientations emerged that attempted to go beyond or above the framework and standards that seemed to be set for narrative analysis by Labov and Waletzky in 1967. Consequently, this volume also seeks to give ample opportunity to take critical stock of the last 30 years and to look forward toward new forms of narrative inquiry. As such, the contributions to this volume equally hold the balance between what enabled narrative inquiry over the last 30 years, what constrained it, and what can be learned from those enabling and constraining factors. It is a pleasure to present Bill Labov's concluding contribution to this volume, which is to be seen as one of those forward orienting voices.

The overwhelming response to our request to "celebrate" 30 years of narrative analysis—in line with the positive reaction to the format of blending brief analyses with critical reflection into a short contribution—led us to take this introductory note to invite more contributions along the same lines for future issues of *Narrative Inquiry*. We assume that this volume has opened up more hot spots than given answers to questions. This was and is the purpose of our journal, and we hope to be able to pursue exactly this for our readership in the future.

---

Requests for reprints should be sent to Michael Bamberg, Department of Psychology, Clark University, Worcester, MA 01610–1477. E-mail: mbamberg@clarku.edu.

[1] Thanks to the generosity of Charlie Piot on behalf of the American Ethnological Society

# Narrative Analysis: Oral Versions of Personal Experience[1]

### William Labov
*Columbia University*

### Joshua Waletzky
*Harvard University*

Most attempts to analyze narrative have taken as their subject matter the more complex products of long-standing literary or oral traditions. Myths, folk tales, legends, histories, epics, toasts, and sagas seem to be the results of the combination and evolution of simpler elements; they contain many cycles and recycles of basic narrative structures; in many cases, the evolution of a particular narrative has removed it so far from its originating function that it is difficult to say what its present function is.

In our opinion, it will not be possible to make very much progress in the analysis and understanding of these complex narratives until the simplest and most fundamental narrative structures are analyzed in direct connection with their originating functions. We suggest that such fundamental structures are to be found in oral versions of personal experiences: not the products of expert storytellers that have been retold many times, but the original production of a representative sample of the population. By examining the actual narratives of large numbers of unsophisticated speakers, it will be possible to relate the formal properties of narrative to their functions. By studying the development of narrative technique from children to adults, and the range of narrative techniques from lower-class to middle-class speakers, it will be possible to isolate the elements of narrative.

In this article, we will present an analytical framework for the analysis of oral versions of personal experience in English. We will first introduce definitions of the

---

Comments should be sent to William Labov, Linguistics Laboratory, University of Pennsylvania, 3550 Market Street, 2nd Floor, Philadelphia, PA 19104. E-mail: labov@central.cis.upcnn.edu

[1]This article was originally published in *Essays on the Verbal and Visual Arts: Proceedings of the 1996 Annual Spring Meeting of the American Ethnological Society* (pp. 12–44), edited by June Helm, Seattle: University of Washington Press. Copyright 1967 by University of Washington Press. Reprinted with permission.

basic units of narrative and then outline the normal structure of the narrative as a whole. Finally, we present some general propositions about the relation of formal properties to narrative functions, based on our examination of a moderate body of data.

The analysis will be *formal,* based upon recurrent patterns characteristic of narrative from the clause level to the complete simple narrative. We will rely upon the basic techniques of linguistic analysis, isolating the invariant structural units, which are represented by a variety of superficial forms. From this analysis it is possible to derive a considerable amount of information on the syntax and semantics of English below the sentence level, but this direction of research will not be exploited here. We will be concerned primarily with the characteristics of narrative itself.

The analysis is *functional:* Narrative will be considered as one verbal technique for recapitulating experience—in particular, a technique of constructing narrative units that match the *temporal sequence* of that experience. Furthermore, we find that narrative that serves this function alone is abnormal: it may be considered empty or pointless narrative. Normally, narrative serves an additional function of personal interest, determined by a stimulus in the social context in which the narrative occurs. We therefore distinguish two functions of narrative: (a) *referential* and (b) *evaluative.*

In most previous studies of folk narrative, the basic unit for analysis has been a substantial piece of thematic material, defined at various levels of abstraction by the type of action referred to. Thus the work of Propp (1958) was devoted to the formal structure of such large semantic units. The present study assumes as a basic task the analysis of narratives that might appear as fundamental, unanalyzable units in Propp's scheme. We will be concerned with the smallest unit of linguistic expression that defines the functions of narrative—primarily the clause, although we will refer to cases where phrases and words are relevant to evaluative function. Colby's work (1966) took as data the frequencies of individual words according to a semantic subcategorization; a linguistic approach is quite opposite in direction, focusing upon the syntagmatic structure of words and phrases operating in clauses and higher levels of organization. Schatzman and Strauss (1955) studied class differences in narrative technique by informal means; it is hoped that the methods developed in the present discussion will permit a more reliable and objective approach to studies of this type.

We will be dealing with tape-recorded narratives taken from two distinct social contexts. One is a face-to-face interview where the narrator is speaking only to the interviewer, a person not a member of a narrator's primary group. In the second situation, the narrator is recorded in interaction with his primary group; he is speaking in part to the members of his group, and in part to an outsider on the margins of the group, who provides only a part of the stimulus for the narrative.

The following pages provide 14 examples of the data on hand, drawn from about 600 interviews gathered in the course of four linguistic studies.[2] The narrators include speakers from Black and White communities, rural and urban areas, and they range in age from 10 to 72 years old. In one respect the range is limited: There are no highly educated speakers represented here; in fact, none of the narrators finished high school.

The ultimate aims of our work, require close correlations of the narrator's social characteristics with the structure of their narratives, since we are concerned with problems of effective communication and class and ethnic differences in verbal behavior.[3] In this article, however, we are concerned with the narratives themselves, and so these fourteen examples appear as anonymous narrations, arranged in descending order of the speakers' ages.

Narrative 1
(Were you ever in a situation where you thought you were in serious danger of getting killed?) I talked a man out of—Old Doc Simon I talked him out of pulling the trigger. (What happened?)

Well, in the business I was associated at that time, the Doc was an old man ... He had killed one man, or—had done time. But he had a—young wife, and those days I dressed well. And seemingly she was trying to make me.

I never noticed it. Fact is, I didn't like her very well, because she had—she was a nice looking girl until you saw her feet. She had big feet. Jesus, God, she had big feet!

Then she left a note one day she was going to commit suicide because he was always raising hell about me. He came to my hotel. Nice big blue 44, too.

I talked him out of it; and says, "Well, we'll go look for her, and if we can't find her, well you can—go ahead, pull the trigger if you want to." I was maneuvering.

So he took me up on it. And we went to where they found her handkerchief—the edge of a creek—and we followed down a little more, and we

---

[2]The materials include: 70 interviews with speakers from various occupations, ethnic membership, and ages on Martha's Vineyard, Massachusetts; 230 interviews with speakers representing a stratified random sample of the Lower East Side of New York City; 250 interviews of children and adults from our current research in Central Harlem; and 50 interviews from exploratory work in Cleveland, Boston, Philadelphia, Chicago, Phoenix, and Beaufort County, South Carolina. The basic interview techniques are described in Labov (1964, 1966) and Labov, Cohen, and Robins (n.d.).

[3]In our current research in Central Harlem, we are concerned with the functional conflicts between standard English and the nonstandard English of Black and Puerto Rican children. Many of these children show great verbal ability in many areas, including the construction of narratives, but cannot read at all. One purpose of this work on narrative analysis is to show how children use language to carry out the functions that are important in their system of values.

couldn't find anything. And got back—it was a tent show—she was laying on a cot with an ice bag on her head. She hadn't committed suicide.

But—however—that settled it for the day. But that night the manager, Floyd Adams, said, "You better pack up and get out because that son of a bitch never forgives anything once he gets it in his head."

And I did. I packed up and got out. That was two.

That was two.

After I came out from New York ...

Narrative 2

I had dogs that could do everything but talk. And by gorry, sir, I never licked 'em.

(When you have small kids, they're always asking for one more thing, like a drink of water, to keep from going to bed at night. I wonder if you had that problem, and what you did about it?) Yeah, but—a lot of the children I've seen, that their excuse they've got to go to the bathroom, and they don't have to go at all. (How do you cope with it. You can't—you never know ... ) No. I don't remember how we coped with it. I never believed a whole lot in licking. I was never—with my children, and I never—when it was with my animals, dogs; I never licked a dog, I never had to. A dog knew what I meant; when I hollered at a dog, he knew the—what I meant. I could—I had dogs that could do everything but talk. And by gorry, sir, I never licked 'em.

I never come nearer bootin' a dog in my life. I had a dog—he was a wonderful retriever, but as I say he could do everything but talk. I could waif him that way, I could waif him on, I could waif him anywhere. If I shot a crippled duck he went out after it; he didn't see it in the water, he'd always turn around look at me, and I'd waif him over there, if the duck was there, or if it was on the other side of where we're on, I could waif him straight ahead, and he'd turn and he'd go. If he didn't see me, he'd turn around, he'd look at me, and I'd keep a-waifin' him on. And he'd finally catch sight of him, and the minute he did, you know, he would bee-line and get that duck.

I was gunnin' one night with that dog—we had to use live decoys in those days—a fellow named Jack Bumpus was with me; I was over at a place called Deep Bottom, darker than pitch. And—uh—heard a quackin' off shore. And, I said to Jack, "Keep quiet. There's one comin' in." And—uh—finally Jack said to me, "I think I see 'im." I said, "Give 'im a gun. Give 'im a gun. Try it."

So he shot, and this duck went for the shore with his wings a-goin' like that for the shore. Went up on the shore. Well this dog never lost a crippled duck on shore, he'd take a track just the same as a hound would take a rabbit track. And I sent him over. I said, "Go ahead."

So he went over there. And—gone a while and come back and he didn't have the duck. And that was unusual—I said, "You git back there and get that duck!" And he went back there; and he stayed a little while longer, longer than he did the first time, and he come back and he didn't have that duck.

And I never come nearer shootin' a dog. By gorry, I come pretty near. *"You git back there and get that duck!"* And that dog went back there, and he didn't come back. And he didn't come back. By gorry, we went over there—I walked over there, and here he was; one of my tame ducks that I had tethered out there had got the strap off her leg, and had gone out there, and when this fellow shot, he hadn't hit the duck. The duck came to the shore, he hadn't hit the duck; but the duck was scared and come for the shore. My dog was over there, and he had his paw right on top of that duck, holdin' him down just as tight as could be, and—by gorry, boy, I patted that dog, I'll tell you if I ever walloped that dog I'd have felt some bad. He knew more 'n I did; the dog knew more than I did. He knew that was that tame duck; he wasn't gonna pick him up in his mouth and bring him, you know. He was just holdin' him right down on the ground.

Narrative 3
(Were you ever in a situation where you were in serious danger of being killed?) My brother put a knife in my head. (How'd that happen?) Like kids, you get into a fight and I twisted his arm up behind him.

This was just a few days after my father had died, and we were sitting shive. And the reason the fight started ... He sort of ran out of the yard—this was out on Coney Island—and he started talk about it. And my mother had just sat down to have a cup of coffee. And I told him to cut it out.

Course kids, you know—he don't hafta listen to me. So that's when I grabbed him by the arm, and twisted it up behind him. When I let go his arm, there was a knife on the table, he just picked it up and he let me have it. And I started bleed like a pig.

And, naturally, first thing was—run to the doctor. And the doctor just says, "Just about this much more," he says, "and you'd a been dead."

Narrative 4
... They didn't believe in calling the law or anything like that. They just took things in their own hands. (Did you ever see any shooting of that sort?) Oh, yes. I can remember real well. I w's just a girl. 'Fact, stayed with me quite a while.

Well, there's a fellow, his name was Martin Cassidy 'n' Bill Hatfield. Mr. Cassidy's mother gave him some money an' tell him to go get a bushel of peaches. An' he went down to Martin's house. An' Martin had some moonshine there.

Back down there, they make their own liquor, you know. So—we call it moonshine. Today, they call it white lightnin'; but at that time we call it moonshine.

An' I remember real well what happened. Bunch of us kids was out there playin'; an' no one meanin' any harm about it. But anyway, Mrs. Hatfield come down an' took away her money from Mr. Hatfield, you know, for the peaches, cause she know what he was gonna buy drinks with it. 'Nd Mr. Cassidy was laying out there in the yard.

And Mr. Cassidy just looked up, and he said to Bill, just—just jokin', just in a kiddin' way, he said "Uh huh," he says, "that's—another dollar bill you won't get to spend for drinks, hunh?"

'Nd Bill said, "I'll fix you, ya so-and-so."

So he walked in Martin Cassidy's *house,* his own house, came out with a double-bitted axe, hit him down 'crost the head once, turned over and hit him again, then throwed the axe down and run through the woods.

Just over two dollars that he was sent for peaches with.

### Narrative 5
(Were you ever in a situation where you were in serious danger of being killed?) Yes. (What happened?) I don't really like to talk about it. (Well, tell me as much about it as you can?)

Well, this person had a little too much to drink, and he attacked me, and a friend came in, and she stopped it.

### Narrative 6
(Were you ever in a situation where you were in serious danger of being killed?)

Yeah, I was in the Boy Scouts at the time. And we was doing the 50-yard dash, racing, but we was at the pier, marked off, and so we was doing the 50-yard dash. There was about eight or nine of us, you know, going down, coming back.

And going down the *third* time, I caught cramps and I started yelling "Help!", but the fellows didn't believe me, you know. They thought I was just trying to catch up, because I was going on or slowing down. So all of them kept going. They leave me.

And so I started going down. Scoutmaster was up there. He was watching me. But he didn't pay me no attention either. And for no reason at all there was another guy, who had just walked up that minute ... He just jumped over and grabbed me.

### Narrative 7
(And what about the street fight?) Then—ah—well, street fight, the most important, lemme see. (You know, the one that you remember the most.) Well, I had quite a lot. Well, one, I think, was with a girl [laughter]. Like, I was a kid, you know.

And she was the baddest girl—*the baddest girl in the neighborhood.* If you didn't bring her candy—to school, she'd punch you in the mouth. And you had to kiss her when she ['d] tell you. This girl was only about twelve years old, man, but she was a killer. She didn't take no junk. She whupped all her brothers.

And I came to school one day, and I didn't have no money; my ma wouldn't give me no money. And I played hookies one day. First time I played hookies, man, put sump'n on me, so I said, you know, I'm not gonna play hookies no more, 'cause I don't want to get a whuppin'.

So I go to school, and this girl says, "Where's the candy?" I said, "I don't have it." She says, powwww!! So I says to myself, "Well, there's gonna be times my mother won't give me money because a poor family, and I can't take this all—and and, you know—every time she don't give me any money. So I say, well, I just gotta fight the girl. She gonna hafta whup me. I hope she [don't] whup me."

And I hit the girl: powwww!!

Narrative 8
(Were you ever in a situation where you were in serious danger of being killed?) I'm gonna die? When I was drownin', I didn't know—like, I was turnin' tumblesauts. But that was the only time.

I—I was in a fight downtown once. Like—I went down to a party, and—this—this guy was a soldier—and this guy was a soldier, and he comes on, "gimme a cigarette."

I said, "I don't have any cigarette"

"Well, lemme search you."

I said, "You're not gonna search me."

"Well—I'm a soldier, and I know judo."

I said, "Well, I don't—I don't care if you're a *cop* and you know karate, you're not gonna search me."

And he hit me, man, like I hit him. And like, I—I got next to the guy. He didn't get a chance to use nothing, and I put sump'm on him.

I had—had a couple of guys with me. So we walked around the corner,—after, you know, I knocked him down a couple of times. I said "Well, you know, we'll soon get it."

I walk around the corner about twenty guys come after us, down by the projects. And we're runnin'—and, like—I couldn't run as fast as the other guys. And they was catchin' up to me. And I crossed the street, and I tripped, man. And, like, when I tripped, they kicked me and they was on me and I said, "Like this is it, man"; I pulled a knife.

But—a guy I know from the projects came over and gave me a hand.

And that—that was it, you know. That was it.

Narrative 9
(Did you ever have a feeling, or a premonition, that something was gonna happen, and it did?) Yes, I did. (Tell me about it.)

I was goin' with a girl, one time; we were layin' on a bed—we weren't doin anything, we were talkin'—and, I don't know, I looked into her face, and I saw, like, horns coming out of her head. You know. You know—like—I said, "You look like the devil!"

She said, "What do you mean, I look like the devil?"

"Don't kid around." I said, "I'm not kiddin'. I saw horns comin' out of your head."

And the girl got very angry and walked out. But, we got together, and we went together for about four months.

And, like, this girl tried to put me in a couple of tricks. Like she tried to get some boys to hurt me. You know. And she was a devil.

So, now, anything I see I believe it's going to happen.

Narrative 10
(Did you ever see anybody get beat up real bad?)

I know a boy name Harry. Another boy threw a bottle at him right in the head, and he had to get seven stitches.

Narrative 11
(What was the last cartoon you saw on television?) I don't know, I was watching the Sandy Becker show. (What was the story about?) About this pig. (What happened?)

See he—they threw him out, you know. So he wanted to get back in, 'cause, you know, it was sn- raining hard. So he got on this boat and tried to—go somewhere else. And the boat went over. And he tried to swim.

So this other man was fishing in the rain. So he seen the pig, and went over there and, and picked the pig up and put it in the boat and brought it back to shore, so he would land there.

And that was that.

Narrative 12
(What was the most important fight you remember?)

When I was in fourth grade—no—it was third grade—there was this boy, he stole my glove.

He took my glove, and say that his father found it downtown on the ground. I told him that he—it's impossible for him to find downtown, 'cause all those people were walking by, and just his father is the only one that find it? So he get all upset.

Then I fought him. I knocked him all in the street. So he say he give. And I kept on hitting him. Then he start crying and run home to his father.

And his father told him, he ain't find no glove.

Narrative 13

... See, Napoleon he took the ring and put it on the maiden. It was a statue of the maiden. Then he put it on her finger where the ring's supposed to be, and then he put it on the 45° angle. And then he looked in, and then he saw the place where the project was made at. And everything wh—the doctor who made it was dead.

So he came. He took him and the boy—the boy asked could he see it, and when the boy started to see it, he had this thing on—this patch or something—on his back. The Japanese leader could trace him by that patch because, you know, by radar.

And then—he started—so he took the patch off the boy and put it on the dog. And he took a stick and threw it in the water and the dog ran after it. And the radar—it went in the water with the dog.

And then—Napoleon and the dog started running—I mean, Napoleon and the boy started running, and they started running to the place where the project was made. And they started running to the place. And then, when they got there, they found that all of it was dried up and everything.

So when they started to leave out, he had a Japanese man first tell him to surrender. And before he told him to surrender, the dog—the dog came in there. The dog had found them. And the Japanese man came and told 'em to surrender.

See, they was inside the cave and the Japanese man was outside. And he told them to surrender. And he didn't surrender. He first—he told them that he made a trap. Then he said, "You can come in and make sure the project is all washed up," 'cause it was no more there. And they came.

When he sent one of his men to India ...

Narrative 14

(Did Calvin do something that was really wild?) Yeah. We made Calvin hit—I say, "Calv—"

See, we—it was on a Sunday, and we didn't have nothin' to do after I—after we came from church. Then we ain't had nothin' to do.

So I say, "Calvin, let's go get out—put our dirty clothes on so we can play in the dirt."

And so Calvin say, "Let's have a rock—a rock war." And I say, "All right."

So Calvin had a rock and we, you know—here go a wall and a faraway go a wall. Calvin threw a rock. I was lookin' and—uh—and Calvin threw a rock. It oh—it almost hit me.

So I looked down to get another rock.

Say "Sssh!" an' it pass me.
I say, "Calvin, I'm bust your head for that."
Calvin stuck his head out. I th'ew the rock, and the rock went up, I mean it went up, came down, and say [slap], and smacked him in the head and his head busted.

These fourteen examples cover a wide variety of types, from extremely short to relatively long, from highly organized structures to simple serial types. In addition to the narrative themselves, enough preliminary quotation is given so that one can obtain some idea of the stimulus to which the narratives respond—a matter quite relevant to the functional analysis of narrative.

Some difficult questions arise as we examine these narratives:

1. Though each is presented as a single narrative, how in fact do we know whether one or more narratives are contained in a given example? Is narrative structure well enough defined that we can answer this question? For instance, is Narrative 5 a narrative or a fragment of a narrative? Is Narrative 13 a fragment of a narrative or three separate narratives?

2. The structural framework of the narrative cannot be studied profitably without saying something about the sequence of events to which it refers. The fundamental question of narrative analysis appears to be this: How can we relate the sequence of clauses in the narrative to the sequence of events inferred from the narrative?

We will attempt to answer these questions in the following discussion.

## THE BASIC FRAMEWORK OF NARRATIVE

### Temporal Sequence

We have defined narrative informally as one method of recapitulating past experience by matching a verbal sequence of clauses to the sequence of events that actually occurred. For example, in Narrative 5 we have four independent clauses that refer to four successive events or situations:

(5)
  a  Well, this person had a little too much to drink
  b  and he attacked me
  c  and the friend came in
  d  and she stopped it.

The temporal sequence of narrative is an important defining property that proceeds from its referential function. Narrative is not the only method for referring to a sequence of events; all recapitulation of experience is not narrative. For example, the events of Narrative 5 might have been presented in the following way:

(5′)
- c  A friend of mine came in
- d  just in time to stop
- a  this person who had a little too much to drink
- b  from attacking me.

This form of presenting events depends on syntactic embedding. However, not all alternatives to narrative require this type of subordination. The following series of four independent clauses presents the same material in reverse order:

(5″)
- d  A friend of mine stopped the attack.
- c  She had just come in.
- b  This person was attacking me.
- a  He had had a little too much to drink.

Despite the fact that these two formulations are perfectly logical, orderly, and acceptable ways of representing a sequence of events, they are not narratives as we are about to define the concept. The basic narrative units that we wish to isolate are defined by the fact that they recapitulate experience in the same order as the original events.

However, inspection of the other examples shows that the relationships between clauses and events are not simple. For instance, in Narrative 3:

(3)
- d  and we were sitting shive.
- e  And the reason the fight started …
- f  He sort of ran out in the yard—
- g  this was out on Coney Island—
- h  and he started talk about it;
- i  and my mother had just sat down to have a cup of coffee
- j  and I told him to cut it out.

The sequence of clauses d through j does not match the sequence of events and situations inferred from the narrative. The situation described in g ("This was out on Coney Island ") certainly did not follow f ("He sort of ran out of the yard"); the event of i ("and my mother had just sat down to have a cup of coffee") did not follow h ("and he started talk about it")—rather, it preceded it; the referent of clause e is not temporally ordered with relation to any of the events ("and the reason the fight started"). The clauses that do refer to events clearly in the sequence are:

(3′)
   f  He sort of ran out in the yard
   h  and he started talk about it
   j  and I told him to cut it out.

So far, we have discussed clauses in general as narrative units. But it can quickly be seen that only independent clauses are relevant to temporal sequence. Subordinate clauses (like the embedded clauses seen in formulation 5′) may be placed anywhere in the narrative sequence without disturbing the temporal order of the semantic interpretation, as in the next example taken from Narrative 1:

(1)
   k  Then she left a note one day
   l  she was going to commit suicide
   m  because he was always raising hell about me.

Here clause l ("she was going to commit suicide") is the familiar construction of indirect discourse in which we refer to the fact that a person in the past referred to an event that would occur sometime in the future. Clause m, on the other hand, refers to events prior to clause k. One can quote any number of examples to show that any subordinate clause is removed from the temporal sequence of narrative, even if it retains its own temporal reference.

These considerations illustrate the motivation for the definitions of the narrative clause to be developed later in this article. These elements will be characterized by *temporal sequence:* Their order cannot be changed without changing the inferred sequence of events in the original semantic interpretation.

## Displacement Sets

The following operations provide a formal basis for establishing temporal sequence among the independent clauses of a narrative. Each clause is assigned a sequential symbol (using lowercase letters), as in the next example from Narrative 8:

(8)
   w  and they was catchin' up to me
   x  and I crossed the street
   y  and I tripped, man.

Each clause is then tested for the potential range of displacement by examining the semantic interpretation that results when the clause in question is moved to all

NARRATIVE ANALYSIS    15

possible positions in the remaining sequence. For example, we find that x can be placed before w without changing the original semantic interpretation, since we can infer that the process of catching up extended throughout the sequence:

(8′)
- x  and I crossed the street
- w  and they was catchin' up to me
- y  and I tripped, man.

But x cannot be placed after y without changing the original interpretation, as in:

(8″)
- w  and they was catchin' up to me
- y  and I tripped, man
- x  and I crossed the street.

The result of these operations is indicated in the following system of subscripts. For the clause c, the symbol $_a c_p$ indicates that c can be placed before any and all of the preceding a clauses and after any of the following p clauses without changing the temporal sequence of the original semantic interpretation.

The set consisting of the clauses before which c can be placed, c itself, and the clauses after which c can be placed, is the *displacement set* of c, symbolized DS(c).

Thus, for the partial sequence of w, x, and y discussed previously, we have

(8‴)
| | | |
|---|---|---|
| $_0 w_2$ | and they was catchin' up to me | DS(w) = {w, x, y} |
| $_1 x_0$ | and I crossed the street | DS(x) = {w, x} |
| $_0 y_0$ | and I tripped, man. | DS(y) = {y} |

## Narrative Clauses and Free Clauses

Two extreme types of displacement ranges that result from this operation are

$$_0 c_0 \text{ and } _{x-1} c_{n-x}$$

in which n is the total number of clauses in a sequence. The $_0 c_0$ clause, with a displacement set of {c}, is locked in position in the sequence; it evidently functions as a *narrative clause* of the simplest kind, maintaining the strict temporal sequence that is the defining characteristic of narrative. The $_{x-1} c_{n-x}$ clause, on the other hand, has a displacement set equal to the entire narrative and can range freely through the narrative sequence. This type may be termed a *free clause*.

## Coordinate Clauses

Although the free clause has no fixed relation to the temporal sequence, and the simple $_0c_0$ narrative clause is strictly ordered by temporal sequence, there are other types of clauses that have more complex relations to narrative sequence. We frequently find sequences of the type $_0c_1$ $_1d_0$, as in this extract from Narrative 14:

(14)
$_0s_0$     [and the rock] came down
$_0t_1$     and smacked him in the head
$_1u_0$     and say (slap!)

Clauses t and u might just as well been reversed:

(14′)
$_0s_0$     [and the rock] came down
$_0t_1$     and say (slap!)
$_1t_0$     and smacked him on the head

Both t and u have identical displacement sets, DS(t) = {t, u}, DS(u) = {t, u}, and they may be freely interchanged without any change in temporal sequence. Clauses with identical displacement sets may be termed *coordinate clauses*. (All free clauses are coordinate in this sense, since they all have the same displacement sets, but it is the coordinate nature of certain narrative clauses that is our primary concern.)

One can, of course, have three or more coordinate clauses in a single sequence, as in the following extract from Narrative 1:

(1)
$_0l_0$     He came to my hotel. Nice big blue 44 too.
$_0m_3$     I talked him out of it,
$_1n_2$     and says, "Well, we'll go look for her,
$_2o_1$     and if we can't find her, well you can—go ahead, pull the trigger if you want to."
$_3p_0$     I was maneuvering.
$_0q_0$     So he took me up on it.

Here clauses m, n, o, and p are coordinate, with identical displacement sets (m, n, o, p ), because they could occur in any of the six possible permutations without altering the temporal sequence of the original semantic interpretation. But none of these could be placed before l ("He came to my hotel") or after q ("So he took he up on it").

## Restricted Clauses

The narrative clauses that we have considered are of two general forms, $_0c_0$ and $_0c_1$ $_1d_0$, and appear to have one feature in common. Their displacement sets range from a left zero subscript to a right zero subscript, with no zeros in between. We also find in narratives a third type of clause that does not range freely over the entire narrative, yet has a wider range than the narrative clause. This type of clause has a displacement set that may range across several left or right zero subscripts. Such clauses, which are neither free nor temporally ordered in the strict sense, may be termed *restricted clauses*.

It may be now helpful to consider a narrative as a whole to illustrate the nature of free clauses, coordinate clauses, and restricted clauses and to show how the displacement sets of such clauses are determined. Narrative 6 may be analyzed as follows:

(6)

| | | |
|---|---|---|
| $_0a_{18}$ | yeh I was in the boy scouts at the time | DS {a–s} |
| $_1b_{17}$ | and we was doing the 50-yard dash | " |
| $_2c_{16}$ | racing | " |
| $_3d_{15}$ | but we was at the pier, marked off | " |
| $_4e_{14}$ | and so we was doing the 50-yard dash | " |
| $_5f_{13}$ | there was about eight or ten of us, you know, going down, coming back | " |
| $_6g_0$ | and, going down the *third* time, I caught cramps | {a–g} |
| $_0h_0$ | and I started yelling "Help!" | {h} |
| $_0i_1$ | but the fellows didn't believe me, you know, | {i–j} |
| $_1j_0$ | they thought I was just trying to catch up because I was going on or slowing down | {i–j} |
| $_0k_1$ | so all of them kept going | {k–l} |
| $_1l_0$ | they leave me | {k–l} |
| $_0m_3$ | and so I started going down | {m–p} |
| $_{13}n_5$ | Scoutmaster was up there | {a–s} |
| $_6o_3$ | he was watching me | {i–r} |
| $_7p_2$ | but he didn't pay me no attention either | {i–r} |
| $_0q_0$ | and for no reason at all there was another guy, who had just walked up that minute ... | {q} |
| $_0r_0$ | he just jumped over | {r} |
| $_0s_0$ | and grabbed me | {s} |

Narrative 6 begins with six free clauses, all of which can range over the entire narrative; for each of these, the sum of the subscripts is 18. The third clause, *racing,* is in apposition with *doing* in the second clause, and is treated as derived from *we was racing.* It must be analyzed separately, because it is possible that such an appositive could be temporally ordered in respect to other clauses.[4] The situation and action described in these six clauses prevails throughout the entire narrative: that is, the *8 or 9 of us* continue racing even when the narrator himself is in trouble.

The first narrative clause is g, with a displacement set of {a, b, c, d, e, f, g}, ranging from the left zero of a to its own right zero. Clauses i and j are coordinate clauses of the type just discussed, and so are k and l.

Clause m is a narrative clause with a displacement set ranging over the three following clauses. These following clauses are not in strict narrative sequence; the first one, n, is a free clause ("Scoutmaster was up there"). It should be understood that the test for displacement range must include a procedure for adjusting anaphoric reference. "Scoutmaster was up there" would be a strange utterance in initial position, but if we supply the referent of "there—at the pier," we have "Scoutmaster was up at the pier," which could stand in initial position without changing the temporal sequence of the original semantic interpretation. The reverse situation would apply if a specific free clause in initial position, with several proper names, was displaced to a point later in the narrative: pronoun substitution would be made.

The second clause, o, ("He was watching me") is a restricted clause, with DS(o) = {i–r} extending before n. It could have been placed at any point after h ("I started yelling 'Help!'"), that is, after the action that called the scoutmaster's attention to the narrator and logically motivated his action. It is worth following the logic of this argument in detail, because it is typical of the method for establishing the displacement sets of restricted clauses.

While it is true that the scoutmaster's job was to watch everyone, we interpret the statement o ("He was watching me") to mean that there was a significant change at one point, from watching everyone to watching the narrator in particular. This interpretation hinges on the word "either"—this word coordinates the negation of "He didn't pay me no attention" with some previous negative statement; the first preceding negative clause is i ("the fellows didn't believe me."). Therefore, we can

---

[4]As in, "We were running, walking, and then creeping down the road." We might better say that an apparent appositive turns out to be a coordinated clause. Coordinate verbs are always analyzed separately if they are independent, and in most cases in which they are subordinated to verbs of saying and telling. See Narrative 2, which follows: "I said, 'You git back there/ and get that duck.'" If the narrator had cited himself as saying, "You get that duck and get back there," he would have been reversing the inferred sequence of events—in this case, two utterances. The same argument holds for the example in Narrative 1 (cited previously), clauses n and o. On the other hand, if someone says: "You try and get it," we cannot understand these as two independent verbs, but rather the use of "and" is equivalent to an infinitive embedding, the same as "You try to get it."

conclude that both of these statements refer to events that responded to clause h ("and I started yelling 'Help!'"). Therefore, the displacement sets of o and p cannot include h without a change in the temporal sequence of the original semantic interpretation.

On the other hand, clause o could range towards the end, at any point up to clause s. If clause o appeared after s, then the same temporal inference that we now draw—that the scoutmaster began watching after the cry for help—would be altered. It would be the grabbing of the narrator by the "other guy" that would mark the beginning of the scoutmaster's watching.

The same argument holds for clause p, which is a restricted clause with the same range as o.

The rest of the narrative consists of simple $_0c_0$ narrative units. Clause q ("for no reason at all there was another guy") has the temporal status of a punctual act, appearance: the viewpoint is clearly that of the narrator.

Figure 1 is a graphic display of these statements about the displacement sets of the clauses concerned. Each clause is represented by a mark opposite the alphabetic symbol, and the vertical line running through this mark represents the displacement

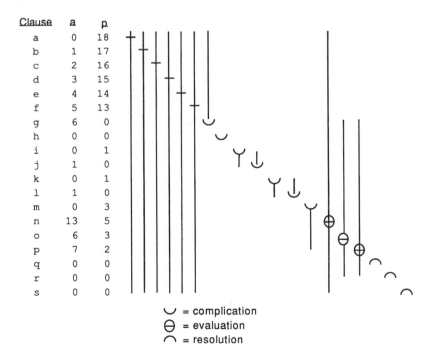

FIGURE 1  Displacement ranges of the clauses of Narrative 6.

set. We will return to this diagram later in discussing the normal structure of narrative as a whole.

## Temporal Juncture

If narrative clauses succeed each other in uninterrupted sequence, the zero subscripts alone would show the temporal segmentation of the narrative. But because any number of free or restricted units can intervene between two narrative clauses, we must define temporal relations between any two clauses in the narrative, not necessarily contiguous. We wish to define formally the condition under which any two clauses are ordered with respect to each other and cannot be interchanged without change in the temporal sequence of the original semantic interpretation. Such a condition is met when the displacement range of a given clause does not extend past the actual location of some following clause, and conversely, the displacement range of this following clause does not extend past the actual location of the given preceding clause. More concisely, their displacement sets do not include each other. Two such clauses are temporally ordered with respect to each other. Their displacement sets may in fact overlap, but the displacement set of c will not include d, and that of d will not include c if c and d are temporally ordered.

Two clauses that are temporally ordered with respect to each other are said to be separated by *temporal juncture*. This juncture has no relation to any free or restricted clauses that may fall in between the temporally ordered clauses. In Narrative 6, given in full previously, we find temporal junctures between g and h, h and i, j and k, l and m, m and q, q and r, r and s. Since i and j, k and l are coordinate, we can best represent these junctures by the following diagram:

| | |
|---|---|
| g | I caught cramps |
| h | and I started yelling |
| ij | the fellows didn't believe; they thought I was |
| kl | all of them kept going; they leave me |
| m | I started going down |
| q | there was another guy |
| r | he just jumped over |
| s | and grabbed me. |

## Definition of the Narrative Clause

We can now proceed to define the basic unit of narrative, the narrative clause, in terms of temporal juncture and displacement sets. It is characteristic of a narrative clause that it cannot be displaced across a temporal juncture without a change in

## NARRATIVE ANALYSIS

the temporal sequence of the original semantic interpretation. Therefore if the displacement set of a given clause does not contain two clauses that are temporally ordered with respect to each other, then that clause is a *narrative clause*. More simply, we can say that a narrative clause has an *unordered displacement set*. If the displacement set is ordered—that is, if some members are temporally ordered with respect to each other—then the given clause is a restricted clause or a free clause. If such an ordered set is equal to the narrative as a whole, the clause is a *free clause;* if not, a *restricted clause.*

We can restate these definitions formally in the following manner. A narrative $N$ may be represented as a set of $n$ clauses

$$c^1, c^2 \ldots c^i \ldots c^n$$

in which $0 \leq I \leq n$. Then

1. $c^i \in DS(c^j)$ if $c^i \ldots c^j$ and $c^j \ldots c^i$ yield the same temporal sequence in semantic interpretation [or if $c^i = c^j$]
2. If $c^i \in DS(c^k)$ and $c^j \in DS(c^k)$
   and $c^i \notin DS(c^j)$ and $c^j \notin DS(c^i)$
   a. and $DS(c^k) = N$, then $c^k$ is a free clause.
   b. and $DS(c^k) < N$, then $c^k$ is a restricted clause.
3. If condition 2 does not hold, $c^k$ is a narrative clause.

### Definition of a Narrative

We can now define quite simply those sequences of clauses that we will consider as narratives. Any sequence of clauses that contains at least one temporal juncture is a narrative. Thus

(10)
  $_0a_2$   I know a boy name Harry.
  $_1b_0$   Another boy threw a bottle at him right in the head,
  $_0c_0$   and he had to get seven stitches.

is a narrative, because a temporal juncture is found between b and c. A statement such as "I shot and killed him" would be a narrative, because it contains a temporal juncture, but not "I laughed and laughed at him." There are many ambiguous cases that allow two distinct interpretations: "I punched him in the head, the mouth and the chest" is normally a list, which does not imply that he was punched first in the head, then in the mouth, and then in the chest. But the temporal interpretation is possible, and it is more likely in "I beat him up and stomped on him."

The upper bound of narrative is not set by this approach, and the question of deciding between one narrative or two must be left to the section that deals with the overall structure of narrative.

### Narrative Heads

The finite verb of a narrative clause, which carries the tense marker of the clause, is the *narrative head* of that clause. Heads of coordinate clauses are coordinate heads.

(2)
| | |
|---|---|
| $_0u_0$ | And—gone a while |
| $_0v_0$ | and come back |
| $_0w_1$ | and he didn't have the duck. |
| $_0x_{31}$ | And that was unusual— |
| $_1y_0$ | I said, "You git back there |
| $_0z_0$ | and get that duck."[5] |
| $_0aa_0$ | And he went back there; |

Here, the narrative heads are *gone, come, did-, was, said, said,* and *went.* The types of grammatical forms and categories that can function as grammatical heads are extremely limited. The principle forms are simple past and simple present. As a rule, no modals appear; abstractly considered, it is possible that *could* could function as a narrative head, though no examples have been found in our materials to date. The progressive (past and possibly present) does appear occasionally as a narrative unit:

(1)
| | |
|---|---|
| $_0u_1$ | and got back |
| $_{21}v_9$ | it was a tent show |
| $_1w_1$ | she was laying on a cot with an ice bag on her head. |
| $_{12}x_7$ | She hadn't committed suicide. |
| $_1y_0$ | But—however—that settled it for the day. |

In this example, "was laying" is in temporal order; it can be displayed before the free unit v and after the restricted unit x, but not before u or after y without changing the temporal sequence of the semantic interpretation. There is considerable semantic and syntactic interest in the questions raised by this use of the past progressive,[6]

---

[5] As noted previously, the subordination of "get back there" and "get that duck" to "I said" is not the type of subordination that removes clauses from temporal sequence. We can consider this coordination: "I said, 'You git back there,' and I said, 'You get that duck.'"

[6] If "was laying" is accepted as a narrative clause, it cannot have the basic grammatical meaning of "simultaneous" as stated by Diver (1963). It would rather differ from the simple past *lay* by the feature

NARRATIVE ANALYSIS   23

and many other such issues are raised by the data of narrative analysis; however, this article is confined to the description of the basic units and framework of narrative, and such questions are not pursued here.

In general, the present perfect does not appear in narrative.[7] The past perfect, as noted before, does not function as a narrative head. However, if the clause with the past perfect refers to an event developed in the narrative, rather than to some event preceding the entire narrative, as is the case in Clause x in Narrative 1. Although x would have been true in initial position, it would not have referred to the particular suicide threatened in Clause k. In its present position, x asserts that the threat of k was not consummated at some time prior to the moment in which x is stated—necessarily before the next preceding narrative unit. Therefore, x can be placed before the disclosure of w, at any point after k. It can also occur at any point after the disclosure w with no change in temporal sequence.

A series of past perfect narrative heads can be used to describe a set of events in temporal sequence, placing the entire set at some point prior to the preceding narrative unit.

(2)
$_0nn_0$    I walked over there
$_0oo_{18}$    And here he was;
$_{42}pp_{17}$    one of my tame ducks that I had tethered out there had got the strap off her leg,
$_{43}qq_{16}$    and had gone out there,
$_{30}rr_{15}$    and when this fellow shot he hadn't hit the duck.

It is true that the three clauses pp, qq, and rr are here in temporal sequence. But no permutation of their order will produce a different temporal sequence in semantic interpretation:

$_0oo_{18}$    and here he was
$_{28}rr_{17}$    and when this fellow shot he hadn't hit the duck
$_{43}qq_{16}$    one of my tame ducks that I had tethered out there

---

"extended." The meaning of "simultaneous" can be supported by arguing that these clauses are equivalent to "When we got back, she was laying ... " In other cases, Diver pointed out, the use of the past progressive may force a metaphorical interpretation "the action was so swift that it was as if it was simultaneous with the preceding," as in "I was on the masthead; the ship gave a lurch; I was falling through the air; I hit the water." These and other interpretations can be subjected to an increasing number of empirical tests through the analysis of narratives such as the ones given here.

[7] Diver (1963) showed this form in his narrative axis with the meaning of "present, before," and gives a constructed example: "All day the sun has warmed the Spanish steps .... " One can find such examples in literary works that use historical present sequences freely, perhaps, but they have not occurred in the material we have examined to date.

     had gone out there
$_{44}pp_{15}$ She had got the strap off her leg.[8]

As indicated by the subscripts, pp and qq are free clauses, and rr is restricted—it cannot precede the shot itself, but can follow at any later point.

## Related Narrative Sequences

The definitions we have given for narrative units are deliberately applied to the linear sequence presented by the narrator. This linear sequence may be considered the *surface structure* of the narrative; there are often many narratives with rather different surface structures, but with equivalent semantic interpretations. In the same way, there are many sentences with different surface structures that correspond to the same underlying string of formatives in the original phrase structure of a grammar:

  a The rock say "shhh!"
  b "shhh!" is what the rock say
  c What the rock say is "shhh!"
  d It's a fact that the rock say "shhh!"
  e The rock's saying "shhh!"

  In previous discussions, we showed that for each series of events described in a narrative, there are other equivalent means of verbal statement besides narrative. There are also equivalent narratives with the same semantic (temporal) interpretation. It is useful to relate all of these to a single underlying form, just as sentences b through e are related to the simplest form, a. To do this, we must consider the fundamental semantic relation in narrative.

  The semantic interpretation of a narrative, as we have defined it, depends on the expectation that the events described did, in fact, occur in the same order as they were told in. Thus the sequence

  $_0a_0$  he attacked me
  $_0b_0$  the friend came in

---

[8]Here the usual adjustments in anaphoric reference have been made. It my be noted that this series of past perfect clauses is one answer to a difficult problem produced by a narrative of this type. The result would lose its surprising effect if these clauses were placed in narrative sequence with regular preterit verbs. By placing the three clauses well out of temporal sequence, it is more difficult for the listener to follow the explanation and surprise is achieved at the risk of a certain awkwardness and confusion. Again, we find that even partial success signals the fact that the narrator of Narrative 2 is a practiced storyteller and has probably told this story many times. We do not take narratives of this type as primary data.

with temporal juncture between a and b, is equivalent in its semantic interpretation to

| $_0a_0$ | he attacked me |
| | then |
| $_0b_0$ | the friend came in |

That is, the temporal juncture is semantically equivalent to the temporal conjunction *then*.

Of course, the a-then-b relation is not the only one at work in narrative. If it were, we would have only a succession of narrative clauses. One also finds implied relations between clauses such as a-and at the same time-b, or a-and now that I think back on it-b. But among these temporal relations, the a-then-b is in some sense the most essential characteristic of narrative. Some narratives (see Narrative 5) may use it exclusively, and every narrative must, by definition, use it at least once.

Though some of these relations are marked explicitly, the majority of them are implied by certain lexical and grammatical features. Moreover, these implicit markers are, in a given situation, often ambiguous: They may stand for more than one relation. Consider the following sequence from Narrative 4:

| $_1b_?$ | Martin Cassidy's mother give him some money |
| $_?c_0$ | an' tell him to go get a bushel of peaches |
| $_0d_0$ | an' he went down to Martin's house |

Though both c and d are connected to the preceding clause by *and*, and though d is clearly ordered with respect to b, b and c are not clearly ordered. The lexical meanings of *give* and *tell* imply a possible simultaneity between b and c. If we substitute for *tell* a verb whose lexical meaning (virtually) denies the possibility or simultaneity with *give*, then b and c are unambiguously ordered:

| $_0b_0$ | Martin Cassidy's mother give him some money |
| $_0c'_0$ | an' bring up a bushel of peaches from the cellar |

One more important point can be drawn from this example. The two possible relations between b and c as they stand are b-then-c and b-and at the same time-c, not c-then-b. This again suggests that the x-then-y relation is the fundamental one in narrative, which is then added to or modified by marked lexical or grammatical forms.

## Isolating Primary Sequences

If we give primacy in narrative to the a-then-b relation, we may wish to select the narrative sequence with the most explicit statement of this relation as the basic underlying form and derive other equivalent narratives from it. Such a basic form we term the *primary sequence*. As we will see, the derivation of other forms from the primary sequence has an important interpretation in the functional organization of the narrative structure as a whole. The procedure for isolating primary sequence can be set out as four steps, and illustrated by the following operations on Narrative 6, previously analyzed in Figure 1:

1. A displacement range is assigned to each clause of the narrative.
   $_0a_{18}\ _1b_{17}\ _2c_{16}\ _3d_{15}\ _4e_{14}\ _5f_{13}\ _6g_0\ _0h_0\ _0i_1\ _1j_0\ _0k_1\ _1l_0\ _0m_3\ _{13}n_5\ _6o_3\ _7p_2\ _0q_0\ _0r_0\ _0s_0$
2. Free clauses are moved to the beginning of the narrative.
   $_0a_{18}\ _1b_{17}\ _2c_{16}\ _3d_{15}\ _4e_{14}\ _5f_{13}\ _6n_{12}\ _7g_0\ _0h_0\ _0i_1\ _1j_0\ _0k_1\ _1l_0\ _0m_2\ _5o_3\ _6p_2\ _0q_0\ _0r_0\ _0s_0$
3. Restricted clauses are moved to a point as early as possible in the narrative without changing the temporal sequence of the original semantic interpretation.
   $_0a_{18}\ _1b_{17}\ _2c_{16}\ _3d_{15}\ _4e_{14}\ _5f_{13}\ _6n_{12}\ _7g_0\ _0h_0\ _0o_8\ _1p_7\ _2i_1\ _3j_0\ _0k_1\ _1l_0\ _0m_0\ _0q_0\ _0r_0\ _0s_0$
4. Coordinate clauses are coalesced to single units.
   $_0a\text{–}n_9\ _1g_0\ _0h_0\ _0o\text{–}p_5\ _1i\text{–}j_0\ _0k\text{–}l_0\ _0m_0\ _0q_0\ _0r_0\ _0s_0$

The string of 10 symbols given here represents the primary sequence of the narrative, in which the a-then-b relation is developed most explicitly. The operation of moving free clauses and restricted clauses as far to the left as possible is a method of minimizing the total amount of delay in the statement of any given event or condition. We can, in fact, define both of these as a specific operation: the minimizing of left subscripts.

Formally, we consider a narrative $c^1, c^2 \ldots c^i \ldots c^n$ with left displacement ranges $a^1, a^2 \ldots a^i \ldots a^n$, in which $0 \leq i \leq n$. A *left displacement function* $y(N_i)$ is defined for each permutation $N_1, N_2 \ldots N_m$ of the clauses $c^2, c^2 \ldots c^n$ that preserves the temporal sequence of the original semantic interpretation:

$$y(N_i) = \sum_{i=1}^{n} a^i$$

When $y(N_i)$ is minimal, any sequence $c^i, c^j$ in which $DS(c^i) = DS(c^j)$ is rewritten as $c^k$ and displacement ranges reassigned. The resulting string is the *primary sequence* of the series $N_1, N_2 \ldots N_m$.

We now proceed to show why in most narratives the linear ordering of clauses departs significantly from the order of the primary sequence. For this purpose, we will have to outline the overall structure of narratives as governed by narrative functions.

## OVERALL STRUCTURE OF NARRATIVES

### Orientation

Figure 1 shows a group of six free clauses occurring together at the beginning of Narrative 6. This is characteristic of most narratives to a greater or lesser degree. Of the 14 examples given in the beginning of this article, 11 have such groups of free clauses. When we examine these groups of free clauses in relation to referential function, we find that they serve to orient the listener in respect to person, place, time, and behavioral situation. We will therefore refer to this structure feature as an *orientation section:* formally, the group of free clauses that precede the first narrative clause. Not all narratives have orientation sections, and not all orientation sections perform these four functions. Furthermore, some free clauses with these functions occur in other positions. Finally, we find that the orientation function is often performed by phrases or lexical items contained in narrative clauses. Despite these limitations, the overall view of narrative shows that the orientation section is a structural feature of a narrative structure. When orientation sections are displaced, we frequently find that this displacement performs another function, evaluation, to be discussed later. Furthermore, we find that orientation sections are typically lacking in narratives of children and less verbal adults whose narratives fail in other ways to carry out referential functions, for example, to preserve temporal sequence. This is the case with Narrative 13, the narrative of vicarious experience from a television show, *The Man From UNCLE.* An interesting example is Narrative 5, where the suppression of full narrative structure is plainly motivated by the explicit reluctance of the narrator to identify persons and places. Here, as in many of the critical issues discussed below, it is essential to preserve the context of the narrative. Because such originating context is often missing and cannot be reconstructed in traditional folk tales, it is more difficult to relate analysis to the originating functions.

### Complication

The main body of narrative clauses usually comprises a series of events that may be termed the complication or complicating action. In Figure 1, complicating action section of Narrative 6 runs from clause g to m.

In many cases, a long string of events may actually consist of several cycles of simple narrative, with many complication sections. This is the case with Narrative 2, the product of a practiced storyteller who is widely known in his community (Martha's Vineyard) as an expert in this traditional art.[9] The subdivisions of

---

[9] As noted previously, Narrative 2 has many formal features that set it aside from the others and identify it as the product of a practiced storyteller. One can point to the embedding of an essentially anonymous "other" in the complicating action, frequent if traditional metaphor, the triple

28  LABOV AND WALETZKY

FIGURE 2   Overall structure of Narrative 5.

Narrative 2 are plainly marked by structural features to be discussed later, but in Narrative 13, this task is much more difficult and must depend upon informal semantic criteria.

The complication is regularly terminated by a result, as in the simple Narrative 5: clause d—or perhaps c and d—is the result that ends the complicating action of a and b, as shown in Figure 2.

To isolate the result in Narrative 5, we are forced to use semantic criteria that are often difficult to apply and seldom consistent. Without further functional analysis, it will usually be hard to tell when a narrative is actually over—when the result begins and when it has been given in full.

### Evaluation

Before proceeding to discuss the result of narratives, we would like to suggest that a narrative that contains only an orientation, complicating action, and result is not a complete narrative. It may carry out the referential function perfectly, and yet seem difficult to understand. Such a narrative lacks significance: it has no point. This is the case with Narratives 11 and 13. Narrative 11 is difficult to follow, although the complicating action and the result seem to be clearly stated.

(11)
$_0a_0$   See he- they threw him out, you know.
$_0b_0$   So he wanted to get back in, 'cause, you know, it was sn-raining hard.
$_0c_0$   So he got on this boat

---

subcycle typical of developed folk tales, strategic repetition, and also the determination shown by the narrator in introducing the story. The preliminary material illustrates how a narrator of this sort will get the topic of his favorite stories into the conversation despite the fact that the original stimulus was only marginally relevant. The transition of the interview theme was accomplished solely by the subject, and the actual stimulus for the narrative was his own.

Despite the fact that features appear in this narrative that are distinct from the simpler examples, a formal analysis of Narrative 2 is possible only after consideration of the simpler narratives or, at least, a formal analysis based on such functional considerations as we have introduced.

| | | |
|---|---|---|
| $_0d_0$ | and he tried to—go somewhere else. | |
| $_0e_0$ | And the boat went over. | |
| $_0f_1$ | And he tried to swim. | |
| $_6g_6$ | And this other man was fishing in the rain. | |
| $_1h_0$ | So he seen the pig | |
| $_0i_0$ | and he went over there | |
| $_0j_0$ | and picked the pig up | |
| $_0k_0$ | and put it in the boat | |
| $_0l_0$ | and brought it back to the shore, so he would land there. | |
| $_0m_0$ | And that was that. | |

There are 13 independent clauses, and 12 of them are narrative clauses. A diagram of displacement ranges for this narrative offers little justification for any internal segmentation (see Figure 3).

Narrative 13 is actually a very detailed statement of a sequence of events and their results—a series of at least three narrative cycles. Yet, the overall effect of Narrative 13 is confusion and pointlessness. This is true for the whole narrative, which is actually 10 times as long as the extract.

Both Narratives 11 and 13 are examples of narratives of vicarious experience, not, as in the other cases, of personal experience. They are lacking the evaluation section that is typical of narratives of personal experience. When we compare Narrative 13 with Narrative 14, a narrative of personal experience, we can appreciate the great difference between unevaluated and evaluated narration.

Narratives are usually told in answer to some stimulus from outside and to establish some point of personal interest. For example, among the narratives given here we find many examples of narratives dealing with the danger of death. When the subject is

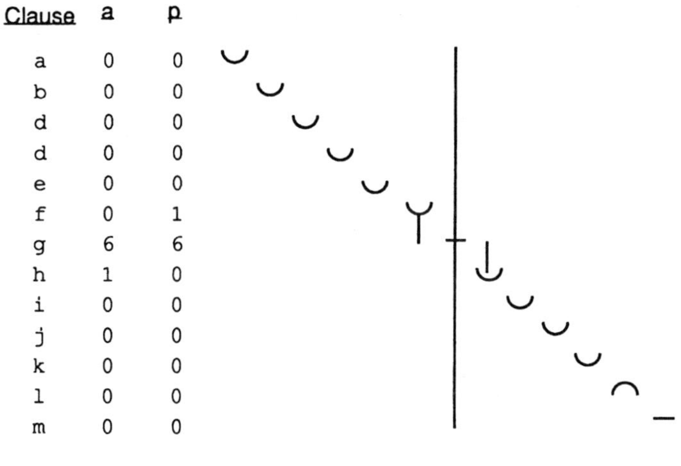

| Clause | a | p |
|---|---|---|
| a | 0 | 0 |
| b | 0 | 0 |
| d | 0 | 0 |
| d | 0 | 0 |
| e | 0 | 0 |
| f | 0 | 1 |
| g | 6 | 6 |
| h | 1 | 0 |
| i | 0 | 0 |
| j | 0 | 0 |
| k | 0 | 0 |
| l | 0 | 0 |
| m | 0 | 0 |

FIGURE 3   Overall structure of Narrative 11.

asked if he were ever in serious danger of being killed, and he says "Yes," then he is asked: "What happened?". He finds himself in a position in which he must demonstrate to the listener that he really was in danger. The more vivid and real the danger appears, the more effective the narrative. If the narrative is weak and uninteresting, he will have made a false claim. (See Narratives 1, 3, 6, and 8.)

Beyond such immediate stimulus, we find that such narratives are so designed as to emphasize the strange and unusual character of the situation—there is an appeal to the element of mystery in most of the narratives. (See Narratives 2, 3, and especially 9.). Then, too, many narratives are designed to place the narrator in the most favorable possible light: a function which we may call self-aggrandizement. (See Narratives 7, 8, and especially 12.)

The functions of narrative have an effect on the narrative structure. A simple sequence of complication and result does not indicate to the listener the relative importance of these events or help him distinguish complication from *resolution.* We also find that in narratives without a point it is difficult to distinguish the complicating action from the result.

Therefore, it is necessary for the narrator to delineate the structure of the narrative by emphasizing the point where the complication has reached a maximum: the break between the complication and the result. Most narratives contain an evaluation section that carries out this function.

Many evaluation sections are defined formally. Multicoordinate clauses or groups of free or restricted clauses are frequently located at the break between the complicating action and the resolution of these complications. This is the case in Figure 1, for the clauses n, o, and p. As the narrator is going down, in the water, the moment of crisis is suspended by three clauses that do not occur in this position by any necessity of temporal sequence. They are restricted clauses that could have occurred much earlier in the narrative—in fact, before the first temporal juncture. After these three clauses, the narrative moves swiftly to a conclusion.

In many narratives, the evaluation section is fused with the result: that is, a single narrative clause both emphasizes the importance of the result and states it. This is the case with Narratives 3 and 12. In Narrative 3, the doctor's statement: "you'd a been dead" tells us simultaneously that the narrator was close to death and that he survived. The evaluation is here shown as related directly to the originating function—to demonstrate that the narrator was indeed close to death.

In the case of Narrative 1, we find more than one evaluation section. Narrative 1 begins with a long orientation section of 10 clauses.

(1)
$_0a_{30}$   Well, in the business I was associated at that time, the Doc was an old man ...
$_1b_{29}$   He had killed one man,
$_2c_{28}$   or—had done time.

| | |
|---|---|
| $_3d_{27}$ | But he had a young wife |
| $_4e_{26}$ | and those days I dressed well. |
| $_5f_{25}$ | And seemingly, she was trying to make me. |
| $_6g_{24}$ | I never noticed it. |
| $_7h_{23}$ | Fact is, I didn't like her very well, because she had—she was a nice looking girl until you saw her feet. |
| $_8i_{22}$ | She had big feet. |
| $_9j_{21}$ | Jesus, God, she had big feet! |
| $_{10}k_0$ | Then she left a note one day she was going to commit suicide because he was always raising hell about me. |
| $_0l_0$ | He came to my hotel. Nice big blue 44 too.[10] |
| $_0m_3$ | I talked him out of it, |
| $_1n_2$ | and says, "Well, we'll go look for her, |
| $_2o_1$ | and if we can't find her, well, you can—go ahead, pull the trigger if you want to." |
| $_3p_0$ | I was maneuvering. |
| $_0q_0$ | So he took me up on it. |
| $_0r_0$ | And we went to where they found her handkerchief—the edge of a creek— |
| $_0s_0$ | And we followed down a little more, |
| $_0t_0$ | And we couldn't find anything. |
| $_0u_1$ | And got back— |
| $_{21}v_9$ | it was a tent show— |
| $_1w_1$ | she was laying on a cot with an ice bag on her head. |
| $_{12}x_7$ | She hadn't committed suicide. |
| $_1y_0$ | But—however—that settled it for the day. |
| $_0z_0$ | But that night the manager, Floyd Adams, said, "You better pack up |
| $_0aa_0$ | and get out, because that son of a bitch never forgives anything once he gets it in his head." |
| $_0bb_1$ | And I did. |
| $_1cc_0$ | I packed up |
| $_0dd_0$ | and got out. |
| $_0ee_0$ | That was two. |

The first narrative unit is k ("Then she left a note one day ... "), followed by l ("He came to my hotel") and m ("I talked him out of it"). We then have two clauses

---

[10] The phrase "Nice big blue 44 too" might as well be considered a narrative clause, derived from "He had a nice big blue 44 too." However, the status of *had* as the head of a narrative clause is still at issue, and it would be tendentious to use a deleted form as evidence. We have therefore been treating this phrase as subordinated to "He came to my hotel," equivalent to "with a nice big blue 44 too."

coordinated with m—clauses n ("And says") and o ("I was maneuvering."). These multicoordinate clauses suspend the action at a critical moment—when the danger of death is greatest, and they contain an explicit statement of the attitude of the narrator. His coolness in a moment of crisis emphasizes the danger and reflects well on himself.

Five narrative clauses follow this suspension, resolving the crisis introduced by l and m. A second evaluation section occurs at a subsidiary point when the situation is further resolved—the fate of the lady in question is determined, and simultaneously the immediate threat to the narrator. The action is suspended at this point by the use of a free clause that might have occurred in the orientation section, v ("it was a tent show"), and a direct comment, x, that might have been inferred from w. The resolution is stated with some finality in y ("that settled it"). Finally, there is an added explicit evaluation of a third party that confirms the implications of the previous evaluation section, followed by a conclusion. The overall diagram shows how evaluation sections outline the structure of the narrative.

It should be apparent here that the evaluation sections are responsible for those deviations from the order of the primary sequence of the narrative that complicate the a-then-b relation of narrative. The functions of the evaluation section must be added to the primary narrative function in order to understand how the primary sequence is transformed into the more complex structure that we see here. All of the evaluation sections shown here are related to the originating function of the narrative. From a structural point of view, the first section is the major break in the complicating action.[11]

Not all evaluation sections have the structural feature of suspending the complicating action, as shown in the Figure 4. In many cases, the evaluation may be present as lexical or phrasal modification of a narrative clause, or it may be itself a narrative clause or coincide with the last narrative clause. For this reason, the fundamental definition of evaluation must be semantic, although its implications are structural.

The *evaluation* of a narrative is defined by us as that part of the narrative that reveals the attitude of the narrator towards the narrative by emphasizing the relative importance of some narrative units as compared to others. This may be done by a variety of means:

Semantically defined evaluation:
1. direct statement: "I said to myself: this is it."
2. lexical intensifiers: "He was beat up real, real bad."
   "I whupped that dude half to death."

---

[11] The three evaluation sections of Narrative 1 raise the possibility that we can analyze this narrative as consisting of three distinct subcycles: that it is a complex narrative consisting of three structural units. This article is limited to the consideration of simple narratives, and this possibility must be postponed to a later study of subcycles and complex narratives.

NARRATIVE ANALYSIS    33

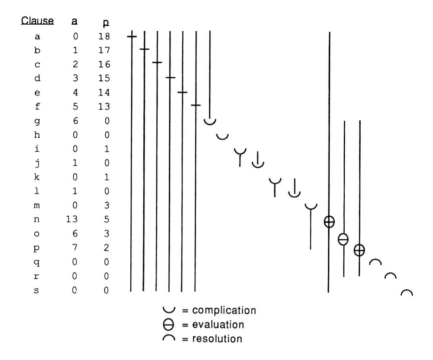

FIGURE 4   Overall structure of Narrative 1.

Formally defined:
3. suspension of the action:
   a. through coordinate clauses and restricted clauses: See Figure 1
   b. repetition (subtype of the above): See Narrative 2, at the moment of crisis when the dog is gone for the 3rd time: "And he didn't come back. And he didn't come back."

Culturally defined:
4. symbolic action: "They put an egg on his door."
   "I crossed myself."
   "You could hear the rosaries clicking."
5. judgment of a third person: here the entire narrative is reported to a person not present at the narrative.

Narrative 12 is a heavily evaluated narrative that shows three of these characteristic forms of evaluation. It is typical of many fight narratives in its two-part structure. The first subcycle deals with the events leading up to the fight, and its conclusion is the beginning of the second subcycle, the fight itself. In this case, the evaluation of the first section is a statement of the narrator:

$_0d_0$      I told him that—it's impossible for him to find downtown, 'cause all those people were walking by, and just his father is the only one that find it?

Although the very length of this closely reasoned argument serves to suspend the action, the structural criteria we have been using show it as a single narrative clause. We identify this clause as an evaluation on semantic grounds: It is an explicit statement by the narrator of his attitude towards the situation.

The conclusion of Narrative 12 is also an evaluative statement that coincides with the last narrative unit: The statement of a third person after the entire sequence of events is reported to him.

$_0j_0$      Then he start crying
$_0k_0$      and run home to his father.
$_0l_0$      And his father told him, he ain't find no glove

In addition, we have the evaluation of the act of clause i

$_0h_0$      So he say he give
$_0i_0$      And I kept on hitting him.

It is normal not to hit someone after he says "I give." This incident evaluates the narrative by indicating that the anger of the narrator was so great—due to excessive and unreasonable provocation—that he was carried away to the extent of violating this norm. The other boy had placed himself outside of normal sanctions by his behavior.

All of these forms of evaluation serve the function of self-aggrandizement, showing the narrator in a favorable position as compared to the other boy. It is evident that there are a great variety of evaluation types, more or less deeply embedded in the narrative. But this variety should not obscure the fact that unevaluated narratives are exceptional as representations of personal experience, and unevaluated narratives lack structural definition.

An important characteristic of narratives is the degree of embedding of the evaluation in the narrative framework. There is a wide range, from the most highly internalized type—a symbolic action or the evaluation of a third person—to the most external—a direct statement of the narrator to the listener about his feelings at the time. In the examples given previously, we find internalized evaluation in Narrative 1, in the dramatic statements of narrator and manager; and in Narrative 3, in the statement of the doctor, ("just about this much more," he says, "and you'd a been dead."). The last narrative, Narrative 14, has a dramatic statement of the narrator ("I say, 'Calvin, I'm bust your head for dat.'").

Sometimes the evaluation occurs in a statement of the narrator to himself, less well integrated into the narrative, as in Narrative 7: "So I says to myself, 'Well, there's gonna be times … '".

The other end of the scale is shown by a comment at the end of the narrative directed towards the listener, as in Narrative 13: "Just over two dollars that he was sent for peaches with." Still more direct is Narrative 2: "I'll tell you if I had ever walloped that dog I'd have felt some bad."

We might construct a scale of degrees of embedding of evaluation, following examples of the following sort:

Internal
1. And when we got down there, her brother turned to me and whispered, "I think she's dead, John!"
2. And when we got down there, I said to myself, "My God, she's dead!"
3. And when we got down there, I thought, "She's dead."
4. And when we got down there, I thought she was dead.
5. Later, the doctors told us she was close to death.
6. I think she must have been close to death.

External
7. You know, in cases like this, it's clear that she was likely as not dead.

## Resolution

With this definition of evaluation, we can now return to the problem of defining the result of a narrative. The problem is now quite simple. We can establish the break between the complicating and resolving action by locating the placement of the evaluation. Thus, the *resolution* of the narrative is that portion of the narrative sequence that follows the evaluation. If the evaluation is the last element, then the resolution section coincides with the evaluation. In the examples given previously, the complicating clauses are symbolized ∪ and the resolving clauses ∩.

## Coda

Many narratives end with a resolution section, but others have an additional element that we may call the *coda*.

The actual sequence of events described in the narrative does not, as a rule, extend up to the present. The coda is a functional device for returning the verbal perspective to the present moment. This is accomplished by a variety of means, so that the codas cannot be identified by such simple tag lines as "And they lived happily ever after."

a. One device used in a coda is *deixis*. This is the linguistic category that points to a referent instead of naming it explicitly: In this case, it has the effect of standing at the present moment of time and pointing to the end of the narrative, identifying it as a remote point in the past.

(1)
$_0aa_0$    I packed up
$_0bb_0$    and got out.
$_0cc_0$    That was two.

(7)
$_0bb_0$    That was one of the most important.

(8)
$_0gg_1$    And that—that was it, you know.
$_1hh_0$    That was it.

(11)
$_0m_0$    And that was that.

This use of the obviate deictic category—*that, there, those*—contrasts sharply with the use of the proximate in the body of the narrative—*this, here, these*. For example, we have the following proximate evaluation in Narrative 8:

(8)
$_0bb_0$    and they was on me and
$_0cc_0$    and I said "Like this is it, man."
$_0dd_0$    I pulled a knife

b. Another device used in codas is an incident in which one of the actors can be followed up to the present moment in actions that may not be totally relevant to the narrative sequence:

And you know that man who picked me out of the water?
he's a detective in Union City,
and I see him every now and again.

c. The effect of the narrative on the narrator may be extended to the present moment:

I was given the rest of the day off,
and ever since then I haven't seen the guy, 'cause I quit.
I quit, you know.
No more problems.

It is interesting to note that all codas are separated from the resolution by temporal juncture. At the same time, it seems that some semantic criterion is necessary to identify codas: The fact that they are frequently not descriptions of events, or of events necessary to answer the question: "What happened?"

The overall structure of the narratives that we have examined is not uniform; there are considerable differences in the degree of complexity, in the number of structural elements present, and how various functions are carried out. However, a composite view of narrative performance leads us to posit a *normal form* for oral versions of personal experience; the degree to which any one narrative approximates this normal form is a significant fact about that narrative—perhaps more significant than any other in terms of fulfilling the originating function of the narrative.

The normal form is quite distinct from the primary sequence of the narrative. As noted above, the need for an evaluation section motivates the transformation of the primary sequence into the more characteristic normal form that appears in the linear sequence presented by the narrator.

One can represent the normal form of narrative using the diagram in Figure 5. Here the originating function of the narrative is applied at the base of the diamond; we proceed up and to the left with the orientation section, then up to the apex with the complication. Frequently, but not always, the evaluation suspends the action at this apex, as represented by the circle. The resolution proceeds downward and to the right, and the coda is represented by the line that returns to the situation (point in time) at which the narrative was first elicited. The simplest possible narrative would consist of the single line of the complication, without a clear resolution; frequently we find minimal narratives that have both complication and resolution ("He hit me hard and I hit him back"). As we proceed to more complex narratives, told by speakers with greater overall verbal ability, we find a higher percentage of narratives that duplicate the exact form of this diagram. Perhaps the most frequent variant is the case in which the evaluation ends the resolution: jokes, ghost stories, and surprise endings take this form, as the story is reshaped by many retellings.

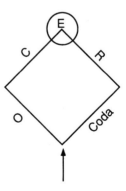

FIGURE 5   The normal form of narrative.

## CONCLUSION

This view of narrative structure helps us to answer the two questions raised at the beginning of this discussion. First, we have related the sequence of narrative elements to the inferred sequence of events in the experience that is being recapitulated, through the definitions of narrative units, restricted clause, free clause, and narrative clause. Secondly, we have outlined the principle elements of simple narratives that perform both referential and evaluative functions. We have shown that the evaluative function requires the transformation of the primary sequence, based on the a-then-b relation, into the more complex normal form of the narrative as presented by the narrator.

With this framework, we are beginning to analyze relative effectiveness and completeness of narrative structure among various subgroups of our population, and, furthermore, to analyze the more complex types of narration developed by skilled storytellers and preserved by oral tradition. It is clear that these conclusions are restricted to the speech communities that we have examined. This view of narrative structure will achieve greater significance when materials from radically different cultures are studied in the same way.

## ACKNOWLEDGMENT

The work described in this article was supported in part by the U.S. Office of Education in connection with Cooperative Research Branch Project No. 3288, "A Study of Non-Standard English of Negro and Puerto Rican Speakers in New York City," under the overall program of Project Literacy.

## REFERENCES

Colby, B. (1966). Cultural patterns in narrative. *Science, 151,* 793–798.
Diver, W. (1963). The chronological system of the English verb. *Word, 19,* 141–148.
Labov, W. (1964). Phonological correlates of social stratification. *American Anthropologist, 66*(6, Pt. 2), 164–176.
Labov, W. (1966). *The social stratification of English in New York City.* Washington, DC: Center for Applied Linguistics.
Labov, W., Cohen, P., & Robins, C. (n.d.). *Final report on Project 3091.* Washington, DC: U.S. Office of Education, Cooperative Research Branch.
Labov, W., & Waletzky, J. (1967). Narrative analysis: Oral versions of personal experience. In J. Helm (Ed.), *Essays on the verbal and visual arts: Proceedings of the 1996 Annual Spring Meeting of the American Ethnological Society* (pp. 12–44). Seattle: University of Washington Press.
Propp, V. (1958). *Morphology of the folk tale* (Publication 10). Bloomington, IN: Research Center in Anthropology, Folklore and Linguistics.
Schatzman, L., & Strauss, A. (1955). Social class and modes of communication. *American Journal of Sociology, 60,* 329–338.

# Narratology and Narratological Analysis

## Gerald Prince
*Department of Romance Languages, University of Pennsylvania*

*Narratology* was born at around the time that Labov and Waletzky's classic article appeared in 1967 (Labov & Waletzky, 1967/this issue). It studies narrative, the representation in any medium (oral, written, and sign languages, still or moving pictures, gestures, etc.) of one or more than one event or change in a state of affairs. Specifically, it investigates what all and only possible narratives (rather than great, literary, fictional, or extant ones) have in common as well as what enables them to differ from one another *qua* narratives, and it aims to describe the narrative-pertinent system of rules governing narrative production and processing. Historically, narratology belongs to the tradition of French structuralism, illustrating both the structuralist tendency to regard texts (in the broad sense of signifying matter) as rule-governed ways in which humans (re)fashion their universe and the structuralist ambition to identify the necessary and the optional components of textual types and to characterize their modes of articulation. It thus constitutes a subset of semiotics, the study of the factors at work in signifying systems and practices. If structuralism generally concentrates on the *langue* or code underlying a given system or practice rather than concentrating on a *parole* or instantiation of that system or practice, narratology specifically focuses on narrative langue rather than narrative paroles. If structuralism can be viewed as extending the notion "unconscious"—the economic unconscious of Marx, the psychological unconscious of Freud, the linguistic unconscious of the grammarians—to every domain of symbolic behavior, narratology can be viewed as depicting a kind of narrative unconscious.

The narratological enterprise became systematic after the appearance of the English translation of Propp's morphological study of the Russian fairy tale (Propp, 1958), and narratology took on many of the features of a discipline in 1966, with the publication of a special number of *Communications* (No. 8) entirely devoted to the structural analysis of narrative. In 1960, Lévi-Strauss—who had earlier provided a structural description of myth and stressed the importance of describing

---

Requests for reprints should be sent to Gerald Prince, School of Arts and Sciences, Department of Romance Languages, University of Pennsylvania, 521 Williams Hall, Philadelphia, PA 19104–6305. E-mail: gerry@babel.ling.upenn.edu

general structural conditions that texts have to satisfy in order to belong to a particular type (Lévi-Strauss, 1958)—reviewed Propp's book and praised its remarkable achievements while criticizing its emphasis on (surface) form rather than (deep) structure, manifest message rather than latent content, and superficial syntactic relations rather than deep logico–semantic ones (Lévi-Strauss, 1960). In 1964, Claude Bremond (1964) began a recasting of the Proppian schema that would be patterned on the logic of action, would show that—at each point in a narrative—there are different ways in which the action might proceed, and would culminate in his *Logique du récit* (Bremond, 1973). The following year, Tzvetan Todorov, who would later coin the very term *narratologie* and develop a narrative grammar accounting for (basic aspects) of Boccacio's *Decameron* (Todorov, 1969), published a French translation of several Russian formalist texts, including one by Propp (Todorov, 1965). In his *Sémantique structurale*, A. J. Greimas (1966) refined Propp's notion of dramatis persona and developed an actantial model involving six actants or basic roles assumable by characters (Subject, Object, Sender, Receiver, Helper, and Opponent). Greimas argued that a narrative constitutes a signifying whole because it can be grasped in terms of the relational structure obtaining among actants. He also performed a paradigmatic analysis of Propp's functions (characters' acts considered in terms of their role in the course of the narrative action) and concluded that basic narrative developments represent modifications from negative beginnings (disruption of order and alienation) to positive ends (establishment of order and integration) effected through the actions of a Subject. As for the 1966 special number of *Communications,* it contained many references to Propp; it featured contributions by Roland Barthes, whose famous "Introduction à l'analyse structurale des récits" provided a global model of narrative description (Barthes, 1966), by Gérard Genette, whose "Discours du récit" would soon champion a "restricted narratology" focusing on verbal telling and would exert enormous influence on the study of narration (Genette, 1972), and Greimas, Bremond, Todorov, et cetera; and it came close to constituting a narratological research program as well as a manifesto. A few years later, narratology was an international field that could boast of many achievements in its exploration of narrative.

It is perhaps the area of narrative discourse (of the narrating as opposed to the narrated, of the signs in a narrative representing the narrating activity, its origin, its destination, and its context) that narratologists have explored most thoroughly. Building on the work of the Russian formalists (Ejxenbaum, 1971a, 1971b; Shklovsky, 1965a, 1965b; Tomashevsky, 1965) and on that of Anglo-Saxon, French, and Germanic students of narration and point of view (Booth, 1961; Brooks & Warren, 1943; Friedman, 1955; Lämmert, 1955; Müller, 1968; Pouillon, 1946; Stanzel, 1955), both Genette (1972, 1983) and Todorov (1973), but also Bal (1977, 1985), Chatman (1978, 1990), Prince (1971, 1973b, 1982), Rimmon-Kenan (1983), and others have described the various orders in which a narrative text can present a series of situations and events, the anachronies (anticipations or retrospections) that it can exhibit, and the undatable structures that it can accommodate. Furthermore, they have characterized narrative speed (the relation between the duration of the narrated and the length of the narrative text) as well as its canonical tempos (ellipsis, summary, scene, stretch, pause). They have, moreover, investigated narrative frequency, the link between the number of times an event happens and the number of times it is recounted. They have analyzed the set of modalities regulating narrative information: the points of view in terms of which the narrated can be rendered and the kind and extent of narratorial mediation a narrative can involve. They have examined the types of discourse (narratized, indirect, free indirect, direct) that a text can adopt to report the characters' utterances or thoughts. They have studied the major kinds of narration (first-, second-, or third-person singular or plural; posterior, anterior, simultaneous, or intercalated) and their modes of combination. They have specified the signs referring to the narrator and the narratee (or audience narrated to, as inscribed in the text), delineated their respective functions, and scrutinized the set of relations obtaining between them as well as the kinds of distance (spatial, temporal, emotional, etc.) separating them from the characters and events in the story.

The narratological investigation of narrated structure has also yielded notable results. For example, in addition to characterizing the minimal constituents of the narrated (goal-directed actions and mere happenings, states and processes, etc.) and the relations (spatiotemporal, logical, thematic, functional, or transformational) that can obtain among them, narratologists have shown that narrative sequences can be said to consist of a series of minimal constituents, the last one of which in time is a (partial) repetition or transform of the first, and they have demonstrated that ever more complex sequences can be said to result from the linking of simpler ones through such operations as conjunction or embedding (Barthes, 1966; Bremond, 1973; Chatman, 1978; Prince, 1973a, 1982; Todorov, 1970, 1973). They have also explored the nature of characters and settings as well as the various techniques through which they are constituted (Barthes, 1966; Chatman, 1978; Hamon, 1981, 1983), and they have analyzed how a story can be described semantically as a world consisting of domains (sets of events pertaining to a character), each of which is governed by modal constraints (alethic, epistemic, axiologic, or deontic) that determine what is or could be the case in the world represented as well as what happens and what does not (Dolezel, 1976; Pavel, 1980, 1985; Ryan, 1985, 1991).

Finally, narratologists have explicitly made certain aspects of narrative pragmatics part of their domain of inquiry, for instance by calling for the development of a feminist narratology that would take into account the role of gender in narrative production and processing (Lanser, 1986; cf. Prince, 1995) or by distinguishing narrativeness (what makes a text narrative, what all and only narratives have in common) from narrativity (what in a text underlines its possibly narrative nature, what emphasizes the presence and semiotic role of narrative structures in a textual economy) and by exploring the factors affecting the latter. Prince (1982, 1983), for example, contended that the narrativity of a text depends on the extent to which the text is taken to constitute a (pointed) autonomous whole (a sequence whose chronological beginning and end are linked by its middle and are transformationally related) that (a) represents an anthropomorphic project; (b) involves some kind of conflict (compare: "The cat sat on the mat" and "The cat sat on the dog's mat"); (c) is made up of discrete, particular, positive (the hallmark of narrative is assurance), and temporally distinct actions that have logically unpredictable antecedents or consequences; and (d) avoids inordinate amounts of commentary about them, their representation, or the latter's context. Prince (1988) also contended that, all other things being equal, the presence of disnarrated elements (representing what did not happen but could have) affected narrativity in a positive manner. Similarly, Ryan (1991) not only showed that an adequate model of plot must represent the relational changes obtaining between the constituents of the factual narrative domain (what is true in the story) and the constituents of the characters' private domains (the virtual narratives fashioned in terms of their knowledge, wishes, obligations, simulations, intentions, or fantasies); she also insisted that "not all plots are created equal" (p. 148) and that narrativity is rooted in the configuration of theses changes and "in the richness and variety of the domain of the virtual" (p. 156). More recently, Ryan (1992) sketched an open-ended taxonomy of different modes of narrativity, including the simple narrativity of fairy tales and urban legends (in which the semantic dimension of the text primarily springs from a linear plot revolving around a single problem), the complex narrativity of Balzac, Dickens, or Dumas (in which narrative structures appear on both the macro- and the microtextual level and semantic integration obtains between the main plot lines and the subordinate ones), the figural narrativity of lyric, historiographic, or philosophic texts (in this case, the sender or the receiver of the narrative message constructs a story by reshaping universal claims, collective entities, and abstract concepts into particular characters and events), and the instrumental narrativity of sermons and debates (in which narrative structures appearing on the microtextual level function merely as illustrations or clarifications of a nonnarrative macrotextual level).

Much work remains to be done on narrativity and the factors affecting it (just as much work is needed on the question of constraints governing the combination of different narrating features, for example, or in the area of narrative semantics). For instance, narrativity factors pertaining to the narrated (the *what* that is represented) should be distinguished from factors relevant to the narrating (the *way* in which that *what* is represented). Moreover, the relative importance of the factors should be explored and so should their interdependences or their incompatibilities. In any case, to fulfill its ambition (and adequately describe narrative competence or the rules presiding over narrative production and processing) narratology should aim at constructing a formal model accounting for narrativity as well as narrativeness. The model might ultimately consist of the following interconnected components: (a) a structural component describing the macro- and microstructures of all and only sequences of narrated situations and events; (b) a narrating component accounting for the way these structures can be presented (speeds adopted, points of view employed, narratorial mediation involved, etc.); (c) a semantic component interpreting the (presented) structures (providing a basis for answering questions about narrative content and for arriving at an understanding of the structures); and (d) a pragmatic component specifying their (degree) of narrativity (and perhaps more generally, specifying the basic cognitive and communicative factors affecting their production and processing). The realization of such a model is, of course, not for the near future, but it is to be hoped that its elaborators will draw not only on the work of their predecessors in narratology but also on the splendid accomplishments of the tradition of narrative analysis inaugurated by Labov and Waletzky.

## REFERENCES

Bal, M. (1977). *Narratologie* [Narratology]. Paris: Klincksieck.
Bal, M. (1985). *Narratology: Introduction to the theory of narrative.* Toronto, Canada: University of Toronto Press.
Barthes, R. (1966). Introduction à l'analyse structurale des récits [Introduction to the structural analysis of narratives]. *Communications, 8,* 1–27.
Booth, W. C. (1961). *The rhetoric of fiction.* Chicago: University of Chicago Press.
Bremond, C. (1964). Le message narratif [The narrative message]. *Communications, 4,* 4–32.
Bremond, C. (1973). *Logique du récit* [The logic of narrative]. Paris: Seuil.
Brooks, C., & Warren, R. P. (1943). *Understanding fiction.* New York: Appleton-Century-Crofts.
Chatman, S. (1978). *Story and discourse: Narrative structure in fiction and film.* Ithaca, NY: Cornell University Press.
Chatman, S. (1990). *Coming to terms: The rhetoric of narrative in fiction and film.* Ithaca, NY: Cornell University Press.
Dolezel, L. (1976). Narrative semantics. *PTL, 1,* 129–151.
Ejxenbaum, B. M. (1971a). O'Henry and the theory of the short story. In L. Matejka & K. Pomorska (Eds.), *Readings in Russian poetics* (pp. 227–270). Cambridge: MIT Press.
Ejxenbaum, B. M. (1971b). The theory of the formal method. In L. Matejka & K. Pomorska (Eds.), *Readings in Russian poetics* (pp. 3–37. Cambridge: MIT Press.
Friedman, N. (1955). Point of view in fiction: The development of a critical concept. *PMLA, 70,* 1160–1184.
Genette, G. (1972). Discours du récit [Narrative discourse]. In G. Gennette, *Figures III* (pp. 65–282). Paris: Seuil.
Genette, G. (1983). *Nouveau discours du récit* [Narrative discourse revisited]. Paris: Seuil.
Greimas, A. J. (1966). *Sémantique structurale: Recherche de méthode* [Structural semantics: Search for a method]. Paris: Larousse.
Hamon, P. (1981). *Introduction à l'analyse du descriptif* [Introduction to the analysis of the descriptive]. Paris: Hachette.
Hamon, P. (1983). *Le personnel du roman* [The personnel of the novel]. Geneva, Switzerland: Droz.
Labov, W., & Waletzky, J. (this issue). Narrative analysis: Oral versions of personal experience. In J. Helm (Ed.), *Essays on the verbal and visual arts: Proceedings of the 1966 Annual Spring Meeting of the American Ethnological Society* (pp. 12–44). Seattle: University of Washington Press. (Original work published 1967)

Lämmert, E. (1955). *Bauformen des Erzählens* [Structures of narrating]. Stuttgart, Germany: J. B. Metzlersche Verlag.
Lanser, S. S. (1986). Toward a feminist narratology. *Style, 20,* 341–363.
Lévi-Strauss, C. (1958). *Anthropologie structurale* [Structural anthropology]. Paris: Plon.
Lévi-Strauss, C. (1960). La structure et la forme [Structure and form]. *Cahiers de l'Institut de Science Economique Appliquée, 7,* 3–36.
Müller, G. (1968). *Morphologische Poetik* [Morphological poetics]. Tübingen, Germany: Max Niemeyer.
Pavel, T. (1980). Narrative domains. *Poetics Today, 1,* 105–114.
Pavel, T. (1985). *The poetics of plot: The case of English Renaissance drama.* Minneapolis: University of Minnesota Press.
Pouillon, J. (1946). *Temps et roman* [Time and the novel]. Paris: Gallimard.
Prince, G. (1971). Notes towards a preliminary categorization of fictional "narratees." *Genre, 4,* 100–106.
Prince, G. (1973a). *A grammar of stories: An introduction.* The Hague, Netherlands: Mouton.
Prince, G. (1973b). Introduction à l'étude du narrataire [Introduction to the study of the narratee]. *Poétique, 14,* 178–196.
Prince, G. (1982). *Narratology: The form and functioning of narrative.* Berlin, Germany: Walter de Gruyter.
Prince, G. (1983). Narrative pragmatics, message, and point. *Poetics, 12,* 527–536.
Prince, G. (1988). The disnarrated. *Style, 22,* 1–8.
Prince, G. (1995). Narratology: Criteria, corpus, context. *Narrative, 3,* 73–84.
Propp, V. (1958). *Morphology of the folktale.* Bloomington: Indiana University Press.
Rimmon-Kenan, S. (1983). *Narrative fiction: Contemporary poetics.* London: Methuen.
Ryan, M.-L. (1985). The modal structure of narrative universes. *Poetics Today, 6,* 717–755.
Ryan, M.-L. (1991). *Possible worlds, artificial intelligence, and narrative theory.* Bloomington: Indiana University Press.
Ryan, M.-L. (1992). The modes of narrativity and their visual metaphors. *Style, 26,* 368–387.
Shklovsky, V. (1965a). Art as technique. In L. T. Lemon & M. J. Reis (Eds.), *Russian formalist criticism* (pp. 3–24). Lincoln: University of Nebraska Press.
Shklovsky, V. (1965b). Sterne's *Tristram Shandy:* Stylistic commentary. In L. T. Lemon & M. J. Reis (Eds.), *Russian formalist criticism* (pp. 25–57). Lincoln: University of Nebraska Press.
Stanzel, F. K. (1955). *Die typischen Erzählsituationen im Roman* [The typical narrative situations in the novel]. Vienna: Braumüller.
Todorov, T. (Ed.). (1965). *Théorie de la littérature* [Theory of literature]. Paris: Seuil.
Todorov, T. (1969). *Grammaire du "Décaméron"* [Grammar of "The Decameron"]. The Hague, Netherlands: Mouton.
Todorov, T. (1970). Les transformations narratives [Narrative transformations]. *Poétique, 3,* 322–333.
Todorov, T. (1973). *Poétique* [Poetics]. Paris: Seuil.
Tomashevsky, B. (1965). Thematics. In L. T. Lemon & M. J. Reis (Eds.), *Russian formalist criticism* (pp. 61–95). Lincoln: University of Nebraska Press.

# Labov and Waletzky in Context

## Cynthia Bernstein
*Department of English, Auburn University*

In a scathing look at a group of literary theorists he calls "Contextualists"—among them Mary Louise Pratt, Barbara Herrnstein Smith, Thomas Leitch, and Susan Lanser—Seymour Chatman (1990) invoked Labov and Waletzky (1967/this issue; henceforth L&W) and Labov (1972) as representing a narrow sociolinguistic perspective in opposition to an inclusive structuralist narratology. For Chatman, at issue is a choice between a contextualist model based upon L&W and a structuralist model based upon the work of such narratologists as Shklovsky, Barthes, and Gennette. I suggest here that this is a false choice. In taking L&W out of context, Chatman misrepresented their stance: "Narrative Analysis" was completely consistent with structuralist analysis of literary narratives. At the same time, however, it provided a foundation for what Toolan (1996) called an "integrational linguistic approach" to the study of narrative texts. What Chatman rejected is not so much L&W's model of natural narrative but the usefulness of natural narrative in the understanding of what he saw as the relative complexity of literary texts. Here, too, I see a false distinction. Although any given story might be classified as natural or literary, oral or written, simple or complex, those classifications are not binary opposites, but merely the definable extremes of endless possibilities.

L&W provided a starting point for examining natural, oral, simple narratives. Although the authors were explicit in rejecting "the products of expert storytellers" in favor of "the original productions of a representative sample of the population," their insights have been persuasive in defining structures that underlie literary narratives as well (see, e.g., Fleischman, 1990; Pratt, 1977). In spite of the fact that their analysis is restricted to "actual narratives of large numbers of unsophisticated speakers," it is consistent with their view of complex narratives as "the result of the combination and evolution of simpler elements" that the essay be seen as a tool for examining the most sophisticated literary narratives. A model that defines funda-

---

Requests for reprints should be sent to Cynthia Bernstein, Department of English, Auburn University, Auburn, AL 36849-5203. E-mail: bernscy@mail.auburn.edu

mental narrative structures to examine more complex ones would seem compatible with structuralist narratology, but Chatman did not see it that way.

A structuralist narratological framework depends essentially upon the distinction between a story's deep structure and surface structure. Chatman (1990) put it this way: "All that narratology argues is the difference between the act of telling (or showing) and the object told, and between their different temporal orders" (p. 312). Chatman accused L&W's model of "blurring ... the distinction between story and discourse, and the separate time orders that each entails" (p. 317) and failing to allow for a deep structure, but seeing "the whole structure right there in the surface of the text itself" (p. 318). In sharp contrast with Chatman's accusation, L&W did go to some effort to establish a structuralist framework that includes the familiar linguistic distinction between deep structure and surface structure (Chomsky 1965). Seeking to analyze "the most fundamental narrative structures," L&W relied upon "the basic techniques of linguistic analysis, isolating the invariant structural units, which are represented by a variety of superficial forms." The contrast between "invariant structural units" and a "variety of superficial forms" suggests the very distinction between deep structure and surface structure that Chatman claimed is absent from the model. Furthermore, L&W distinguished between "the sequence of events inferred from the narrative" (comparable to story) and "the sequence of clauses in the narrative" (comparable to discourse); relating the two is what they perceive to be the "fundamental question of narrative analysis." They stated explicitly that "the linear sequence presented by the narrator ... may be considered the *surface structure* of the narrative; there are often many narratives with rather different surface structures but with equivalent semantic interpretations." Because "superficial forms" are what vary, discussion of the 14 stories presented in "Narrative Analysis" is concerned primarily with surface structure. Still, the main purpose of L&W's analysis is to suggest an underlying model:

> A composite view of narrative performance leads us to posit a *normal form* for oral versions of personal experience; the degree to which any one narrative approximates this normal form is a significant fact about that narrative—perhaps more significant than any other ...

The contrast, then, between an invariant normal form and variable superficial forms reflects Chomsky's (1965) distinction between deep structure and surface structure and suggests the same story–discourse, *fabula–sjuzhet, histoire–discours* distinctions made by structuralist narratologists.[1]

---

[1]See Prince (1987) and Toolan (1988) for discussions of these narratological dichotomies. Toolan drew another appropriate linguistic analogy, comparing the story level to phonology (in that both are abstractions) and the discourse level to phonetics (in that both are actual realizations).

Others have readily connected this analysis (or its counterpart in Labov, 1972) with Formalist narratology. Pratt (1977) asserted: "If it weren't for the fact that his data are not literature, Labov's analysis could have provided valuable linguistic support for the Formalists' ideas about the aesthetic organization of narrative" (p. 68), a claim that is particularly ironic in view of Chatman's connection of Pratt and L&W with the Contextualists. Pratt compared the Russian Formalist distinction between fabula and sjuzhet with Labov's distinction between narrative core and evaluation (Pratt, 1977, p. 68). Along similar lines, Fleischman (1990) associated fabula with L&W's inferred sequence of events. It seems, then, that there is little support for Chatman's position that L&W ignored a distinction between the deep structure of a story and the act of telling it.

Another of Chatman's criticisms is that the sociolinguistic model is "monochronic" (p. 318, fn. 11), that it prohibits "the exchange or 'twisting' of (surface) clauses out of their causal-sequential order" (p. 318). It is true that L&W asserted: "The basic narrative units that we wish to isolate are defined by the fact that they recapitulate experience in the same order as the original events" (pp. 20–21), but it should also be kept in mind that such temporal ordering refers not to the entire range of possibilities but to the unmarked "basic narrative units" of unpracticed storytellers. All of Chatman's references to Labov or to L&W are quoted out of context from Pratt (1977), including Labov's definition of a *minimal narrative* as "a sequence of two clauses which are *temporally ordered*" (Labov, 1972, p. 360; quoted in Chatman, 1990, p. 318; quoted in Pratt, 1977, p. 44). A minimal narrative is not intended to define a literary narrative, a folk tale, or even a personal experience story. A minimal narrative is a unit by which larger structures may be analyzed. Even in the limited corpus presented in "Narrative Analysis," there is an example of a story told by a more practiced storyteller who deviates from the expected temporal sequence and whose story is rejected as primary data for that very reason (L&W, fn. 9). It is essential to ascertain what constitutes the unmarked form of natural storytelling in order to understand the departures that make some storytellers seem practiced. Fleischman (1990) observed that artificial narratives typically do depart from the linear representation suggested by L&W, but that "the artistic effects produced by these departures depend on an assumption that sequential presentation constitutes a norm for the ordering of material in a narrative" (p. 167). That is, rather than defining what constitutes the norm for a literary narrative, "Narrative Analysis" describes the typical means for telling simple stories. L&W reserve for a later study consideration of "sub-cycles and complex narratives" (fn. 11).

If narrative served only a referential function, the syntax of simple narratives might adhere more regularly to temporally ordered independent clauses. What complicates most natural narratives is their corresponding *evaluative* function, defined by L&W as "that part of the narrative which reveals the attitude of the narrator towards the narrative by emphasizing the relative importance of some narrative units as compared to others."[2] When evaluation is weak or lacking, the narrative appears insignificant, pointless, difficult to understand. Labov's method of collecting data encouraged tellable narratives. The "Danger of Death" question used to elicit narratives was something like: "Were you ever in a situation where you were in serious danger of being killed, where you said to yourself—'This is it'?" (Labov, 1972, p. 354; L&W, 1967/this issue). The point is that what stimulates the telling is "a matter quite relevant to the functional analysis of narrative" (L&W, this issue). In contrast, Chatman argued that "tellability" is a worthless criterion by which to judge literary narratives. Although he acknowledged the likelihood of tellability governing a storyteller's success in a vernacular context, he argued against extending a "model of audience power" (p. 325) to the literary situation.

One problem, as Chatman saw it, is that "Contextualism evidently prefers real authors and readers" (p. 314), as opposed to a model that posits an audience built into the text. This argument is directed not so much at L&W but at literary theorists who appropriate a model for narrative in conversation as the basis for the structure of fictional narrative. Apart from the fact that many writers and theorists do posit an originating oral context for the literary narrative,[3] a model based on an oral context can indeed account for multiple audiences, both internal and external to the narrative proper. Labov's Observer's Paradox—"[t]o obtain data on the most systematic form of language (the vernacular), we must observe how people speak when they are not being observed" (Labov, 1972, p. xvii)—accounts for the notion that the structure of speech is likely to vary with the speaker's perception of audience. A speaker's awareness of the observer as audience, then, is likely to become part of the structure of that speaker's utterances. As Bell (1996) and others have suggested, an oral context may involve not only one or more addressees but also overhearers as well as imagined and unimagined audiences who may later hear recorded versions of the original presentation.[4] Chatman recognized theatrical performance as a context that blurs the distinction between real and imagined audiences, but there are many others. A technological environment that involves frequent recording and replaying of conversational exchange through a variety of media allows for a wide range of possible audiences, some of whom may be imagined by speakers or authors and thereby represented in their oral or written utterances. A similar argument may be made regarding the range of possible

---

[2] Labov (1972) modified somewhat the treatment of evaluation as a separate section of a narrative, treating it instead as something that permeates all parts of the narrative structure.

[3] See, for example, Tannen (1984), who concluded that "all narrative, spoken or written, is modeled on the oral storytelling genre" (p. 39). For a discussion of the oral quality of narrative, see Bernstein (1987). See also Enkvist (1985) for a comparison of literary and nonliterary storytelling and their application to courses in creative writing.

[4] See Bernstein (1987) on the subject of internal and external audiences. For another context addressing the intricacies of speaker and audience, see Tannen (1988).

speakers or narrators. Even in an actual conversational context, the speakers may to a greater or lesser degree be representing their own voice or opinions. People may act as spokespersons for others, they may speak in an ironic tone, they may quote directly or indirectly the voices of others, and so on. Rather than positing categories of real or imagined speakers, authors, or narrators, narrative theory must allow for the widest range of possibilities.

Another problem that Chatman had with tellability as a criterion is that subjective judgment is required in order to evaluate it, thereby eradicating the "hard-won distinction between literary theory and literary criticism" (p. 324). Whereas the speaker in a conversational context has only the floor at stake, a writer's dependence for approval upon an interpretive community risks failure of a greater magnitude.[5] Chatman posed the rhetorical question: "What if a manuscript by some mute, inglorious Joyce is turned down by every publishing-house-as-'selector' forever? Would that mean that the text had *never* been 'tellable,' never a literary narrative?" (p. 326). The underlying issue deserves a thoughtful response. Unfortunately, Chatman's use of "Joyce" within the question as a metonym for "a great author whose work is unarguably tellable" makes the question he has phrased a circular one. If the question were phrased simply as: "What if a manuscript is turned down by every publisher ...," one could respond that the work might be tellable to some other audience but not to the ones imagined by the publishers to whom the work was submitted; it might be appreciated more by another culture or at another time. If one ignores issues of tellability and audience, one loses the opportunity to explain—not critically but theoretically—why some kinds of stories are valued by some cultures and not by others. As Tannen (1984) and others pointed out, not only the point of a story but also the strategies used to evaluate it and interpret it are culturally bound.[6] Chatman himself, arguing for a theory that is independent of context, slipped in the notion of culture when he asked: "[W]hy should we worry about the speech-act situation at all, instead of simply concentrating on the intrinsic properties of the 'detachable' text-type that our culture calls 'narrative'?" (p. 324). In response, it is the speech-act situation that leads to the definition of narrative held by "our culture." There is considerable loss, then, in maintaining a model of narrative structure that fails to account for the effects of culture.

I have argued here that placing L&W in the camp of the Contextualists in opposition to Structuralists is a consequence of taking them out of context. Further,

---

[5]See Bernstein (1993) for a discussion of how real and fictional interpretive communities impact narrative structure.

[6]Nationality, gender, and history are among the cultural factors affecting the evaluative function in storytelling. See Polanyi (1985) for a discussion of American cultural constraints on storytelling. Abney (1994) found that males used evaluation more often than females in their storytelling. De Beaugrande (1980) found that "value assignments" (his term for evaluation) in an 1878 folk tale occur more frequently at "turning points" (p. 269).

I have suggested the value of a sociolinguistic conversational model in analyzing narrative. I am not proposing, however, that such a model replace the valuable contributions made by Chatman and others, but that structuralist narratology must incorporate pragmatics in order to account for textual structures resulting from cultural contexts surrounding actual and fictional speakers and writers, audiences and readers. Supporting an expanded model of narratology is the multidisciplinary interest taken by the contributors to this special issue of the *Journal of Narrative and Life History*. Sternberg (1990) recognized the need for blending the boundaries of discipline when he wrote that linguists, sociologists, and others have been "working in complete isolation from literary material and methodology" (p. 921, fn. 15). Sternberg misread Labov (1972), however, when he complained that Labov excluded fictional narrative "by definition" (Sternberg, 1990, p. 921, fn. 15; see also p. 912, fn. 7). Labov (1972) and especially L&W saw the analysis of natural narrative as essential to the understanding of complex fictional narratives. Movement toward an interdisciplinary approach is also evident in Toolan (1996), whose "integrational linguistic approach" is applied to both literary and nonliterary texts. Likewise, Herman (1995) referred to a "Narratology After Structuralism," an upcoming project whose approach is both structural and pragmatic (p. 225, fn. 1). Elsewhere (Bernstein 1994a, 1994b) I argued for an approach that accounts for both the structural forms and the pragmatic functions of narrative. A workable narratology cannot afford to maintain such binary oppositions as Structuralism and Contextualism. I agree with Toolan's argument that: "we are much too confident in thinking that we know just what is text and just what is context" (Toolan, 1996, p. 4). The new narratology will need to reexamine such binary oppositions as oral–written, actual–fictional, contextual–structural in order to recognize that most of those distinctions are not categories by which narrative devices can be labeled but ranges of possibilities by which some strategies might be usefully described.

## REFERENCES

Abney, L. (1994). Gender differences in oral folklore narratives. *The SECOL Review, 18,* 62–79.

Bell, A. (1996, October). *Sociolinguistics of style.* Paper presented at New Ways of Analyzing Variation in English 25, Las Vegas, NV.

Bernstein, C. (1987). *The internal audience in literary and rhetorical discourse.* Unpublished doctoral dissertation, Texas A & M University, College Station.

Bernstein, C. (1993). Reading *The scarlet letter* against Hawthorne's fictional interpretive community. *Language and Literature, 18,* 1–20.

Bernstein, C. (1994a). The contextualization of linguistic criticism. In C. Bernstein (Ed.), *The text and beyond: Essays in literary linguistics* (pp. 3–14). Tuscaloosa: University of Alabama Press.

Bernstein, C. (1994b). Language and literature in context. *The SECOL Review, 18,* 45–61.

Chatman, S. (1990). What can we learn from contextualist narratology? *Poetics Today, 11,* 309–328.

Chomsky, N. (1965). *Aspects of the theory of syntax.* Cambridge: MIT Press.

de Beaugrande, R. (1980). *Text, discourse, and process: Toward a multidisciplinary science of texts.* Norwood, NJ: Ablex.

Enkvist, N. E. (1985). Text and discourse linguistics, rhetoric, and stylistics. In T. van Dijk (Ed.), *Discourse and literature* (pp. 11–38). Amsterdam: John Benjamins.

Fleischman, S. (1990). *Tense and narrativity: From medieval performance to modern fiction.* Austin: University of Texas Press.

Herman, D. (1995). *Universal grammar and narrative form.* Durham, NC: Duke University Press.

Labov, W. (1972). The transformation of experience in narrative syntax. *Language in the inner city* (pp. 354–396). Philadelphia: The University of Pennsylvania Press.

Labov, W., & Waletzky, J. (this issue). Narrative analysis: Oral versions of personal experience. In J. Helm (Ed.), *Essays on the verbal and visual arts: Proceedings of the 1966 Annual Spring Meeting of the American Ethnological Society* (pp. 12–44). Seattle: University of Washington Press. (Original work published 1967)

Polanyi, L. (1985). *Telling the American story: A structural and cultural analysis of conversational storytelling.* Norwood, NJ: Ablex.

Pratt, M. L. (1977). *Toward a speech act theory of literary discourse.* Bloomington: Indiana University Press.

Prince, G. (1987). *A dictionary of narratology.* Lincoln: University of Nebraska Press.

Sternberg, M. (1990). Telling in time (I): Chronology and narrative theory. *Poetics Today, 11,* 901–948.

Tannen, D. (1984). Spoken and written narrative in English and Greek. In *Coherence in spoken and written discourse* (pp. 21–41). Norwood, NJ: Ablex.

Tannen, D. (1988). The commingling of orality and literacy in giving a paper at a scholarly conference. *American Speech, 63,* 34–43.

Toolan, M. J. (1988). *Narrative: A critical linguistic introduction.* London: Routledge.

Toolan, M. J. (1996). *Total speech: An integrational linguistic approach to language.* Durham, NC: Duke University Press.

# From Labov and Waletzky to "Contextualist Narratology": 1967–1997

### Joyce Tolliver
*Department of Spanish, Italian, and Portuguese*
*University of Illinois–Urbana*

When I was asked by the editor of this volume to write up a short "piece" for this special commemorative issue, I immediately (once I recovered from the flush of self-importance his flattering invitation brought) began to imagine a little essay in which I would recapitulate the ways in which Labov and Waletzky (1967/this issue; henceforth L&W) influenced narratology and narrative theory.[1] Clearly that 1967 attempt to sketch out a tentative model for at least some aspects of narrative structure was fundamental to the project that Chatman (1969, 1978), Prince (1973), Todorov (1969, 1971, 1973, 1977), Genette (1972), Culler (1975a, 1975b), and other structuralists would eagerly undertake in the 60s and 70s.[2] As Toolan (1988) rightly pointed out, it has largely been L&W's *referential* function that has been discussed at length by narratologists, to the relative neglect of their *evaluative* function. Without a doubt, the concept of minimal narrative units and indeed the entire project of establishing what narratives (and only narratives) might have in common was at the heart of the structuralist narratological enterprise, an enterprise that was largely conceptualized and elaborated after the appearance of the L&W essay. And yet, the notion of the evaluative function has also influenced later discussions of those interested in narrative theory; certainly it was crucial to the development of the

---

Requests for reprints should be sent to Joyce Tolliver, Department of Spanish, Italian, and Portuguese, University of Illinois, Urbana, IL 61801. E-mail: joycet@uiuc.edu

[1] I distinguish *narratology*, which is explicitly structuralist and relatively narrow in focus, from the larger category of *narrative theory*, which includes a much greater variety of theoretical departure points and areas of interest.

[2] Barthes (1966/1977b) deserves a mention apart here. Not only because, as it happens, his groundbreaking "Introduction to the Structural Analysis of Narratives," although reprinted in *Image-Music-Text* in 1977, was first published in French in 1966, the year before L&W, and thus disrupts my neat vision of L&W as originating, engendering figures; but also because his work in large part took literary theory in very different directions than did the work of the other narratologists I have named.

concepts of tellability and "point," and in many ways it was central to reader-response theories of literature. This is not to imply that Culler, Prince, and other literary theorists had heard the presentation given at the 1966 American Ethnological Society in Philadelphia; or even that they had read the Proceedings in which the paper appeared the following year. I do want to suggest that that work suggests a model, if not a method, that reflected the central concerns of narratologists working and publishing in the years just after 1967.

Nevertheless, the more I thought about the ways in which students of narrative theory—those theorizing primarily about literary texts, that is—had, consciously or not, been influenced by L&W, the more I was forced to recognize the more crucial ways in which the project outlined in that fundamental essay had not been exploited by those working "in" literature. When I first read the essay as a graduate student, I found the identification of the "invariant structural units" of narrative "which are represented by a variety of superficial forms" (L&W, this issue) rather dizzying and ultimately considerably less interesting than the discussion of narrative's evaluative functions, barely begun there but developed more fully in Labov (1972). By the time I read the essay, it was the mid-80s, nearly two decades after its original publication; a time when structuralism was ceding to poststructuralism and concepts such as "invariant structural units" (or, indeed, invariant anything) were no longer accepted without question by literary theorists and critics. Yet, curiously to my mind, narratologists had done relatively little with L&W's assertion that "normally, narrative serves an additional function of personal interest determined by a stimulus in the social context in which narrative occurs." It was precisely this social context that interested me at the time and that in fact still interests me; yet, as Toolan (1988) politely put it: "narrative has not always been properly related to its contexts of occurrence, its role as an instrument or resource for its human 'users'" (p. 147), especially, I would add, by those whose interests lie fundamentally in the field of literary theory.

Perhaps it should not have surprised me, after all, that structuralist narratologists should have taken up only what turned out to be a relatively small part of L&W's project. For, clearly, from the beginning the narratologists shared what Christine Brooke-Rose (1990) called a "dream of a 'science' of literature with universal rules" (p. 287). Barthes (1966/1977b) draws an analogy between narrative, whose existence he sees as universal across cultures and across time, and language itself. For Barthes, linguistics can and should provide our model for the study of narrative—but remember that Barthes also confidently added: "as we know, linguistics stops at the sentence" (p. 82). I wonder now if perhaps 1966 marked, not the sealing of the coming together of linguistics and literary criticism (begun decades earlier), but indeed a splitting off between the two disciplines, a parting of ways. For, if the paper L&W presented at the 1966 meeting of the American Ethnological Society shows anything, it shows that in fact linguistics does not "stop at the sentence" and certainly that the study of narrative must focus on the relation between and among sentences. Within linguistics, the study of narrative would inevitably become a discourse-based study, but narratologists, working within literary theory, would eventually renounce the linguistic model rather than expand it beyond the level of the sentence.

For Barthes (1966/1977b), then, writing in 1966, just as "structuralism's constant aim [is] to master the infinity of utterances [paroles] by describing the 'language' [langue] of which they are products and from which they can be generated" (p. 80), so students of narrative should generate the models of narrative structure that underlie all (and only) narratives. The work of other structuralists followed this same logic and posited this same goal. Yet, curiously, in a field of study of which "universality was the point" (Brooke-Rose, 1990, p. 286), the variety of narratives taken as primary corpora was remarkably limited. All of the early narratologists examined only written narrative fiction in their search for universals, and for the most part they limit their examination to male-authored, canonical European and North American prose fiction of the last two centuries.[3] The two most famous (and in some ways most brilliant) examples of narrative theory from this period are both extended analyses of single French novels: Barthes's (1970) *S/Z,* which examined the various "codes" at work in Balzac's *Sarrasine,*[4] and Genette's (1981) *Narrative Discourse: An Essay in Method,* which is an extended meditation on Proust's *Remembrance of Things Past.*[5]

The early narratologists, then, claimed universal generalizability for their models, but, working as they were within the context of literary theory, they excluded precisely those narratives that L&W suggested might present an ideal starting point: relatively simple conversational narratives told by speakers with a limited formal education (which is not, of course, to imply a parallel limitation on their storytelling skills, a point that is made abundantly clear in Labov, 1972). L&W, on the other hand, made no claims about the universality of their findings. In fact, they framed their analysis in language with a tentativeness (or a caution) that is rarely found in works of literary theory, especially those of the late 60s and the 70s: "We are *beginning* to analyze relative effectiveness and completeness of narrative structure *among various subgroups of our population*" (1967/this issue, p. 38; italics added). Indeed, they are explicit about the nonuniversality of their claims: "It is clear that these conclusions are restricted to the speech communities that we have examined. This view of narrative structure will achieve greater significance when materials from radically different cultures

---

[3]Barthes's "Introduction" (1966/1977b) does take *Goldfinger,* a James Bond novel by Ian Fleming, as its primary text of praxis, while also referring to Poe and Flaubert, and Todorov's (1969) early narratological work proposed a "grammar" of the *Decameron* (following Propp). All of the early narratological models search for their "universal" rules in the written text.

[4]To be more precise, *Sarrasine* is a novella.

[5]Genette's landmark work was first published in French in 1972 *(Figures III),* and its translation to English appeared in 1981.

are studied in the same way" (1967/this issue, p. 38). Their socio-linguistic perspective necessarily calls for a recognition of the crucial role played by narrator–audience dynamics and by such variables within this dynamic as age, race, class, and cultural background. Thirty years later, standard narratological models, although building in many ways on this pioneering essay, still routinely ignore these crucial factors. In this sense, L&W's elision of gender as a key variable seems less remarkable, for the importance of this aspect to narrative structure has been downplayed even by those Seymour Chatman (1990) has (rather disparagingly) called "contextualist" narratologists.

Looking back, now, at the development of narratology and narrative theory since the appearance of L&W, I am no longer able to outline the simple linear "progress" I had initially imagined. The structuralist enterprise of narratology, claiming universality but ignoring conversational narratives, taking linguistics as its model but limiting itself to an application of sentence-level syntax whereby the literary narrative text was compared to the sentence, limped through the 70s and was, by the early 80s, clearly in trouble. As early as 1981, Susan Sniader Lanser called for a new narrative poetics, one that would not excise narrative from the social context L&W saw as integral to a study of stories and storytelling. In particular, she called for an inclusion of the element of gender in narratological models, a call for action that she later formalized in her landmark 1986 article. The year before, Mieke Bal (1985) also called for a consideration of narrative's cultural and social grounding, specifically highlighting the aspect of gender studies.[6] The response to the proposals of Lanser, Bal and other "new" narratologists is illustrative of the sorts of tensions existing within the field of narratology during the 80s, tensions that have not yet been resolved.

Lanser published her essay outlining the project of a "feminist narratology" in 1986, the same year that Mary Louise Pratt called into question the ethnocentricity of speech-act theory and thus sharply called into question, as well, her own earlier work applying speech-act theory to the literary text. It was a time of rapid change, of revisioning, within literary theory. Lanser (1988) would find herself obligated to point out, indeed, that it was time of "paradigm shift" (this was, of course, not yet a cliché).[7] She was responding to an article appearing in *Style,* where her article on "feminist narratology" had appeared, that took issue not only with her proposal for a feminist narratology, but with the very notion of any narratology that considered "extratextual" aspects. Evidence that narratology could no longer complacently exist in isolation from trends in linguistics and the rest of the literary theory was readily available, in the form of contributions such as Rimmon-Kenan's (1989) critique of "the crisis of narratology" and Michael Toolan's (1988) lucid and eloquent melding of literary theory and discourse linguistics which appeared

---

[6] Bal's 1985 book is a revision and a translation of her 1977 *Narratologie* (Bal, 1977).
[7] I have recently seen an advertisement for a t-shirt that reads: "Do you have change for a paradigm?"

the previous year. However, the multiple appeals for a more socially situated narratology have met considerable resistance. A 1990 issue of *Poetics Today,* the first of two issues whose topic is "Narratology Revisted," offers a case in point. It is here that Seymour Chatman (1990) poses the question I alluded to earlier: "What can we learn from contextualist narratology?" By "contextualist narratology," he refers to a loosely defined group whose "chief objection to narratology is that it fails to take into account the actual setting in which literature [note that he refers to *literature,* rather than to *narrative*] is situated" (p. 309). In this category Chatman placed such disparate theorists as Susan Lanser (with reference to her 1981 work), Mary Louise Pratt (most surprisingly, because of her 1977 book, which does not address itself explicitly to questions of narrative per se) and Thomas Leitch (1986). His answer to the question he posed is readily apparent: What can we learn from those who want to take into account questions of the "context" of narrative? Not much. Surprisingly, most of his criticism is aimed at Pratt (1977)—this, 4 years after she herself had already disassociated herself from that work (but for reasons that have nothing to do with the flaws Chatman found in her model). Chatman also takes aim at L&W and Labov (1972) in this article. Much of his rejection of their work seems to depend on questionable readings of the article we are now all discussing today. Chatman claims that his rejection of the Labovian choice to speculate on narrative structure via an investigation of "vernacular stories" "is not elitist" (p. 317). Yet, what are we to think when he rhetorically asks: "Why give up a broad base for an evidently narrower and less informative choice?" (p. 317). Apparently, studies of Proust's *Remembrance of Things Past* constitute a "broad base"; preliminary findings based on a corpus of 600 oral narratives are "narrower and less informative."

Chatman's (1990) article coexists in the same issue of *Poetics Today* with an article by Gerald Prince (1990) that proposes a move toward a typology of narratives and Brooke-Rose's (1990) article, "Whatever Happened to Narratology?" Brooke-Rose clearly considers narratology to be already dead and gone; Chatman is energetically resisting what he (rightly) perceives as a threat to orthodox narratology—a threat posed years before the publication of his 1990 article—and Prince seems oblivious to the fact that the field has changed at all in the previous decade and a half. We find the same tensions within narratology, the same resistance to considering the social context so crucial to Labovian approaches to narrative, a full 5 years later, this time in the pages of *Narrative.* The players are, by now, familiar figures: Susan Lanser (1995), who returns to her call for a "sexing" of narrative (her title alludes to Jeannette Winterson's *Sexing the Cherry*), and Gerald Prince (1995), who roundly rejects any intrusion of the external into the object of narratological study.

Brooke-Rose's (1990) death knell to narratology, sounded now these 7 years ago, may have been a bit premature then. But now, I am beginning to wonder if perhaps its time has, indeed, come. I would be convinced of it were it not for the appearance on the scene, even as recently as 1996, of studies of narrative such as Monika Fludernik's (1996) most recent book, studies that are thoroughly contemporary, in touch, and authoritative—and that unapologetically situate themselves within narratology. However, Fludernik's work goes far beyond the scope of orthodox narratology. It does seem to me that narratology, the way the orthodox narratologists insist on defining it, has indeed come—and gone. This is not to say that L&W's insistence on narrative's situation in social interaction has been ignored completely; it's just that the social grounding of narrative has been much more widely considered by those literary critics and theoreticians working outside of narratology; largely, these days, in culture studies.

The most recent issue of *Narrative,* in fact, is full of calls for a critical practice that not only remembers literature's—especially narrative's— social, cultural, and historical grounding, but that even allows for the (re)entry of such old-fashioned elements as emotion (even though it still seems more acceptable, in academic circles, to speak of "affect"). Evaluation, in both the Labovian and the regular senses, has returned, it seems. Wayne C. Booth (1997) speaks of judging (yes, judging!) the efficacy of one type of self-reflexive narrative in overtly affective, evaluative terms: "The ultimate test is not, 'Did the story grip me?' but 'Is the person I lived with—always finally the implied author—a good day-by-day mate?'" (p. 54). Ross Chambers (1997) rejects a tendency in his earlier work by which he "fell in with the general thrust of academic theories of reading, which ... are uninterested in reading as a social practice" (p. 68) and, while reviewing Barthes's "Death of the Author" (1966/1977b) suggests that we direct our attention toward "an issue of theoretical responsibility: what responsibility, toward the author, is entailed by a reader whose reading displaces—however inevitably—an authorial sense?" (p. 69). Nancy K. Miller (1997) sees the sorts of changes exemplified in Chambers's piece as good signs indeed for the health of narrative studies: "I see as a hopeful turn in the study of narrative ... the return—or is it the arrival—of emotions, of affective engagement" (p. 64). Quoting Michele Barrett and Anne Phillips, she encourages us to resist "the generational fallacy," which assumes that "later theory is therefore better theory, and that the best theory of all is the position from which we happen at the moment to be speaking" (p. 63).[8] I share Miller's optimism and can think of no better illustration of the aptly named generational fallacy than the vivid relevance that L&W holds for all of us interested in narrative theory now, 30 years later.

## REFERENCES

Bal, M. (1977). *Narratologie: Essais sur la signification narrative dans quatre romans modernes* [Narratology: Essays on narrative meaning in four modern novels]. Paris: Klincksieck.
Bal, M. (1985). *Narratology: Introduction to the theory of narrative* (Christine van Boheemen, Trans.).

---

[8]The quotation from Barrett and Phillips (1982) appears on page 7 of their work.

Toronto, Canada: University of Toronto Press.
Barrett, M., & Phillips, A. (1982). Introduction to *Destabilizing theory: Contemporary feminist debates.* Stanford University Press, Stanford, CA.
Barthes, R. (1970). *S/Z.* Paris: Seuil.
Barthes, R. (1977a). The death of the author. In S. Heath (Ed. and Trans.), *Image-music-text* (pp. 142–148). New York: Hill & Wang.
Barthes, R. (1977b). Introduction to the structural analysis of narratives. In S. Heath (Ed. and Trans.), *Image-music-text* (pp. 79–124). New York: Hill & Wang.
Booth, W. C. (1997). The struggle to tell the story of the struggle to get the story told. *Narrative, 5*(1), 50–59.
Brooke-Rose, C. (1990). Whatever happened to narratology? *Poetics Today, 11,* 283–293.
Chambers, R. (1997). Reading, mourning and the death of the author. *Narrative, 5,* 67–76.
Chatman, S. (1969). New ways of analyzing narrative structures. *Language and Style, 2,* 3–36.
Chatman, S. (1978). *Story and discourse: Narrative structure in fiction and film.* Ithaca, NY: Cornell University Press.
Chatman, S. (1990). What can we learn from contextualist narratology? *Poetics Today, 11,* 309–328.
Culler, J. (1975a). Defining narrative units. In R. Fowler (Ed.), *Style and structure in literature* (pp. 123–142). Oxford: Blackwell.
Culler, J. (1975b). *Structuralist poetics: Structuralism, linguistics, and the study of literature.* Ithaca, NY: Cornell University Press.
Fludernik, M. (1996). *Towards a "natural" narratology.* New York: Routledge.
Genette, G. (1972). *Figures III.* Paris: Seuil.
Genette, G. (1981) *Narrative discourse: An essay in method* (J. E. Lewin, Trans.). Ithaca, NY: Cornell University Press.
Labov, W. (1972). The transformation of experience in narrative syntax. In W. Labov (Ed.), *Language in the inner city* (pp. 354–396). Philadelphia: University of Pennsylvania Press.
Labov, W., & Waletzky, J. (this issue). Narrative analysis: Oral versions of personal experience. In J. Helm (Ed.), *Essays on the verbal and visual arts: Proceedings of the 1966 Annual Spring Meeting of the American Ethnological Society* (pp. 12–44). Seattle: University of Washington Press. (Original work published 1967)
Lanser, S. S. (1981). *The narrative act: Point of view in prose fiction.* Princeton, NJ: Princeton University Press.
Lanser, S. S. (1986). Toward a feminist narratology. *Style, 20,* 341–63.
Lanser, S. S. (1988). Shifting the paradigm: Feminism and narratology. *Style, 22,* 52–60.
Lanser, S. S. (1995). Sexing the narrative: Propriety, desire, and the engendering of narratology. *Narrative, 3,* 85–94.
Leitch, T. (1986). *What stories are: Narrative theory and interpretation.* University Park: Pennsylvania State University Press.
Miller, N. K. (1997). Time pieces. *Narrative, 5,* 60–66.
Pratt, M. L. (1977). *Toward a speech act theory of literature.* Bloomington: Indiana University Press.
Pratt, M. L. (1986). The ideology of speech act theory. *Poetics Today, 7,* 59–72.
Prince, G. (1973). *A grammar of stories.* Berlin: Mouton.
Prince, G. (1990). On narrative studies and narrative genres. *Poetics Today, 11*(2), 271–282.
Prince, G. (1995). On narratology: Criteria, corpus, context. *Narrative, 3*(1), 76–85.
Rimmon-Kenan, S. (1989). How the model neglects the medium: Linguistics, language, and the crisis of narratology. *Journal of Narrative Technique, 19,* 157–166.
Todorov, T. (1969). *Grammaire du Décameron* [A grammar of the Decameron]. The Hague, Netherlands: Mouton.
Todorov, T. (1971). *La Poétique de la prose* [The poetics of prose]. Paris: Seuil.
Todorov, T. (1973). *Poétique* [Poetics]. Paris: Seuil.

Todorov, T. (1977). *The poetics of prose* (R. Howard, Trans.). Ithaca: Cornell University Press.
Todorov, T. (1981). *Introduction to poetics* (R. Howard, Trans). Minneapolis: University of Minnesota Press.
Toolan, M. (1988). *Narrative: A critical linguistic introduction.* New York: Routledge.

# Labov and Waletzky Thirty Years On

## Jerome Bruner
### School of Law, New York University

It is rather a moving experience "retroreading" the classic paper by Labov and Waletzky (1967/this issue; hereafter L&W) 30 years on, reading it in a mood of critical retrospect rather than to refresh memory when one has assigned it to a class yet again. One realizes how much L&W were caught in the time warp of their day—call it the structuralist warp—but at the same time, were fighting valiantly to be free of it. If the paper "failed" to achieve the structural linguistic ideal of its day in its formal "clausal analysis," it nonetheless succeeded in blazing a trail for students of overall narrative structure. L&W truly created a landmark, but it may not have been the one that they had in mind. Indeed, *landmark* may be the wrong word, for L&W is still as much of a fresh challenge as it ever was.

In what follows, I shall be particularly concerned with the dissonance between these two "missions" of their article: the decompositional objective of their clausal analysis on the one hand, and their effort to characterize the overall features or "segments" of a well-formed narrative on the other.

I think the failure of L&W's decompositional structuralism was inherent in the analytic model they chose to follow. It was the model that, following Hockett (1960), we have come to call "duality of patterning," the model that works so elegantly in the analysis of the "sound system" of language as one goes from distinctive features to phonemes to morphemes. It was *the* structuralist model of its day, made famous by the brilliant study of Jakobson and Halle (1956).[1] For any given language, for example, a *phoneme* is a sound unit a change in which alters the meaning of the word or morpheme it composes. That change, however, is also defined by the packet of contrasting distinctive features at a "lower level" that compose the phoneme. Thus, because the distinctive feature contrast palatal–dental

---

Requests for reprints should be sent to Jerome Bruner, School of Law, Faculty of Law, New York Unviersity, Fuchsberg Hall, 29 Sullivan Street, New York, NY 10012. E-mail: bruner@acf2.nyu.edu.

[1]See also Jakobson (1978), in which he attributes the discovery of such "duality" to the Polish linguist Baudoin de Courtenay, who had been professor of linguistics at Moscow in the late 19th century and whose discovery helped launch Russian Formalism, to which structuralist linguistics is so indebted (see also Levi-Strauss's preface to Jakobson, 1978).

does not apply in Japanese, Japanese phonemes remain invariant across a shift in this feature. So, for example, native Japanese speakers learning English cannot "hear" the difference between such English words as rob and lob, and use the two words interchangeably. An English /p/, conversely, sounds the "same" whether aspirated as in *pin* or unaspirated as in *spin*—at least to an English speaker, though not to others. Because such variants as the aspirated and unaspirated /p/ for English speakers are not distinguished (we say they are *allophones* of the same phoneme) they cannot be used at the next level up for distinguishing two morphemes. Perhaps, however, they cannot be distinguished because they are irrelevant to morpheme formation.

The compositional architecture that imbeds distinctive features, phonemes, and morphemes is exquisite—indeed, miraculous. Alas, as one mounts the language ladder from the sound system to systems of meaning, the structurally tight link between adjacent levels becomes more complex and fuzzier, more context bound and contingent. The relation between words and sentences is an intermediate case: Sentence syntax establishes rules for well-formedness. But syntactically defined well-formedness has little to do with meaning, as with the famous example, "Colorless green ideas sleep furiously." Sentence meaning depends not just upon well-formedness, not just upon words, but also upon word markers (like -*es* and -*ed*), intonation, and above all upon "context," which in turn is affected by the background knowledge of a listener and even by the existence of speech–act conventions, genres, conventional semantic and metaphoric clustering, and the like. By the time one gets to the forming constituents of a narrative text, the neat top-down/bottom-up duality miracle of the Jakobson–Halle formalism has been left long behind. Efforts to make sense of a "garbled" story seem to be guided much less by the interlocking multilevel constituents in the text than by some sort of seeming opportunism steered by a general search for "what's this all about." The big question in understanding narrative is what guides this "general" search. Are there simply constituent features of narrative *text* that guide us in bringing narrative meaning to a garbled, often narratively ill-formed account we hear? Or is there some narrative model in our minds that guide us?

Now back to L&W. Typical for its times, it is full of structuralist optimism. L&W propose that constituent *clauses* have a tightly defined structural relation to the narratives they comprise, much as with the structural link between distinctive features, phonemes, and morphemes. And so they begin their account by presenting an elaborate though rather conventional system for analyzing clause structures, clausal sequences, and displacement ranges, which are presumed to be the formal constituents of narratives. Having done so, they then proceed to a description of the "overall" structure of narrative, a discussion full of powerful and original ideas that, on close inspection, has trivially little to do with the clausal analysis they have just presented. There are some relations, but they seem neither strict nor convincing, almost artifactual spinoffs of the loose relations that exist between clauses and the discourse they constitute. I return to this matter, but first I need to set out L&W's treatment of the "overall structures" of narrative.

They propose five general features of narratives: *orientation, complication, evaluation, resolution,* and *coda*. These are characterized as sequential segments of a story. The function of the *orientation* segment is to orient a listener at the outset to "person, place, time, and behavioral situation." So far, so good. But then back to the clauses. Can orientation be "define[d] formally [as] the group of free clauses which precede the first narrative clause" (p. 30)? What of Kafka's novels—particularly *The Castle* and *The Trial*, where the narrative artifice depends upon "holding back" or minimizing on such orientational clauses? Granted, many stories begin by letting you know about the who, what, when, and where of what is to follow. But isn't this fulsome orientation more a genre specification—"newspaper story," for example—rather than a property of narrative text? Isn't it possible to provide "orientation" in the form of analepsis and prolepsis, flashbacks and flashforwards (see Goodman, 1980)? We seem to hold places in mind where we can fit these flashbacks and flashforwards. All of which suggests that narrative structure is created or exists not so much on the page as in the head of the listener. Texts evoke expectancies, though they may not fulfil them.

If an account begins, for example, "He staggered down the street, blood seeping from the stab wound in his arm ..., " we know that the story is well on its way; we also know in some intuitive way that an orientation is coming or, in any case, is due us. Indeed, if we actually came on the victim, we'd doubtless ask him what had happened, hoping for some orientation; but if he refused to speak, we'd also doubtless come up with some sort of hypothesis about what happened (a kind of pro tem orientation of our own)—for example, he'd been walking down an empty street and was mugged, he was a tough who'd been the victim of gang war, whatever. We would be trying to figure how this poor fellow had got from "ordinary" existence to his present bloodstained state. We don't need a segment of "free-standing clauses preceding the first narrative clause" to get our minds moving narratively. We search for orientation in creating a narrative, because a story requires some baseline canonical state to be disturbed or disrupted if it's to be a story.

But we're getting ahead of *our* story—to the issue of complication, L&W's second feature or "segment." *Complication* is the disturbance in a story. To understand its full sense, it helps to go back to Kenneth Burke's (1945) earlier, celebrated "dramatistic Pentad." For Burke, the requisite elements of a story are Agent, Action, Goal, Instrument, and Scene, not unlike L&W's orientation ensemble. But for him, the "engine" of dramatic narrative is not simply their interaction, but an imbalance between two or more of these elements—a mismatch, say, between Agent and Goal, Action and Scene, or whatnot. It is this imbalance that generates a sixth element, Trouble (Bruner, 1991). And it is Trouble that defines complication. Indeed, L&W take Trouble so much for granted as the heart of complication that they even gathered their corpus of narratives so as to guarantee its presence. Recall that they asked their subjects to tell about a time when their lives were endangered—the ultimate trouble! And, of course, it's virtually in the structure of narrative that if a story contains a troubled complication, it requires some explication about how things were before it got that way—that is, an orientation, telling how things were before the trouble erupted.

Complication will, of course, be familiar to students of Aristotle's *Poetics*. It is his *peripéteia*, a disruption of some canonical or legitimate order of things, a disruption specific to the time, situation, and protagonists of the tale that "locates" a story in a time and culture, as White (1981), Mink (1978), and Turner (1982) have subsequently demonstrated for historical and "preliterate" narratives. I think it was L&W who first made us sensitive to the cultural and historical specificity of narrative—that, as it were, stories are always local.

And I think it was their own sensitivity to this localness of trouble that led them to recognize the importance of evaluation, their third segment. Though brief, their discussion of it is nothing short of breathtaking, even today. *Evaluation* is the feature of a narrative that elucidates the relation between what happens in the story's complication with what might legitimately be expected to have happened, given its orientation. Evaluation, as it were, provides a narrative rationale for the fourth narrative feature, resolution. It is through evaluation that we are able to see the appropriateness (or inappropriateness) of the action taken by protagonists to achieve a resolution of the story's complication. And, of course, it is principally through evaluation that a storyteller introduces the perspectives of the story's protagonists—and his own perspective, if the story requires it, though most classic stories hide the narrator's perspective behind a screen of seemingly transparent omniscience.

The four features (I hesitate to call them *segments* for reasons I've already made clear) provide the coherence in a story. The fifth, the *coda*, serves a different function beyond that. It permits the listener "to tell the dancer from the dance," in Yeats's lovely line. It transports both the teller and hearer from the story's then-and-there to the here-and-now of the telling—a feature of narrative too often overlooked. It can take the form of a moral as in Aesop's fables, or implicitly leave listeners in a state of suspension with respect to the reality of the present here-and-now in contrast with the story's then-and-there, as in the more postmodern stories of an Italo Calvino, a Franz Kafka, or even a Gustave Flaubert.

I think it can be said without exaggeration that L&W's fivefold characterization of overall narrative structure transformed the study of narrative profoundly. It set many of us thinking about the cognitive representation of reality imposed by narrative structure on our experience of the world and on how we evaluate that experience. In that sense, it can be placed alongside such other classic "breakthroughs" as Burke's (1945), Mink's (1978), and Ricoeur's (1984). I happily admit that it set me thinking about narrative not simply as a form of text, but as a mode of thought (Bruner, 1986).

To be sure, there were many scholars thinking about the role of narrative in the "construction of reality" even 30 years ago: Vernant (1965), Levi-Strauss (1955), and Bartlett (1932) among them. But though the L&W paper was not explicitly "about" this topic, it provided a powerful impetus to further work along these lines—even to Labov's own work on Black English, the role of mobility on class-related idiolects, and the like. Hard to say why exactly. The consensus of colleagues I've consulted is that it was the clarity and "the detailed workability" of their approach that gave others courage.

I want to return now to L&W's "failed" clausal analysis. Why (at least in my opinion) did it not pay off? Let's explore this matter a little further. L&W justify the clause as the appropriate "unit of analysis" by criticizing the folklorist, Vladimir Propp (1956), for using too large a unit of analysis (the "functions" that comprise a tale structure as a whole, of which more presently), and then criticize the anthropologist Benjamin Colby (1966) for choosing too small a unit (single words whose frequencies he counted with the aim of distinguishing stories of different ethnic origin). Colby had no intention of analyzing narrative structure; he wanted only to differentiate different ethnic narratives. But were Propp's units, his functions, really too large?

Propp had argued (rather convincingly, I think) that the constituents of a tale, its functions as he called them, had to take their meanings from the tale as a whole, else they could not serve as a reflection of the tale's overall structure. He illustrated his point with the widely distributed folkloric "wonder tales" he was studying. Such tales always run an invariant course, starting with (a) some sort of shortage, lack, or loss, that (b) affects the well-being of a privileged principal protagonist, who (c) then goes on a quest, (d) in the course of which he meets a stranger who offers him a magic gift, and so forth, on through a baker's dozen of other functions. In any given version, a tale can tolerate deletions of functions so long as the sequential order of the remaining function is maintained. Note that Propp's analysis operates with open "slots" that permit "tokens of a type" to be inserted within them, thus allowing the contents of a story to vary while holding narrative structure invariant. Thus, the variorum texts of a wonder tale can tell of a young prince left alone who sets forth to discover the world and meets a fakir who offers him the gift of an endless golden thread, et cetera; or it can be about a musical prodigy who outgrows his teachers and sets forth to find the secret of music and meets an old fiddler who offers him the secret of the music of the spheres, et cetera. The coherence of the tale as a whole (as well as the meaning of its parts) depend upon the tale's overall structure, not upon its autonomous words or clauses. In Propp's view, as in the example, overall narrative structures and their constituent functions were genrelike, capable of encompassing variations in specific content, as with his widely varying yet structurally invariant wonder tale.

Given that functions could be deleted from a tale without destroying its coherence, it is an easy step to conclude that the overall properties of the genre did not exist in the clauses but in the expectancies or belief structures of hearer and teller. Indeed, one can also question Propp's insistence upon his functions following a strict sequence, for as already noted, sequence can and often is violated with dramatic effects by such narrative devices as flashbacks and flashforwards. But the central point is that the structure of narrative is as much in the head as on the page.

Were Propp's constituent functions really too large for L&W or were they just not textual, on-the-page enough? Did L&W, perhaps, dislike the textual vagueness of functions? One can see their attachment to text by a crucial example they cite, one in which a story is transformed by a reversal of clausal order:

/the king died :: the queen cried/ (1)
/the queen cried :: the king died/. (2)

But the story can also be transformed by changing intonation contours, as when one shifts from a straight to a sarcastic rendering of either clause sequence. And no doubt too, the context of telling would similarly affect the interpretation of either sequence. So why, then, should clauses be given exclusive importance as units of analysis? Why not context, why not intonation contours, why not such tropological features as sarcasm, irony, and so forth; or genre, as when one inserts either sequence into the tale of Juana La Loca displaying the propped-up dead King all around Aragon in a glass carriage so as not to imperil her position on the throne.

We might still ask, 30 years after L&W, where the underlying structure of a narrative comes from. Many people now believe that it has its origin either in some sort of "image schema," to borrow Johnson's (1987) term, in a loose generic "script," to borrow Schank and Abelson's (1977), or simply in some sort of "prototype cognitive construction." Any of these might derive its underlying properties from the very sensorimotor schemas in terms of which we organize experience of our own actions and interactions: the kind of SOURCE–PATH–GOAL schemas that Johnson (1993, p. 168) sees as having "sufficient internal structure to determine the structure of prototypical stories" in much the same sense as they provide a prototype for our most often used metaphors. Indeed, such schemas probably provide the beginning–middle–end armature on which stories are built—as Aristotle suggested as long ago as the *Poetics*. Beyond that, we know that such schemas come to be seen as "standing for" a culture's typical plights, ones that are emblematic of the everyday situations that need negotiating socially—matters relating to maintaining a normative balance in our own life stories and in our relations with others, like balancing personal autonomy and social authority, giving and getting affection, and the like. Such culturally embodied prototypes typically involve some normative balance between competing goods or between costs and benefits. It is often this delicate requirement of balance that generates the complication of a story—its *agon* or *peripéteia*. Such prototypes are also generic enough to be realized through different exemplification, as in Propp's wonder tales discussed earlier. Moreover, such prototypes seem also to be combinable enough to be formed into sagas, genres, and even "lines of precedent" in common law.

There remains the question of how to *linearize* a story based on such prototypes, how to transmute it into intersubjectively compelling language. Is it by such phrase Lego-like maneuvers as putting together the "right" clauses, intonation contours, markers, and all the other means we have for "linearizing" (Levelt, 1989)? Cognitively inclined linguists like Fillmore (1978) and Langacker (1987, 1991) seem to doubt it. There is a growing conviction that, both in acquisition and in historical change, we begin by constructing narrative utterances as holistic configurations, and that only later do we master (or invent) finer-grained grammatical distinctions for decomposing these larger scale constructions (Bruner & Lucariello, 1989). Grosser narrative constructions are forever being modelled by adult speakers in the child's language environment. We know from Peggy Miller's (1982) work, for example, that young children hear on average seven narratives per hour spoken by significant adults around them. It seems beyond belief that all that children learn from such a rich and action-apposite linguistic input is some abstract, context-independent clausal syntax. The fluency and virtuosity with which even quite young children complain narratively of thwartings imposed upon them, the linguistic fluency (and the extended utterances) with which they justify their own transgressions (Dunn, 1988)—such observations force one to suppose that there is some sort of larger scale mapping of holistic utterance on referent scenarios, much as Langacker (1987, 1991) suggests. It may even be the case that grammatical form classes originally emerged out of the need to fine-tune prototypic utterances to local circumstances better. Tomasello (in press) poses the problem well: "All constructions—whether composed of one words, or many categories of words in specific orders and with specific markers and intonations—derive from recurrent events, or types of events, with respect to which people of a culture have recurrent communicative goals. This means that a major function of all linguistic construction is attentional: to take one or another point of view on a situation or event, with particular participants in focal or background attention," and, he adds, with various rhetorical requirements, like speech act intentions, taken duly into account (Fillmore, 1978; Goldberg, 1995; Langacker, 1987, 1991; Taylor, 1996).

If there is anything to this line of speculation, and I believe there is plenty, then what one should look for as the constituents of narrative is not an underlying clausal structure, but the processes of linguistic constructions by which prototype narratives are adapted to different and varying situations, whether in the course of individual growth (e.g., Nelson, 1989), or with historical change (Lord, 1981). Surely, the young infant's intonationally colored *Allgone!* is an early holophrastic rendering of a prototype narrative, just as a preference for aspectual rather than tense-marked verbs suggests that young children are "tracking" a narrative rather than a "time" line in putting utterances together (Bruner, 1983). And Lord (1981) has also suggested, to shift to the historical side, that narrative modules are created for standard scenarios that can then be combined to meet local requirements encountered by the "singer of tales."

The only thing one can say in conclusion is that it has been a rich 30 years since L&W, and that much of that richness is an abundance that grew from the seeds they planted back then.

# REFERENCES

Bartlett, F. C. (1932). *Remembering*. Cambridge, England: Cambridge University Press.
Bruner, J. (1978). Learning how to do things with words. In J. S. Bruner and A. Garton (Eds.), *Human growth and development: The Wolfson lectures 1976*. Oxford, England: Clarendon.
Bruner, J., & Lucariello, J. (1989). Monologue as narrative recreation of the world. In K. Nelson (Ed.), *Narratives from the crib* (pp. 73–97). Cambridge, MA: Harvard University Press.
Bruner, J. (1983). *Child's talk*. New York: Norton.
Bruner, J. (1986). *Actual minds, possible worlds*. Cambridge, MA: Harvard University Press.
Bruner, J. (1991). *Acts of meaning*. Cambridge, MA: Harvard University Press.
Burke, K. (1945). *The grammar of motives*. New York: Prentice-Hall.
Colby, B. (1966). Cultural patterns in narrative. *Science, 151,* 793–798.
Dunn, J. (1988). *The beginnings of social understanding*. Cambridge, MA: Harvard.
Fillmore, C. W. (1968). The case for case. In E. Bach & R. Harms (Eds.), *Universals in linguistic theory*. New York: Holt, Rinehart & Winston.
Goldberg, A. (1995). *Constructions: A construction grammar approach to argument structure*. Chicago: University of Chicago Press.
Goodman, N. (1980). The telling and the told. In W. J. T. Mitchell J. T. (Ed.), *On narrative* (pp. 1–23). Chicago: University of Chicago Press.
Hockett, C. F. (1960, Septmeber). The origin of speech. *Scientific American, 203,* 121–130.
Jakobson, R. (1978). *Six lectures on sound and meaning*. Cambridge, MA: MIT Press.
Jakobson, R., & Halle, M. (1956). *Fundamentals of language*. S'Gravenhage, Netherlands: Mouton.
Johnson, M. (1987). *The body in the mind: The bodily basis of meaning, imagination, and reason*. Chicago: University of Chicago Press.
Johnson, M. (1993). *Moral imagination: Implications of cognitive science for ethics*. Chicago: University of Chicago Press.
Labov, W., & Waletzky, J. (1967). Narrative analysis: Oral versions of personal experience. In J. Helm (Ed.), *Essays on the verbal and visual arts: Proceedings of the 1966 annual spring meeting of the American Ethnological Society* (pp. 12–44). Seattle: University of Washington Press.
Langacker, R. (1987). *Foundations of cognitive grammar* (Vol. 1). Stanford, CA: Stanford University Press.
Langacker, R. (1991). *Foundations of cognitive grammar* (Vol. 2). Stanford, CA: Stanford University Press.
Levelt, W. J. M. (1989). *Speaking: From intention to articulation*. Cambridge, MA: MIT Press.
Levi-Strauss, C. (1955). The structural study of myth. *Journal of American Folklore,* 68, 428–444.
Lord, A. B. (1981). *The singer of tales*. Cambridge, MA: Harvard University Press.
Miller, P. J. (1982). *Amy, Wendy, and Beth: Learning language in South Baltimore*. Austin: University of Texas Press.
Mink, L. O. (1978). Narrative form as a cognitive instrument. In R. H. Canary and H. Kozicki (Eds.), *The writing of history: literary form and historical understanding*. Madison: University of Wisconsin Press.
Nelson, K. (1989). *Language from the crib*. Cambridge, MA: Harvard University Press.
Propp, V. (1956). *Morphology of the folktale*. Bloomington: Indiana University Press.
Ricoeur, P. (1984). *Time and narrative* (Vol. 1). Chicago: University of Chicago Press.
Schank, R. C., & Abelson, R. P. (1977). *Scripts, plans, goals, and understanding: An inquiry into human knowledge*. Hillsdale, NJ: Lawrence Erlbaum Associates, Inc.
Taylor, J. (1996). *Linguistic categorization*. New York: Oxford University Press.
Tomasello, M. Cognitive linguistics. In W. Bechtel & G. Graham (Eds.), *A companion to cognitive science*. Oxford: Basil Blackwell.
Turner, V. (1982). *From ritual to theater: The human seriousness of play*. New York: Performing Arts Journal Publications.
Vernant, J. P. (1965) *Mythes et pensée chez les Grecs*. Paris: Maspero.
White, H. (1981). The value of narrativity in the representation of reality. In W. J. T. Mitchell (Ed.), *On narrative* (pp. 1–23). Chicago: University of Chicago Press.

# A Matter of Time: When, Since, After Labov and Waletzky

## Elliot G. Mishler
*Department of Psychiatry, Harvard Medical School*

I have tried to pinpoint when I first read Labov and Waletzky's paper (1967/this issue; henceforth, L&W), proposing a model of narrative analysis for "oral versions of personal experience." I imagine other contributors to this celebratory issue have also searched for the "beginnings" to their stories of L&W's influence on their work. After rummaging through files of teaching memos, early drafts of both my book on research interviewing (Mishler, 1986b) and my first application of L&W to an interview narrative (Mishler, 1986a), my best guess is that the "when" for me was during the 1982–83 academic year.

In the Fall of 1982, after completing the manuscript of a book on clinical discourse (Mishler, 1984), I began a new project centered on a critique of standard methods of interviewing in both the social sciences and medical encounters. My memos from that period refer to Labov's coauthored book on therapeutic discourse (Labov & Fanshel, 1977). Cited earlier in my work on medical interviews, it retained its relevance for my analysis of interviewing practices, offering an alternative, sociolinguistic model of interviewing as "conversation." It includes a brief section on narrative with references to the two earlier papers on L&W, which I then tracked down (Labov, 1972; L&W, 1967/this issue).

A year later, my work on interviewing had moved beyond critique to a formulation of interviews as "speech events," dialogic encounters in which narrative accounts would appear if they were not suppressed by standard approaches. Further, I argued that methods of narrative analysis had become available—others in addition to L&W—that allowed for systematic research on "stories" and the interview process through which they were produced.

By the early Fall of 1983, my memos refer not only to the two earlier papers and the Labov–Fanshel (1977) book, but also to the later—and until now—the last of Labov's papers on narrative (Labov, 1982). In that paper, he retreated from the analytic approach represented in L&W, rejecting its assumptions and offering an

---

Requests for reprints should be sent to Elliot G. Mishler, 105-6 Trowbridge Street, Cambridge, MA 02138. E-mail: emishler@ix.netcom.com

alternative model of analysis and interpretation. Appearing while I was deeply involved in trying both to learn how to do narrative work and in developing a general perspective on narrative methods as an alternative to traditional approaches to interviewing and other forms of psychological and social research, this paper became a prominent focus in both my book and my first exercise in narrative analysis (Mishler, 1986a, 1986b).

While describing the "setting" for this story of my encounter and dialogue with L&W, I have been outlining two chronologies: the temporally ordered sequences of narrative-relevant events for Labov and myself. This seems appropriate given the centrality of temporal sequence in L&W. Labov's trajectory of interest in narrative, as expressed in his publications, has the form of an episodic story with a beginning and end, marked off in 5-year intervals: 1967, 1972, 1977, 1982. My path was more continuous, with shifts and turns reflecting other influences.

For me and my students during the early and mid-1980s, the impact of L&W was immediate and powerful. We were, it seems, already prepared to hear the message and apply it to our own studies. Of course, we were listening to our own special understanding of the message, translating it into our discipline-based languages and making it relevant to our particular interests. Through different routes and in varying degrees, we—along with many others in psychology and the social sciences—had become disenchanted with the traditional positivist-based "science" in which we had been trained and which dominated research in our fields. I had already turned away, a decade earlier, from the experimental-quantitative research paradigm in my own field of social psychology toward alternative ways of studying naturally occurring discourse, first in classrooms (Mishler, 1972) and later in clinical encounters (Mishler, 1984), and had also published a critique of positivist approaches (Mishler, 1979).

So, I was "ready," and L&W had a special combination of features that seemed to match my requirements for a new methodological approach. It displayed theoretical rigor with formal definitions of narrative and nonnarrative clauses and provided methods for empirical research through specification of coding categories for narrative functions. In these ways, it mirrored the "scientific" perspective of our home disciplines to which I and my students were still loyal though dissatisfied citizens.

It also met our other theoretical and empirical interests in studying "meaningful" units of language and social action by focusing on personal narratives elicited in interviews. L&W was a bridge to the study of narratives for those of us struggling to find an alternative way of doing "science." My first efforts to analyze interview narratives (Mishler, 1986a, 1986b) were based on L&W, as were the studies of my postdoctoral Fellows in the 1980s who adopted a narrative approach (Attanucci, 1993; Bell, 1988; Riessman, 1990).

However, the story told so far is incomplete. There is a counterplot, and the narrative takes an ironic turn. These initial studies were framed by the "fundamental question of narrative analysis" asserted in L&W: "how can we relate the sequence of clauses in the narrative to the sequence of events inferred from the narrative?" We relied on the definition of a narrative "as one method of recapitulating past experience by matching a verbal sequence of clauses to the sequence of events which actually occurred" (L&W, 1967/this issue).

Nonetheless, there were early signs that these were problematic and restrictive assumptions. In my exposition of L&W, I pointed to its relative inattention to the interview context in the production of narratives and to the "limited usefulness" of the requirement of "concrete equivalence or 'identity'" in the temporal ordering of narrative clauses and actual events (Mishler, 1986b, p. 86). Others also urged caution. For example, in a May 1985 letter commenting on a draft of my paper on the analysis of interview narratives, Dell Hymes urged me to consider an alternative perspective: "Stories have form of their own in terms of lines. Not every cultural tradition or community observes the purposed universals of Bill's schemes. ... it's only fair to say that if the material includes narratives, I would look for recognition of line and groups of lines." He warned that if I "rely on it (L&W), it will perpetuate part of what you want to transcend."

The "story," that is, the fate of L&W in my own work, gets complicated right from the start because of the increasing influence of alternative conceptions of narrative analysis I was also learning about in this early period. For example, *On Narrative* (Mitchell, 1981), the 1980 special issue of *Critical Inquiry,* became a critical resource, although it is cited only in the Appendix of "suggested readings" in my research interviewing book. Its direct influence appears later: for example, in the varied "exemplars" presented in my paper on validation in narrative research (Mishler, 1990), in a focus on structural approaches and the retrospective character of life history narratives (Mishler, 1992), and my proposed "typology" of alternative models of narrative analysis (Mishler, 1995).

*On Narrative* (Mitchell, 1981) plays an important role in this story, in part because it sharpened my awareness of the relative insulation from each other of different groups of narrative scholars and researchers—a problem I have often addressed in my teaching and writing, as in the papers noted previously. Essays by a dozen eminent scholars were included in the volume—philosophers and literary critics, novelist and historian, anthropologist and psychoanalyst. We learn from the Editor's introduction that the issue was the "product" of a 1979 "symposium on: 'Narrative: The Illusion of Sequence'" (p. 1). L&W's "fundamental question of narrative analysis" is itself interrogated by the title. Referring to the "inevitable temptation" to "try to tell the story of the symposium," the Editor asks "which story would be the right one to tell?" The symposium organizers' "plot" was the "first plan to go awry, as one speaker after another quarreled with the assumption that sequence is either illusory or is definitive of narrativity" (p. 1).

What is significant in the present context is that though the 1981 collection of papers focused on the problematic of sequence there is not a single reference by any contributor to any of the three earlier publications on L&W. This may reflect the notable absence of linguists or sociolinguists among the contributors. It appears that "turnabout is fair play," because it is rare to find reference to any of them in studies of discourse and narrative by sociolinguists. One example will have to serve: the recent encyclopedic and quite exceptional text by Schiffrin (1994) on discourse analysis includes a brief section on L&W citing the key references, but does not refer to any of the symposium authors, whose collective corpus of work on language and narrative is voluminous.

Reflecting back on our first attempts at narrative analysis, I think our "readiness" for alternative approaches to research led us to push the problems raised by Hymes and the symposium authors to the fringes of consciousness. We could not hear the cautions about the overzealous focus on temporal order and chronology but had to come to the problems in the course of our own work. The irony in all this is that in our effort to escape positivism we had grasped a "positivism with a human face."

The story does not end there. Each of us discovered one or another limitation of L&W as we tried to make sense of our own materials. For example, in intensive life history interviews, respondents rarely provided chronological accounts. Finding a temporally ordered sequence of events was a task of analytic reconstruction, and the technical apparatus of narrative and nonnarrative clauses had to be subordinated to or displaced by other methods (Mishler, 1992). Respondents also told storylike accounts that did not depend on a sequence of event clauses but reflected a course of affective experiences or the impact of events of extended duration, that is, habitual narratives (Riessman, 1990). Or they told several stories, and there were problems of boundaries and connections not addressed by L&W (Bell, 1988).

As I mentioned earlier, Labov was well aware of deep problems with the original version of L&W. In his 1982 paper, he shifted away from the conception of narrative as a sequence of temporally ordered clauses toward a model, drawn from Goffman, of social "moves." Providing detailed analyses of instances of "unexpected violence" in terms of the denial of the legitimacy of requests, he offered a functional perspective based on his analysis of requests as speech acts in his work on therapeutic discourse (Labov & Fanshel, 1977).

L&W is not a static fixture but a source of many stories, including Labov's own. For many of us, it opened up a world of possibilities we are still exploring. In my first detailed analysis of an interview narrative, I used a combination of L&W with Labov's later speech-act approach (Mishler, 1986a). Since then I have used it only in teaching novice narrative researchers and as an example of one among other approaches (Mishler, 1995). In more recent work (Mishler, 1997) I have borrowed another sociolinguist's approach that relies on a line and stanza model (Gee, 1985, 1991), as Hymes earlier recommended.

This has been a brief story of a long journey that remains as exciting as it was at the beginning. I recently introduced a group of students to work on narrative analysis with examples of new questions emerging from current studies to explain "Why I love doing narrative research." One was drawn from a discussion in my ongoing Narrative Study Group about problems of working with translations of stories in other languages. The value and limits of L&W for this problem had an important place in our discussion. My thanks to Labov and Waletzky for giving me the key to the garden. It turns out that there are many entries, but it was that first look that captured me.

## REFERENCES

Attanucci, J. S. (1993). Timely characterizations of mother–daughter and family–school relations: Narrative understandings of adolescence. *Journal of Narrative and Life History, 3,* 99–116.

Bell, S. E. (1988). Becoming a political woman: The reconstruction and interpretation of experience through stories. In A. D. Todd & S. Fisher (Ed.), *Gender and discourse: The power of talk* (pp. 97–123). Norwood, NJ: Ablex.

Gee, J. P. (1985). The narrativization of experience in the oral style. *Journal of Education, 167,* 9–35.

Gee, J. P. (1991). A linguistic approach to narrative. *Journal of Narrative and Life History, 1,* 15–39.

Labov, W. (1972). The transformation of experience in narrative syntax. In W. Labov (Ed.), *Language in the inner city* (pp. 354–396). Philadelphia: The University of Pennsylvania Press.

Labov, W. (1982). Speech actions and reactions in personal narrative. In D. Tannen (Ed.), *Analyzing discourse: Text and talk* (pp. 219–247). Washington, DC: Georgetown University Press.

Labov, W., & Fanshel, D. (1977). *Therapeutic discourse: Psychotherapy as conversation.* New York: Academic.

Labov, W., & Waletzky, J. (this issue). Narrative analysis: Oral versions of personal experience. In J. Helm (Ed.), *Essays on the verbal and visual arts: Proceedings of the 1966 Annual Spring Meeting of the American Ethnological Society* (pp. 12–44). Seattle: University of Washington Press. (Original work published 1967)

Mishler, E. G. (1972). Implications of teacher strategies for language and cognition: Observations in first-grade classrooms. In C. B. Cazden, V. P. John, & D. Hymes (Ed.), *Functions of language in the classroom* (pp. 267–298). New York: Teachers College Press.

Mishler, E. G. (1979). Meaning in context: Is there any other kind? *Harvard Educational Review, 49,* 1–19.

Mishler, E. G. (1984). *The discourse of medicine: Dialectics of medical interviews.* Norwood, NJ: Ablex.

Mishler, E. G. (1986a). The analysis of interview narratives. In T. Sarbin (Ed.), *Narrative psychology: The storied nature of human conduct* (pp. 233–255). New York: Praeger.

Mishler, E. G. (1986b). *Research interviewing: Context and narrative.* Cambridge, MA: Harvard University Press.

Mishler, E. G. (1990). Validation in inquiry-guided research: The role of exemplars in narrative studies. *Harvard Educational Review, 60,* 415–442.

Mishler, E. G. (1992). Work, identity, and narrative: An artist-craftsman's story. In G. C. Rosenwald & R. L. Ochberg (Ed.), *Storied lives: The cultural politics of self-understanding* (pp. 21–40). New Haven, CT: Yale.

Mishler, E. G. (1995). Models of narrative analysis: A typology. *Journal of Narrative and Life History, 5,* 87–123.

Mishler, E. G. (1997). Narrative accounts in clinical and research interviews. In B. -L. Gunnarsson, P. Linell, & B. Nordberg (Ed.), *The construction of professional discourse* (pp. 223–244). London: Longman.

Mitchell, W. J. T. (Ed.). (1981). *On narrative.* Chicago: University of Chicago Press.

Riessman, C. K. (1990). *Divorce talk: Women and men make sense of personal relationships.* New Brunswick, NJ: Rutgers.

Schiffrin, D. (1994). *Approaches to discourse.* Oxford, England: Blackwell.

# Dualisms in the Study of Narrative: A Note on Labov and Waletzky

## Paul J. Hopper
*Department of English, Carnegie Mellon University*

The classical status of a paper is confirmed when it becomes recognized that a close reading of the paper is the only way to understand the entire nexus of research that arose around it. In my course on discourse analysis at Carnegie Mellon I often ask my doctoral students in Rhetoric to read Labov and Waletzky's "Narrative Analysis: Oral Versions of Personal Experience" (1967/this issue; henceforth L&W). Over the years a critique has emerged during our discussions, whose outlines I briefly reproduce here.

The L&W model of narrative is actually laid out not only in their coauthored article, but in a second (solo) paper by Labov published in 1972 as a chapter in *Language in the Inner City*. In this article, I use both these sources.

The model is grounded in two parallel assumptions about the relation between an experience and the linguistic report of that experience. Both of these assumptions involve a *dualism* between meaning and language. One of them is rooted in the precept that a linguistic form has a *deep structure,* which is distinct from its *surface structure,* and which is linked to a *semantic interpretation.* These terms, which were first made explicit in Noam Chomsky's *Aspects of the Theory of Syntax* (1965), were commonly used in linguistic analyses in the 1960s and in the middle years of the decade were a prerequisite to having one's work read and taken seriously by linguists. By the end of the same decade, however, they had become to a large extent obsolete under the attacks of the Generative Semanticists. L&W had adopted some of the thought and terminology of late 1960s transformational grammar. The terms surface structure and semantic interpretation are used quite liberally in the 1967 paper, though not deep structure, which is, however, strongly implied by surface structure. For deep structure, L&W use the alternative *underlying form,* a term that

---

Requests for reprints should be sent to Paul J. Hopper, Department of English, Carnegie Mellon University, 259 Baker Hall, Pittsburgh, PA 15213. E-mail: phlu+@andrew.cmu.edu

persisted in phonological theory long after deep structure had disappeared from the scene in syntax. The 1972 version of the model (Labov, 1972) eschews this terminology entirely, reflecting the vigorous rejection of Chomsky by the linguistic avant-garde at around this time. (Chomsky, of course, later made an astonishing comeback, but that is another story.)

It is clear that L&W were impressed with the success of 1960s transformational grammar and saw their own work as solidly in this theoretical camp. Formulations such as the following suggest the degree to which the thought of this school had been appropriated:

> The definitions we have given for narrative units are deliberately applied to the linear sequence presented by the narrator. This linear sequence may be considered the surface structure of the narrative; there are often many narratives with rather different surface structures, but with equivalent semantic interpretations. In the same way, there are many sentences with different surface structures that correspond to the same underlying string of formatives in the original phrase structure of a grammar. (1967/this issue, p. 24)

The underlying form of a narrative is the form that is linked to the semantic interpretation. However, despite what seems like an explicit attempt by L&W to relate them, there are some crucial differences between the underlying form of a narrative and the deep structure of a Chomskyan sentence. One of these is that the conception of deep structure that was elaborated in *Aspects* (Chomsky, 1965) was an abstract one. In the *Aspects* model of syntactic structure, there was no such thing as a surface sentence that was identical to its own deep structure. In the L&W conception of narrative, however, some clauses are privileged narrative clauses, and the set of these in a discourse is defined as the narrative:

> Of course, the *a*-then-*b* relationship is not the only one at work in narrative. If it were, we would have only a succession of narrative clauses. One also finds implied relationships between clauses such as *a*-and at the same time-*b,* or *a*-and now as I think back on it-*b*. But among these temporal relationships, the *a*-then-*b* is in some sense the most essential and characteristic of narrative. Some narratives ... may use it exclusively, and every narrative must, by definition, use it at least once. (1967/this issue, p. 25)

Furthermore, in L&W's model of narrative, actual utterances of the speaker are equated with surface structure. This was in fact one of the most widespread misapprehensions by the consumers of linguistic theory at the time, and the transformationalists were forced to divert considerable political capital towards correcting it. For Chomsky and his followers, the study of actual utterances is a taboo subject, relegated to what is called *performance* as opposed to *competence.* In L&W's model of narrative, speakers (unconsciously) manipulate basic (deep structure) narrative clauses in order to achieve (surface structure) effects such as Evaluation.

It should be added that, despite the superficial appropriation of Chomskyan ideas, the conception of language and of the goals of analysis is in fact non-Chomskyan, as is revealed in the introductory paragraphs:

> The analysis will be *formal,* based upon recurrent patterns characteristic of narrative from the clause level to the complete simple narrative. We will rely upon the basic techniques of linguistic analysis, isolating the invariant structural units, which are represented by a variety of superficial forms. From this analysis it is possible to derive a considerable amount of information on the syntax and semantics of English below the sentence level. ... (L&W, 1967/this issue, p. 4)

It is the Bloomfieldian technique dismissed by Chomsky as a "discovery procedure," the allegedly forlorn project of arriving at an analysis by comparison of recurrent patterns in texts. In actual fact, it is only what linguists have always done and still do, because the identification of recurrent patterns is an unavoidable step in any kind of meaningful analysis; in the context of the time, an explicit statement of commitment to the procedure was enough to place even the most serious study beyond the pale of theoretical respectability. P. H. Matthews (1993), trying to place Labov in the mainstream of American linguistics at this time, claimed that

> the theoretical problems which Labov addressed before and after 1970 concerned the nature of rules and grammars, and the nature of change in language conceived as a change in grammar, in a way that entered directly into the debate with Chomsky. (p. 43)

The (sociolinguistic) "rules" for which Labov argued were almost always phonological rules, and there is, in any case, little evidence that the flow of ideas between Labov and the Chomskyans went both ways. Labov's name does not appear in the index to the most celebrated phonological work of the decade, Chomsky and Halle's massive 1968 book *The Sound Pattern of English.* I was present at many orally delivered papers during this period, including the first public presentation of the paper on sound change by Weinreich, Labov, and Herzog in Austin in 1966 to which Matthews refers, and do not recall any real substantive debate; rather, the sociolinguists and the formal grammarians listened politely to one another—which in those polemical days was a sure sign of the hopeless gap between the two schools—and eventually founded their own conferences (e.g., New Ways of Analyzing Variation, North Eastern Linguistics Society), created their own heroes, and simply drifted apart.

Evidently, then, the first duality, that between semantic interpretation and form, is only an apparent one because the implied appropriation of transformational grammar was incomplete. The attempt to co-opt syntactic theory for narrative was a half-hearted one, adopting its terminology without its doctrines and abandoning it as soon as it became politically possible to do so.

However, the second duality, between the experienced event and the narrated event, is much more real and fundamental, and goes through both the 1967 article by L&W and the 1972 chapter by Labov. Repeatedly, the supposition is made that the speaker has independent access to an original event sequence that is distinct from his verbalization of it. The speaker seems to have the events in mind, and can "recall" them, rather as if he—Labov's informants at this time are all male—has mentally recorded them on an internal VCR, and can replay them at will. It is easy to document this assumption from the texts:

> The semantic interpretation of a narrative, as we have defined it, depends on the expectation that the events described did, in fact, occur in the same order as they were told in. (L&W, 1967/this issue, p. 24)

> ... the speaker becomes deeply involved in rehearsing or even reliving the events of his past. (Labov, 1972, p. 354)

> ... because the experience and emotions involved here form an important part of the speaker's biography, he seems to undergo a partial reliving of that experience, and he is no longer free to monitor his speech as he normally does in face-to-face interviews. (Labov, 1972, p. 355)

> We define narrative as one method of recapitulating past experience by matching a verbal sequence of clauses to the sequence of events which (it is inferred) actually occurred. (Labov, 1972, pp. 359–360)

> ... in each case we have four independent clauses which match the order of the inferred events. (L&W, 1967/this issue, p. 12)

> The basic narrative units that we wish to isolate are defined by the fact that they recapitulate experience in the same order as the original events. (L&W, 1967/this issue, p. 13).

> These elements will be characterized by temporal sequence: their order cannot be changed without changing the inferred sequence of events in the original semantic interpretation. (L&W, 1967/this issue, p. 14)

> We wish to define formally the condition under which any two clauses are ordered with respect to each other, and cannot be changed without change in the temporal sequence of the original semantic interpretation. (L&W, 1967/this issue, p. 20)

In the introductory section of L&W, this conjecture becomes an explicit methodological postulate that makes the analytic enterprise a functional one: "The analysis is *functional:* Narrative will be considered as one verbal technique for recapitulating experience—in particular, a technique of constructing narrative units that match the temporal sequence of that experience" (L&W, 1967/this issue, p. 4).

These two statements together could be characterized as a *structural-functional* approach (for a more general description of Labov's work in these terms, see Williams, 1992, pp. 67–92). At no point is it ever suggested that this is a problematic assumption, yet it raises some profound questions. The speaker's experiences are explicitly said to be "temporal," that is, they are chronologically ordered. The past is, of course, gone and materially inaccessible to us. We cannot verify an account of the past in the same way that we can verify, say, the existence of the Taj Mahal. Western mythology compensates for this inaccessibility of the past by insisting on a mental faculty called "memory" in which, we believe, past events are somehow inscribed (or stored) and await recovery by us. We can accomplish this recovery selectively, choosing to extract this event, and that event, but not that other one. We can manipulate the linguistic form of the account we give, changing how we "present" this event-memory in order to attain a certain effect, but the event itself as it is stored in our memory is unchangeable.

The same is true of the sequence of events as it is stored in our memory. This too cannot be changed. Suppose that I illegally divest myself of stock after I receive privileged ("inside") information about an imminent bankruptcy, but tell everyone, including the SEC investigators, that these two events happened in the reverse order. Then I have "lied"; for the "real" order of events was first getting the information, then divesting, and I am only too aware of this and hope the investigators won't "find out the truth." Isn't this a clear case of my account of an event sequence and the real event sequence being different? How could it be otherwise?

One problem is that, as has been noted, no one has access to the true, original order of events. For to establish the "true" order of events is not to travel back in time and rewitness them, but to rely on yet another account underwritten by evidence viewed by others as more authoritative and reliable than my own. In Barbara Herrnstein Smith's formulation (1981), we have no privileged, omniscient view of events, only more and more versions of events. This is an epistemic problem, because it has to do with how we establish events and their sequencing.

A second problem is an ontological one, the nature of the event itself. Roy Harris, at a recent conference, reduced a questioner to silence on this topic by asking, first: "Are events enumerable?" When the questioner admitted that yes, events were enumerable, Harris asked him quite simply how many things had happened to him that day. The point, of course, is that outside of a social context, we cannot identify the boundaries of an event. What is stored in our minds, if the metaphor can be made to make sense, is not sequences of events, but, in Barbara Herrnstein Smith's words, "a motley collection of images, recollections, and ideas from the past" (Smith, 1981, p. 225). Only the act of narration gives this random and unordered mass a structured form.

Consider, as an example, a narrative segment like the following (L&W, 1967/this issue, p. 17):

| | |
|---|---|
| $_0k_1$ | so all of them kept going |
| $_1l_0$ | they leave me |
| $_0m_3$ | so I started going down |

In this story, the narrator is afflicted with cramps during a swimming race. It is extraordinarily hard to think of the sequence as having its origin in a set of objectively ascertainable discrete events occurring in a previously established order, which is then later "recapitulated," on demand by a storyteller, no matter how talented and gifted. Almost as unimaginable is the notion that L&W would postulate such an a priori construct. How could it ever be verified except through yet another narrative? The uncertainty over events extends to the analysts' decision as to where to draw such linguistic boundaries as "clause" and "verb," decisions that bear crucially on the determination of event boundaries. Quite often this decision seems an arbitrary one, not obvious but requiring argument, as the authors seem to acknowledge when they discuss coordinated clauses in Footnote 4: "Co-ordinate verbs are always analyzed separately if they are independent" (L&W, 1967/this issue, pp. 17–18). However: " ... if someone says 'You try and get it,' we cannot understand these as two independent verbs, but rather the use of 'and' [is] equivalent to an infinitive embedding, the same as 'You try to get it'" (p. 18).

In another footnote (10), we read:

> The phrase "Nice big blue 44 too" might well be considered a separate narrative clause, derived from "He had a nice big blue 44 too." However, the status of *had* as the head of a narrative clause is still at issue, and it would be tendentious to use a deleted form as evidence. We have therefore been treating this phrase as subordinated to "He came to my hotel," equivalent to "with a nice big blue 44 too." (L&W, 1967/this issue, p. 31)

The point is important enough to need a reasoned argument. Yet what L&W give us is not an argument, but special pleading ("we cannot understand these as ... "; "it would be tendentious to ... ") Now, if there is no objectively achieved certainty about the linguistic boundaries of events, how can it be plausibly claimed that they are stored in memory as a sequence? As so often in formal kinds of linguistics, an appearance of objectivity imparted by the quasi-mathematical notation rests uneasily on prior analytic and epistemic decision making that is not free from dispute.

Smith (1981) pointed out that

> Our knowledge of past events is usually not narrative in structure or given in story-like sequences; on the contrary, that knowledge is most likely to be in the form of general and imprecise recollections, scattered and possibly inconsistent pieces of verbal information, and various visual, auditory, and kinesthetic images—some of which, at any given time, will be more or less in or out of focus and all of which will be organized, integrated, and apprehended as a specific "set" of events only in and through the very act by which we narrate them as such. (p. 225)

The constructed framework that holds this fragmentary record together is a social one. The social dimension is of course very prominent in L&W's article. They note, for example, that: "The ultimate aims of our work will require close correlations of the narrator's social characteristics with the structure of their narratives, because we are concerned with problems of effective communication and class and ethnic differences in verbal behavior" (L&W, 1967/this issue, p. 5). The technique of asking a simple question that elicits a fully formed narrative points to an underlying assumption that the narrative obtained is somehow purified of its contaminating social context. Yet formulations of this kind suggest strongly a third dualism, that between the structure of a linguistic event and the social context to which that linguistic event is adapted. Alternative conceptions of this relationship have set aside the purely individual contribution, seeing the social "context" and the individual's performance as being one. Smith (1981) suggested that narrative is to be seen as a transaction rather than as an individual achievement. More generally, Middleton and Edwards (1990) pleaded for "a reversal of the usual approach to the relationship between human consciousness and communication" (p. 11). Of particular relevance to the present topic is their statement that

> Rather than wondering about how internal mental processes might represent past experience, we are interested in how people construct versions of events *and* their own mental process within the practice of ordinary conversation ... People's accounts of past events are treated not as a window onto the cognitive workings of memory, but as descriptions that vary according to whatever pragmatic and rhetorical work they are designed for, such that no single, decontextualized version can be taken as a reflection of the "contents" of a person's memory. (p. 10)

Middleton and Edwards (1990) go even further in suggesting that the notion of memory should be replaced by that of "remembering," a term which emphasizes narration—the production of a socially endorsable version of the past—as a collaborative rather than an individual enterprise. They add to the dualism real event–narrated event others:

> It makes no sense to talk in terms of what is an individual as compared with what is a social memory, what is specifically social and what specifically physical, what part of memory is internal and what is externally located. (p. 10)

The life cycle of a "classic" paper, such as L&W, is the following. It brings to the fore a theme that has hitherto been marginal to a discipline, such as the genre Narrative in linguistics, and treats it in a way that shows how a novel combination of data and method makes this theme no longer marginal but one of crucial relevance to the discipline. Its existence attracts to that theme researchers who would not previously have thought of it as a central concern, and it becomes the point of diffusion of numerous important studies. Subsequently, although it continues to be read for the importance of its ideas and its place in the history of the science, its premises have become the target of critiques that would not be remotely possible were it not for the brilliance of the original conception. Those that indulge in this critique are often conflicted, feeling bound to present the reasons for their reservations while acknowledging the incomparable and lasting value of the original contribution.

## REFERENCES

Chomsky, N. (1957). *Syntactic structure*. The Hague, The Netherlands: Mouton.
Chomsky, N. (1965). *Aspects of the theory of syntax*. Cambridge: MIT Press.
Chomsky, N., & Halle, M. (1968). *The sound pattern of English*. New York: Harper & Row.
Labov, W. (1972). The transformation of experience in narrative syntax. In W. Labov (Ed.), *Language in the inner city* (pp. 354–396). Philadelphia: University of Pennsylvania Press.
Labov, W., & Waletzky, J. (this issue). Narrative analysis: Oral versions of personal experience. In J. Helm (Ed.), *Essays on the verbal and visual arts: Proceedings of the 1966 Annual Spring Meeting of the American Ethnological Society* (pp. 12–44). Seattle: University of Washington Press. (Original work published 1967)
Matthews, P. H. (1993). *Grammatical theory in the United States from Bloomfield to Chomsky*. Cambridge, England: Cambridge University Press.
Middleton, D., & Edwards, D. (1990). Introduction. In D. Middleton & D. Edwards (Eds.), *Collective remembering* (pp. 1–22). London: Sage.
Smith, B. H. (1981). Narrative versions, narrative theories. In W. J. T. Mitchell (Ed.), *On narrative* (pp. 209–232). Chicago: University of Chicago Press.
Weinreich, U., Labov, W., & Herzog, M. I. (1968). Empirical formulations for a theory of language change. In W. P. Lehrmann & Y. Malkiel (Eds.), *Directions for historical linguistics* (pp. 95–188). Austin: University of Texas Press.
Williams, G. (1992). *Sociolinguistics: A sociological critique*. London: Routledge.

# Narrative Authenticity

## Elinor Ochs
*Department of TESL and Applied Linguistics*
*University of California Los Angeles*

## Lisa Capps
*Department of Psychology, University of California Berkeley*

Narrators of personal experience work to make their stories sound credible. As Labov (1982) noted:

> Reportable events are almost by definition unusual. They are therefore inherently less credible than nonreportable events. In fact, we might say that the more reportable an event is, the less credible it is. Yet credibility is as essential as reportability for the success of a narrative. (p. 228)

Credibility depends in part upon the plausibility of a chain of objective events and whether they can be corroborated. Narrators, however, couch these events within subjective events that can not be contradicted. The narrators studied by Labov (1972, 1982, 1986) threaded their narratives with subjective events such as thinking ("I thought he was gonna *hit* me"), knowing ("I didn't know what it was"), talking to oneself ("I said to myself, 'There'll be times I can't put up with this ... '"), intending ("I was about to hit him"), and feeling ("boy that was an *eery* night for me comin' home").

Remembering is also a subjective event. However, although remembering itself is an unobservable and therefore unverifiable mental state, a thought cast as remembered is presented as true. *Remember* is a factual mental verb (Chafe & Nichols, 1986) that presupposes the certainty of a proposition. Thus: "I remember going to the House of Fabrics with you in my red corduroy pants" presupposes that the speaker went "to the House of Fabrics with you in my red corduroy pants."

---

Requests for reprints should be sent to Elinor Ochs, Department of TESL and Applied Linguistics, University of California Los Angeles, 3300 Rolfe Hall, Los Angeles, CA 90095–1531. E-mail: ochs@humnet.ucla.edu

Remembering, then, is an authenticating act: Rememberers publicly claim to have brought to conscious awareness a state, event, or condition that is real in their eyes; they believe it to be true.

In this sense, acts of remembering are attempts to seize authority with respect to a topic of concern. For the presupposed truths to become recognized as such, however, these acts require validation by others. When such validation is not forthcoming, the authenticity of the remembered experience and by implication the reliability of the rememberer is called into question (Taylor, 1995). Contested memories can concern personal and collective events of consequence for groups and nations. Contestation of memory, however, can also concern events of import only to family members or acquaintances directly involved. In the following family encounter between 3-year-old Evan, his older brother Dick, and their parents, the event contested concerns whether or not Dad promised Evan ice cream for dessert if he ate a good dinner. Towards the end of dinner, Evan attempts to remind Dad about the promise (Ochs, 1994, p. 116):

    Evan:    YOU *'MEMBER* I COULD HAVE A—

Dad is occupied talking to Dick and Evan has to repeat his reminder to Dad and then to Mom:

    DADDY? YOU (**'MEMBER**) IF I EAT A *GOOD* DINNER I—
    ... ((*Evan is tapping Dad's arm for attention*))
    MO:MMY *Mo*mmy.—you—you *'mem***ber**—( um ) if I eat a good ... *din*ner I could have a *ice* cream

At this point Dad contests Evan's memory, while the rest of the family side with Evan:

| | |
|---|---|
| Dad: | An ice cream?—Who said that |
| Evan: | You |
| Dick: | *You* |
| | (0.4 pause) |
| Mom: | Oooooooo ((*laughing*))hehe |
| Dad: | *I* didn't say that |
| Dick: | **Remember**?—he—you said "Daddy—could I have a i:cecrea:m?" |
| | ... |
| Dad: | Where *was* I? |
| | ... |
| Dad: | I don't even **remember** telling you that— |

|  | What was I doing when? |
|---|---|
| Dick: | Daddy I'll tell you the *exact* words you said. |
| Dad: | Tell m- What was I doing—where *was* I first of all? |
| Dick: | You were sitting right in that chair where you are now. |
|  | (0.4 pause) |
| Mother: | ((*laughing*)) hehehaha—It's *on* film—they have you. |

In this exchange, it is not enough for Evan to have remembered Dad's promise or for Evan to have the supported recall of his older brother. Dad denies the remembered event and demands the exact details as positive proof. In the face of Dad's challenge, the children supply further evidence of the remembered event. Dick tells him he can quote his exact words and cites the precise locale of the promise: "You were sitting right in that chair where you are now." Mom, who first signals Dad's sinking position with her incriminating "Oooooooo" and snickering, provides the clinching source of evidence, namely, that the researchers have captured this entire episode on film. Her comment "They have you" may be interpreted to mean both that the researchers have Dad on tape and that the children have Dad boxed into a corner.

In this family interaction, a child's memory prevails, but often this is not the case, particularly when children are unable to garner support from more mature persons: In dyadic adult–child encounters, for example, children's rememberings often give way to adult reformulations, backed by their authoritative status in the family. This phenomenon is the object of focus in family therapies, in which parental accounts frequently prevail over those of children (Aronsson & Cederborg, 1994; Cederborg, 1994; Minuchin & Fishman, 1981). In their study of Swedish family therapy, Aronsson and Cederborg articulated the linguistic and interactional resources that family members routinely bring to their talk to display authoritative stance, including evidential adverbs like *actually* and *absolutely* and recruitment of authoritative support, as in the following narrative dispute between adolescent Sam and his father (Cederborg, 1994, p. 126):

| Father: | Your clothing allowance was suspended for five months because you consistently spent it on things other than clothes, and then went and asked your mother to buy you clothes. |
|---|---|
| Sam: | That's **not actually** *true*. |
| Father: | *That's* **ABSOLUTELY true, ask your mother**. |

Another consistent marker of high certainty is reference to *exact numbers*. For instance, Sam and his father conflict in their accounts of the amount of time that Sam devoted to studying, Sam supports his position that he has indeed studied hard by specifying the exact time he spent on this task:

Sam: The week before I went back I did **2.5** hours every day revising for my exams.

Of note here is that not only does he use numbers, he formulates the number as a statistic—2.5—as if he had arithmetically calculated average time per day across number of days studied. Sam's father is not to be outdone by such displays. He himself gets into the numbers game, claiming:

Father Three days you didn't do anything AT ALL. You were watching television all day and went off to Tom's in the afternoon.

Sam and his father continue to clash over the truth:

Sam: That just **ISN'T true**
Father: It **IS true,**
Sam: No.

At this point, father not only appeals to other authorities, he specifies the exact number who he believes will back him up:

Father: Well **three** people will **tell** you it is.

Displays of relative certainty and displays of positive and negative affect are the building blocks of identities. Each display of high certainty in the dispute between Sam and his father may be seen as an attempt to establish themselves as authorities and at the same time establish the addressee as a liar or culprit. Sam and his father become gridlocked in their unwillingness to accept the identities they have attempted to assign one another. Therapists work to establish a more balanced dialogue between parental and child perspectives on past events. This process involves helping family members relinquish their sense of absolute certainty about what they remember, in part through the therapist's modeling of less absolute stances and in part through making explicit the subjectivity and malleability of memory.

Sam and his father are not alone in their sense that their narrative tells the true story. Eyewitness testimonies, for example, are used in court to establish what actually happened. Research, however, suggests that memory of eyewitnessed events is affected by prior life experiences and biases and by postevent experiences, reflections, and conversations, including the testimony of others and the displayed dispositions of lawyers (Loftus, 1979). Loftus and her colleagues (Loftus, 1979, 1980; Loftus & Ketcham, 1991) conducted *misinformation* experiments, in which participants (generally college students) are shown videos of simulated accidents and crimes. These studies demonstrated that witnesses are highly suggestible and can be led into modifying their perceptions through questioning techniques that contain presuppositions (e.g., "Did you see *the* dent in the car?", rather than "Did you see a dent?").

The issue of veracity versus subjectivity of narrative and memory plagues clinicians, litigators, and philosophers, among others. For those who believe there is a truth to recall, an important question is: Can a past truth ever be accessed? Kundera (1995, pp. 128–129) airs perhaps the most despairing response to this issue:

> Try to reconstruct a dialogue from your own life, the dialogue of a quarrel or a dialogue of love. The most precious, the most important situations are utterly gone. Their abstract sense remains. ... perhaps a detail or two, but the acousticovisual concreteness of the situation in all its continuity is lost ... And not only is it lost but we do not even wonder at this loss. We are resigned to losing the concreteness of the present ... Remembering is not the negative of forgetting. Remembering is a form of forgetting ... We die without knowing what we have lived.

For those who are more optimistic about the recoverability of memory, a driving question is: How can we ascertain the accuracy of a memory? Is resistance to suggestion and refusal to modify one's account indicative of truth? The resistance displayed by Sam and his father suggests that being impervious is no assurance of accurate recall. Is implicit memory in the form of, for example, somatic sensations, fragmented flashbacks, or dreams indexical of the true occurrence of a past event? Unanswered, this question remains hotly contested (Sarbin, 1995). Although some believe that therapists or clients themselves can induce implicit memories (creating false memories) and that behavioral manifestations can be feigned, others insist on their unequivocal authenticity (e.g., Loftus, 1980; Terr, 1994). The issue has profound emotional and legal consequences for the lives of would-be victims and perpetrators. What are the consequences for one's sense of reality and self-identity when one's memory of even seemingly insignificant events is repeatedly overruled? Or when one becomes convinced that an emotionally significant event did not happen or happened in a radically different manner than one's memory? The risks can include social isolation, persecution, and excruciating self-doubt, which are frequently associated with psychiatric disorders.

There is no simple resolution of the tension between subjectivity and truth of a remembered past. This tension may be an inherent property of selfhood. As Bergson (1911) noted, and others like Kundera (1981, 1985, 1995) and Ricoeur (1988) later concurred, we can't reflect upon ourselves in the present, as we experience the moment. Rather, the nonpresent—the past and the possible—is the modality for self-making. As Bruner (1987) noted: "We seem to have no other way of describing 'lived time' save in the form of a narrative" (p. 12). Knowledge of past and potential selves in turn is grounded in beliefs about the past and the possible and in our assumption that these beliefs are true. The activity of self-reflection, however, also engenders the awareness that beliefs vary in certainty, can be contested, and are vulnerable to change. As such, the process of grounding ourselves is infused with doubt and motion. Havel (1988, p. 225) alluded to this dynamic when he reflected: "man is the only creature who is both a part of being (and thus a bearer of its mystery), and aware of that mystery as a mystery. He is both the question and the questioner, and cannot help being so." We come to define ourselves as we grapple with our own and others' ambiguous emotions and events. As a result, uncertainty as well as certainty plays an important role in configuring selves. Paradoxically, we are perhaps most intensely cognizant of ourselves when we are unsure of ourselves, including our memories. The tension between certainty and doubt drives narrative activity in pursuit of an authentic remembered self.

## REFERENCES

Aronsson, K., & Cederborg, A. -C. (1994). Co-narration and voice in family therapy: Voicing, devoicing and orchestration. *Text, 14,* 345–370.
Bergson, H. (1911). *Creative evolution.* Boston, MA: University Press of America.
Bruner, J. (1987). Life as narrative. *Social Research, 54*(1), 11–32.
Cederborg, A.-C. (1994). *Family therapy as collaborative work.* Unpublished doctoral dissertation, Linkoping University, Sweden.
Chafe, W., & Nichols, J. (1986). *Evidentiality: The linguistic coding of epistemology.* Norwood, NJ: Ablex.
Havel, V. (1988). *Letters to Olga* (Paul Wilson, Trans.). New York: Henry Hold.
Kundera, M. (1981). *The book of laughter and forgetting.* Harmondsworth, England: Penguin.
Kundera, M. (1985). *The unbearable lightness of being.* New York: Harper & Row.
Kundera, M. (1995). *Testaments betrayed.* New York: HarperCollins.
Labov, W. (1972). The transformation of experience in narrative syntax. In *Language in the inner cities: Studies in Black English Vernacular* (pp. 354–396). Philadelphia: University of Pennsylvania Press.
Labov, W. (1982). Speech actions and reactions in personal narrative. In D. Tannen (Ed.), *Georgetown University round table on languages and linguistics 1981: Analyzing discourse: Text and talk* (pp. 219–247). Washington, DC: Georgetown University Press.
Labov, W. (1986, March 10). *On not putting two and two together: The shallow interpretation of narrative.* Pitzer College Invited Lecture, Claremont, CA.
Loftus, E. F. (1979). *Eyewitness testimony.* Cambridge, MA: Harvard University Press.
Loftus, E. F. (1980). *Memory.* Reading, MA: Addison-Wesley.
Loftus, E. F., & Ketcham, K. (1991). *Witness for the defense.* New York: St. Martin's Press.
Minuchin, S., & Fishman, C. H. (1981). *Family therapy techniques.* Cambridge, MA: Harvard University Press.
Ochs, E. (1994). Stories that step into the future. In D. F. Biber & E. Finegan (Eds.), *Perspectives on register: Situating register variation within sociolinguistics* (pp. 106–135). Oxford, England: Oxford University Press.
Ricoeur, P. (1988). *Time and narrative* (Vol. 1–3; K. Blarney & D. Pellauer, Trans.). Chicago: University of Chicago Press.

Sarbin, T. (1995). A narrative approach to "repressed memories." *Journal of Narrative and Life History, 5,* 51–66.
Taylor, C. E. (1995). *Child as apprentice-narrator: Socializing voice, face, identity, and self-esteem amid the narrative politics of family dinner.* Doctoral dissertation, University of Southern California, Los Angeles.
Terr, L. (1994). *Unchained memories.* New York: Basic Books.

# Struggling Beyond Labov and Waletzky

## Janet Holmes
### Department of Linguistics, Victoria University of Wellington

When I began working in the area of narrative, one of my colleagues (a great admirer of Labov, it should be said) commented: "Let's see if you can manage to get beyond Labov and Waletzky—no one else has yet!" In narrative analysis, as in so many other areas of sociolinguistics, Labov's research is where one starts. I certainly began analyzing narratives from the Wellington Corpus of Spoken New Zealand English with the intention of examining aspects of narrative other than their basic internal structure, but as I proceeded I found that in whatever direction I attempted to develop the analysis, I kept inescapably returning to the need to first establish the basic structure of the narratives.

In many ways this personal experience seems to be reflected in the field of narrative analysis more generally. The structure identified and described by Labov and Waletzky (1967/this issue; henceforth L&W) 30 years ago is not only cited in every text concerned with narrative structure, it is also actively drawn on and used, with little if any modification, in current work analyzing narrative structure in a very wide range of contexts, for example, women's gossip (Coates, 1996), news stories (A. Bell, 1991, 1995), and ethnographic interviews (Linde, 1993). Indeed L&W has proved so rich a source that even the specific stories they analyzed frequently appear as illustrative material in papers and books primarily describing narratives from different corpora. Yet, clearly much progress has been made. L&W developed their analysis in part to demonstrate the structural complexity evident in the discourse of Black adolescents (see L&W, this issue, fn. 3). Thirty years later, their analytical framework is used as a tool across the social sciences, for countless different purposes.

In this short article, I use my own research on ethnic and gender contrasts in narrative structure to assess the current relevance of L&W's paper in discourse analysis. After briefly describing the database, I make just three points; firstly,

---

Requests for reprints should be sent to Janet Holmes, Department of Linguistics, Victoria University of Wellington, P.O. Box 600, Wellington, New Zealand. E-mail: janet.holmes@vuw.ac.nz

L&W continues to provide an adequate descriptive framework for much narrative analysis; secondly, many of the developments in the last 30 years were suggested by L&W as areas for further research; thirdly, recent research suggests that contextual factors deserve much greater attention in narrative analysis than was recognized in L&W.

## NARRATIVE DATABASE

L&W's data was collected in an interview context, and there has been much debate (which I do not pursue here) about the structural differences between elicited and spontaneous narratives (e.g., Linde, 1993; Polanyi, 1989; Wolfson, 1982). My database consisted of 96 spontaneous narratives from relaxed conversations between 30 pairs of friends of the same age, gender, social class, and ethnicity collected for the Wellington Corpus of Spoken New Zealand English. Twenty-four of the conversationalists were Maori and 36 Pakeha; half were women and half men. The conversations were recorded by the participants themselves in their homes.

## L&W AS AN ANALYTICAL FRAMEWORK

It should first be recognized that as a basic description of narrative structure, L&W's framework continues to serve well for many purposes. It provided a valuable basis for comparative research, for example, as well as a sound starting point for more sophisticated interpretive research in a range of disciplines. It enabled me to identify a number of interesting contrasts in the way the Maori and Pakeha in my sample told stories to their friends (Holmes, in press-a). The data illustrated the ways in which different cultural groups may exploit the optional elements in narrative structure. So, for example, Maori narrators sometimes dispensed with components such as the resolution and the coda. By contrast, Pakeha narrators generally spelled out the significance of their stories overtly with a clause expressing a resolution (often introduced by *so*). As a result, Maori stories sometimes seemed incomplete to Pakeha ears. Moreover, the expression of the *evaluation* by Maori storytellers tended to be very inexplicit judged by Pakeha norms (cf. Scollon & Scollon, 1981), a point discussed later in this article. Hence, the narrative components identified by L&W proved useful in identifying ethnic differences in the way stories were structured, and their framework seems to provide an adequate descriptive model.

## EXTENDING L&W'S FRAMEWORK

Many of the research developments in narrative analysis over the last 30 years were signalled in L&W's paper, albeit sometimes in embryonic form. So the complexity of form (e.g., lexical, syntactic, prosodic, paralinguistic, nonverbal) and position (often extending throughout the action component) associated with the evaluative component, which has been discussed in some detail by researchers (e.g., Linde, 1993; Toolan, 1988; Wolfson, 1982), was first identified in L&W's paper. They noted, for instance, that the evaluation "may be present as lexical or phrasal modification of a narrative clause, or it may be itself a narrative clause, or coincide with the last narrative clause"; the evaluation section may be "fused with the result," and there may be "more than one evaluation section" (L&W, this issue). The evaluation may be "highly internalized" or explicitly "external" (L&W, this issue), a source of variation that Labov (1972, p. 373) identified as class-related.

The significance of the evaluative component, and the potential sophistication in the means by which it is expressed, is particularly evident in current research on identity construction in discourse (e.g., S. E. Bell, 1988; Bruner, 1987; Coates, 1996; Harré, 1987; Schiffrin, 1996). Narration is one obvious means of constructing a particular type of identity—ethnic, professional, political, parental, social, and so forth. In my data, New Zealand women and men used stories to actively construct their gender identities. These stories predominantly reproduce and reinforce societal gender divisions, but sometimes challenge traditional patterns and expectations. As L&W (this issue) demonstrated, the point of a story is conveyed through the evaluative component. Examining the ways in which narrators construct their gender identity reveals that often the most important "point" of a story is far from explicit: The evaluative component is sometimes deeply embedded in the context within which the story is told.

My analysis of an extended story told by a middle-aged New Zealand woman, Helen, illustrates this (see Holmes, in press-b). At one level, the point of the story is Helen's account of a visit to the swimming pool, updating her friend Joan on the daily frustrations involved in the ongoing story of her life (cf. Coates, 1996; Linde, 1993). At another level, the story constructs Helen's identity as a "good" daughter and a "good" mother, illustrating Linde's (1993) observation that narrative is "an extremely powerful tool for creating, negotiating, and displaying the moral standing of the self" (p. 123). The analysis of this story reveals the verbal dexterity narrators may demonstrate in expressing such an evaluation. It clearly illustrates the extent to which evaluation is a complex and somewhat slippery concept, as L&W signalled 30 years ago. Since then, discourse analysts have developed a range of sophisticated tools for unpacking its expression.

## CONTEXT IS CRUCIAL

My third point is hinted at in different ways in both preceding points and focusses on an aspect of narrative analysis that was largely neglected in L&W's paper—the significance of the context of narration not only to an adequate interpretation of the narrative, but also to an adequate account of its structure. Recent research has explored the extent to which a narrative is embedded in the social context within which it is produced.

I noted that Maori narrators often left components of narrative relatively inexplicit, relying on the context and the extent of shared background with their interlocutors to fill these apparent gaps. Contextual information is here crucial to an adequate interpretation. Similarly, when identity is constructed through narrative, the evaluative component that expresses, as Linde (1993) suggested, an inescapably moral basic proposition may be conveyed by implicit rather than explicit means. Unpacking the underlying message is often only possible with extensive ethnographic research to supply necessary contextual detail. Meaning derives from the interplay between language, text, and context, as Bakhtin (1981) pointed out. Hodge and Kress (1988) made the same point in the context of critical discourse analysis: "The site in which a text occurs typically contains instructions as to how it should be read and what meanings should be found in it" (p. 68). Interpreting the evaluative component of a narrative in particular—its moral significance—always requires attention to the context in which it was produced.

Even more compelling is the evidence from recent narrative research regarding the extent to which narratives may be jointly constructed by participants (e.g., S. E. Bell, 1988; Corston, 1993; Duranti, 1986; Goodwin, 1986; Riessman, 1993; Rymes, 1995). L&W identified narrative as essentially a solo performance. The concept of a single narrator, for instance, is implicit in Labov's (1972) description of the power of a story to compel attention, in a paper that clearly builds on L&W: "[narratives] will command the total attention of an audience in a remarkable way, creating a deep and attentive silence that is never found in academic or political discussion" (p. 396). However, the structural development of a narrative may depend to a much greater extent than L&W recognized on the cooperation of the coparticipants. Minimally, coparticipants attend to the narration. Going further, Linde (1993) identified the evaluation as "socially the most important part of the narrative" (p. 72) and argued that participants must agree on the evaluative component for a text to qualify as a narrative. Others have demonstrated the varying extents to which so-called "listeners" may actually contribute to the emerging narrative structure (e.g., Corston, 1993; Duranti, 1986). Such jointly constructed narratives are best described as collaborative, interactive, or "dialogic" in structure (Bakhtin, 1981; Cheepen, 1988, p. 54). Pursuing this point in a range of cultural contexts, the concept of "audience" is clearly inappropriate in contexts in which the narrative emerges as the joint product of a group performance (Besnier, 1990; Boggs, 1972; Heath, 1982, 1983; Moerman, 1988; Watson, 1975).

In the analysis of my New Zealand sample, this aspect of narrative structure was an area that provided both ethnic and gender contrasts. Pakeha listeners contrasted with Maori in providing more explicit verbal encouragement of various sorts during the narration. This was true even of minimal responses in which Pakeha listeners provided significantly more than Maori. In addition, Pakeha listeners were much more likely to ask the narrator questions (e.g., where was that? when was this?), thus not only affecting the level of detail provided in various components of the narrative (especially the orientation), but in some cases influencing the direction in which the story developed. Maori were much more likely to indicate attention nonverbally or by relevant matching stories or postnarrative reflections. There was also evidence of a gender contrast in this area, with a tendency for New Zealand women to use verbal strategies that explicitly expressed support for the narrator more often than men. Women used more supportive minimal responses than men, and the questions asked by Pakeha New Zealand men sometimes disrupted the story, or seemed to disconcert the narrator, whereas the women were more likely to ask facilitative questions that assisted the development of the story (see Holmes, in press-b). The contribution of listeners to the structure of a narrative clearly warrants analyst's attention, as does attention to the wider context in which the narrative is produced.

## CONCLUSION

L&W's analytical framework has provided a sound basis for descriptive and comparative research on narrative structure for the last 30 years. The components they identified have proved remarkably robust in the face of extensive use for many and varied purposes by researchers in a very wide range of disciplines. Moreover, in identifying areas of complexity, such as the differing degrees of sophistication with which the evaluation could be realized and the problems involved in identifying its expression, they anticipated an important area of future development for narrative research. In recent research, the crucial contribution of context, including different levels of participants' contributions to a narrative, has been increasingly recognized. As narrative analysis moves into its fourth decade, one would predict that attention to context will continue to hold its place at the core of narrative analysis, demonstrating the importance of detailed ethnographic information, not only to an adequate analysis of the meaning of narratives, but equally to a fuller appreciation of the complexities of their structure.

## REFERENCES

Bakhtin, M. (1981). *The dialogic imagination* (M. Holquist, Ed.; C. Emerson & M. Holquist, Trans.). Austin: University of Texas Press.
Bell, A. (1991). *The language of the news media*. Oxford, England: Blackwell.
Bell, A. (1995). News time. *Time and Society, 4*, 305–328.
Bell, S. E. (1988). Becoming a political woman: The reconstruction and interpretation of experience through stories. In A. D. Todd & S. Fisher (Eds.), *Gender and discourse: The power of talk* (pp. 97–123). Norwood, NJ: Ablex.

Besnier, N. (1990). Conflict management, gossip, and affective meaning on Nukulaelae. In K. A. Watson-Gegeo & G. M. White (Eds.), *Disentangling: Conflict discourse in Pacific Societies* (pp. 290–334). Stanford, CA: Stanford University Press.

Boggs, S. T. (1972). The meaning of questions and narratives to Hawaiian children. In C. Cazden, V. P. John, & D. Hymes (Eds.), *Functions of language in the classroom* (pp. 299–327). New York: Columbia Teachers' College Press.

Bruner, J. (1987). Life as narrative. *Social Research, 54,* 11–32.

Cheepen, C. (1988). *The predictability of informal conversation.* London: Pinter.

Coates, J. (1996). *Women talk.* Oxford, England: Blackwell.

Corston, S. (1993). On the interactive nature of spontaneous narrative. *Te Reo, 36,* 69–97.

Duranti, A. (1986). The audience as co-author. *Text, 6,* 239–247.

Goodwin, C. (1986). Audience diversity, participation and interpretation. *Text, 6,* 283–316.

Harré, R. (1987). The social construction of selves. In K. Yardley & T. Honess (Eds.), *Self and identity: Psychosocial perspectives* (pp. 41–52). New York: Wiley.

Heath, S. B. (1982). What no bedtime story means? *Language in Society, 11,* 49–76.

Heath, S. B. (1983). *Ways with words.* Cambridge, England: Cambridge University Press.

Hodge, R., & Kress, G. (1988). *Social semiotics.* Cambridge, England: Polity.

Holmes, J. (in press-a). Narrative structure: Some contrasts between Maori and Pakeha story-telling. *Multilingua.*

Holmes, J. (in press-b). Story-telling in New Zealand women's and men's talk. In Ruth Wodak (Ed.), *Gender, discourse and ideology.* London: Sage.

Labov, W. (1972). The transformation of experience in narrative syntax. In W. Labov (Ed.), *Language in the inner city* (pp. 354–96). Philadelphia: University of Pennsylvania.

Labov, W., & Waletzky, J. (this issue). Narrative analysis: Oral versions of personal experience. In J. Helm (Ed.), *Essays on the verbal and visual arts: Proceedings of the 1966 Annual Spring Meeting of the American Ethnological Society* (pp. 12–44). Seattle: University of Washington Press. (Original work published 1967)

Linde, C. (1993). *Life stories: The creation of coherence.* Oxford, England: Oxford University Press.

Moerman, M. (1988). *Talking culture, ethnography and conversation analysis.* Philadelphia: University of Pennsylvania Press.

Polanyi, L. (1989). *Telling the American story: A structural and cultural analysis of conversational storytelling.* Norwood, NJ: Ablex.

Riessman, C. K. (1993). *Narrative analysis.* London: Sage.

Rymes, B. (1995). The construction of moral agency in the narratives of high-school drop-outs. *Discourse and Society, 6,* 495–516.

Schiffrin, D. (1996). Narrative as self-portrait: Sociolinguistic constructions of identity. *Language and Society, 25,* 167–203.

Scollon, R., & Scollon, S. B. (1981). *Narrative, literacy and face in interethnic communication.* Norwood, NJ: Ablex.

Toolan, M. J. (1988). *Narrative: A critical linguistic introduction.* London: Routledge.

Watson, K. A. (1975). Transferable communicative routines: Strategies and group identity in two speech events. *Language in Society, 2,* 53–72.

Wolfson, N. (1982). *The conversational historical present in American English narratives.* New York: Foris.

# "Narrative Analysis" Thirty Years Later

## Emanuel A. Schegloff
*Department of Sociology, UCLA*

For the most part, people tell stories to do something—to complain, to boast, to inform, to alert, to tease, to explain or excuse or justify, or to provide for an interactional environment in whose course or context or interstices such actions and interactional inflections can be accomplished (M. H. Goodwin, 1989, 1990). Recipients are oriented not only to the story as a discursive unit, but to what is being done by it, with it, through it; for the story and any aspect of its telling, they can attend the "why that now" question (Schegloff & Sacks, 1973). It should not be surprising that the projects that are being implemented in the telling of a story inform the design and constructional features of the story, as well as the details of the telling (Sacks, 1978). They inform as well the moment-to-moment manner of the story's uptake by its recipients (C. Goodwin, 1984; C. Goodwin & M. H. Goodwin, 1987), and that uptake in turn is taken up by the teller (if indeed there is a single teller; cf. Duranti & Brenneis, 1986; C. Goodwin, 1986; Lerner, 1992; Mandelbaum, 1993) and feeds back to affect the next increment of telling.

Design and constructional features of stories are shaped as well by an orientation to who the recipient(s) is, to how many of them there are, and who they are to one another and to the teller and what they can (or should) be supposed to know (C. Goodwin, 1981, 1986). Such quotidian storytellings arise in, or are prompted by, the ongoing course of an interactional occasion or the trajectory of a conversation or are made to interrupt it (Jefferson, 1978; Sacks, 1974, 1992). On the story's completion the interaction and its participants have been brought to some further state of talk and interaction, transformed or not—talk and interaction whose further trajectory will in some fashion be related to that story's telling (Jefferson, 1978; Sacks, 1974, 1992; Schegloff, 1992). Ordinary storytelling, in sum, is (choose your term) a coconstruction, an interactional achievement, a joint production, a collaboration, and so forth.

---

Requests for reprints should be sent to Emanuel A. Schegloff, Department of Sociology, UCLA, 264 Haines Hall, Box 951551, Los Angeles, CA 90095–1551.

Although the 1967 Labov and Waletzky paper, "Narrative Analysis: Oral Versions of Personal Experience" (this issue; henceforth L&W), was important in attracting attention to the interest of ordinary persons' stories of personal experience,[1] it obscured part of what is involved in their very constitution by setting their formative examination in the context of the sociolinguistic interview, an interactional and situational context masked by the term "oral versions [of personal experience]." This formulation of their subject elevated the issue of "oral vs. written" into central prominence and glossed the telling differences (if I may put it that way) between contrasting auspices of speaking and organizations of talking in the interview on the one hand and less academically occasioned settings of storytelling on the other. Although we are celebrating the positive consequences of their paper on its 30th anniversary, it is worth detailing its unintended, less beneficial consequences in the hope of redirecting subsequent work toward a differently targeted and more compelling grasp of vernacular storytelling.

This tack may strike readers as tangential to the occasion, and in a sense it is. It starts not from an interest in *narrative* as a field for whose development L&W is central, but from a more general interest in quotidian talk-in-interaction—a domain into which most occurrences of "oral versions of personal experience" are likely to fall. Taking narrative as the focus, one opts for a discursive unit, genre, and activity across contexts of realization, pushing to the background the consequences of those contexts—however conceived—for the actual constitution of stories. Taking "talk-in-interaction" as the relevant domain, an analyst is constrained to take into account

---

[1] It may be worth recalling "the times" in which L&W was produced by reference to other work and workers active in related areas, in order to complement the line drawn from L&W to this issue of *Journal of Life History and Narrative*. Recall, then, that the special issue of the *American Anthropologist* on "The Ethnography of Communication," edited by John Gumperz and Dell Hymes, appeared in 1964. Goffman's influential "The Neglected Situation" appeared in that special issue, as did Labov's "Phonological Correlates of Social Stratification," in which the basic interview techniques used by L&W are described (L&W, 1967, fn. 5). Garfinkel's *Studies in Ethnomethodology* appeared in 1967. The first of Sacks' *Lectures on Conversation* (1992) were delivered in 1964 and mimeographed transcripts began circulating informally shortly thereafter. The lectures for Spring 1966 began with several lectures on storytelling (later published as "On the Analyzability of Stories by Children," Sacks, 1972), including observations on the mapping of sentence order to event order (Sacks, 1992, Vol. 1, pp. 236–266; cf. the notes for an earlier version of these lectures in Fall 1965, Vol 1., 223–231). Schegloff's "Sequencing in Conversational Openings" appeared in the *American Anthropologist* in 1968. There was an informal meeting during the 1966 Linguistic Institute at UCLA at which many of these people—Garfinkel, Gumperz, Labov, Sacks, Schegloff—and others—Aaron Cicourel and Michael Moerman come to mind—met, some for the first time. For example, though Bill Labov and I had then been colleagues at Columbia for a year, we met for the first time at that UCLA encounter; it was also the first meeting of Labov and Sacks, as I recall. A few days later, there was an informal meeting at Bill Bright's house involving a partially overlapping set of people—including Goffman, for example, but not Garfinkel or Sacks—to discuss the teaching of sociolinguistics. In short, the mid-60s was a time when a range of related ways of addressing a related range of subject matters at the intersection of language, interaction, discourse, practical action and inference, and the like was being explored.

the different settings of "orality" (henceforth "talking")—in which different speech-exchange systems with different turn-taking practices differentially shape stories and the practices of storytelling, not to mention the different practical activities in whose course, and on whose behalf, storytelling may be undertaken. An analyst is so constrained because the participants embody these differences in their conduct.[2]

Taking the practices of conversation as a baseline for talk-in-interaction, what can be said about the sociolinguistic interview as a setting in which to describe an object generically formulated as "oral versions of personal experience" or narrative?

For one thing, the context of the sociolinguistic elicitation plays havoc with the motive force of the telling—the action and interactional precipitant of the telling—by making the elicitation question itself the invariant occasion for telling the

---

[2]"Personal experience" in this way emerges as a "type" of the larger class "narrative," a taxonomy fitted to academic and investigatory preoccupations—such as the task of collecting examples of narrative by soliciting their telling and needing to specify "what kind of story" is wanted. This, however, is an unusual way for the matter to come up in ordinary interaction. Rather than starting with "narrative" and choosing some "type," participants are likely to have something to tell, with design considerations bearing on whether to tell it minimally in a single-unit utterance, as a story, and so forth, and, if as a story, what design features for story construction to adopt. For example, in the brief excerpt that follows, Hyla and Nancy are two college students with tickets to the theater that evening to see The Dark at the Top of the Stairs. In this telephone conversation several hours before they are to meet, Nancy asks Hyla how she came to get the tickets.

```
Hyla, 5:06-17
 1                   (0.8)
 2   Hyla:    [·hhhhhh]
 3   Nancy:           [How did]ju hear about it from the pape[r?
 4   Hyla:                                                    [·hhhhh I sa:w-
 5                   (0.4)
 6   Hyla:    A'right when was: it,
 7                   (0.3)
 8   Hyla:    The week before my birthda:[y,]
 9   Nancy:                              [Ye] a[:h,
10   Hyla:                                     [I wz looking in the Calendar
11            section en there was u:n, (·) un a:d yihknow a liddle:: u-
12            thi:ng, ·hh[hh
13   Nancy:              [Uh hu:h,=
```

Here the question asked at Line 3 is ostensibly to be answered with a simple response: "I saw ... " ("ostensibly" because this may be belied by the audibly deep in-breath which precedes it ("·hhhhh") and which may project a rather longer telling in the works). That initial response-in-progress is abandoned shortly after onset, and a storytelling format begins to be deployed, the story going on for a good two pages of single-spaced transcript. This is one type of instance of having something to tell and choosing among alternative formats of telling, in contrast with starting with a story-to-be-told and choosing among types of story.

story.[3] Though the authors would surely now disavow or reject it, this seems to have embodied something of an ideal of a "null context" in which one might get at the pure shape of storytelling itself, freed of the diverse situated motives and contingencies of actual tellings. It would not be the first time in the western intellectual and scientific tradition, or even in the context of contemporary linguistics, in which an ideal form is extracted from transient "distortions" of its idiosyncratic situated occasions, however ironic such an effort appears in the midst of otherwise sustained and innovative preoccupation with linguistic variation. However, the variationism of sociolinguistics has been couched more in terms of groups and sociodemographic categories than in terms of situations and interactional contexts (Goffman, 1964).[4]

Actually, the image at work here appears to take the story or narrative as already formed, as waiting to be delivered, to fit in or be trimmed to fit the context into which it is to be inserted. In this regard it resembles common conceptions of speech acts, whose constitutive conditions and properties are autonomous, which have their origins in the psychology of the individual (whether in intentions or experiences and memories) and which are then stitched into the occasions on which they are enacted. One does not find here the sense of an ongoing interaction in which consequential next moments of the participants' lives are being lived together (in contrast to the content of the stories being elicited, in which that property is valued) with the stories being touched off or mobilized by those moments, with the telling constituted to serve the exigencies of those moments and being shaped thereby.

This image of narrative was (and is) both reflected in, and fostered by, the data with which L&W worked, at least as displayed in the 1967 paper. Although it was an important step to present the data, to devote a whole separate section of the paper to the "texts," when we look at "the data" today, a number of striking observations present themselves:

1. They report nothing (no talk or other conduct) by the recipient(s) in the course of the telling.
2. They report nothing (no talk or other conduct) by the recipient(s) at the end, on the completion of the story.
3. They report no silences "in the course" of the story to indicate where else (earlier) the story might have been (designed to be) possibly complete, without fruition.

---

[3] If the inquiry for a story was designed to implement some other action or interactional tack, or was so understood by its recipients, L&W do not tell us. The same goes for the telling that ensued, though we might suppose the common "motive" of "helping science" to have been mobilized (cf. Orne, 1959, 1962; Rosenthal, 1966).

[4] The problem is not the aim of arriving at some underlying practices or structures of narrative, only the effort to do so by stripping away naturally occurring circumstantial detail by intervening in the data collection (thereby distorting the data), rather than by arriving at it by analysis of naturally occurring "specimens."

4. They report no hesitations, hitches, or other deviations from smooth delivery in the course of the telling, nor any problems in its uptake during the course of the telling.

In short, there is nothing interactional in the data at all other than the eliciting question, which takes on a role much like that of an experimental stimulus to occasion the production of the already formed story waiting to be told.

Of course, L&W could not do everything, could not take everything into account, could not anticipate developments that were still embryonic at the time of the 1967 paper. Still, it is striking to what degree features of the 1967 paper have remained characteristic of treatments of narrative. This analytic tack has remained acceptable, and indeed celebrated, because it has fit so well with the academic tradition of ex cathedra decisions on analytic focus. I speak here of the academy, not of L&W.

Academics—whether literary, linguistic, psychological, and so forth—have wished to focus on narrative per se, so that is what they studied or how they formulated what they studied. A focus on the structure of narrative as an autonomous discursive form was consistent with the structuralism that dominated academic culture in the 1960s from the anthropology of Lévi-Strauss to the then-recent turn of literary studies, and which allowed an extension of themes familiar from literary studies to the study of the vernacular. They have collectively disattended the fact that, unlike the narratives examined in literary studies that are ordinarily singly authored (however sensitive to social and cultural context), in the natural social world narrative—in the form of the telling of stories in ordinary talk-in-interaction—is an organic part of its interactional environment. If it is disengaged from its environment, much is lost that is constitutive of its occurrence there. Even many of those otherwise committed to "coconstruction" as a theme of social, cultural, and linguistic practice might be drawn to disengage stories from the detailed interactional context of their telling by this effort to focus on narrative structure per se or by the uses to which it may be put. Thereby, the "product-narrative," or an idealized version of narrative structure, logic, rhetoric, and so forth, has been disengaged from its context of production and reception and has become reinforced as a rich discursive resource, deployable for a wide variety of other interpretive undertakings, unconstrained by the symbiotic relation otherwise obtaining between a story and the occasion of its telling. But back to L&W.

L&W took the key problems of securing oral narratives of personal experience for analysis to be those of authenticity and spontaneity—how to get their tellers to transcend Labov's version of the observer's paradox (Labov, 1970, p. 47), the formality and hypercorrection of speech that set in with overt observation by outsiders, a problem which Labov had already encountered and described in other work. Part of the solution was to elicit stories so exciting and engaging to tell that the tellers would lose themselves in the very drama of the telling (hence stories about "a time you were almost killed," etc.). At the same time, avoiding "contamination" by the observer led to an enforced reserve in the uptake of stories by the elicitor that could not but problematize the trajectory of the telling and the shape of the resultant story—especially in the case of a dramatic or "exciting" story. In this respect, in treating the recipient as basically extraneous (and hence a source of "bias"), in treating the narrative as "belonging to" the basic unit of western culture—the individual doing the telling (the talking head)—the opportunity was missed to re-situate the narrative in social context, to see that the recipient(s) is an irremediable component of a story's telling. Even if recipients stay blank (and perhaps especially then), their presence and conduct enters into the story's telling. Nor are the consequences of having proceeded in this way trivial or incidental. They go to the heart of the matter—the characterization of the anatomy of ordinary storytelling. For example, the presence of a summary theme or evaluation in L&W's account may well reflect the formative effect of the elicitation session and the eliciting inquiry as the occasion for telling. When stories come up "naturally," such summings-up by teller are often not present (they may rather be articulated by recipients as part of a receipt sequence), and if they are present, it can testify to "trouble" in the uptake of the story (Jefferson, 1978, pp. 228–237).

Or consider the possible effects of the decision to solicit "stories of almost being killed" for their capacity to secure involved and spontaneous telling. This seems to be predicated on the view that "type of story" or "topic of story" is nonconsequential for its anatomy or structure and that only spontaneity is specially associated with it. This may well be so, but there is some past experience with this issue and some evidence that what stories are about (given their recipients, etc.) may be nonarbitrarily related to the trajectory of telling.

Jefferson (1980, 1988), for example, observed that she was initially reluctant to get involved in a proposed study of "talk about troubles," suspecting that it was a structurally nonconsequential matter, focussed on a topic designed to be of interest for analytically extraneous reasons. Once engaged with the data, however, she found that "troubles-telling" mobilized distinctive interactional stances from both teller and recipients, engendered distinctive trajectories of telling and uptake (Jefferson & Lee, 1981), and so forth. Similarly, Schegloff (1976/1984) found that "opposition-type stories in which teller was one of the protagonists" served to pose issues of alignment for recipients which could in turn have consequences for how the telling was brought to a close.

However "obvious" in retrospect, neither of these distinctive features, nor that these were relevant ways of "typologizing" stories, was accessible in advance. Whatever the virtues of stories about having almost been killed, when disengaged from the details of the context of their telling and in particular from their uptake-in-their-course by their recipients, we cannot know what distinctive features of structure or interactional enactment they occasion.[5]

To sum up, there have been some developments over these 30 years in our understanding of talk-in-interaction and conversation in particular, and they suggest some directions of inquiry that merit more serious attention by those interested in narrative as a dressed-up version of storytelling. For example:

Consider the differences between storytellings by reference to their conditions of launching—between those which themselves launch a sequence and those which are "responsive," that is, between storytellings that have to "make their own way" and those that are responsive to inquiry, to invitation, to solicitation, or can be introduced under that guise. Here we are noting not only the special character of stories "in second position" in the sense of being produced in answer to a question as compared to ones that launch a spate of talk, but that there can be striking differences between stories that have been *sol*icited (and further between those already-known stories that are solicited and those not previously known) and those that are *el*icited, in which a question gets a story without having specifically asked for one (as in the excerpt reproduced in Footnote 2).

Consider the differences between stories analyzably used to do something and those apparently told "for their own sake."

Consider the relation between a story proper and the practices of storytelling, and the storytelling sequence, by which it is constructed and conveyed.

Consider the fact that one consequence of a storytelling can be the touching off of another storytelling (Sacks, 1992, Vol. 1, pp. 764–772; Vol. 2, pp. 3–17, 249–68). Subsequent stories are mobilized in recipients' memory by a story's telling just because they can serve as displays of understanding of, and alignment (or misalignment) with, prior stories. Such a consequence is both background and prospect for storytelling in conversation. A "subsequent story" is designed for the place in a course of tellings that it is to occupy. Consider, then, the differences in storytellings by reference to their place in such a sequence of tellings. This is especially relevant for stories of personal experience, and much is lost by not incorporating it, for

---

[5]Here again there are analytic particulars, not hypothetical speculations, to be considered. For example, in the stretch of talk taken up in C. Goodwin, 1986, and Schegloff, 1987, 1992, the telling of a story is prompted for its dramatic, exciting character to escape the displayed boring character of the talk otherwise going on. However, the telling is no sooner launched than the auspices of its telling, the premise of its dramatic character, are challenged, and turn out to compromise the course of the telling. Where "excitement" is offered as relief from ennui, it may be taken as a complaint about the current active speakers and prompt responses which impact the teller quite differently from the "exciting" stories elicited in the L&W. These too might have been compromised (or differently told) had others, familiar with the tale and the events it reported, been present to the telling. However, the elicitation setting provides a more antiseptic and hothouse environment, and in this respect at least, an unnatural one.

example, in collecting stories of the Holocaust. However, this is a consequence of severing narratives from their origins as stories told in real-life interaction.

Whatever findings may emerge from such inquiries, given that story recipients may contest the initial premises of the telling (C. Goodwin, 1986, pp. 298–301; Sacks, 1974, pp. 340–344), that the telling can be substantially shaped by such contestation (C. Goodwin, 1986, 301–302), or by other "interpolations" by recipients (Lerner, 1992; Mandelbaum, 1993), and that whether, where, and how the story and storytelling end can be contingent on the occurrence and form of recipient uptake (Jefferson, 1978, pp. 228–237; Schegloff, 1992, pp. 203–214), one might entertain the possibility that the constitutive practices of storytelling incorporate recipients and that storytelling abstracted from its interactional setting, occasioning, and uptake is an academically hybridized form. A search for the vernacular or quotidian counterpart to literary narrative could benefit from a redirection from this path.

A body of conversation-analytic work over the last several decades has found that the organization and practices of talk-in-interaction in specialized (often work) settings is generally best described as a modification or transformation of the organization of talk in ordinary conversation (Drew & Heritage, 1992a, 1992b; Heritage, 1984; Heritage & Greatbatch, 1991). For example, the practices and organization of talk in classrooms, courts, news interviews, therapy sessions, and so forth all stand in systematic, describable relations to the organization and practices of ordinary conversation.[6] "Elicitation sessions" appear to be a specialized setting and speech exchange system (Sacks, Schegloff, & Jefferson, 1974) as well. They ought to be understood by reference to ordinary interaction, as should the activities (like storytelling) that occur in them—and not the other way around.

Just because L&W was an early entry, very likely the first, in the effort to describe "ordinary" narrative does not mean that other story types, otherwise contexted and occasioned, should be described by comparison to their account. Although stories like those described by L&W surely get told, in ordinary conversation they take work to achieve, work that may vary from occasion to occasion, yielding stories that vary from occasion to occasion, or ones whose invariance took doing. We do not get to see any of that in L&W or to suspect it.

I have focused attention on the half of the cup that is empty, not the half that is full. L&W sought to bring attention from the stories that preoccupied students of high literature to those of ordinary folks. They sought to bridge the chasm between

---

[6]This goes specifically to the practices of storytelling in such settings as well. For example, with respect to talk in therapy sessions, Sacks (1992, vol. 1, pp. 767–768) called attention to Fromm-Reichmann's observation that a key problem in the training of therapists and in the practice of therapy is listening to the stories of others without having those stories mobilize in the therapist subsequent stories ("second stories") of their own experience. Her remarks exemplify the notion of specialized settings as transformations of ordinary conversational practice—therapists-in-training have to neutralize or suppress practices of story reception in ordinary conversation in favor of ones fitted to the technical tasks of therapeutic interaction. For another setting, see also Pomerantz (1987).

formalism and functionalism by taking on both jobs. This is the full half. They isolated the ordinary folks in the artificial environment of the academic elicitation and thereby suppressed the possibility of observing the very functions they hoped to link to their formal account. This is the empty half. There is, then, ample work remaining to be done.

## ACKNOWLEDGMENTS

This article was prepared in response to an invitation to contribute to a special issue of the *Journal of Narrative and Life History,* assessing and reflecting on the article, "Narrative Analysis: Oral Versions of Personal Experience" by William Labov and Joshua Waletzky, 30 years after its publication. My thanks to Steven Clayman, Charles and Marjorie Goodwin, and John Heritage for reacting to earlier versions of this contribution.

## REFERENCES

Drew, P., & Heritage, J. (1992a). Analyzing talk at work: An introduction. In P. Drew & J. Heritage (Eds.), *Talk at work* (pp. 3–65). Cambridge, England: Cambridge University Press.
Drew, P., & Heritage, J. (Ed.). (1992b). *Talk at work.* Cambridge, England: Cambridge University Press.
Duranti, A., & Brenneis, D. (Eds.). (1986). The audience as co-author. *Text, 6,* 239–347.
Garfinkel, H. (1967). *Studies in ethnomethodology.* Englewood Cliffs, NJ: Prentice-Hall.
Goffman, E. (1964). The neglected situation. *American Anthropologist, 66*(6, Part II), 133–136.
Goodwin, C. (1981). *Conversational organization: Interaction between speakers and hearers.* New York: Academic.
Goodwin, C. (1984). Notes on story structure and the organization of participation. In M. Atkinson & J. Heritage (Eds.), *Structures of social action* (pp. 225–246). Cambridge, England: Cambridge University Press.
Goodwin, C. (1986). Audience diversity, participation and interpretation. *Text, 6*(3), 283–316.
Goodwin, C., & Goodwin, M. H. (1987). Concurrent operations on talk: Notes on the interactive organization of assessments. *IPrA Papers in Pragmatics, 1*(1), 1–52.
Goodwin, M. H. (1989). Tactical uses of stories: Participation frameworks within girls' and boys' disputes. *Discourse Processes, 13,* 33–71.
Goodwin, M. H. (1990). *He-said-she-said: Talk as social organization among black children.* Bloomington: Indiana University Press.
Gumperz, J. J., & Hymes, D. (Eds.). (1964). The ethnography of communication [Special issue]. *American Anthropologist, 66*(6, Part II).
Heritage, J. (1984). *Garfinkel and ethnomethodology.* Cambridge, England: Polity.
Heritage, J., & Greatbatch, D. (1991). On the institutional character of institutional talk: The case of news interviews. In D. Boden & D. H. Zimmerman (Eds.), *Talk and social structure* (pp. 93–137). Cambridge, England: Polity.
Jefferson, G. (1978). Sequential aspects of storytelling in conversation. In J. Schenkein (Ed.), *Studies in the organization of coversational interaction* (pp. 219–248). New York: Academic.
Jefferson, G. (1980). *End of grant report on conversations in which "troubles" or "anxieties" are expressed* (Rep. No. HR 4805/2). London: Social Science Research Council.

Jefferson, G. (1988). On the sequential organization of troubles—Talk in ordinary conversation. *Social Problems, 35,* 418–441.

Jefferson, G., & Lee, J. L. (1981). The rejection of advice: Managing the problematic convergence of a "troubles-telling" and a "service encounter." *Journal of Pragmatics, 5,* 399–422.

Labov, W. (1964). Phonological correlates of social stratification. *American Anthropologist, 66*(6, Part II).

Labov, W. (1970). The study of language in its social context. *Studuim Generale, 23,* 30–87.

Labov, W., & Waletzky, J. (this issue). Narrative analysis: Oral versions of personal experience. In J. Helm (Ed.), *Essays on the verbal and visual arts: Proceedings of the 1966 Annual Spring Meeting of the American Ethnological Society* (pp. 12–44). Seattle: University of Washington Press. (Original work published 1967)

Lerner, G. (1992). Assisted storytelling: Deploying shared knowledge as a practical matter. *Qualitative Sociology, 15,* 247–271.

Mandelbaum, J. (1993). Assigning responsibility in conversational storytelling: The interactional construction of reality. *Text, 13,* 247–266.

Orne, M. T. (1959). The nature of hypnosis: Artifact and essence. *Journal of Abnormal and Social Psychology, 58,* 277–299.

Orne, M. T. (1962). On the social psychology of the psychological experiment: With particular reference to demand characteristics and their implications. *American Psychologist, 17,* 776–783.

Pomerantz, A. (1987). Descriptions in legal settings. In G. Button & J. R. E. Lee (Eds.), *Talk and social organisation* (pp. 226–243). Clevedon, England: Multilingual Matters.

Rosenthal, R. (1966). *Experimenter effects in behavioral research.* New York: Appleton-Century-Crofts.

Sacks, H. (1972). On the analyzability of stories by children. In J. J. Gumperz & D. Hymes (Eds.), *Directions in sociolinguistics: The ethnography of communication* (pp. 325–345). New York: Holt, Rinehart & Winston.

Sacks, H. (1974). An analysis of the course of a joke's telling in conversation. In R. Bauman & J. Sherzer (Eds.), *Explorations in the ethnography of speaking* (pp. 337–353). Cambridge, England: Cambridge University Press.

Sacks, H. (1978). Some technical considerations of a dirty joke. In J. Schenkein (Ed.), *Studies in the organization of conversational interaction* (pp. 249–269). New York: Academic.

Sacks, H. (1992). *Lectures on conversation* (Vols. 1 & 2). Oxford, England: Blackwell.

Sacks, H., Schegloff, E. A., & Jefferson, G. (1974). A simplest systematics for the organization of turn-taking for conversation. *Language, 50,* 696–735.

Schegloff, E. A. (1968). Sequencing in conversational openings. *American Anthropologist, 70,* 1075–1095.

Schegloff, E. A. (1984). On some questions and ambiguities in conversation. In J. M. Atkinson & J. Heritage (Eds.), *Structures of social action: Studies in conversation analysis* (pp. 28–52). Cambridge, England: Cambridge University Press. (Reprinted from Pragmatics Microfiche, 22, D8-G1, 1976, Department of Linguistics, Cambridge University)

Schegloff, E. A. (1987). Analyzing single episodes of interaction: An exercise in conversation analysis. *Social Psychology Quarterly, 50,* 101–114.

Schegloff, E. A. (1992). In another context. In A. Duranti & C. Goodwin (Eds.), *Rethinking context: Language as an interactive phenomenon* (pp. 193–227). Cambridge, England: Cambridge University Press.

Schegloff, E. A., & Sacks, H. (1973). Opening up closings. *Semiotica, 8,* 289–327.

# Toward Families of Stories in Context

## Marjorie Harness Goodwin
*Department of Anthropology, UCLA*

This essay addresses three features of Labov's and Waletzky's (1967/this issue; henceforth L&W) important article on narrative: (a) L&W's definition of narrative as a genre dealing with past events, (b) their procedures for data eliciting, and (c) their notion of *evaluation*.

In their classic article on stories, L&W (1967/this issue) argued that narrative provides "one method of recapitulating past experience by matching a verbal sequence of clauses to the sequence of events which actually occurred." Stories in this study were collected in a dyadic interview situation, in response to questions about past events posed by an interviewer. Although the last utterances of a teller's narrative frequently tied back to the interviewer's initial questions, in L&W's study the questions the interviewers put forward were not considered part of the storytelling process. This ignoring of the researcher's impact on the data-gathering process is similar to what happens frequently in cultural anthropology, in which the ethnographer's work in eliciting statements about culture is virtually erased.

In this short essay I describe how ethnography affords the researcher a process for gathering stories that is alternative to interviewing and results in different understandings about the structure that stories exhibit. By examining naturally occurring stories we can see how narrative structure is related to the participation framework of the moment and current social projects, often encompassing multiple participants. Narratives told at different times may be linked to each other. Moreover, some of these linked stories provide for the description of future and possible as well as past events. Stories told in interaction with others (rather than in response to questions a researcher poses) constitute a powerful tool for building social organization, often sanctioning untoward behavior.

Inspired by Labov's studies of "the logic of nonstandard English" (Labov, 1970), as well as his push towards getting the vernacular speech events of a speech

---

Requests for reprints should be sent to Marjorie Harness Goodwin, Anthropology, UCLA, Los Angeles, CA 90095–1553. E-mail: mgoodwin@anthro.ucla.edu

community, I undertook fieldwork in the early 1970's among working-class African American children in Philadelphia (see Goodwin, 1990). My concern was to document the naturally occurring talk within focused encounters (Goffman, 1961), through which a particular neighborhood group of children built their social order. For a year and a half I tape-recorded the children as they played together on the street, after school, on weekends, and during the summer. Rather than focusing on particular speech events, I instead tape-recorded everything that the children did. I wanted to capture the structure of events in children's lives as they unfolded in the ordinary settings in which they habitually occurred, rather than to control the data-gathering process.

In their study of narrative, L&W found that narratives adhered to a basic structural pattern, which they viewed as inherent to the process of storytelling itself. By way of contrast, in my own work involving ethnographic research, I found that the immediate local context as well as the longer-term social projects (i.e., ostracism) that participants are engaged in are critical in shaping the way events are reported. A storyteller builds her story with attention to the participation structure of the moment; this includes both the current audience and their alignment towards figures in the story, as well as the place of the story within a larger plan of activity. In that stories in naturally occurring interaction are rarely prompted by an interviewer's question about the interviewee, the principal figure need not therefore include the storyteller (the central character in L&W's "danger of death" stories).

When girls in the Maple St. community I studied wish to sanction others in the group who through their actions show they "think they cute" or better than other group members, they initiate an elaborate dispute process called he-said-she-said. In that talking about someone in her absence constitutes a serious breach, a culturally recognizable offense, girls usually frame grievances towards other girls in terms of this offense. For example, girls accuse one another in statements such as "Kerry said you said that I wasn't gonna go around Poplar no more." Stories constitute important ways in which girls learn that they have been talked about behind their backs. Through *instigating,* a girl who will stand as neither accuser nor defendant describes how a nonpresent party was talking about her current addressee behind her back. Whereas within personal narratives it is common for the principal figure to be the current teller, the principal character in instigating stories is generally an absent party.

The larger framework of the he-said-she-said dispute provides organization for the characters in a story, as well as their actions. The teller reports actions of an absent party towards the present hearer. When the present audience changes, so do the cited characters in the story; teller adapts the story continuously to the interaction of the moment.

Stories are often told with the purpose of realigning the current social order. Wanting to create social drama leading to a confrontation, the storyteller attempts to elicit from the offended party a commitment to confront the absent party. In order to accomplish this, she reports incidents of her own encounters with the absent party and describes how she herself responded in an aggravated manner. She suggests to the listener the type of behavior that is appropriate with the offending party by providing models of her own past interaction, even quoting herself in the past:

Example 1
Bea:   Oh yeah. Oh yeah.=*She* was, *she-* was-
       she was in Rochele house you know,
       and she said that um, that-
       I heard her say um, (0.4) um um uh uh
       "*Juli*a said y'all been talking behind my back."
       I said I'm a- I'm a say "Honey, I'm *gla:*d,
       that *you* know I'm talking **behind your back**.
       because *I-* because I *meant* for you to know *any*way."
       An' she said, I- said
       "I don't have to talk behind your back.
       =I can talk in front of your *face too*."

In discussing the role of evaluation, Labov stated (1972) that evaluation, the means by which the narrator indicates "the point of the narrative, its raison d'etre: why it was told, and what the narrator is getting at" is perhaps "the most important element in addition to the basic narrative clause" (p. 366). As argued by Labov (p. 392), using direct speech in reporting experiences provides a way to intensify certain narrative events, thereby warding off indifferent stances to the reported talk (p. 396). In the interview-gathering situation used by Labov, talk into the narrative by the interviewer was minimal. Consequently, there was very little opportunity to judge how internal evaluative strategies affected audience response; by way of contrast, in naturally occurring interaction it is possible to look at the next utterances of those listening to a story to see if tellers are indeed successful in warding off a "so what?" response. In such recipient response to stories we can locate yet another form of evaluation of the story.

Through stories such as Example 1, told with direct quotation, the teller attempts to encourage a reaction of righteous indignation so that the listener will promise to confront the offending absent party in the future. Immediately upon completion of the prior story, for example, the offended party produces a *future story* in which she projects what she will do when she confronts the offender (Kerry):

Example 2
Barbara:   So, she got anything t'say
           she come say it in front of my face. (1.0)
           I better not *see **Kerr**y* today.

> I ain't gonna say- I'm-a-say
> "Kerry *what you say* about me."

Future stories such as these have social consequences. Following this type of future enactment from the offended party, the instigator informs other people in the neighborhood that such a statement has been made. Subsequently, if the offended party backs down from her commitment, she can be accused of having "moled" or "swagged," which is viewed seriously by the children as loss of character.

In the stories relayed to others in the neighborhood who are not central figures in the upcoming event, the instigator emphasizes the offended party's past statements that are important to the future confrontation, but eliminates or minimizes her own work in soliciting such statements. For example, in Example 3, Bea underplays her own talk in soliciting a statement from the offended party. Although her own reporting prior to the commitment to confront statement (Example 2) had taken some 141 lines of text, she summarizes her own past interaction with a single utterance in indirect speech: "I had told **Bar**bara, what um, what Kerry said about her?" before elaborating in direct quotation the offended party's commitment to confront her offender:

Example 3
Bea:   Hey you- you n- you know- You know I- I-
       I had told **Bar**bara, what um,
       what Kerry said about her?
       And I- and she said
       "I better not see um um **Ker**ry, because"
       she said she said
       "Well I'm comin around Maple
       and I *j*ust better not *see* her b'cause I'm-
       b'cause I'm gonna tell her behind her-
       in front of her face and not behind her-
       I mean in front of her *face*."

In the initial storytelling session (Example 1), the crucial events at issue were the actions of an offending party (Kerry). When a story is retold to someone who may be a future witness to the confrontation, a detailed chronology of past events is not key to the activity of involving a listener in some future state of the he-said-she-said event. What is important is the reaction of the offended party to the report of how she was talked about in her absence.

Following the instigator's reports, members of the children's community actively evaluate the insitgator's reportings by building yet a third story type: *hypothetical stories*. In response to stories about the possible confrontation developing, others in the neighborhood who are neither offended nor offending party express their alignment towards the possible spectacle. For example, Martha, on hearing Bea's story about Barbara's response states:

Example 4
Martha: Can't wait t'see this
A::C*tion*. Mm*fh,* Mm*fh.*
Bea: But if ***Bar****b*ara say
[she
Martha: [I laugh- I laugh I laugh if Kerry say- Bea s-
I laugh if Barbara say, "I ***wrote*** it
so what you gonna ***do*** about it."
Bea: ***She*** say, she- and- and she
and she probably gonna back out.
Martha: I know.
Bea: Bouuh boouh bouuh
Martha: And then she gonna say
"You didn't ***have*** to ***write*** that about me Barbara."
She might call her Barbara ***fat*** somp'm.
Barbara say "Least I don't have no long: bumpy legs and
bumpy neck. Spot legs,
Least I don't gonna fluff my hair up
to make me look like I hadda bush."

Here the girls utilize ritual insults, actions which are rarely used in someone's presence to construct a hypothetical drama. This informing about a past meeting with an offended party thus can recruit potential spectators to the event.

In building the he-said-she-said event, children of Maple Street make use of a whole family of structurally different stories; these stories are deeply embedded within the structure of a larger social and political process. In delivering her stories, the instigator carefully crafts them to elicit from her listeners responses that will promote involvement in a future confrontation. In the case of interaction with the offended party, the instigator's *past stories* generate the offended party's future stories. With other children in the neighborhood, who are neither offending nor offended parties, however, involvement takes the form of playing out hypothetical stories. Each story type is situated within a different kind of encounter, with differentiated forms of hearers and different story characters; however, stories occurring at different times and in different places are linked in a complex speech event, a dispute process.

Evaluative activity occurs not only through the ways in which the narrator recounts past events in direct speech but also the ways in which listeners use direct quotation to build future and possible stories of their own design. If one were to look only at elicited stories, none of the ways in which hearers actively coparticipate in building subsequent linked stories would be evident. In addition, the ways that stories are used by girls to put people in their place and reshuffle alignments would be obscured.

Still other structural complexities of the storytelling participation frame may occur when stories are told to multiple recipients, not all of whom display the engagement of a rapt listener. Although with the Maple Street girls, responses of recipients promote the spectacle that the instigator attempts to design, in other circumstances hearers may oppose the framework a speaker's actions make relevant (Goodwin, 1997); in such circumstances evaluation can also take the form of byplay or heckling.

Sacks (1963) argued that stories need to be considered in light of ongoing social projects. Within the retold, future, and hypothetical stories examined here, the present interaction and larger social projects of tellers rather than properties of the past events influence how characters and their actions will be depicted. Extended ethnography permits us to see how stories unfold in the everyday events of people's lives and permits us to view language in terms of its functions—in Malinowski's (1923, pp. 312–313) terms, "as a link in concerted human activity."

This is important for anyone seriously interested in the enterprise of ethnography, which relies on informants' accounts of events. Rather than accepting reports as instances of the events they describe, social science researchers need to seriously investigate the process of reporting itself as a situated conversational activity.

## REFERENCES

Goffman, E. (1961). *Encounters: Two studies in the sociology of interaction.* Indianapolis, IN: Bobbs-Merrill.

Goodwin, M. H. (1990). *He-said-she-said: Talk as social organization among Black children.* Bloomington: University of Indiana Press.

Goodwin, M. H. (1997). By-play: Negotiating evaluation in story-telling. In G. R. Guy, J. Baugh, D. Schriffin, & C. Feagin (Eds.), *Towards a social science of language: Papers in honour of William Labov: 2. Social interaction and discourse structures* (pp. 77–102). Philadelphia: John Benjamins.

Labov, W. (1970). *The study of nonstandard English.* Champaign, IL: National Council of Teachers.

Labov, W. (1972). The transformation of experience in narrative syntax. In W. Labov, (Ed.), *Language in the inner city: Studies in the Black English vernacular* (pp. 354–396). Philadelphia: University of Pennsylvania Press.

Labov, W., & Waletzky, J. (this issue). Narrative analysis: Oral versions of personal experience. In J. Helm (Ed.), *Essays on the verbal and visual arts: Proceedings of the 1966 Annual Spring Meeting of the American Ethnological Society* (pp. 12–44). Seattle: University of Washington Press. (Original work published 1967)

Malinowski, B. (1923). The problem of meaning in primitive languages. In C. K. Ogden & I. A. Richards (Eds.), *The meaning of meaning* (pp. 296–336). New York: Harcourt, Brace.

Sacks, H. (1963). Sociological description. *Berkeley Journal of Sociology, 8,* 1–16.

# Narrative Structure and Conversational Circumstances

## Aylin Küntay and Susan Ervin-Tripp
*Department of Psychology, University of California, Berkeley*

Labov and Waletzky (1967/this issue; henceforth L&W) established fundamental properties in narrative structure and the linguistic realizations of those structural categories. They made possible the opening up of new questions in narrative analysis, giving grounds for cross-genre, cross-cultural, and developmental comparisons.

Our concern with the conversational context of fledgling and expanded narration has led us to reopen the question of what constitutes a narrative and to address a new question of how production circumstances alter the structural features of a narrative. In eliciting personal narratives, L&W used a prompting frame that called for high-point stories by drawing on the tellers' most shaped, retold, and dramatic experiences. Our concern is with less auspiciously launched narratives, which are incidental to conversation and provide a wider range of types.

When we set out to identify personal experience narratives in natural conversations, we noticed that stories launched into a conversational situation do not exhibit many of the prototypical narrative genre features that were put forward by L&W. They were not always recognizable by criteria such as explicit orientation, presence of a climactic complicating action, or closure of the story line with a resolution. Indeed, sometimes they even lacked temporal juncture. In this article, we examine the conversational circumstances surrounding structural organization both in marginal cases of narrative and in those that display the structure outlined by L&W.

## DATABASES FOR STUDY

### American Adult Data

The adult data, labeled UC Disclab, consists of 180 transcripts collected in a variety of contexts, but primarily from informal natural groups of friends taped by students in California.

---

Requests for reprints should be sent to Aylin Küntay, Department of Psychology, University of California, Berkeley, Berkeley, CA 94720. E-mail: kuntay@cogsci.berkeley.edu

## Turkish Preschool Data

The Turkish data, labeled Eryavuz, come from child–adult conversations at two preschool sites in Istanbul. There were 40 children, 3 to 5 years of age, from whom both *elicited* and *spontaneous* extended discourse was collected. For the examples included in this article, 60 hours of spontaneous audio-taped talk were analyzed.

## OCCASIONS FOR NARRATIVES

A type of story that tended to exhibit a full-fledged structure in the Turkish preschool context was spontaneous breaking into performance. In the Turkish preschools, such narratives were not very common, given that the teachers, at times explicitly, discouraged children from telling stories except in the time allotted for storytelling. The following narrative is from a 4-year-old boy (Hasan) retelling a particularly dramatically reported near-death experience of a neighbor as if it were of a sibling.[1]

During a gymnastic session at the preschool, Hasan (4;11)[2] spontaneously launched into a dramatic story about his nonexistent younger brother. When he was asked to retell the story (for the tape recorder), the content of the second telling was very like the first, and there was the same animated tone of voice (H = Hasan; A = adult):

Example 1: Brainwashing [translated from Turkish]
1  A:  tell it again.
2  H:  my sibling opened medicine/medicine box—ook it?
3      was able to open it?
4      broke that lid?
5      ate them up?
6      ate all all all of them up?
7  A:  a-ah! [=expressing surprise]
8      eee? [=so then?]
9  H:  ate them?
10     the ones which were mine?
11     he/she deserved it, so he got sick
12 A:  then?
13 H:  then we took him to doctors

---

[1] A later interview with Hasan's father revealed that Hasan did not have any brothers or sisters. However, the father reported that their neighbor's son, to whom Hasan may be referring as a sibling, had been hospitalized recently for swallowing some headache pills.
[2] The numbers in parentheses indicate the child storytellers' ages in years and months.

14  A:  what did they do at the doctor's?
15  H:  what's this? {re: tape recorder}
16  A:  this—we will listen to it later
17  H:  are you going to listen to it?
18  A:  yes
19      what did they do then at the doctor's?
20  H:  doctors ehh.. ee tube— they inserted a tube towards his/her belly
21  A:  hmmh
22  H:  and after that e eh.. his/her stomach— e they cleansed his/her brain
23  A:  Uuuuh! [=expressing astonishment]
24  H:  yes!
25  A:  is he/she fine now?
26  H:  ee if they hadn't washed his/her brain,
27      he/she would have died
28  A:  god forbid!
29      now he/she is fine, that means
30  H:  they washed his/her brain
31      after that he/she got well
32      and never took medicine without permission again.
          Hasan (boy, 4;11); Küntay: Eryavuz preschool

From the perspective of the 4-year-old boy, the events as he heard them are so impressive that he seems to be carrying them around in a story-package awaiting opening in the first possible occasion. His excitement is reflected in his animated tone of voice. The temporal sequencing of the events into a personally evaluated complicating action (2–11), the building up of suspense through an extended resolution (20–22), which also receives an evaluation by the presentation of a counterfactual event (26–27), and the usage of a narrative-ending coda to return to the present time (32) depict most of the essential elements of a complete structure outlined by L&W.

It is the contrast of elicited or *prefaced* stories to other occasions that best demonstrate that the structure of stories is strongly related to the circumstances of their telling. Researchers' probing questions constitute obvious motivations for speakers to initiate and sustain a prototypic narrative. The elicitation signals that the respondent has to undertake a performance, and so narrators are, in some sense, accountable to the public standards for a story.

Researchers (Berman, 1995; Fivush, 1991; McCabe, 1997; Peterson & McCabe, 1994) suggested that the origins of narrative development lie in adult-structured interactions, wherein the children's contributions are not autonomous but are prompted to match the prototype. In Turkish and American schools we find children usually do not tell stories to other children; it is adults who support children's elicited stories with prompts to get started and to continue.

In the following example, the adult stimulates a story, but the probes also alter the display of narrative clauses. Emre (4;11) has been talking to the adult researcher about a children's entertainment center that he visited over the weekend (E = Emre):

Example 2: Alligator game [translated from Turkish]
1   E:  here is a scoreboard, shows our score
2   A:  is that so? How did you— did you make a lot of points?
3   E:  I did
4       *but once* I won a lot of things
5       that alligator-shooting game did not give us
6       because some part of it was broken
7   A:  is that so? what happened?
8   E:  got broken
9       we had won a lot of shillings [=coins, tokens]
10      at that time it got broken
11  A:  my gosh!
12  E:  *but then*— *but* at that time then you know
13      those people who are at Piramit [= a children's entertainment center]
14      those people who control Piramit— they fixed that
15      and *then* we got all that shilling.
                    Emre (boy, 4;11); Küntay: Eryavuz preschool

This story has a classic construction with a high point and resolution, but the temporal marking appears to be affected by the audience prompting. The audience question (2) takes the teller from a timeless description to a specific event. In answering the question, the child begins by a short reply to the question, yet the *but* signals a newsworthy issue or violation of expectation (4). The story then begins marked with *once*. After the complicating action, the audience question interrupts the flow (7). At this point the teller repeats and moves back in time to recapitulate the sequence of winning before the equipment broke (9), even using a past perfect suffix to mark anteriority before the time evoked by the question. He then continues the time sequence, marking the resolution of the problem with *but then* (12). The audience effect in this example is relatively delicate, but in some cases in our data, stories prompted by questions or conversational issues often begin in the middle or even at the resolution, so the time line and relative focus is radically different from the prototypic narrative (Ervin-Tripp & Küntay, 1996).

*Rounds* are occasions in which certain elements can be taken for granted. Example 3 occurred in a spontaneous conversation during a series of rounds about different facets of the 1989 Loma Prieta earthquake experience. In consequence, the following example lacks even the fundamental feature of narrative, temporal juncture. It was recorded by a student after the earthquake as part of his assignment to tape natural interaction.

Example 3: Earthquake story
Albert (A) and Ned (N) are two brothers. Olga (O) is Ned's friend, Cynthia (C) her roommate. All are college students.
53  A:  you know that-
54      that *nice *glass *china *display case in our *dining room?
55  N:  =in the *dining room=
56  C:  =o-o-oh=
57  A:  **trashed/
58  C:  =forget it/=
59  N:  =*absolutely= trashed/
60  A:  whole thing a=bsolutely..yeah =
61  N:  =*every *single bit= of *glass and
62      *pottery in th-
63  O:  and *crystal?
64  N:  *all the crystal..*trashed/
65  A:  crystal
66  N:  *everything ..*trashed/
67  C:  =o-o-oh my go-o-o-d=
68  A:  =oh a er *antiques *genuine= *antiques
69  N:  =and the *amount of *money= we have lost
70      is going to be **astronomical/
                                    UCDisclab:QUAKE

The story is about an implicit temporal sequence—an earthquake followed by the outcomes of the earthquake. To have restated the obvious, to have given a temporal, causal sequence such as "we were in the classroom and suddenly it shook" would have made no sense because everyone present already had experienced the complicating action. Despite being similar in content to the adventurous "near-death" narratives collected by L&W, this conversational segment does not meet the usual criteria of narrative. There is no animate protagonist, no narrative clauses, no temporal juncture, no conflict. However, the orientation (53–54), the rhythm of the telling, the alternation between ellipsis and expansion, the lexical and syntactic repetitions, the evaluation by the listeners (56, 67) and by the tellers (68–70), the probing by the participants (63), and the coda (69–70) are appropriate to a dramatic story, so it seems to listeners to be a story.

As told later to audiences who do not share the same history of the earthquake, the same story would be reshaped to provide orientation and temporal sequences to fill in what is not shared. In fact, when Luebs (1992) interviewed 14 people 2 months after the Loma Prieta earthquake, the speakers provided full-fledged narrative structures to convey their experiences of the earthquake.

Naturally occasioned narratives can be told in response to narrow prompts, can support conversational moves such as claims, or can describe problem situations. Consequently, the outcome structures display selective elaboration of certain narrative components and absence of others. Some identify the resolution to illustrate a point, giving the complication as background. Some stories are simply vivid quotations; others constitute examples or allusions to personal characterizations. Some narratives invoke audience participation in the conflict to help solve problems. Ochs, Smith, and Taylor (1989), who studied what they call "detective stories" during dinnertime talk in families, noticed that such narratives can be characterized by interactive negotiation of an incomplete resolution. The following is an example of a *problem solving* story from a Taiwanese engineering student who is conversing with two Asian American women about the topic of race and gender relations (Y = Yuan, H = Hel, M = Min):

Example 4: Asian women
40  Y:  well, I just met a Caucasian guy yesterday
41      and we were just talking right?
42      and he he he speaks a little bit of Chinese
43      and he got a job uh got a job with a company like
44      uh doing tradings and stuff
45      and he was just telling me
46      yeah ... you know ... some Asian women ... man
47      some Chinese women you just take them and
48      bang them ... you know
49      like have sex with them
50      yeah bang them ... and then yeah so y'know
51      I'm just going to work here a couple of years
52      and then go back to Taiwan and get a wife
53      you know what am I supposed to response-
54      to response to that?
55  H:  you can bop him
56  Y:  all I can say is you know
57  M:  tell him you're pissed
58  Y:  all I can say is being in this world
59      there's somebody who like to hit other people
60      and there's somebody who like to get hit ... you know
61      so what can you say?
62  H:  did you hit him?
63  Y:  no
64  H:  why not?

65  Y: cause whoever the girl that wants to go out with
66     him, that's her problem ... that's not my problem.
                                    UC Disclab: ASDAT

The story in Example 4 begins as a prototypic narrative involving a conflict, but without a resolution. The businessman's statement (46–49) is presented without evaluation, so the conflict is implicit. There is a possible narrative transition marker *then* (50), but no overt reply is reported, and the action shifts to interior reflection. Yuan describes information about his own plans (51–52) implying a conflict with the stance of the businessman. He leaves the story with a question about what he should have done (61). In the context of the preceding conversation about racial anger, the two women have no hesitation in taking Yuan's frustration for granted and in providing an answer to his question (55, 57). Helen elicits a resolution of inaction (62), with an account of the teller's reasoning only when prompted (64–66). The story has two unusual features: the failure to report the ending, which had to be prompted, and the solicitation by the teller of alternative outcomes.

## CONCLUSIONS

The differences between conversational circumstances surrounding abbreviated and full-fledged narratives allow us to see that the structural complication is not an inherent feature of the narrative genre, but is highly dependent on the conversational occasions and production contexts of stories. Volunteered or elicited often-practiced stories like those studied by L&W are most likely to be elaborated to a full schema. Rounds, besides emulating what came before, promote omission of presupposed elements. Narratives that are produced in response to probes or questions or to make conversational points systematically focus on some narrative components and omit others.

## REFERENCES

Berman, R. A. (1995). Narrative competence and storytelling performance: How children tell stories in different contexts. *Journal of Narrative and Life History, 5,* 285–313.

Ervin-Tripp, S. M., & Küntay, A. (1996). The occasioning and structure of conversational stories. In T. Givón (Ed.), *Conversation: Cognitive, communicative and social perspectives* (pp. 133–166; Typological Studies in Language, No. 34). Amsterdam: John Benjamins.

Fivush, R. (1991). The social construction of personal narratives. *Merrill–Palmer Quarterly, 37,* 59–81.

Labov, W., & Waletzky, J. (this issue). Narrative analysis: Oral versions of personal experience. In J. Helm (Ed.), *Essays on the verbal and visual arts: Proceedings of the 1966 Annual Spring Meeting of the American Ethnological Society* (pp. 12–44). Seattle: University of Washington Press. (Original work published 1967)

Luebs, M. (1992). Earthquake narratives. *Proceedings of the eighteenth annual meeting of the Berkeley Linguistic Society* (pp. 157–165). Berkeley: University of California, Linguistics Department.

McCabe, A. (in press). Developmental and cross-cultural aspects of children's narration. In M. Bamberg (Ed.), *Narrative ability—Six approaches*. Hillsdale, NJ: Lawrence Erlbaum Associates, Inc.

Ochs, E., Smith, R., & Taylor C. (1989). Detective stories at dinnertime: Problem-solving through co-narration. *Cultural Dynamics 2,* 238–257.

Peterson, C., & McCabe, A. (1994). A social interactionist account of developing decontextualized narrative skill. *Developmental Psychology, 30,* 937–948.

# Were You Ever in a Situation Where You Were in Serious Danger of Being Killed? Narrator–Listener Interaction in Labov and Waletzky's Narratives

### Uta M. Quasthoff
*University of Dortmund, Germany*

It is one of the characteristics of a "classic" that everyone in the field—and many more readers outside of it—think they know it by heart. Only, when the work is reread for some special reason, it turns out that it contains aspects that had not been noticed in the course of previous readings. In the conviction that my own theoretical perspective on narrative has remarkably changed over the past 30 years, and assuming that Labov and Waletzky (1967/this issue; henceforth L&W) is indeed a "classic," I will reread the original article for the purposes of this article, looking for hints that can be taken as an early fundament of an interactive concept of narrating (see Quasthoff, 1990, 1997, for a more detailed description of this interactive approach).

## NARRATOR–LISTENER INTERACTION IN L&W

The descriptive format presented in L&W is a structural one in the classical linguistic sense. This means that each linguistic unit to be described must be attributed to one speaker, because a structural concept including more than one participant was not available (and not asked for) in the linguistic methodology of the 60s. Once the reader's attention is focussed on the interactive quality of narrating, however, a variety of traces hinting at the narrator–listener cooperation can be discovered in the article. For reasons of space I only follow up on one, which

---

Requests for reprints should be sent to Uta M. Quasthoff, Hackstueckstrasse 38, Hattingen-Bredenscheid, D–45527, Germany.

concerns an empirical feature of the narratives documented by L&W as a result of their elicitation technique.

## The Danger-of-Death Question

When the subject is asked if he were ever in serious danger of being killed, and he says "Yes," he is then asked, "What happened?" He finds himself in a position where he must demonstrate to the listener that he really was in danger. The more vivid and real the danger appears, the more effective the narrative. (L&W, this issue)

In many of the narratives given in L&W (this issue), I noticed precisely the same kind of cooperation between listener and narrator in the opening of the story that we found in our developmental data (Hausendorf & Quasthoff, 1992, 1996), with the reservation that this pattern was limited in our data to the interaction of adult listeners with 5-year-old narrators (as opposed to 7-, 10- or 14-year-olds):

Example 1
[1] (Were you ever in a situation where you thought you were in serious danger of getting killed?) I talked a man out of— Old Doc Simon I talked him out of pulling the trigger. (What happened?) (L&W, Narrative 1; similar in Narratives 3, 4, 5, 6, 8, 9, 10, 11, 14)

Example 2
| Adult: | Hast du das mitgekriegt Da war doch plötzlich n Krach da ne? | Did you notice that there was suddenly a bang huh? |
|---|---|---|
| Child: | Ja ich habs mitgekriecht | Yeh, I saw what happened |
| Adult: | Mensch erzähl mir mal wat warn da los? | Man, tell me what happened? |

(Hausendorf & Quasthoff, 1992, p. 248; 1996, p. 212)

Of course, this does not imply that the narrative skills of the adults or adolescents in L&W operate at the same level as 5-year-olds. Rather, the structural similarity might be related to the orderedness of narrator–listener interaction in general and the contextualizing power of specific patterns of this interaction, which results in the constitution of different kinds of (social) context (Quasthoff, 1994). In particular, I therefore scrutinize these structural patterns of narrative interaction in the next section.

## STRUCTURAL DESCRIPTIONS OF NARRATIVE INTERACTION

Unlike the classic structural orientation in narrative analysis, the interactive orientation requires a level of structural description that is interindividual, representing the interactive achievement, which is more than the addition of single speaker- or listener-bound units. We solved this problem of how to describe this level by condensing a sequential model of narrative interaction from empirical analyses. The basic idea of this model of narrative production is a three-fold analysis of *jobs* (or *tasks*), *devices,* and *forms* in the reconstruction of the interactive process. The descriptive level of the jobs covers the global tasks to be fulfilled jointly by both participants in dyadic conversation. Consequently, this descriptive level does not yet allow the differentiation into narrator and listener.

The tasks are structural in nature and sequentially ordered. They are assumed to be generally applicable to all instances of the realization of the respective discourse unit and are thus context-free: If a narrative was successfully told, the organizational jobs must have been done, no matter how and no matter by whom. Methodologically, the jobs are the *tertium comparationis* (the common third) for developmental or sociolinguistic comparison—aside from their providing the structural concept for the dyad's achievement.

The devices, on the other hand, are formulated narrator- and listener-specific. They are sequentially ordered on the basis of local implicativeness: If someone realizes Move A, then a move of the Type B (or C) is to be expected on the basis of local "conditional relevances," which are framed globally. In other words, these conditional relevances operate on a local as well as on a global basis. They constitute the sequential implications, which in turn constitute the predictions of our empirical model in that they form an ordered sequence of local turns as moves in the respective fulfillment of global tasks.

These sequential dependencies form the specific interactive patterns that are typical of adult–child interaction or other situational frames—such as the one documented in L&W. In our developmental data, it is essentially the adult's use of the global and local constraints on the child's successive activities that could be reconstructed as developmental mechanism.

The forms refer to the linguistic surface realizations of the semantic-pragmatic units of the devices. Only at this level of description do language- or code-specific structures come into play. Forms as well as devices have been found to be not only different for the narrator and listener, but also for children of different age groups (as opposed to adults) and even for adults in interaction with children of different age levels.

Figure 1 shows an illustration of the organizational jobs required by the conversational realization of a narrative discourse unit.

Narrative discourse units have to be prepared by the display of thematic relevance with respect to the narrative's content (or the display of formal relevance with respect to narrating as an activity). In other words, the turn-by-turn talk has to provide a contextual condition for the sequential placement of a narrative; it has to reach (or to be driven to) a point where topicalizing of a narrative is at least a possible next turn in the interaction.

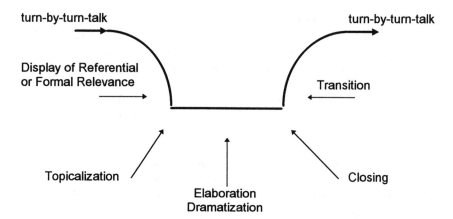

FIGURE 1  Organizational tasks of a narrative discourse unit in conversation.

In noninterviewlike, ordinary conversation, a context thematically relevant to the danger-of-death stories could be talk about danger or fights or killings in big cities. These topics would make the narrative-topicalizing question "Were you ever in a situation ... " a possible next turn. This question represents a listener device structurally oriented towards some nonspecific but reportable event, thus governing the narrator into his or her topicalization device, which often has the form of an *abstract* (Labov, 1972):

Example 3
I talked a man out of—Old Doc Simon I talked him out of pulling the trigger (L&W, 1967/this issue, p. 5).

Example 4
My brother put a knife in my head (L&W, 1967/this issue, p. 7)

The contingent topicalization of a reportable event by narrator and listener represents the structurally decisive point in narrative interaction, which has to be followed by a global next turn—a narrative discourse unit. If such a unit is withheld after topicalization, there must be an account (cf. narrative No. 5 in L&W, this issue, which is our Example 5, following).

On the basis of this structural description we can reconstruct more precisely the type of opening represented previously in Example 1:

Interviewer: topicalization: question/reportability in a nonspecific sense
(*situation where you thought you were in serious danger ...* )
Narrator: topicalization: answer/reportability in a specific sense (abstract: *I*

*talked a man out of—Old Doc Simon I talked him out of pulling the trigger*)
Interviewer: topicalization: question/elaboration (*What happened?*)
Narrator: answer/beginning of elaboration (orientation: *Well, in the business I was associated at that time, the Doc ...* )

The structural description shows how the interviewer, by use of the local device of adjacency pairs (yes–no question, wh-question), establishes global conditional relevances step by step. The (future) narrator's first answer, which still can be heard locally, receives its global nature—becomes an abstract—due to the interviewer's succeeding question: "What happened?"

When this kind of opening is compared to a prototypical self-initiated story, in which the narrator ties the abstract directly to the topically coherent context, one can see that L&W's elicitation technique expands topicalization by localizing this structural juncture, which is the same technique adult listeners intuitively use to ensure narrative communication with children, whose mastery of global-structural demands is limited (Hausendorf & Quasthoff, 1992, 1996; Quasthoff, 1997).

In the next section I discuss possible reasons for this structural similarity in different kinds of narrative interaction.

## COMPARISON TO ONTOGENETIC DATA

If we compare the interaction with a 5-year-old child in Example 2 with the elicitation of a narrative told by a 72-year-old speaker in Example 1 more explicitly, we find the following structural similarities: In both cases the listener starts with a yes–no question that—if affirmatively answered—puts the narrator under the obligation to tell a story according to the global conditional relevances shared by socialized members of the respective discourse culture. This is the way L&W describe the general procedure in the quotation given previously. Consequently, the structural analogy so far can be easily explained by the fact that it seems to be an effective elicitation technique, used in both settings by listeners who are interested in steering their interactive partner into storytelling.

At first glance, the structural analogy seems to exclude the narrators' devices: Due to a lack of global competence, the child seemingly explicitly acknowledges the structural obligation ("Yeh, I saw what happened"), but still does not proceed to follow up on it before the adult makes the structural obligation explicit ("tell me what happened"). The adult narrator in the L&W example (Example 1), however, does not explicitly answer the yes–no question, but immediately produces what can be heard as an abstract. What makes the comparison so irritating, however, is the fact that the 72-year-old speaker, just as the child, does not open the narrative proper immediately after the abstract, but seems to wait for his listener's elaborating question: "What happened?"

Having reached this degree of analytic sensitivity in relation to the phenomenon, we find a number of narratives in the L&W data in which the narrator in fact does answer the yes–no question explicitly:

Example 5
[5] (Were you ever in a situation where you thought you were in serious danger of being killed?) Yes. (What happened?) I don't really like to talk about it. (L&W, 1967/this issue, p. 8)

Example 6
[9] (Did you ever have a feeling, or a premonition, that something was gonna happen, and it did happen?) Yes, I did. (Tell me about it.) (1967/this issue, p. 9)

Example 6 in particular is in total analogy to Example 2, including the explication of the global conditional relevance into narrating ("Tell me about it").

In our ontogenetic study, we analyzed not only the developmental progress of narrative skills in children but also the intuitive variation of adult listeners' devices and forms in adjustment to the child's age. As was mentioned previously, we found the described pattern of narrative topicalization only in the interaction between adult and 5-year-old narrators. In informal interaction with 7-, 10-, and 14-year-old children, listeners reduced the described two steps to one compact interactive move by simply displaying a lack of knowledge regarding the event in question. That is, they neither localized nor explicated global narrative constraints. Rather, they implied the global relevance of their activities simply by establishing the eventability and reportability of a specific event. This pattern is illustrated in Example 7, showing a fragment of a conversation with a 7-year-old child.

Example 7

| | |
|---|---|
| Wat warn da unten | "What kind of bang was that |
| fürn Krach | down there |
| wer hat da so rumgeschrien? | who was shouting? |
| n Erwachsener und ganz böse | an adult and very angrily |
| hab ich schreien gehört | I heard shouting |
| bis oben ins Erzieherzimmer | all the way up in the teacher's lounge |
| hab ich das gehört | I heard that |
| wat warn da los?" | what happened there?" |

07–112–07

The fact that in interaction with 7-year-olds in our data, adults did not use this localizing and explicating elicitation technique and that the children did not rely on it anymore clearly excludes an analysis in terms of competence. It rather leads to the assumption that the interactants mutually display a particular relationship towards each other that includes a certain unwillingness on the part of the interviewees to tell even highly reportable stories: Although 5-year-olds, who wait for a request to elaborate a topicalized story, display a lack of structural competence, fully competent speakers, who do the same, appear to be reluctant to tell the story. Remembering L&W's remark that the data stem either from face-to-face interviews or group situations in which the interviewer did not necessarily play the central role (1967/this issue, p. 4), we are steered into an ethnographic issue: The mutual display and thus the interactive establishment of an outside or inside relationship. Obviously, the different types of narrative topicalizations produced and mutually displayed the issue of a (sub)cultural boundary between narrator and listener to different degrees. The use of a localizing pattern by listener and narrator, resulting in the display of a low degree of readiness to tell a personal experience, (re)produces a frame (Goffman, 1974) of cultural distance.

By looking for traces of narrating as an interactive process in L&W, we have not only found these traces but also indications of the "interactive" function of narratives (Quasthoff, 1980): Situational contexts are established via narrative interaction. Thus, L&W has been proven to be a real "classic"—ahead of its time in many aspects.

## REFERENCES

Goffman, E. (1974). *Frame analysis: An essay on the organization of experience.* New York: Harper & Row.

Hausendorf, H., & Quasthoff, U. M. (1992). Patterns of adult–child interaction as a mechanism of discourse acquisition. *Journal of Pragmatics, 17,* 81–99.

Hausendorf, H., & Quasthoff, U. M. (1996). *Sprachentwicklung und Interaktion: Eine linguistische Studie zum Erwerb von Diskursfähigkeiten bei Kindern* [Language development and interaction: A linguistic study of the acquisition of discourse abilities in children]. Wiesbaden, Germany: Westdeutscher Verlag.

Labov, W., & Waletzky, J. (this issue). Narrative analysis: Oral versions of personal experience. In J. Helm (Ed.), *Essays on the verbal and visual arts: Proceedings of the 1966 Annual Spring Meeting of the American Ethnological Society* (pp. 12–44). Seattle: University of Washington Press. (Original work published 1967)

Quasthoff, U. M. (1980). *Erzählen in Gesprächen* [Narrating in conversations]. Tübingen, Germany: Narr.

Quasthoff, U. M. (1990). Narrative universals? Some considerations and perspectives. In U. Ammon, & M. Hellinger, (Eds.), *Constrastive sociolinguistics* (pp. 475–496). Berlin: Mouton de Gruyter.

Quasthoff, U. M. (1994). Context. In R. E. Asher (Ed.), *The encyclopedia of language and linguistics* (pp. 730–737). Oxford, England: Pergamon.

Quasthoff, U. M. (1997). An interactive approach to narrative development. In M. Bamberg (Ed.), *Narrative development: Six approaches* (pp. 51–83). Mahwah, NJ: Lawrence Erlbaum Associates, Inc.

# Stories in Answer to Questions in Research Interviews

## Deborah Schiffrin
*Department of Linguistics, Georgetown University*

The collection and analysis of narratives played an important role in the courses that I took with William Labov when I was a graduate student at the University of Pennsylvania, as well as in the Project on Linguistic Change and Variation in which I participated as a research assistant. After summarizing how the analytic directions that we pursued were embedded in the sociolinguistics of the 1970s, I analyze how a small set of narratives were situated in response to interview questions designed not to elicit narratives (e.g., "Have you ever been in a situation where you were in serious danger of getting killed?"), but to elicit one or two word answers about local communication *networks* (e.g., "How often do you see your neighbors?") My conclusion briefly assesses how my methods fit within narrative analysis, discourse analysis, and sociolinguistics in the 1990s.

## THE 70s: NARRATIVES AND SOCIOLINGUISTICS

Readers of this journal are familiar with the methods developed by Labov (Labov, 1972c; Labov & Waletzky, 1967/this issue) to study syntactic and textual patterns in personal narratives. These methods, however, were interwoven with Labov's more general development of sociolinguistics.

One of Labov's goals was to provide a linguistically grounded explanation of the relations between standard and nonstandard dialects to help combat the view that economically underprivileged and disempowered African American children were verbally deprived and genetically inferior (Labov, 1972b, pp. 201–202). Labov showed that the children's use of complex syntax to evaluate their informally elicited personal narratives contrasted dramatically with the simple syntax used in

---

Requests for reprints should be sent to Deborah Schiffrin, Department of Linguistics, Georgetown University, Washington, D.C. 20057. E-mail: schiffrd@guvax.acc.georgetown.edu

their responses to questions asked during interviews with unfamiliar adults in authoritative positions. This difference suggested that grammatical competence is reflected in language performance that is socially situated: Because the rules of our grammar are evinced through speech, and because ways of speaking are sensitive to social situations, knowledge of the rules may be concretely manifested only during particular situations of language use.

Although the telling of personal narratives was indeed sensitive to social situation, Labov proposed that certain narratives could be elicited during certain interviews. The retelling of some experiences (e.g., those whose topic was personal danger) was so very invested with personal meaning—and so likely to place an interactional demand upon the speaker to justify that meaning—that the speaker would be unlikely to monitor his or her own speech when transforming those experiences into stories. Self-monitoring of speech was important, because it was believed to be related to different styles of speaking (Labov, 1972a). Maximum attention to speech (e.g., reading a list of words in a formal elicitation situation) was thought of as "careful style" and the most imitative of superposed norms of standard language. Minimum attention to speech (e.g., arguing with a friend or spouse at home), however, was thought of as "casual style"—the style providing the best lens through which to reveal the early acquired rules of vernacular grammar. Narratives about certain topics, then, could provide analysts with "casual" speech, and, thus, with a performative window into the rules of grammar (Labov, 1972b, p. 210).

Our two-semester course in field methods, as well as our work on the Language, Change and Variation project, included long and repeated interviews with residents of Philadelphia neighborhoods. In addition to finding the narratives told during these interviews, we coded all speech for style and analyzed sociolinguistic variables. Our interviews were guided by sets of topically arranged questions in interview modules (Labov, 1984) that we used to help overcome the Observer's Paradox: "the aim of linguistic research in the community must be to find out how people talk when they are not being systematically observed ... (but) we can only obtain these data by systematic observation" (Labov, 1972b, p. 209).

The interview format was relatively fluid and open-ended: We were encouraged to bring up topics in our own ways and to follow up on topics introduced by respondents. Yet some questions were required, and these were marked on our modules with asterisks. Questions marked with double asterisks were not only required, but had to be asked in the same way by each interviewer and in each interview. These questions formed a surprising set. Some were attempts to standardize requests for demographic information: Questions such as: "How many years of school did you get a chance to finish?" were expected to elicit short, easily codable, and scalable answers. However, others were meant to elicit long answers that would shift style away from careful speech. Questions such as: "Have you ever been in a situation where you were in serious danger of getting killed? Where you said to yourself 'This is it?'" were meant to elicit narratives—narratives so powerful that they might "command the total attention of an audience in a remarkable way, creating a deep and attentive silence" (Labov, 1972c, p. 396). Notice that underlying this methodological practice was a tacit assumption that possible variability in listeners' interpretation of questions would alter neither the form nor content of their response: Just as people could be prompted to provide brief demographic information in a uniform manner, so too, could they be prompted to tell long and powerful stories.

What we did with our narratives reflected the concerns of Labovian sociolinguistics in the mid-1970s. We isolated the narratives in our data and then transcribed them in ways that facilitated analysis of variants used in narrative (e.g., the historical present tense) and of the various devices used to evaluate the narrative (i.e., to "make the point"; Labov, 1972c). Our transcription tools—separating clauses, identifying different types of clauses, placing constituents in columns—served as preliminary coding devices. They provided an overview of the temporally ordered versus displaced clauses (Labov & Waletzky, this issue) in the narrative, of their constituents and their syntactic structures.

The distinctions that we transcribed and coded were crucial to our analyses of linguistic variants and evaluative devices. Our analyses at the time fit squarely within the ongoing development of variation analysis not only because of our interest in quantitative comparisons, but also because some of our methods and assumptions were similar to those underlying analyses of phonological variation (Schiffrin, 1994, chap. 8). Our interest in the syntactic and textual devices through which a speaker revealed the point of a fully developed story (i.e., abstract, orientation, complicating action, evaluation, and coda; Labov, 1972c) meant that we paid little attention to minimal narratives (i.e., two clauses with temporal juncture) or jointly told narratives. Likewise, we ignored narrator's talk before and after a narrative, as well as interlocutors' talk during a narrative. In brief, we coded only what we thought mattered and only what we planned to analyze.

Our analyses of the narratives also bypassed the fact that they had been told during interviews, many of them as answers to questions. Yet, this was just the sort of situation that had potential to become what we wanted to avoid: an asymmetric interview in which speakers told stories in an interactional capacity not as storytellers, but as informants fulfilling requests from researchers (cf. Wolfson, 1976).

## STORIES IN ANSWERS TO NETWORK QUESTIONS

Linguistic change and variation is influenced by peoples' positions not only in macrolevel global structures of society (and the access to power and privilege attendant with those positions), but also in microlevel, local structures in their communities. Just as we included standardized demographic questions in our 1970s interviews, then, so too, did we include questions about involvement in community networks. We hoped that answers to these "network questions" could be easily coded in a uniform manner—so that we could quickly discover, for example, with whom one played cards (spoke on the phone, and so on) and where they lived (on the block, in the neighborhood, and so on).

When I examined the answers given to 45 network questions that I asked one particular couple (Henry and Zelda; Schiffrin, 1987, pp. 41–47), however, I found them extremely difficult to code. Even when the requested information was provided (in 38 of the 45 answers), Henry and Zelda continued (in 18 of their answers) to argue, provide explanations or descriptions, give directions, and, in 9 of their answers, to tell stories. Once someone began an answer, what was said would open its own sequential possibilities for "next" talk: An explanation, for example, could be followed by a disagreement, then a defense, and then a story justifying one's initial claim.

The stories that Labov alerted us to in the 1970s often revolved around conflict (see also Labov, 1981). When I examined the nine stories in my data, I found that they, too, often clustered around resolved (or unresolved) conflict, for example, a disagreement among card players or an unfair parking ticket. Other stories addressed a conflict in the ongoing interaction; for example, Zelda told a story about her intimacy with an old friend that challenged Henry's contention that the two were not truly close. Still other stories dealt with conflict in both story and interactional worlds: A story told jointly by Henry and Zelda recounted conflicting diagnoses of a friend's illness, but also justified an opinion that doctors are not always a good source of medical advice. Thus, the general points of the nine stories were not only similar, they were familiar: By seating themselves on the "right" side of a conflict, Henry and Zelda were justifying their moral positions and their sense of a righteous self in a story world or an interactional world.

As discussed previously, Labovian analyses often pursued a more formal direction of segmenting, categorizing, and counting syntactic units in narrative in order to quantitatively assess linguistic and social constraints on variation. I decided to apply these procedures to the network questions, first, to see how the questions were structurally differentiated from each other and, second, to see if there was a relation between the form of my questions and the content of the answers.

The structural differences I wanted to compare were those relating questions either to "prior" talk *(discourse markers)* or "upcoming" talk *(question type, length)*. I knew that the markers I had used with my questions *(well, okay)* could be structural demarcations of a shift from prior talk: *Well* marks a next move as not immediately predictable by prior talk (Greaseley, 1994; Jucker, 1993; Schiffrin, 1987, chap. 5); *okay* closes prior talk and marks upcoming talk as a next move (Beach, 1993; Merritt, 1984; cf. Heritage & Sorjonen, 1994, on *and*). Both question type and length impinge upon upcoming talk because each helps provide options for a response. Question type *(yes–no* or *wh)* influences what information is required to complete the incomplete proposition opened by a question: Whereas yes–no questions open a choice between two options (confirm or deny a proposition), WH-questions open a set of choices (temporal, spatial, etc.) that allow selection among a relatively larger range of options. Question length *(single or multiple utterances)* also indicates response options. I coded each question according to how many intonation units I used in my turn before a next speaker self-selected: "single" if a next speaker began after a single intonation unit; "multiple," after several intonation units. Because my longer turns reformulated my initial question, turns with multiple utterances presented more response options than those with single utterances

I found a surprising relation between the question features tying the question to prior talk (markers) and those leading to upcoming talk, as shown, first, in Table 1. Whereas markers opened 80% (16 of 20) of the WH questions, they opened only 24% (6 of 25) of the yes–no questions. Thus, I used *well* or *okay* to mark a structural shift from prior talk more often when I asked a question that offered a larger range of response options.

Table 2 shows a similar pattern. Whereas markers opened 71% (15 of 21) of the multiple utterance questions, they opened only 29% (7 of 24) of the single utterance questions. Table 2 shows, then, that questions structurally marked as shifts from prior talk more frequently needed reformulation before a next speaker self-selected to answer. Thus, questions with discourse markers gave respondents a wider range of options through which to answer the question, either through the form of a question or through reformulation of the initial question.

Let us turn, now, to the content of answers. Table 3 shows the relation between features of the questions and the referential content of answers, that is, whether the information referentially anticipated by the question was provided alone (Information), with something else (Information Plus), or not at all (Other).

We see a consistent distribution of answers depending on the options opened through questions and on the marked shift from prior talk. That is, in contrast to the 38 Information and Information Plus answers, the 7 Other answers follow WH more than Yes–No questions (5 vs. 2) and questions marked by *well* or *okay* (6 vs. 1).

We can now focus more narrowly on the 25 answers from the Information Plus and Other rows to see which contained the nine stories.

The most notable trend in Table 4 is in the Markers column: Stories were in 50% (7) of the 14 Information and Information Plus answers to the questions opened with markers, compared to 18% (2) of the 11 Information and Information Plus answers to questions without markers. Thus, the questions that were structurally differentiated from prior talk could be treated by respondents as opportunities to not only inform me about their involvement in community networks, but to illustrate that involvement through the (often conflictual) worlds created in their stories. More generally, these questions provided opportunities in which one could not only

TABLE 1
Markers and Question Type in Network Questions

|  | WH Question | Yes–No Question | Total |
|---|---|---|---|
| Marker | 16 | 6 | 22 |
| No Marker | 4 | 19 | 23 |
| Total | 20 | 25 | 45 |

*Note.* WH = *who, what, where, when, why, how* question.

TABLE 2
Markers and Question Length in Network Questions

|  | Single | Multiple | Total |
|---|---|---|---|
| Marker | 7 | 15 | 22 |
| No Marker | 17 | 6 | 23 |
| Total | 24 | 21 | 45 |

TABLE 3
Network Questions and Content of Answers

| | Question ||||||
|---|---|---|---|---|---|---|
| | Type || Length || Marker ||
| Answer | WH | Yes–No | Multiple | Single | Marker | No Marker |
| Information | 7 | 13 | 9 | 11 | 8 | 12 |
| Information plus | 8 | 10 | 8 | 10 | 8 | 10 |
| Other | 5 | 2 | 4 | 3 | 6 | 1 |
| Total | 20 | 25 | 21 | 24 | 22 | 23 |

*Note.* WH = *who, what, where, when, why, how* question.

TABLE 4
Stories in Answer to Network Questions

| | Question ||||||
|---|---|---|---|---|---|---|
| | Type || Length || Marker ||
| | WH | Yes–No | Multiple | Single | Marker | No Marker |
| Stories | 6 | 3 | 5 | 4 | 7 | 2 |
| No stories | 7 | 9 | 7 | 9 | 7 | 9 |
| Total | 13 | 12 | 12 | 13 | 14 | 11 |

*Note.* WH = *who, what, where, when, why, how* question.

answer a question as an "informant," but (re)create an experience as a "performer" (i.e., storyteller) and "character" (i.e., storyworld figure; Blum-Kulka, 1993; Goffman, 1981).

At the outset of this section, I noted the difficulty of coding the answers to the network questions. Showing the distribution of the stories (as well as the other unanticipated information) in the slots designed for answers pinpoints some of the locations where I had the most difficulty. However, quantitative analyses that segment, categorize, and count can never be enough—certainly this was never Labov's intention.

In Example 1, I ask a WH question prefaced by *well;* the turn occupies multiple utterances; following was an argument about family and recommendations for restaurants.

Example 1
Debby:   (a) Well, let's see, em: wh- who do you go out with?
         (b) Like, if you want to go out t'eat, say.
         (c) Would y'call anybody up and say, "Hey: let's go."
Zelda:   (d)                              [Um: Well we go with our old friends.
         (e) And um most of the time when we go out to eat, it's with either his brother,
         (f) or my: sisters..Or- family. We're very family minded.
Henry:   (g)                     [Family!   Family.

Zelda answers the question with *old friends* (d), *his brother* (e), *my sisters* (e)—all relatively easy to code. However, as Henry overlaps in (g) with Zelda to generalize to *Family!* Zelda changes the direction of her answer (note the truncated *or-* preceding her own *family* ). Although we might then code Zelda's answer as "family," this response could actually be a local product of Henry's insertion, rather than an accurate answer to my question.

An overview of the talk prior to Example 1 also complicates the coding of Zelda's answer. Prior to my question in Example 1, I had asked whether Zelda and Henry still saw any of their old friends. After Zelda's answer, both Henry and Zelda talk at length about their old neighborhoods, their previous homes, the vacation apartment they now share with Henry's brother, and the closeness of their family. After Henry tells a story about the one fight he did have with his brother, Zelda hopes that her sons will be close, and Henry argues that family relationships are changed by wealth. It was after I agreed with Henry's claim that "money can sure change the personality" that I asked: "Who do you go out with?" (Example 1). Thus, the "family" answer in Example 1 is not only a local response to a question, but a continuation of a global theme of "family closeness."

In this section, I have situated a set of stories in a question–answer series: The stories concerned conflict and they tended to be told after questions that marked a structural shift from prior talk. Doubts about the reliability and validity of the answers to some of my network questions make it all the more important to understand both the distributional and sequential location of the stories in Henry and Zelda's answers. Indeed, the information that was not referentially anticipated by my questions, but was instead presented as stories, arguments, descriptions, explanations, may be telling us something about respondents' involvement in their social networks: In fact, it may be doing so in a more "telling" way than the one or two word answers we anticipated.

## THE 1990s: NARRATIVES, DISCOURSE ANALYSIS, SOCIOLINGUISTICS

In 1977, the stories in the answers to network questions seemed paradoxical: Why would someone tell me a story when I asked them how many neighbors they would invite to a party? In 1997, the locations of the stories are not surprising at all: Asking people about communication patterns seems to provide an ideal interactional site in which to describe, argue about, explain, and illustrate one's communicative experiences.

Why did I first ignore the stories told in responses to network questions? Just as our 1970s analyses were part of ongoing developments of variation analysis, our 1990s analyses cooccur with developments in discourse analysis. In fact, the course on "Narrative analysis" that is now taught at Georgetown (where I teach) is part of a sociolinguistics curriculum in which "Variation analysis" is also included, but the narrative course itself is an alternative to "Conversation analysis." The faculty who teach this course (either me, Deborah Tannen, or Heidi Hamilton) believe that both courses are part of sociolinguistics, and that either course also provides an entry to discourse analysis.

The demonstration in this article of some general linguistic patterns in a question–answer series during an interview, then, applies the general empirical methodology that Labov pioneered to the discourse in which stories were told. However, these methods of analysis should not be seen as alternatives to more recent interpretive and contextual approaches, but as complementary. Stories are sequentially embedded not only in question–answer series, but in all of the other worlds that we simultaneously create when we talk. Labov's linguistic and quantitative methods of narrative analysis can be fruitfully joined with other discourse and sociolinguistic analyses to help reveal the patterns in the many intersecting worlds that emerge when we talk to each other.

## REFERENCES

Beach, W. (1993). Transitional regularities for "casual" "Okay" usages. *Journal of Pragmatics, 19,* 325–352.
Blum-Kulka, S. (1993). "You gotta know how to tell a story": Telling, tales and tellers in American and Israeli narrative events at dinner. *Language in Society, 22,* 361–402.
Goffman, E. (1981). Footing. In *Forms of talk* (pp. 124–159). Philadelphia: University of Pennsylvania Press.
Greaseley, P. (1994). An investigation in the use of the particle "well." *Journal of Pragmatics, 22,* 477–494.
Heritage, J., & Sorjonen, M. (1994). Constituting and maintaining activities across sequences: "And" prefacing. *Language in Society, 23,* 1–30.
Jucker, A. (1993). The discourse marker "well": A relevance-theoretical account. *Journal of Pragmatics, 19,* 435–452.
Labov, W. (1972a). The isolation of contextual styles. In W. Labov (Ed.), *Sociolinguistic patterns* (pp. 70–109). Philadelphia: University of Pennsylvania Press.
Labov, W. (1972b). The study of language in its social context. In W. Labov, *Sociolinguistic patterns* (pp. 183–259). Philadelphia: University of Pennsylvania Press.
Labov, W. (1972c). The transformation of experience in narrative syntax. In W. Labov (Ed.), *Language in the inner city* (pp. 354–396). Philadelphia: University of Pennsylvania Press.
Labov, W. (1981). Speech actions and reactions in personal narrative. In D. Tannen (Ed.), *Analyzing discourse: Text and talk* (pp. 219–247). Washington DC: Georgetown University Press.
Labov, W. (1984). Field methods of the project on linguistic change and variation. In J. Baugh & J. Sherzer (Eds.), *Language in use* (pp. 28–53). Englewood Cliffs, NJ: Prentice Hall.
Labov, W., & Waletzky, J. (this issue). Narrative analysis: Oral versions of personal experience. In J. Helm (Ed.), *Essays on the verbal and visual arts: Proceedings of the 1966 Annual Spring Meeting of the American Ethnological Society* (pp. 12–44). Seattle: University of Washington Press. (Original work published 1967)
Merritt, M. (1984). On the use of "okay" in service encounters. In J. Baugh & J. Sherzer (Eds.), *Language in use* (pp. 139–147). Englewood Cliffs, NJ: Prentice Hall.
Schiffrin, D. (1984). How a story says what it means and does. *Text, 4,* 313–346.
Schiffrin, D. (1987). *Discourse markers.* Cambridge, England: Cambridge University Press.
Schiffrin, D. (1988). Sociolinguistic approaches to discourse: Topic and reference in narrative. In K. Fererra (Ed.), *Linguistic change and contact: Proceedings of the Sixteenth Annual Conference on New Ways of Analyzing Variation* (pp. 1–28). Austin: University of Texas Press.
Schiffrin, D. (1994). *Approaches to discourse.* Oxford, England: Basil Blackwell.
Schiffrin, D. (1996) Narrative as self portrait: The sociolinguistic construction of identity. *Language in Society, 25,* 167–204.
Wolfson, N. (1976). Speech events and natural speech: Some implications for sociolinguistic methodology. *Language in Society, 5,* 189–209.

# Structure and Function in the Analysis of Everyday Narratives

### Derek Edwards
*Department of Social Sciences, Loughborough University*

A major contribution of Labov and Waletzky (1967/this issue; henceforth L&W) was the demonstration that everyday spoken narratives, especially those of "unsophisticated speakers," could be systematically studied without resort to the types and schemas already developed for literary works. This remains a lesson only half heeded, in that literary schemas continue to provide an interpretative basis for theorizing about oral narratives and their psychological *functions*. Another important feature was the emphasis on function as well as *structure*: "unevaluated narratives are exceptional as representations of personal experience" (L&W, this issue). Narratives in L&W are stories "told," recorded natural phenomena that have functionally driven systematic properties. Yet, I want to argue that it is the interactional functions of storytelling that the L&W model underestimated and that pursuing those functions starts to threaten the structural categories themselves.

L&W's reduction of function, to a set of ordered structural categories, stems partly from the structural linguistics framework that was brought to bear and partly from the method by which the stories were gathered. Many were obtained in interview, rather than produced spontaneously (i.e., as part of everyday, nonresearch activities), and others came from group talk in the presence (and somewhat for the benefit of) an observer-recorder. It is not a matter of naturalness, but of activity. In pursuing what storytelling does, what kind of local activities it may accomplish, we would have to obtain data from spontaneous activity settings and bring analysis closer to that of talk in general, or talk-in-interaction (Schegloff, 1989). One of the less beneficial consequences of L&W has been the widespread application of the scheme as a ready-made data coding device, to which narratives get interpretatively fitted.

---

Requests for reprints should be sent to Derek Edwards, Department of Social Sciences, Loughborough University, Loughborough, Leicestershire LE11 3TU, England. E-mail: d.edwards@lboro.ac.uk

L&W's data were presented and analyzed as set-piece narratives, minimally contextualized (if at all) by repeated, general purpose interviewer questions, such as: "Were you ever in a situation where you were in serious danger of being killed?" (p. 9), and "What was the last cartoon you saw on television?" (p. 10). The questions were seemingly asked out of polite interest and for the record, for the collection. The questions themselves were not performative of any business outside of that, with anything much at stake in the current interaction, and so neither were the stories. This is something we can contrast with, say, a police interview concerning a crime, a lawyer doing cross-examination, or contested narratives in a marital dispute. There is a strong "oral tradition," "campfire tales" element in L&W, a study of narratives as set piece productions, collected and compared for their structural properties—collected as a set, rather than as part of some activity in which they may have occurred. The questions were stimulus questions, part of the methodology of obtaining stories, rather than part of the phenomenon under investigation. L&W (this issue) emphasized the importance of this issue, without giving it analytic prominence.

Interview data can be rich and revealing, providing many of the elements and moves that make up discursive life. However, they are likely (and may even be designed) to underplay what talk "does," how versions accomplish actions and counter alternatives, how stories are themselves activities and are not just about activities or provided as offstage recollections and commentaries. It depends largely on what we want to do: formulate generalizations and comparisons between literary, oral, and cultural genres (which narratology is good at) or understand what is going on in particular conversational occurrences (which conversation analysis is good at). In contrast to L&W, my own interest in everyday narratives is as potential phenomena for "discursive psychology" (Edwards, 1997; Edwards & Potter, 1992), in which the analytic focus is on how people, within the social actions that talk accomplishes, produce constructive descriptions of the world, while attending rhetorically to issues such as truth and error, reality and mind, identity and relationship, motive and interest. It is from that perspective that I write this article.

In L&W's (this issue) pursuit of narrative structure, function remains a somewhat restricted concept, being a matter of "recapitulating experience" according to "personal interest" and "evaluation." These functions are analyzed by deriving formal categories and rules for the semantic content of clauses. This produces a commitment to the notion that any function will be realized by whole clauses considered as propositions (the traditional ideational units of logic and grammar), rather than, say, by subtle details of lexical choice (Toolan, 1988). The L&W notion of function is rather mechanical, when viewed from a more interaction-oriented perspective. Physical activities are typically coded as narrative events (Complicating Actions), whereas quoted comments (e.g., direct speech) and emotional reactions are typically classed as Evaluations. However, Toolan (1988) made the Austinian point that talk is also action (the range of speech acts served by narratives are more available in Labov's later work: Labov, 1982; Labov & Fanshel, 1977). Similarly, emotional reactions are also events-in-sequence, and it may even be a story's central concern to relate precisely how and when they occur (Edwards, 1997). The structural requirement, that functions should ideally correspond to discrete clause types, inevitably leads to procrustean categorizations of talk's interactional business.

Both the *referential function* and the *evaluative function* in L&W underestimate important interactional concerns that narrators may be dealing with. The notion of "recapitulating experience," as a gloss on narrative's referential function, underestimates the constructive work done by descriptions. Descriptions, being undetermined by objects and events themselves, are intrinsically selective and categorial and are thereby evaluative, irrespective of the presence of separate, free-floating "evaluative clauses" (Culler, 1981). The constructive and consequential nature of descriptions is effectively side-stepped by notions of an "original semantic interpretation," which is equated with the presumed order in which "the events described did, in fact, occur" (L&W, this issue). This means resorting to "deep structure" syntax and semantics for the underlying propositions expressed in clauses, which is a way of disattending to the business done by specific things said. It also involves imagining actual event sequences of the sort narrated and constructing plausible, normative, and logical sequences for those.

For example, one story in L&W (pp. 14–15) included the sequence:

w   and they was catchin' up to me
x   and I crossed the street
y   and I tripped, man.

The claim is that a "formal basis for establishing temporal sequence among the independent clauses of a narrative" can be defined, by testing for the "potential range of displacement" between these kinds of clauses. Thus, the order "xwy" is considered an inconsequential alternative to "wxy" because it changes nothing in the "original" event sequence, on the basis that "we can infer that the process of catching up extended throughout the sequence." In contrast, wyx would alter event order, effectively becoming a different story. However, it is not the semantic content of these clauses that impose those constraints. Crossing the street may well have been a response to seeing the pursuers catching up, a way of gaining time or camouflage, say, by putting some street traffic between narrator and pursuer, and one can always trip and get up and run on.

The thing that establishes the order wxy is not the intrinsic, deep structural content of those clauses with regard to each other, but their location in the rest of the narrative *as told.* Immediately prior to "w" we are told "I couldn't run as fast as the other guys" (i.e., the "catching up" was a general rather than temporary problem), and immediately after "y" the narrator says "And, like, when I tripped, they kicked me ... "—in other words, it was straight after his tripping that they caught him. Each clause has a local relevance with regard to what precedes and follows it.

Note the specific placement of the generalizing (nonnarrative) clause: "I couldn't run as fast as the other guys." Despite being a "free clause" in L&W, it does actually occur at a specific juncture in the narrative, and it is a proper task of narrative analysis to explicate what it is dong there, if possible. Its specific relevance is for what is said next—that he was being caught up—and that is interpretable as an event-in-sequence. The point is that it is not only a clause's status with regard to events following one after another that specifies the relevance of its placement in a narrative. Conversation analysis, with its concern for the specifics of talk in sequence, undermines any such analytic categories such as "displacement set" and, especially, the free clause. Categories of that sort start to look like artifacts of L&W's analytic requirement for a structural-linguistic separation of event narration from evaluation. Clauses are "free" only according to how L&W define narrative. They are not free in any general purpose kind of way, and in fact they can often be tied to their precise locations in the talk, once we look beyond "original event" criteria for the basis of their sequential placement.

The analytic procedure of imagining the original events and using that as a basis for how freely clauses can come one after another, obscures the way that telling an "accurate" story, achieving authenticity, verisimilitude, and so on, may themselves be analyzable as textual accomplishments or worked-up rhetorical concerns (Edwards & Potter, 1992; Lynch & Bogen, 1996; White, 1987). Effectively, both the referential and the evaluative functions in L&W are inadequate bases for studying talk's actions, or narrative's psychology, because they separate description (as reference) from interaction (as evaluation)—they tend to close off, rather than open up, investigation of talk's business. Of course, I recognize that these kinds of analytic interests were not the primary concerns of L&W, which was narrative structure. However, the narrative structures identified have been influential well beyond their original remit, and it is that broader range of influences and applications that I am addressing.

Let us pursue some consequences of L&W's primary focus on how narratives recapitulate event order by examining the structural categories Orientation and Evaluation. Orientation clauses are ones that typically occur early in a narrative, setting the scene for the events that follow, providing *who?*, *where?*, and *when?* kinds of information. Evaluation clauses answer the question (or forestall its asking), "so what?" A basic analytic motivation for such categories is the pursuit of formal rules of event sequencing. The motivation is that Orientation and Evaluation clauses are ones that have a relative freedom of placement with regard to the logical order of events.

Thus, an orienting expression such as "this was out on Coney Island" (L&W, this issue) might be inserted within an action sequence that all took place on Coney

Island and thus produces a problem for the notion that stories should be narrated in the order in which events occurred. One way out of that, of retaining canonical event order, would be to classify "this was out on Coney Island" as a special Orientation clause type, rather than as an out-of-sequence "event." That makes good semantic sense. The trouble is that solving the problems of formal analysis starts to underspecify what the item was doing there and then, where it occurred, including its role within (rather than as generalized context for) the narrated event sequence.

In fact, the item "this was out on Coney Island" followed "he sort of ran out in the yard," and it may be not until "the yard" was mentioned that the action's more general location had any explanatory relevance—perhaps the place where they lived had no yard, and the relevance of Coney Island was restricted to this fact and positioned for that relevance, rather than serving as some kind of explanatory setting for the story as a whole. Contrast that with: "I was in the Boy Scouts at the time ..." (L&W, 1967/this issue), a detail which provides a general explanatory relevance for who the participants were, what their relationships were, and what activity they were engaged in and enhances the "near death" nature of the experience (the topic requested by the interviewer), given that the boy's savior from drowning was not a member of his scouting group, who all ignored him, but some fortuitous passer-by. It is this idea of contextual, scene-setting Orientations as having explanatory relevance (or evaluation relevance), being specifically formulated for that purpose, and occurring at some juncture where that relevance arises that I want to emphasize. It is both a way into the kind of analysis that I do and also an angle on what gets sidelined when analysis boils down to assigning structural categories to discrete items of talk. (For exemplary conversation analytic studies of what people are doing when they "formulate place," see Schegloff, 1972; Drew, 1978).

The following is a brief extract from a relationship counselling session, in which Mary and Jeff are talking to the counsellor about their marital problems. Mary starts to tell how she and Jeff recently had an argument after her Friday night out, which occurred while Jeff was at work. Mary has recently had an extramarital affair, and Jeff generally objects to her continuing to have unchaperoned nights out.

1 I went out Friday night
2 and Jeff was working on call
3 and um the place that I went to
4 like closed at half past twelve
5 and I got home about one o'clock

This includes what, in L&W, is called an Orientation sequence, establishing time, place, actors, circumstances, prior to Mary's detailing the argument she had with Jeff. However, note how line 2, a free clause in L&W's scheme (describing background circumstances rather than a particular event-in-sequence), nevertheless occurs specifically at this juncture. Following line 1, it accounts for why Mary was not out with her husband. So, although Jeff's "working on call" is a pervasive backdrop to the whole night's events, including their eventual argument (which happened on the telephone with Jeff still at work), it nevertheless has a specific relevance at the juncture where it occurs.

Sequential narrative events are also included (lines 3–5), which both set the scene for the events that follow and recount events-in-sequence. They have a general relevance. Mary's late homecoming is narrated as an event in a sequence wherein the place she had been to "closed at half past twelve." That is to say, the time she got home was routinely and externally provided for, rather than, say, a more blameworthy and provocative matter of personal choice. So specific events can be narrated in sequence and yet have general evaluative relevance, just as generalized backdrops are formulated at specific junctures and may have local relevance to specific events. Furthermore, the sequential events that Mary goes on to narrate (see Edwards, 1997, for fuller details of this sequence), turn out to be mostly speech acts, including Jeff's utterances "what hour do you think this is?" and "you shouldn't be home this late." Although these are the kinds of quoted speech that figure as Evaluation clauses in L&W, and they certainly are evaluative, they are also the central, in-sequence actions (narrative events) that make up Mary's story. They are not, without doing Mary's talk an injustice, separably codable Evaluation clauses pertaining to the "actual" narrative events of coming home late. They are the very events she is narrating.

Evaluation is a pervasive concern when stories are told, rather than a separate and identifiable clause type (Kernan, 1977), occurring in an Evaluation section. That is the case, at least, if we are primarily interested in how evaluation gets done, rather than in defining the functions of discrete clause types. Evaluation may also arise as an oriented-to participants' concern, as L&W recognize in defining it as the answer to a potential "so what?" Something I would want to pursue is the extent to which the various structural categories, defined by L&W in terms of semantic content, also arise as participants' interactional concerns. For example, there are presumably occasions when storytelling is interrupted with questions such as "where or when exactly did all this happen?", and "who did you say was chasing him?", as well as the dreaded "so what?" The advantage of such uptakes and pursuits is that general elements of story content might be identified not only as analysts' categories, but as features that participants themselves may treat as absent and necessary, for which they may have criteria of adequacy and relevance, and for which, on specific occasions, they may provide ways of doing some kind of interactional business (rather than just, let us say, naively getting the facts straight). Any such interactional status is best examined within the framework of conversation analysis, which is designed for doing that, rather than retrieved from the internal semantic structures of narratives themselves.

Formal definitions of narrative clause types and order rules are accompanied by cautions about variability and multifunctionality. For example, it turns out that

Evaluation clauses may occur virtually anywhere (Labov, 1972). Evaluation may be expressed by an Orientation clause, particularly if the latter occurs after the start of the main narrative sequence; it may be expressed in the guise of an event-in-sequence (a narrative clause), such as "I crossed myself," when that action is considered to be an evaluative cultural symbol (cf. "what hour do you think this is?"); and it may also coincide with the story's Resolution (L&W, 1967/this issue). It appears that a Coda might look like an Evaluation too (e.g., "That was one of the most important"; L&W, this issue). The more variable, simultaneous, or overlapping these structural categories are, then, of course, the less convincing the analytic scheme is. The more categories such as Orientation, Evaluation, and Coda depend on sequential placement, rather than semantic content, the more circular the scheme becomes. It can only weaken the notion of rules for sequential placement operating on independently defined content categories. Certainly, in many applied uses of the scheme that I have seen, a category's ascription seems more arbitrary, and more location-dependent, than the formally defined structural model in L&W would suggest.

Circularity also enters, the more normative (rather than descriptive) the scheme becomes: "As we proceed to more complex narratives, told by speakers with greater over-all verbal ability, we find a higher percentage of narratives which duplicate the exact form of the diagram given above [the 'diamond']" (L&W, this issue). This means that exceptions to the pattern can be dismissed as not being "well formed" instances, rather than empirical disproofs. If narrative structures are to have a normative rather than descriptive status, then a sounder basis for that would be participants' oriented-to norms (the "so what?", etc.), rather than norms imposed by the analyst's efforts to retain a model in the face of examples that do not fit it. Normative idealization makes L&W's structural categories dangerous when used as a set of precoded analytic slots for an actual story's contents. The temptation for analysts is to start with the categories and see how the things people say can be fitted to them. In that role, as a coding scheme, structural categories tend to obscure the particularity of specific details and how that particularity is crucial for the occasioned, action-performative workings of discourse.

Studying stories told for interest's sake, on a "well what do you know!" kind of basis, looks toward the roots of oral traditions. These are stories of the kind studied in L&W, told for the telling, to whomsoever was present. However, the interests of discursive and narrative psychology and of conversation analysis require the inclusion of more mundane stories. These are told not just on, let us say, a "round the campfire" basis, but in the performance of some other activity. Like Labov's narratives, they are factual rather than fictional, or at least that is the basis for their telling: These are events that reportedly happened. However, in being told as part of an ongoing social interaction, for that interaction, a lot of what is said, its "point" and evaluation, will be built into what occasions it and into its descriptive detail.

Consider, for example, police interviews (Linell & Jönsson, 1991), courtroom testimony (Drew, 1992), stories told in therapy and counselling (Edwards, 1995), or gossip (Bergmann, 1993). In providing an alibi you do not also have to address what is "interesting" about it, as if that were some feature of the tale itself. There is surely far more to all this than "interesting." Returning to my initial remarks, if we want to understand the content and functions of mundane narratives, we need to bring their study closer to the study of mundane talk in general, to everyday reports and descriptions, and the interactional business they perform. This is something that, in contrast to literary traditions of narrative analysis, Labov and Waletzky's ground-breaking and inspirational work clearly started to do.

## REFERENCES

Bergmann, J. R. (1993). *Discreet indiscretions: The social organization of gossip.* Hawthorne, NY: de Gruyter.
Culler, J. (1981). *The pursuit of signs.* London: Routledge & Kegan Paul.
Drew, P. (1978). Accusations: The occasioned use of members knowledge of "religious geography" in describing events. *Sociology, 12,* 1–22.
Drew, P. (1992). Contested evidence in courtroom cross-examination: The case of a trial for rape. In P. Drew & J. Heritage (Eds.), *Talk at work: Interaction in institutional settings* (pp. 470–520). Cambridge, England: Cambridge University Press.
Edwards, D. (1995). Two to tango: Script formulations, dispositions, and rhetorical symmetry in relationship troubles talk. *Research on Language and Social Interaction, 28,* 319–350.
Edwards, D. (1997). *Discourse and cognition.* London: Sage.
Edwards, D., & Potter, J. (1992). *Discursive psychology.* London: Sage.
Kernan, K. T. (1977). Semantic and expressive elaboration in children's narratives. In S. Ervin-Tripp & C. Mitchell-Kernan (Eds.), *Child discourse* (pp. 91–102). New York: Academic.
Labov, W. (1972). The transformation of experience in narrative syntax. In W. Labov (Ed.), *Language in the inner city* (pp. 352–396). Philadelphia: University of Pennsylvania Press.
Labov, W. (1982). Speech actions and reactions in personal narrative. In D. Tannen (Ed.), *Analyzing discourse: Text and talk* (pp. 219–247). Washington, DC: Georgetown University Press.
Labov, W., & Fanshel, D. (1977). *Therapeutic discourse: Psychotherapy as conversation.* New York: Academic.
Labov, W., & Waletzky, J. (this issue). Narrative analysis: Oral versions of personal experience. In J. Helm (Ed.), *Essays on the verbal and visual arts: Proceedings of the 1966 Annual Spring Meeting of the American Ethnological Society* (pp. 12–44). Seattle: University of Washington Press. (Original work published 1967)
Linell, P., & Jönsson, L. (1991). Suspect stories: On perspective setting in an asymmetrical situation. In I. Marková & K. Foppa (Eds.), *Asymmetries in dialogue* (pp. 75–100). Hemel Hempstead, England: Harvester Wheatsheaf.
Lynch, M., & Bogen, D. (1996). *The spectacle of history: Speech, text, and memory at the Iran-Contra hearings.* Durham, NC: Duke University Press.
Schegloff, E. A. (1972). Notes on a conversational practice: Formulating place. In D. Sudnow (Ed.), *Studies in social interaction* (pp. 75–119). Glencoe, IL: Free Press.
Schegloff, E. A. (1989). Harvey Sacks—Lectures 1964–1965: An introduction/memoir. *Human Studies, 12,* 185–209.
Toolan, M. (1988). *Narrative: A critical linguistic introduction.* London: Routledge.
White, H. (1987). *The content of the form: Narrative discourse and historical representation.* Baltimore: Johns Hopkins University Press.

# Intertextuality and the Narrative of Personal Experience

### Deborah Keller-Cohen and Judy Dyer
*Program in Linguistics, University of Michigan*

Labov and Waletzky's (1967/this issue; hereafter L&W) "Narrative Analysis: Oral Versions of Personal Experience" occupies an unparalleled place in the history of narrative analysis. Although concerns with narrative take us back to Aristotle's *Poetics,* L&W turned linguists' attention to the study of discourse at a time when most were occupied with the sentence level considerations raised by Chomskian generative grammar. The authors' stated purpose was to analyze what they characterized as the "simplest" narratives to discover the micro-units of narrative and then to examine how these basic components of narrative were put to use to communicate the macrofunctions of narrative.

Although both strands of this agenda pointed decidedly toward the internal workings of a narrative, the authors were acutely aware of the impact of textual context in shaping personal narratives. Despite this fact, to our knowledge no attention has been given to this aspect of their work.[1] We therefore take the occasion of this celebration of "Narrative Analysis" as an opportunity to map out how they understood intertextuality. Because the three decades since the writing of "Narrative Analysis" have witnessed a burgeoning awareness that textual context is critical in understanding how and why texts are shaped as they are and express what they do, it seemed worthwhile to establish what constituted an early conception of intertextuality. Although there are many fronts on which one might wish to criticize the assumptions or methods of L&W, our goal is to draw out what their assumptions seemed to be and to try to understand the work in the context of their own time with the benefit, where appropriate, of contemporary thinking.

---

Requests for reprints should be sent to Deborah Keller-Cohen, 1076 Friez Bldg., Program in Linguistics, University of Michigan, Ann Arbor, MI 48109–1285. E-mail: dkc@umich.edu

[1] L&W were concerned with this issue in a more limited way in their choice of prompts for the narratives. (See a later report of this research in Labov, 1972a).

Intertextuality has been interpreted in various ways, but at the center of these understandings is an appreciation that a text is related to other texts including that in which it is embedded. (Bakhtin, 1979/1986; Barthes, 1977; Becker, 1995; Fairclough, 1992; Foucault, 1972; Kristeva, 1966/1986). Intertextuality presupposes that a text can be detached from its context and related to other texts (Baumann & Briggs, 1990), and L&W's paper may certainly be seen as operating within this notion of text. Following Baumann and Briggs' definition of entextualization as the process of rendering discourse extractable, of making a stretch of linguistic production into a unit—a text—that can be lifted out of its interactional setting (p. 73). L&W's narratives have been lifted out of their surrounding linguistic and social context (decontextualized), presented as independent texts (entextualized), and recontextualized in the seminal paper. The entextualization of the narratives has further implications with regard to their interpretation within the new context, as will be seen in our discussion of the importance of anterior text.

Three particular understandings of intertextuality are implicated in L&W's article: the relation between a text and other distant texts to which it is related—texts to which it bears historical or genre relations; antecedent authorial texts—those which create earlier or alternative constructions of the text's author; and anterior text—in the stream of discourse the text immediately prior to the studied text.

## HISTORICALLY PRIOR TEXTS

That intertexuality was an early consideration in the work of L&W can be seen in the opening statement in "Narrative Analysis."

> Most attempts to analyze narrative have taken as their subject matter the more complex products of long-standing literary or oral traditions. Myths, folktales, legends, histories, epics, toasts and sagas seem to be the results of the combination and evolution of simpler elements; they contain many cycles and recycles of basic narrative structures; in many cases, the evolution of a particular narrative has removed it so far from its originating function that it is difficult to say what its present function is. (L&W, 1967/this issue)

Two concepts of intertextuality seem to be operating here. For one, L&W acknowledge that some types of narratives such as myths and folktales grow out of long-standing cultural traditions, either spoken or written. L&W's intellectual progenitor, Propp (1928/1968), recognized that cultural contact altered the form of such narratives (p. 100), complicating an understanding of why a particular genre of narrative assumes the shape it does. Neither Propp nor L&W conceived of narratives as synchronically mutable, treating them as fixed at a single point in time. As such, L&W's views of narrative structure apparently had not been influenced by studies of oral literature beginning as early as the 1930s (Chadwick & Chadwick, 1932–40) and continuing on the American scene (see Parry & Lord, 1954, on Yugoslav heroic poetry) to challenge prevailing conceptions about oral literature as fixed. Their efforts, as well as subsequent research by Lord (1968) and others in the oral formulaic school, argued that oral literature is variable, each telling actually a combined effort of the narrator and audience.[2]

Second, by using interview questions to elicit personal narratives, L&W sought to limit the effect of textual context on the narratives. Ironically, in selecting narratives of personal experience, they chose texts that are deeply embedded in the ongoing text of the narrator's life. Thus, personal narratives not only have the immediate textual context for interpretation but also all the past and future texts of that narrator's life. A friend telling another about a car accident, a client telling a therapist about a problem at home, and a child recounting the events at a birthday party are all instances of narratives of personal experience. The pervasiveness of such narratives creates as well as is facilitated by their embeddedness in the normal flow of discourse. Furthermore, personal experience narratives are generally seen as the product of repeated externalized recollections of an experience. Personal narratives, as much as folk stories, are repeated, rehearsed, and reshaped for each new telling. Who cannot recall the loud groans from family members as one of their own tells a story for the $n$th time? Likewise, spousal critiques of each others' retold stories have been a rich source of humor in cartoons, television, and film for decades.

## ANTECEDENT AUTHORIAL TEXT: NARRATORS AND NARRATIVE IDENTITIES

Concern with managing intertextuality was also evident in the individuals L&W chose for narrators. Having identified a type of narrative they believed was not grounded in cultural tradition, L&W selected speakers they regarded as likely to be little influenced by the full range of narratives available in the culture at large. Drawing on Propp (1928/1968), who argued that "uncorrupted tale construction [was] peculiar only to the peasantry—to a peasantry, moreover, little touched by civilization" (p. 100), L&W selected "unsophisticated speakers," not "expert storytellers" whose background, they seem to imply, would have limited their exposure to both oral and literate narrative traditions. Unaware of the rich narrative

---

[2] It could be argued that L&W were well aware of the variability of orally produced narratives and as such viewed it as a methodological challenge, controlling for it through the way in which they elicited the narratives of personal experience. In their study, the interviewer offered little feedback (except occasionally to encourage more talk) so as not to influence the form of the narrative. If that is the case, the narratives elicited may have departed from the form of such narratives in everyday talk in interaction.

repertoire that speakers from oral traditions possess (Finnegan, 1988; Heath, 1983), they adopted Propp's assumptions about narrators from oral cultures.

In contemporary scholarship it has become commonplace to observe that speakers use the site of narratives to construct particular identities (Bruner, 1987; Gergen & Gergen, 1986; Langellier, 1989; Ochs & Capps, 1996; Polkinghorne, 1988; Schiffrin, 1996; Somers & Gibson, 1994), the construction of identity being understood not as a single act, but as a process that is constantly active, each telling of a story offering the narrator a fresh opportunity to create a particular representation of herself. The interface of the narrative context with the narrator's presentation of self is evident in L&W's data, as they themselves acknowledge (this issue). In fact, they saw this as connected to why speakers tell narratives, in their terms "the significance" of a narrative. This focus was articulated in their analysis of evaluation, which they defined as "that part of the narrative which reveals the attitude of the narrator towards the narrative by emphasizing the relative importance of some narrative units as compared to others" (this issue). Among the types of evaluation they observed, they noted that speakers make narrative choices in order to display a particular portrait of themselves (p. 38). The self that the narrators depict is inevitably constructed for that particular context, as verbal interaction does not take place in a vacuum, and narratives, even less personal narratives, are particular—told by a given individual in particular ways to an identifiable audience in accordance with the occasion. As Goffman (1959, p. 15) observed: "when an individual appears before others he will have many motives for trying to control the impression they receive of the situation," and there is no reason why this should not be so in a sociolinguistic interview. Bruner (1990, p. 101) referred to this as the self being "dialogue dependent." Although examples of narrative portraiture are evident in their data (see Narratives 2 and 7 as examples), L&W were less concerned with the problem of multiple narrative identities than with being able to draw generalizations across the narrative structures. For them the narrator's identity was stable although the narrative goals may vary.

## ANTERIOR TEXT AND ELICITATION CONTEXT

With a target narrative and narrator in place, L&W took further steps to constrain the intertextuality of the data. L&W believed the structure and function of these narratives would be readily interpretable because they were produced "in direct connection with their originating function," that is, in response to a known prompt, a question. The stories reported in "Narrative Analysis" were drawn from four different studies that the authors report employed the same interview techniques.[3]

---

[3]L&W (1967/this issue), fn. 2.

Although not described in the 1967 publication, a description of the methods appeared in "The Isolation of Contextual Styles" (Labov, 1972a). This latter work was deeply concerned with the way the formality of a situation influences the production of linguistic variables, in which a speech situation that elicited more monitoring of one's speech relative to other situations was defined as *formal*. The contrast, taken to be central to the variation examined, was between (a) formal speech: the language elicited in response to the interview questions and its associated formal contexts (reading aloud word lists and minimal pairs) and (b) *casual* speech: language occurring more spontaneously, such as talk to another during the interview, talk to the interviewer not related to the questions of the interview, and emotionally charged responses to formal elicitation questions (such as questions about the danger of death).

It is the speech elicited in the more casual contexts that serves as the data for the analysis in L&W. Those narratives were drawn from two linguistic contexts: responses to a formal elicitation question about dangerous situations and narratives arising in casual conversation with the interviewer participating more marginally. In " ... Contextual Styles" Labov (1972a) provided more information about the elicitation of the narratives, maintaining that speakers pay much less attention to their speech as they become caught up in retelling the experience their narrative describes, producing casual rather than formal talk.

As indicated in the preceding section, we now recognize that narratives of personal experience are greatly influenced by the many retellings of which they are a part. Even so, "Narrative Analysis" makes an important contribution to recognition of the role of the immediately anterior text in the shape a narrative takes. Indeed, in Labov's (1972b) continuation of this work, he offered additional discussion of the way the interviews were designed to foster the production of narratives (p. 354). There he noted that elicitation of the narratives was set up through the use of a paired sequence of questions, the first designed to assess whether a speaker had a tellable story and the second used to elicit the story.

Again we see that L&W took intertextuality to be a resource to manage, this time in the elicitation of the narratives themselves. Since that time, scholars have come to understand the multiple ways in which adjacent text serves as an important resource in creating and understanding narratives. For example, Basso's (1986) analysis of Native American discourse illustrates how adjacent text elicits and creates subsequent text. Her study of Kalapalo narrative discourse showed that the narrative that gets told arises out of the interaction between the narrator and the "what-sayer or responder-ratifier" (p. 119) who uses several devices, including repetitions and questions, to elicit more of the narrative.[4] Capps and Ochs (1995)

---

[4]The vast literature employing conversational analytic methods likewise demonstrates the role of anterior text in the interpretation of prior text, through the concept of double contextuality (Heritage, 1984, p. 242).

showed how anterior text is a resource for interpreting subsequent text. In their conversational study of narratives of agoraphobia, they found that the causes of agoraphobic panic attacks can be discovered by coordinating assessments provided earlier in an interaction with subsequent narratives of panic. Although the literature on the role of anterior text is too vast to deal with adequately here, suffice it to say that our understanding of this aspect of intertextuality has grown exponentially in the decades since L&W.

In this essay we attempted to introduce the reader to a heretofore unexplored topic, the role of intertextuality in L&W's "Narrative Analysis." Our goal has been to show that L&W acknowledged, mitigated, and exploited intertextuality: They aimed to avoid culturally practiced genres by choosing narratives of personal experience, they selected speakers they thought could lay no claim to the full range of cultural resources available for narrative expertise, and they chose contexts designed to elicit casual speech taken not to be influenced by literary conventions. It will be important for us to continue to work out how speakers make use of other texts as they talk about their personal experiences if we are to refine our understanding of how such narratives are constructed.

## REFERENCES

Bakhtin, M. M. (1986). *Speech genres and other late essays.* Austin: University of Texas Press. (Original work published 1979)

Barthes, R. (1977). An introduction to the structural analysis of narrative. In R. Barthes (Ed.), *Image, music and text* (pp. 79–124). New York: Heath.

Basso, E. (1986). Quoted dialogues in Kalapalo narrative discourse. In J. Sherzer & G. Urban (Eds.), *Native South American discourse* (pp. 119–168). Berlin: Mouton De Gruyter.

Baumann, R., & Briggs, C. (1990). Poetics and performance as critical perspectives on language and social life. *Annual Review of Anthropology, 19,* 59–88.

Becker, A. L. (1995). *Beyond translation.* Ann Arbor: The University of Michigan Press.

Bruner, J. (1987). Life as narrative. *Social Research, 54*(1), 11–32.

Bruner, J. (1990). *Acts of meaning.* Cambridge, MA: Harvard University Press.

Capps, L., & Ochs, E. (1995). Out of place: Narrative insights into agoraphobia. *Discourse Processes, 19,* 407–439.

Chadwick, H. M., & Chadwick, N. K. (1932–40). *The growth of literature* (Vol. 1–3). Cambridge, England: Cambridge University Press.

Fairclough, N. (1992). Intertextuality in critical discourse analysis. *Linguistics and Education, 4,* 269–293.

Finnegan, R. (1988). *Literacy and orality.* Oxford, England: Basil Blackwell.

Foucault, M. (1972). *The archaeology of knowledge.* London: Tavistock.

Gergen, K., & Gergen, M. (1986). Narrative form and the construction of psychological science. In T. Sarbin (Ed.), *Narrative psychology* (pp. 22–44). New York: Praeger.

Goffman, E. (1959). *The presentation of self in everyday life.* New York: Doubleday Anchor.

Heath, S. B. (1983). *Ways with words.* Cambridge, England: Cambridge University Press.

Heritage, J. (1984). *Garfinkel and ethnomethodology.* Cambridge, England: Polity.

Kristeva, J. (1986). *The Kristeva reader*. New York: Columbia University Press. (Original work published 1966)

Labov, W. (1972a) The isolation of contextual styles. In W. Labov (Ed.), *Sociolinguistic patterns* (pp. 70–109). Philadelphia: University of Pennsylvania Press.

Labov, W. (1972b). The transformation of experience in narrative syntax. In W. Labov, (Ed.) *Language in the inner city* (pp. 354–396). Philadelphia: University of Pennsylvania Press.

Labov, W., & Waletzky, J. (this issue). Narrative analysis: Oral versions of personal experience. In J. Helm (Ed.), *Essays on the verbal and visual arts: Proceedings of the 1966 Annual Spring Meeting of the American Ethnological Society* (pp. 12–44). Seattle: University of Washington Press. (Original work published 1967)

Langellier, K. (1989). Personal narratives: Perspectives on theory and research. *Text and Performance Quarterly, 9,* 243–276.

Lord, A. B. (1968). *The singer of tales.* New York: Atheneum.

Ochs, E., & Capps, L. (1996). Narrating the self. *Annual Review of Anthropology, 25,* 19–43.

Parry, M., & Lord, A. B. (1954). *Serbocroation heroic songs.* Cambridge, MA: Harvard University Press.

Polkinghorne, D. (1988). *Narrative knowledge and the human sciences.* Albany: State University of New York Press.

Propp. V. (1968). *Morphology of the folktale.* Austin: University of Texas Press. (Original work published in 1928)

Schiffrin, D. (1996). Narrative as self-portrait: Sociolinguistic construction of identity. *Language in Society, 25,* 167–203.

Somers, M., & Gibson, G. (1994). Reclaiming the epistemological "other": Narrative and the social constitution of identity. In C. Calhoun (Ed.), *Social theory and the politics of identity* (pp. 37–99). London: Basil Blackwell.

# A Short Story About Long Stories

## Catherine Kohler Riessman
*Department of Sociology and School of Social Work, Boston University*

I encountered Labov and Waletzky's original article (1967/this issue, henceforth L&W) in the context of very specific problems in working with qualitative textual data. It was 1983, and I was a (not so young) postdoctoral fellow wrestling with talk about marriage, in the form of transcripts of interviews with more than 100 separating and divorcing women and men. My sociological training in research methods called for fragmenting the data in service of interpretation (Strauss, 1987) and, accordingly, I was moving through the lengthy interviews cutting, categorizing, and grouping responses into a common set of thematic elements.

A recently separated man challenged my fragmentation efforts: responding to an interview question asking for the "reasons for his separation," he laughed and said, "Well, you know, that's a real long story. Maybe I can sum it up by saying ... ." He then gave a list of complaints. Only later did I realize the full significance of his message: He had knitted the disparate events of his marriage into "a real long story," but traditional social science methods of interviewing and coding fragmented and decontextualized them (Mishler, 1986). The insight, and an alternative way to approach interviews, crystallized when I was handed Labov's (1982) paper on personal narratives of violence by my postdoctoral mentor, Elliot Mishler. From that paper—which transformed forever my way of working with textual data—I worked my way back to L&W.

The fundamental structures of oral versions of personal experience, and their functions, provided a way into the "long stories" about divorce. In addition to healing biographical discontinuities (Bury, 1982) and facilitating the construction of identities, I also came to see how stories justify decisions to divorce (Riessman, 1990). That women and men needed to go to such narrative lengths to explain to the listener what "really happened" in their marriages (our questions did not ask

---

Requests for reprints should be sent to Catherine Kohler Riessman, Department of Sociology and School of Social Work, Boston University, 264 Bay State Road, Boston, MA 02215. E-mail: riessman@bu.edu

for this information, or even encourage narrativization as a discourse strategy) challenges the conventional wisdom that divorce is no longer deviant. Narratives serve a persuasive function in social interaction, in addition to the referential and evaluative functions L&W identify. Looking back, it is hard to imagine we didn't always know the fundamental structures out of which stories are made (orientation, complicating action, evaluation, etc.), because they are so intuitive, logical, and clearly "there" in a wide variety of contexts.

However, not all tales about marriage involve protagonists, events, complications, and consequences. A central problem I encountered with the model is the very definition of narrative. Some of the long stretches of talk about marriage were unanalyzable units in L&W's terms, yet they recapitulated the past, "felt" like narratives in the interview interaction, and were responded to as such (e.g., the teller held the floor for a lengthy turn in the interview conversation and was interrupted only for clarification). They were accounts, they functioned to construct and interpret the past (a perspective I prefer to the authors' implicit correspondence theory), they were recipient-designed, and they were efforts to persuade. How could they be analyzed as formal narratives?

Ultimately, I resolved the problem by developing a beginning typology of narrative *genres* that builds on the work of Linde (1986) and Polanyi (1985). Genre refers to types of narrative that are distinguished by a definite style and are constituted by specific conventions and codes of speech, including verb tense, temporality, sequencing, discourse markers, and other linguistic elements. I reserved the term *story* for the structure identified by L&W. Other genres of narrative include habitual narratives, which emplot durative events and blur time with the conditional past tense. In my research, this narrative form was used persuasively to convey the gradual downward spiral of a marriage and the experience of deadness or heavy hanging time. The hypothetical narrative genre, by contrast, uses the subjunctive to emplot events that never happened, but should have. Like an elaborate fantasy, the form was typically juxtaposed with a story in the simple past to construct a moral opposition—what marriage should have been and what was. Another set of genres attempted to recapitulate emotional "events." Narrators pulled the listener into the unfolding experience of disruption and upheaval of divorce in long passages that are highly structured and metaphored (Riessman, 1991). To interpret these narratives of distress, I needed to reach beyond a Labovian framework and used Gee's (1985, 1986, 1991) structural analysis instead. In sum, extensions of the method were necessary to render the divorce accounts meaningful, given all their diversity. The divorce narratives became analyzable as presentations of self (Goffman, 1959) and as cultural products (Rosenwald & Ochberg, 1992), over and beyond their reference to events that may (or may not) have happened in the marriage.

Perhaps the most controversial stretch of talk I attempted to analyze as a formal narrative was the lengthy (25 min) account of a working-class Puerto Rican woman

("Marta"). I was drawn to it initially precisely because it was not temporally organized and consequently confused the listener-interviewer (Riessman, 1987). The text alerted me to taken-for-granted assumptions about time in research interviews—violated in this case—and their possible connection to class and culture. Labov, of course, studied language and social class (Labov, 1972), but his work is curiously silent about how the story form might vary with culture, although L&W (1967/this issue) had earlier suggested the research topic (p. 38). In the sequence of my own evolving understanding of what differentiates narrative from other forms of talk (such as question and answer exchanges, chronicles, arguments, etc.), Marta's account represented a turning point. It raised fundamental theoretical questions about the boundaries of narrative, which subsequent work has examined systematically. Peterson and Langellier (1995) argue that interpretation is fundamentally affected by how one locates the boundary between text and context, that is, where the analyst chooses through transcription practices to begin and end a narrative segment.

Marta's account raised additional questions about time. As Michaels (1981) showed with children's narratives, a particular kind of temporal ordering is expected in institutional settings that evaluate children on a regular basis, and those who deviate from these preferred styles are evaluated negatively. Marta's narrative, like the Black children's talk that Michaels analyzed, is organized topically rather than temporally—it is a series of linked "episodes" in the life story of courtship and marriage, with moves and shifts between settings that signal the narrator's experience of migration. Like the children's narratives, its meaning was problematic for the listener, but the text becomes artfully senseful when L&W's assumptions about linear time and narrative structure are suspended.

Personal narratives, in all their diversity, offer social scientists a window into personal experience, specifically human agency in the face of life events. Individuals craft their tales collaboratively with listeners—two human agents make sense of personal experience in interaction. Crucial meanings are lost if the form of telling is ignored, and the text is fragmented and decontextualized into symptom counts and lists. There is reciprocity between form and meaning: The way individuals craft their tales, including the narrative genres they select, carry crucial interpretive understandings. Methods that allow for the examination of narrative form—and diverse ways of telling—counter tendencies (all too frequent in social science research) to objectify the subject.

As a conclusion to these brief thoughts about "long stories," I suggest that what's at stake here is more than academic disputes about the defining features of narrative. Narrative has now become a household world in the social sciences and a common tool for evaluation in clinical and educational settings. However, there is a danger: the tyranny of the narrative. How can we open up the concept so that a diversity of styles of telling about consequential events can be honored, but at the same time avoid the pitfall of banalizing the concept—treating all talk as narrative? Can we develop meaningful and useful typologies of narrative than counter restrictive definitions, but avoid reifying narrative form? Given the increasing trend toward the use of storytelling as an evaluative device in educational and clinical settings, what is to forestall the tendency to label those who narrate "differently" as "deficient"? In a word, narrative runs the danger of becoming the new hegemony. I have no clear answers to these problems and questions, though I have pointed in this essay to some directions for future theory and research. In a sense, the problems are a testimony to the success of an intellectual movement that started 30 years ago with L&W's generative paper.

## REFERENCES

Bury, M. (1982). Chronic illness as biographical disruption. *Sociology of Health and Illness, 4*, 167–182.
Gee, J. P. (1985). The narrativization of experience in the oral style. *Journal of Education, 167*, 9–35.
Gee, J. P. (1986). Units in the production of narrative discourse. *Discourse Processes, 9*, 391–422.
Gee, J. P. (1991). A linguistic approach to narrative. *Journal of Narrative and Life History, 1*, 15–39.
Goffman, E. (1959). *The presentation of self in everyday life.* New York: Doubleday.
Labov, W. (Ed.). (1972). *Language in the inner city: Studies in the Black English vernacular.* Philadelphia: Pennsylvania University Press.
Labov, W. (1982). Speech actions and reactions in personal narrative. In D. Tannen (Ed.), *Analyzing discourse: Text and talk* (pp. 219–247). Washington, DC: Georgetown University Press.
Labov, W., & Waletzky, J. (this issue). Narrative analysis: Oral versions of personal experience. In J. Helm (Ed.), *Essays on the verbal and visual arts: Proceedings of the 1966 Annual Spring Meeting of the American Ethnological Society* (pp. 12–44). Seattle: University of Washington Press. (Original work published 1967)
Michaels, S. (1981). "Sharing time": Children's narrative styles and differential access to literacy. *Language and Society, 10*, 423–442.
Mishler, E. G. (1986). *Research interviewing: Context and narrative.* Cambridge, MA: Harvard University Press.
Peterson, E. E., & Langellier, K. M. (1995). The politics of personal narrative methodology. *Text and Performance Quarterly, 17*, 135–152.
Polanyi, L. (1985). *Telling the American story: A structural and cultural analysis of conversational storytelling.* Norwood, NJ: Ablex.
Riessman, C. K. (1987). When gender is not enough: Women interviewing women. *Gender & Society, 1*, 172–207.
Riessman, C. K. (1990). *Divorce talk: Women and men make sense of personal relationships.* New Brunswick, NJ: Rutgers University Press.
Riessman, C. K. (1991). Beyond reductionism: Narrative genres in divorce accounts. *Journal of Narrative and Life History, 1*, 41–68.
Rosenwald, G. C., & Ochberg, R. L. (1992). Introduction: Life stories, cultural politics, and self-understanding. In G. C. Rosenwald & R. L. Ochberg (Eds.), *Storied lives: The cultural politics of self-understanding* (pp. 1–18). London: Yale University Press.
Strauss, A. L. (1987). *Qualitative analysis for social scientists.* New York: Cambridge University Press.

# The "Labovian Model" Revisited With Special Consideration of Literary Narrative

## Suzanne Fleischman
*Department of French, University of California Berkeley*

Commemorating the 30th anniversary of Labov and Waletzky's (this issue) now classic investigation of oral narratives of personal experience (henceforth L&W), this Special Issue offers cross-disciplinary testimony to the impact of this study, together with its sequel, Labov (1972), in launching a new paradigm in the field of narratology. In my own research on narrative (Fleischman 1985, 1986a, 1986b, 1990, 1991), the "Labovian model" has proven its utility in helping to untangle issues of tense and temporality, primarily in "artificial" (van Dijk, 1975) narrative texts of the type we now regard as literature—*avant la lettre*, to be sure, because at the time many of these texts were composed, Literature had not yet evolved into the institution of belles lettres we have come to know. Crucial to an understanding of tense in narrative, are both the *macrostructure* categories of narrative identified by L&W (Abstract, Orientation, Complication, Evaluation, Resolution, Coda) and the narrative units they distinguish at the *microstructure* level of the discourse (the various clause types). In what follows, then, I begin by proposing some refinements to the model at these two levels, as suggested by the texts I have worked with, followed by a discussion of issues that have emerged in attempts to apply L&W's model—which, it must be emphasized, was developed specifically to account for the unplanned (Ochs, 1979) stories of personal experience that have come to be known as *natural narratives*—to longer and more complex planned narratives of literary fiction and film.

---

Requests for reprints should be sent to Suzanne Fleischman, Department of French, University of California, Berkeley, CA 94720–2580. E-mail: suzanne@socrates.berkeley.edu

## MACROSTRUCTURE CONSIDERATIONS

### Peaks and Narrative Tension

Per L&W's model, the Complicating Action of a narrative consists of the set of *narrative events,* reported in *narrative clauses,* that collectively make up a story. This is as a rule the longest section of a narrative, into which both Orientation and Evaluation may be embedded; its termination is marked by one or more narrative clauses that comprise the Result, or Resolution (L&W, this issue). Though the model makes provision for episodic narration—L&W's Narrative 2, for example, is described as containing a long string of events consisting of several cycles of simple narrative, with many complication sections—, it contains no formal mechanism for representing rises and falls in narrative tension, nor does it deal with narratives the lack a well-defined Resolution.

An alternative model for the macrostructure of narrative, not incompatible with L&W's, is Longacre's "profile" model (1981), according to which the flow of a narrative—and of other types of discourse—can be analyzed in terms of the build-up and relaxation of tension around a series of Peaks that collectively define the profile of the text. The profile model can be easily superimposed onto L&W's Complicating Action, thereby building in the recursivity needed to describe the structure of more complex narrative forms. Peaks mark a point in the Complicating Action at which discourse tension reaches a climax, after which it decreases, either to rise again or to decline definitively toward a Resolution, if there is one. Peaks are frequently marked in surface syntax by various devices for "rhetorical underlining," including repetition and paraphrase (discussed further later), insertion of a mass of detail beyond what is called for in routine narration, and, notably, direct speech—all formal devices to "slow down the camera" so that the Peak does not go by too quickly (pp. 347–349).

### Narratives Without a Resolution

Per L&W's model, the Result, or Resolution, of a narrative is normally reported in the final clause(s) of the Complicating Action. Complication builds to a final Peak (according to the modification proposed previously), after which comes a clause answering the question "What *finally* happened?" L&W acknowledged that Resolutions are not always easy to identify. For one of their sample texts they find themselves obliged to resort to semantic criteria "which are often difficult to apply and seldom consistent," adding that "[w]ithout further functional analysis, it will usually be hard to tell when a narrative is actually over—when the result begins, and when it has been given in full" (this issue)). Centineo (1991) found similarly that a number of the personal-experience narratives she collected lacked an identifiable Resolution, being "just a series of evaluative statements about some ill-defined narrative event" (p. 83, fn. 7). The crucial question raised by such texts—more common than one might imagine but often excluded from analysis as "bad data"—is: Should they be regarded as defective narratives, or is this a problem with the model? As listeners frustrated by such texts, we would probably incline to the former position, that is, not all narrators are created equal; some do it badly, and the model is valid. However, if we enlarge the database to include more elaborated varieties of narrative, notably literary fiction and film (see following), then the inadequacy of the model becomes more apparent. It must be reiterated, however, that the Labovian model was not designed to account for the structure of these complex, artificial narrative forms, which rely on different genre conventions and generate different expectations in readers and viewers.

## Repetition

L&W took up the business of repetition in the context of their discussion of *evaluation* (this issue; Labov, 1972, pp. 379–80). However, they focused solely on repetition in successive clauses and specifically as a device for suspending the action. They did not discuss repetitions of the same narrative event at a distance of several clauses, a practice fairly common in "performed stories" (Wolfson, 1978) of various types. Consider the following example, excerpted from a 14th-century narrative detailing the circumstances of composition of a song-poem by the troubadour Peire Vidal (narrative clauses are lettered):

    a. ... Peire Vidal, frightened by this business, boarded a ship
    b. and set off for Genoa.
    **c. And he remained there**
       until he later crossed the sea with King Richard.
       For he was frightened
       lest Lady Adelaide seek to have him put to death.
    **c.′ He remained there for a long time**
       and there composed many beautiful songs
       recalling the kiss that he had stolen.
       And he said—in a song that said "Ajostar e lasar"—
       [*song fragment*]
       and in another place he said: [*song fragment*]
    **c.″ And so he stayed overseas a long time,**
       for he didn't dare return to Provence.[1]

---

[1]From the *razo* of Peire Vidal, my translation from Old Occitan. The full text with translation appears in Fleischman, 1990, pp. 345–348.

This is a simple example involving three repetitions of the "event" of Peire's remaining for a long time in Genoa. As in natural narratives, in which this same phenomenon occurs commonly in the Complicating Action, the repetition functions to reestablish the event (plot) line, which has been broken by an interruption of some sort (cf. Polanyi, 1978), for example, an insertion of commentary or other nonsequential material (snippets of song text in our example).

For simple narratives such as these, it is easy enough to build event repetition formally into the Labovian model, for example, by maintaining the same clause letter with as many primes as necessary, as in our example. But once we enter the domain of literary or cinematic narrative, in which repetition is used strategically for a variety of "artistic" purposes (cf. Fleischman 1989, 1990; Genette, 1980, chap. 3), then the model, with its assumption of a "primary sequence" of events that defines the plot, may be altogether inappropriate.

## MICROSTRUCTURE CONSIDERATIONS

### Summative Result Clauses

At the level of discourse microstructure, the Labovian model distinguishes several different clause types, specifically *narrative* (including *coordinate*) *clauses, restricted clauses,* and *free clauses.* I will assume familiarity with these clause types and their relation to the components of the narrative macrostructure. In my analyses I have found it advantageous to nuance this clause typology. In addition to the repetition of narrative clauses, discussed previously, I find it useful to distinguish a particular type of restricted clause that I have labeled *summative result clause* (Fleischman, 1990, pp. 160–61). Unlike narrative clauses, which normally report unique countable events, summative result clauses function as retrospective summaries of a series of previously reported situations. Insofar as they involve a configurational judgment on the part of the narrator, they are evaluative. At a certain point in his narrative of the Fourth Crusade, apropos of a battle between the Greek and the Latin Christians, the Old French chronicler Villehardouin states: "and the Greeks put up a great show of resistance." This clause telescopes into a single event—and at the same time evaluates—the individual defense maneuvers subsumed under the deverbal noun *resistance.* The summative result clauses given here (see following), from this same narrative, turn out to have a text-demarcating function of instituting midlevel boundaries, chunking the episode—or the text as a whole for structurally very simple narratives—into smaller subunits (without context this may not be immediately apparent):[2]

---

[2] These clauses are all from a section of Chapter 4 of Geoffroy of Villehardouin's chronicle of the Conquest of Constantinople (early 13th century), which I discuss in greater detail elsewhere (Fleischman, 1985, 1990, pp. 160–161, 332–338).

(a) And there our men collected a great deal of booty.
(b) And he performed so well that he received great praise for his service.
(c) There were a great number captured and killed.
(d) There were many prisoners and casualties.

## APPLICATION TO LITERATURE

L&W began the 1967 article by pointing out that "most attempts to analyze narrative have taken as their subject matter the more complex products of long-standing literary or oral traditions" (this issue). This was undeniably true at the time their study was undertaken, whence the radical nature of an inquiry into unplanned storytelling by ordinary people. Although the model they produced was not intended as a structural template for "more complex" narrative forms, their opinion that "it will not be possible to make much progress in the analysis and understanding of these complex narratives until the simplest and most fundamental narrative structures are to be found in oral versions of personal experiences" (this issue) clearly left the door open for an extension of their model to more complex narrative forms, including literary fiction. Within a decade of the appearance of their article, literary scholars began experimenting with the Labovian model as an analytic tool for narrative fiction generally (Adam, 1982; Pratt, 1977, pp. 38–78; Traugott & Pratt, 1980, pp. 247–255; Vetters, 1991; Watts, 1984), and in particular, for texts from cultures or historical periods whose modes of thought and expression are fundamentally oral and thus closer in certain respects to natural narrative (Fleischman, 1990; Fludernik, 1996; Herring, 1991).[3] In a sense, then, we have come full circle, from the days when L&W had to lobby for the inclusion of natural narrative within a broader narratology, to a point where the natural-narrative model they developed could be considered as a heuristic device for furthering our understanding of the workings of complex, artistic narrative forms. On balance, however, the Labovian model has not had a significant impact on the analysis of literary fiction. Most literary narratologists would probably agree with Ryan's (1988) statement that: "The verbal art displayed in conversational storytelling relates to the art of literary narrative as a wild species of plant relates to a cultural variety" (p. 143). It thus seems appropriate in this context to look briefly into features of the Labovian model that have undermined its application to literature. Four issues in particular are targeted here: *iconic sequence, narrative closure* (L&W's Resolution), *primary sequence and its connection to the textual foreground,* and *evaluation.*

---

[3]Interestingly, Fludernik (1996) redefined natural narrative to include both oral and written texts, with neither modality privileged. I use the term here in the traditional sense of L&W, this issue, and Labov, 1972.

## Iconic Sequence

L&W (this issue) defined narrative as: "one verbal technique for recapitulating experience, in particular, a technique of constructing narrative units which match the temporal sequence of that experience." This definition established iconic sequence as the norm for narrative temporality, that is, the discourse marches in step with the world. L&W elaborated this principle further on: "the narrative units that we wish to isolate [narrative clauses] are defined by the fact that they recapitulate experience *in the same order as the original events*" (p. 21, my emphasis). As it turns out, this is rarely if ever the case in literature (especially contemporary literature) or film, in which "anachronies"—beginnings in medias res, flashbacks, flash forwards, revisits to the same events—are the rule rather than the exception (see Genette, 1980, chap. 1). In fact, chronological ordering has long been regarded as an *inferior* method of arrangement in literature, being "too akin to the way of the world, too mimetic and transparent for art" in many analysts' view (cited by Sternberg, 1990, p. 903). "To qualify for art," these narratologists would argue: "chronology needs to undergo such deformation in the telling as to be only gradually reformed or reconstructed in the reading ... " (pp. 903–904). However, as I have argued at various points in my own investigations into narrative temporality (especially Fleischman 1990, 1991), if our cultural and literary competence did not include a narrative norm, one component of which is iconic sequence, then the anachronies of literary and cinematic narrative could not produce the effects they do on readers and spectators. In fact, given how often even natural narrators depart from chronological reporting, this ordering principle might best be viewed as a "norm" validated as much if not more in the breach as in actual observance.

## The Resolution and Narrative Closure

The point was raised previously that some personal-experience narratives lack an identifiable Resolution. This is true a fortiori in modern literature and film, in which typically the story just breaks off at some point that does not correspond to a notable decline in narrative tension and fails to provide any real sense of closure. Sternberg (1978) showed in exhaustive detail how many novels continue "orienting" and "complicating" even after the plot's "resolution" (Chatman, 1990, p. 318). What does this say about the Labovian model? If we limit ourselves to natural narration and most varieties of traditional story performance, we might, as suggested previously, simply write off texts that lack closure as failed narratives. However, once we include Literature, especially modern literature, then we are forced to recognize a mismatch between the Labovian model, with its insistence that narratives have an identifiable Resolution, and a considerable number of novels, short stories, and films. Once again, rather than invalidating the Labovian model, or being taken as evidence that modern fiction and film have abandoned narrativity altogether, this mismatch might simply be viewed as evidence of change. Just as languages change over time, so too art forms, and conceivably in response to analogous pressures.

## Primary Sequence and Foreground

What has come to be known as the primary sequence of a narrative is the skeleton of plot events reported in temporally ordered narrative clauses. From what has been said previously regarding iconic sequence and narrative closure, it should be clear that the notion of primary sequence is problematic, if not irrelevant, for much modern fiction. Whereas the essence of simple stories may still be preserved after the removal of *background* material, leaving only the primary sequence—Weinrich (1973) performed this exercise on a short story by Maupassant—, one cannot, as Vetters (1991, p. 372) noted, do this exercise on the novels of Balzac, Flaubert, or Proust. The essence of Proust in particular lies in repetitious background events and not in singular foreground actions. Two solutions to this problem suggest themselves. Either acknowledge that the foreground–background distinction, tied as it is to primary sequence,[4] does not work for novelistic fiction and other artistic narratives. Or, alternatively, and in line with the spirit of the original Gestalt distinction, redefine foreground such that it is sensitive to genre specificities and not rigidly tied to singulative narrative events and primary sequence (see Fleischman 1985, 1990, §§ 6.1–6.2).

## Evaluation and Modern Fiction

Evaluation is a key component of L&W's model—without evaluation you don't have a narrative—and the one that underwent most substantial revision in Labov, 1972, in which it was shown that rather than being confined to particular junctures in the narrative macrostructure, evaluation is overtly or covertly embedded throughout the text. Regarding the pertinence of the Labovian model to literature, Chatman (1990) observed that "the insistence that every narrative include an evaluation of the experience narrated seems to fly in the face of the efforts by novelists since James and Flaubert to eliminate judgment and other commentary from the narrator's pronouncements" (p. 317–18, fn. 9). True enough. However, this statement presupposes that evaluation in fiction emanates from the narrator, as in natural narration. However, in fiction, I would argue, the issue of evaluation is complicated by the

---

[4]The terms *foreground* and *background* are not used in either L&W or Labov, 1972, but those who established the opposition for narrative discourse (notably Hopper, 1979a, 1979b) based it on the Labovian model.

fact that evaluations can in principle emanate from several sources: the real author, the "implied author," the narrator (if the text has a narrator and not simply a "speaker function"), or characters. So although I agree with Chatman's statement, I would be hard pressed to accept the idea that literary texts are therefore value-free. The problem then becomes one of assigning evaluations to their proper source from among the available options. Evaluations at the *global* level (the text as a whole) seem best assigned to the implied author, to whom the formal devices elaborated by Labov (1972, §§ 3–4) cannot be applied, for the simple reason that the implied author does not speak. At the local level (specific elements of the text—events, characters, setting), evaluations may emanate from characters and from certain varieties of narrator.

Pratt (1977) was convinced of the similarity between "Labov's evaluation devices ... [and] those used in literary narrative to control the reader's attitude and point of view" (p. 63). The devices she invoked in this context include author interruptions instructing us what judgments we should form (Labov's external evaluation), long passages of internal monologue in which characters can reflect on their situation, and dialogues assessing a state of affairs from several viewpoints (Pratt, 1977). Let's look at these devices briefly. Author interruptions have virtually disappeared from fiction, and where present are often ironic. Ironic too (in the sense of dramatic irony) are many interior monologues. In Tom Wolfe's *Bonfire of the Vanities,* for example, the interior monologues of the major characters allow us to "eavesdrop" on thoughts too self-incriminating—that is, evaluative at a higher level—to be uttered aloud. None of Labov's evaluation devices can "instruct us" to read these statements ironically, because irony is an evaluation that emanates from the implied author, a "position" absent from narratives of personal experience. As for reported speech assessing a situation from multiple characters' perspectives, it is once again from a higher level—in this instance the narrator or the implied author—that the instruction comes as to which of these perspectives we should choose. To my knowledge, among scholars who have endeavored to apply the Labovian model to narrative fiction, no one has succeeded in accounting for evaluation at the level of the implied author or by nonjudgmental narrators of the type referred to in Chatman's statement.

## CONCLUSION

Lest this essay terminate, like certain of the narratives it describes, without a bona fide Resolution, let me conclude by reiterating my belief that the model put forth by L&W 30 years ago has provided narratologists—in various disciplines—with an invaluable tool for analyzing the structure of narrative texts. The proof of the pudding is in the ways the model has been modified and adapted to accommodate varieties of narrative other than the oral versions of personal experience for which it was originally formulated. In my own work on performed stories from the Romance Middle Ages, the macro- and microstructure categories of the Labovian model have greatly facilitated an understanding of seemingly idiosyncratic uses of tense and aspect in narrative. If attempts to apply the Labovian model to fiction and film have yielded less than impressive results, the exercise itself has been useful in illuminating the distinctive features of different varieties of narrative.

## REFERENCES

Adam, J. (1982). The macro-structure of the conventional narrative. *Poetics Today, 3*, 135–68.
Chatman, S. (1990). What can we learn from contextualist narratology? *Poetics Today, 11*, 309–328.
Fleischman, S. (1985). Discourse functions of tense-aspect oppositions in narrative: Toward a theory of grounding. *Linguistics, 23*, 851–882.
Fleischman, S. (1986a). Evaluation in narrative: The present tense in medieval "performed stories." *Yale French studies, 70*, 199–251.
Fleischman, S. (1986b). "Overlay" structures in the *Song of Roland:* A discourse-pragmatic strategy of oral narrative. *Berkeley Linguistics Society, 4*, 108–123.
Fleischman, S. (1990). *Tense and narrativity.* Austin: University of Texas Press.
Fleischman, S. (1991). Toward a theory of tense-aspect in narrative discourse. In J. Gvozdanovic & T. Janssen (Ed.), in co-operation with O. Dahl, *The function of tense in texts* (pp. 75–97). Amsterdam: North Holland.
Fludernik, M. (1996). *Towards a "natural" narratology.* London: Routledge.
Genette, G. (1980). *Narrative discourse: An essay in method* (J. E. Lewin, Trans.). Ithaca, NY: Cornell University Press (Translation of "Discours du récit," a portion of *Figures III,* Paris: Seuil, 1972).
Herring, S. C. (1991). *Functions of the verb in Tamil narration.* Doctoral dissertation, University of California, Berkeley.
Hopper, P. J. (1979a). Aspect and foregrounding in discourse. In T. Givón (Ed.), *Syntax and semantics: 12. Discourse and syntax* (pp. 213–241). New York: Academic.
Hopper, P. J. (1979b). Some observations on the typology of focus and aspect in narrative language. *Studies in language, 3*, 37–64.
Labov, W. (1972). The transformation of experience in narrative syntax. In *Language in the inner city* (pp. 354–396). Philadelphia: University of Pennsylvania Press.
Labov, W., & Waletzky, J. (this issue). Narrative analysis: Oral versions of personal experience. In J. Helm (Ed.), *Essays on the verbal and visual arts: Proceedings of the 1966 Annual Spring Meeting of the American Ethnological Society* (pp. 12–44). Seattle: University of Washington Press. (Original work published 1967)
Longacre, R. E. (1981). A spectrum and profile approach to discourse analysis. *Text, 4*, 337–359.
Ochs, E. (1979). Planned and unplanned discourse. In T. Givón (Ed.), *Syntax and semantics: 12. Discourse and syntax* (pp. 51–80). New York: Academic.
Polanyi, L. (1978). False starts can be true. *Berkeley Linguistics Society, 4*, 628–639.
Pratt, M. L. (1977). *Toward a speech-act theory of literary discourse.* Bloomington: Indiana University Press.
Ryan, M. (1988). Review of Katharine Galloway Young, *Taleworlds and storyrealms* (Dordrecht, The Netherlands: M. Nijhoff). *Style, 22*, 143–146.
Sternberg, M. (1978). *Expositional modes and temporal ordering in fiction.* Baltimore: Johns Hopkins University Press.
Sternberg, M. (1990). Telling in time (1): Chronology and narrative theory. *Poetics today, 11*, 901–948.
Traugott, E., & Pratt. M. L. (1980). *Linguistics for students of literature.* New York: Harcourt, Brace.

van Dijk, T. A. (1975). Action, action description, and narrative. *New literary history, 6,* 273–294.
Vetters, C. (1991). Foreground and background: Weinrich against Labov. In M. Kiefer & J. van den Auwera (Eds.), *Meaning and grammar: Cross-linguistic perspectives* (pp. 367–381). Berlin: de Gruyter.
Watts, R. J. (1984). Narration as role-complementary interaction: An ethnomethodological approach to the study of literary narratives. *Studia Anglica Posnaniensia, 17,* 157–164.
Weinrich, H. (1973). *Le temps* (M. Lacoste, Trans.). Paris: Seuil. (Originally published in German, 1964 as *Tempus*, Stuttgart, Germany: Kohlhammer)
Wolfson, N. (1978). A feature of performed narrative: The conversational historical present. *Language in society, 7,* 215–237.

# Why Narrative? Hermeneutics, Historical Understanding, and the Significance of Stories

## Mark Freeman
*Department of Psychology, College of the Holy Cross*

Although narrative studies and narrative analysis have unquestionably gained some measure of credibility in certain quarters of the social sciences in recent years, there nevertheless remains the need to articulate further the primary reasons for their value in studying human beings. Those of us who pursue work in narrative may of course know these reasons well. For those who do not, however—that is, for the vast majority of researchers and theorists in the social sciences—it may not be quite so clear. Many of these people have no knowledge whatsoever about the field; others, who may have made some contact with it at some point, may simply suspect that it's the latest fad or bandwagon, the newest gathering place for the disaffected. We should therefore be prepared when they ask: Why narrative?

Acknowledging that there are numerous ways of answering this question—depending on whether we are psychologists, anthropologists, or sociolinguists; whether we are interested more in lives than texts; whether we are drawn more into the thickets of interpretation than the structures of analysis (and so on)—I focus my efforts on the discipline of psychology and suggest that there are two fundamental planes on which it might profitably be answered. The first is methodological and is essentially concerned with the issue of what the idea of narrative can "do" for psychology and, hence, with why at least a portion of the discipline ought to embrace it. The second is theoretical and is much more concerned with the specifics of narrative thinking, particularly with why narrative provides not only a useful but a uniquely fitting language for studying human beings.

My takeoff point is a talk I gave to my own department late last year. The title of the talk was "Narrative Psychology and the Study of Human Lives (Or, The

---

Requests for reprints should be sent to Mark Freeman, Department of Psychology, College of the Holy Cross, Worcester, MA 01610. E-mail: mfreeman@holycross.edu

Significance of Category C)." What I tried to do in it, basically, was argue that both the discipline of psychology in general and our own departmental curriculum in particular needed to include in their purview something quite different than the standard fare—not as a replacement, I had to emphasize, but as a much-needed supplement. By way of background, our curriculum at Holy Cross requires that all students take Introductory Psychology, Statistics, Research Methods and its associated lab, History and Systems of Psychology, a seminar, some electives, and two courses each in what are called Category A (Psychology as a Natural Science) and Category B (Psychology as a Social Science).

Under Category A, there are such courses as Learning, Sensation and Perception, Cognition and Memory, and Physiological Psychology. To the extent that these areas of inquiry seek to address those features of human behavior that might plausibly be considered natural processes, at least in significant part, there is a special interest here in fixed regularities and lawful relationships, the overriding presumption being that a portion of human behavior operates quite predictably and can in fact be objectified, that is, isolated as an object of inquiry and studied in causal, explanatory fashion. Under Category B, there are such courses as Personality, Social, Developmental, and Abnormal Psychology. Common though some of its presumptions are, this category differs from the previous one in a number of notable ways. First, with few exceptions, it is largely about uniquely human—rather than organismal—phenomena and is in that sense not so much about the realm of nature per se as it is that realm which exists at the intersection of nature and culture. Personality, for instance, is generally understood to be a function of constitutional factors as well as socialization and enculturation. Development is understood to be a function of the dialectical interplay between an experiencing child and the physical, social, and moral world, and so on. This category therefore deals with phenomena that occur within—and are, strictly speaking, inseparable from—social relations. Moreover, and precisely because of this inseparability, there is less talk about causes and if–then type laws than about correlations and the like, about broad relations between variables, often formulated in probabilistic terms, that allow for the creation of empirically based accounts of certain features of psychological life. By and large, nevertheless, the methods of the natural sciences remain operative, as does the aim of isolating variables, manipulating them, and predicting and controlling behavior. What is different, more than anything, are the phenomena. Category B is thus a kind of hybrid category, with one foot in nature, the other in culture.

Now, it is certainly the case that a good number of explorations into narrative are basically of the Category B variety. In Labov and Waletzky's (1967/this issue) landmark work on narrative analysis, for instance, the emphasis is largely formal: "based upon recurrent patterns characteristic of narrative from the clause level to the complete simple narrative" (p. 4). It is also atomistic, in a manner reminiscent of that of the early structuralists; they seek to isolate, via their encounter with complex narratives: "the simplest and most fundamental narrative structures," which are to be analyzed "in direct connection with their originating functions" (p. 4). Narrative, from this perspective, may be deemed an important and heretofore insufficiently appreciated aspect of human experience—in terms of development, communicative competence, storytelling ability, or whatever—but is still fully assimilable to empirical social science as traditionally conceived.

Valuable though this perspective has been in advancing the cause of narrative inquiry, my own interest is in something different. Returning to that department talk for a moment, the question I posed after discussing the natural science and social science components of our curriculum, was: What—if anything—was left after Category A and B? That is, what was it that remained of structured psychological interest after we had subtracted Category A and B phenomena? What remained, I suggested, was the living, loving, suffering, dying human being. Or, to put the matter a bit more academically, what remained were human lives, existing in culture and in time. I therefore proposed that we include in our curriculum another category: Category C, which would bear as its noble title "Psychology as a *Human* Science." Time will tell whether it flies. This category, in any case, is precisely the terrain of that segment of narrative psychology devoted to the study of lives.

With this brief story of curricular convince-work in mind, I would suggest that the first set of reasons for turning toward narrative has to do with the unduly strict methodological demands of much of contemporary academic psychology, its tendency still to focus on what is observable, objectifiable, quantifiable, and so forth. Also relevant in this context, of course, is academic psychology's relative neglect of human lives as such. The fact that the study of lives may be considered a radical endeavor is ironic, to say the least. It is unfortunate as well.

Thus far, I have referred to two major realms of human behavior and experience: that of nature and that which exists in the intersection or space between nature and culture. Narrative, in turn, gives us a language—a very appropriate language, I believe—for exploring a third realm, namely that of culture itself. In saying this, I am not suggesting that human lives as such are somehow set wholly apart from nature. Nor am I suggesting that human lives and the narratives told about them are mere "effects," as it were, of culture. In fact, I go on to suggest, following Ricoeur (e.g., 1980), MacIntyre (e.g., 1981), and others, that narratives themselves grow out of certain inherent features of our historical condition and that they are at least as much constitutive of culture as they are emergent from it. For now, though, I simply want to offer what might be considered the most straightforward answer to the question Why Narrative? It is time we started looking more closely at people, and there is no more valuable a way of doing so than through the stories they tell of their lives. What follows are some defining features of a narrative psychology of the sort being proposed.

First, and most basically, it is *idiographic* in orientation, the primary unit of analysis being the individual life. This does not mean that it's the only possible unit of analysis or that no generalizations can emerge from inquiries of this sort; they can and often do. All that is being said here is that, insofar as the individual life is focal, the methodological approach will be more idiographic (i.e., aiming toward the singular and specific) than nomothetic (i.e., aiming toward the formulation of general laws or principles of behavior). As a corollary of sorts to this emphasis on the idiographic, narrative inquiries into lives also tend more toward the qualitative than the quantitative.

A narrative psychology of lives is geared toward the experiential and is thus *contextual* in orientation as well, the notion being that people are to be studied not in the somewhat contrived situation of the lab or the controlled experiment—important though they are—but in their "natural habitat," as they actually live. There is no doubt but that this is a rather more cumbersome way of studying people than the more traditional "isolation of variables" approach. There is also no doubt but that the resultant data may be decidedly less "clean" than some may wish. However, human lives are lived *in* context, not outside it, and at least a portion of the discipline should be willing to endure the consequences of this fact in its inquiries.

By extension, a narrative psychology of the present sort is avowedly *cultural* in its understanding of human lives. Radical once again though the idea may seem to many mainstream psychologists, it is actually a quite straightforward one: Insofar as we seek to study lives naturalistically, as discussed, and insofar as lives are lived in culture—in language, in social relations, in communities, in the web of quite specific rules, conventions, beliefs, discourses, and so on—then in studying lives we are, as a matter of course and necessity, studying culture as well. Indeed, rather than considering the individual life per se as the primary unit of analysis, perhaps we should speak of the "life-in-culture." Bruner (1990) put the matter well: "It is man's participation *in* culture and the realization of his mental powers *through* culture that make it impossible to construct a human psychology on the basis of the individual alone" (p. 12). There is, in a way, a paradox at work in this notion: Focusing on the individual life requires at the very same time that we move beyond it, into the cultural surround within which it takes shape.

A further consequence of our thoroughgoing participation in culture is that the narrative study of lives, as envisioned here at any rate, must be interpretive—or, more appropriately, *hermeneutic*—in its fundamental methodological approach. Dealing with the life-in-culture commits us to the symbolic and the semantic, to the domain of *meaning,* and the domain of meaning requires as its condition of appraisal the process of interpretation. How hermeneutics enters the picture is somewhat more complicated. A familiar aspect of what has been called the "hermeneutic circle" is that the parts of a given text exist in relation to the whole and the whole in relation to the parts. In reading a novel, for instance, we gather certain strands of meaning as we begin reading, gradually sketch out a preliminary sense of the whole—a sense of "what's going on"—and keep this sense of the whole in mind as a kind of schema, refining and differentiating it all the while as we continue to read. Further episodes are thus situated in relation to the whole, which in turn evolves and expands as a function of these episodes themselves. Reading, therefore, is a process of tacking back and forth between part and whole; meanings that had emerged earlier both contribute to, and are retroactively transfigured by, what occurs later. Hence the idea of the hermeneutic circle, and hence the relevance of the hermeneutic circle to the specific domain of narrative as it pertains to human lives: The relation between episodes and plot, insofar as it entails the more general movement between part and whole emblematic of the hermeneutic circle, suggests that narrative understanding is a species of hermeneutic understanding. What it also suggests is that, valuable though the structural analysis of narrative a la Labov and Waletzky may be, it is but a part or moment in a larger process of hermeneutic explication (see especially Ricoeur, 1976, 1981). Ricoeur (1981) argued: "The diachronic reading of the narrative cannot be absorbed into the achronic reading" (p. 285). Structural analysis must therefore be supplemented by interpretation, founded upon that "temporal dialectic ... implied in the basic operation of eliciting a configuration from a succession" (Ricoeur, 1980, p. 274); otherwise, the specifically narrative aspect of the text in question will have effectively been suppressed.

Moving further still into the nexus of the connection between hermeneutics and narrative, interpretation of the sort that is involved in the study of lives carries within it two distinct dimensions, which Ricoeur (e.g., 1980, 1984) referred to as the *episodic*—the various happenings or events that comprise the "stuff" of the past, and, in line with what was said previously, the *configurational*—the imaginative and indeed on some level *poetic* process of seeing-together these happenings or events, so as to discern patterns, constellations of meaning. A human life from this perspective, therefore, is not to be understood in terms of mere succession, as a series of disconnected events, but as a temporal whole organized around a more or less distinct plot (see also Brooks, 1985; White, 1978).

It is at this point that we move fully into the heart of narrative understanding. This is because once we begin speaking about the configurational dimension, plot, and so forth, we are speaking in large measure of a distinctly *retrospective* mode of interpretive activity: to be able to extract the plot of a story involves returning to earlier episodes, seeing how they relate to subsequent ones and to the evolving whole that is the narrative itself. When one is dealing with life histories or autobiographies or, for that matter, the process of self-understanding—which is in many ways the narrative act par excellence—this retrospective aspect is fairly obvious. However, I would suggest that in prospective inquiries too, inquiries that follow lives forward across some span of time, there is again a distinctly retrospective aspect at work (see Freeman, 1984); for one does not and cannot know what leads to what until after all the entries are in—that is, until one has arrived at that vantage point from which one can craft a "narrative context" inclusive of the data at hand. Along these lines, I would argue that much of what goes on in social scientific thinking—obviously in life histories and the like, less obviously in other areas—not only makes use of but is essentially dependent upon narrative understanding, hermeneutically conceived.

A final dimension of a narrative psychology fashioned along the lines being set forth presently and implied in much of what has been said already is that it is *historical* in orientation: This segment of psychology, in being tied to the interpretive study of lives through time, is fundamentally and necessarily bound up in significant ways in and with history. It is here, in fact, that we move into some of the most specific—and most compelling—answers to the question at hand. Let me therefore work toward a conclusion by focusing on how history enters the narrative picture.

The first and most obvious way it does so is in the idea of life history, that is, the idea that a human life is itself a history, an historical phenomenon, stretched out in time between birth and death. Second, there is the idea that a life history is itself a part of a larger history, the idea that we ourselves are living entries *into* history, contributing to its specific form and the specific nature of its movement. In this sense, turning to narrative, to concrete human lives, is a way of becoming engaged with history—with memorializing or commemorating not only the life in question but its cultural–historical surround. Third, we have what Gadamer (e.g., 1979) referred to as "historical consciousness." What this refers to, in brief, is the notion that we bring to bear our own time-specific and culture-specific understanding of things—our own historically constituted "prejudices"—to any given act of historical interpretation, whether it is of ourselves or others. In this sense, any act of historical interpretation involves a communicative or dialogical aspect, a "fusion of horizons," as Gadamer put it, a bringing-together of my own world, as an interpreter, and the world of the text or event or person being considered (see Gadamer, 1975; also Bakhtin, 1986; Jauss, 1982; Ricoeur, 1976). Narrative, therefore, can serve as a bridge between people, a way of bringing people into human contact with each other, even across significant gulfs of time or space.

These ideas are mainly about history as "object" or "phenomenon," which is of course one common way of speaking about it. The other way has more to do with the *telling* of history, the idea being that the act of narration is inextricably tied to the process of historical understanding itself, of seeking to make sense of the past from the perspective of the present. Taking this idea one step farther, we confront the notion that our very identities, our very selves, predicated as they are upon the process of historical understanding, are also tied to narrative (see Freeman, 1993; also Brockelman, 1985; Carr, 1986; Kerby, 1991). How are we to understand this apparent fact? At this point, we take the question Why Narrative? to another, more theoretical plane, asking in effect: Why does narrative have the prominent place in human thought and experience that it in fact has? We're "story-telling animals," MacIntyre (1981) told us. "Narrative starts with the very history of (hu)mankind," Roland Barthes (1975, p. 237) added. It is simply "one of the ways in which we speak, one of the large categories in which we think" (Brooks, 1985, p. 323).

If in fact these pronouncements are valid, there are two interrelated implications particularly worth noting. The first is that *narrativity* (see especially Danto, 1985)—which we might think of as that dimension of human existence in time that becomes actualized in narratives—may very well be a universal category, which is to say, an essentially human way of figuring reality: "stories lived and imagined, told and untold, constitute the very sphere in which we live .... [Narrative] reflects and actualizes nothing less than our experience as essentially temporal beings; it reproduces and verbalizes our very shaping of the flux of time" (Danto, 1985, p. 252). This does not mean that everyone the world over *tells* narratives the way we do or that everyone is interested in "history" or that everyone reckons with time the same way. What it does mean is that spread throughout all of the quite different ways of speaking, historicizing, reckoning with time, and so forth, is a basic human inclination to see actions together, as temporal patterns, configurations of meaning, and to situate these configurations within larger wholes—whether myths, histories, or what have you—that serve ultimately to organize and make sense of temporal existence. We therefore see the intimate connection between our historical condition and the act of narrativizing. Indeed, Ricoeur (1981) wrote: "The form of life to which narrative discourse belongs is our historical condition itself" (p. 288). Narrative, in short, appears to arise out of an inherent inclination to narrativize; it is part and parcel of being in time and using language to bind experience into sensible form.

The second implication is that, contra those who suppose that narrative entails a kind of fictive imposition on experience (which is assumed to be essentially formless and perhaps meaningless), from the point being offered here it is more appropriately seen as being woven into the fabric of life itself. Ultimately, then, I would answer the question Why Narrative? on this second plane by saying that narrative is the basic medium in which human beings speak, think, grow into selves and understand others. In this sense, as I suggested earlier, it is the most fitting and appropriate language we could use to comprehend human lives in culture and in time.

## REFERENCES

Bakhtin, M. M. (1986). *Speech genres and other late essays.* Austin: University of Texas Press.
Barthes, R. (1975). An introduction to the structural analysis of narrative. *New Literary History, 6,* 237–272.
Brockelman, P. (1985). *Time and Self.* New York: Crossroad.
Brooks, P. (1985). *Reading for the plot: Design and intention in narrative.* New York: Vintage.
Bruner, J. (1990). *Acts of meaning.* Cambridge, MA: Harvard University Press.
Carr, D. L. (1986). *Time, narrative, and history.* Bloomington: Indiana University Press.
Danto, A. C. (1985). *Narration and knowledge.* New York: Columbia University Press.
Freeman, M. (1984). History, narrative, and life-span developmental knowledge. *Human Development, 27,* 1–19.
Freeman, M. (1993). *Rewriting the self: History, memory, narrative.* London: Routledge.

Gadamer, H.-G. (1975). *Truth and method.* New York: Crossroad.
Gadamer, H.-G. (1979). The problem of historical consciousness. In P. Rabinow & W. M. Sullivan (Eds.), *Interpretive social science: A reader* (pp. 103–160). Berkeley: University of California Press.
Jauss, H. R. (1982). *Toward an aesthetic of reception.* Minneapolis: University of Minnesota Press.
Kerby, A. P. (1991). *Narrative and the self.* Bloomington: Indiana University Press.
Labov, W., & Waletzky, J. (this issue). Narrative analysis: Oral versions of personal experience. In J. Helm (Ed.), *Essays on the verbal and visual arts: Proceedings of the 1966 Annual Spring Meeting of the American Ethnological Society* (pp. 12–44). Seattle: University of Washington Press. (Original work published 1967)
MacIntyre, A. (1981). *After virtue.* South Bend, IN: University of Notre Dame Press.
Ricoeur, P. (1976). History and hermeneutics. *Journal of Philosophy, 73,* 683–694.
Ricoeur, P. (1980). Narrative time. In W. J. T. Mitchell (Ed.), *On narrative* (pp. 165–186). Chicago: University of Chicago Press.
Ricoeur, P. (1981). *Hermeneutics and the human sciences.* Cambridge, England: Cambridge University Press.
Ricoeur, P. (1984). *Time and narrative, Vol. 1.* Chicago: University of Chicago Press.
White, H. (1978). *Tropics of discourse.* Baltimore: Johns Hopkins University Press.

# Sequentiality and Temporalization in the Narrative Construction of a South American Cholera Epidemic

## Charles L. Briggs
*Ethnic Studies, University of California, San Diego*

> Time becomes human to the extent that it is articulated through a narrative mode, and narrative attains its full meaning when it becomes a condition of temporal existence. (Ricoeur, 1984, p. 52)

An aspect of Labov and Waletsky's (1967/this issue; henceforth L&W) analysis of narrative that has engendered much discussion is the emphasis they place on sequentiality as a link between narrative structure and lived experience. Writers who have commented on this formulation, of whom there have been too many to review in this brief article,[1] have largely followed L&W in assuming that iconic relations between narrative structures and events are immanent in and form crucial components of narratives. A number of authors have suggested, however, that narrative sequences and events do not stand in simple one-to-one relations. For example, Goffman (1974) and Goodwin (1990) showed how narrative structures are sensitive to participation frameworks that emergence in social interaction. Briggs (1988) pointed to the way that sequentiality, including reiterations of key events, is closely tied to both back-channel cues and to power relations between narrators and audiences. Culler (1981) argued that narrators construct cause-and-effect relations through a range of poetic properties.

Two studies in particular provide points of departure for reformulations of the sequentiality framework. First, Bauman (1986) argued that events do not consist of what "actually occurred," as L&W (1967/this issue) suggested; rather events are themselves created by narratives. Second, Heath (1983) urged us to see sequential-

---

Requests for reprints should be sent to Charles L. Briggs, Ethnic Studies, University of California, San Diego, 9500 Gilman Drive, La Jolla, CA 92093-0522. E-mail: clbriggs@weber.uscd.edu

[1] Toolan (1988, pp. 146–176) provided a useful review of some of these works.

ity as playing functionally distinct roles in different communities. I would like to go on to argue for the need to investigate sequential structure as forming part of the process of temporalization in narrative. To be sure, a host of other features, such as tense–aspect alternations and deictics, also play crucial roles in this process.

In concrete terms, I am proposing a shift away from a theoretical and methodological orientation that leads researchers to simply look for sequential structures in narratives, taking them to be immanent features that are necessarily present if the discourse is regarded as narrative. We should similarly not assume that the experiences represented in a given narrative necessarily take the form of discrete, sequentially ordered events. Rather, a major task of the analyst should be assessment of the degree to which a given body of discourse is structured sequentially and the extent to which experience is objectified as a series of bounded events. I argue that such a perspective is crucial not only for resolving the formal questions raised in L&W but also in addressing Labov's (1982) equally provocative if somewhat less developed observations regarding "a close connection between speech acts and [nonverbal physical] actions that implies a causal relation" (p. 220).

## NARRATIVES FROM A SOUTH AMERICAN CHOLERA EPIDEMIC

I now turn to an example that illustrates how important temporalization is and how much variation narratives exhibit in terms of the extent to which they are ordered temporally. In 1992–93, a cholera epidemic killed some 500 persons, who generally refer to themselves as belonging to an indigenous group known as "the Warao," in the Delta Amacuro of eastern Venezuela.[2] It is hard to imagine the psychosocial impact of the epidemic. Because cholera had not been present in South America for nearly a century, no one had any experience with the disease. Nevertheless, public health officials made almost no efforts to warn the 24,000 residents of Warao communities that it was extremely likely to come to the delta. Cholera is a bacterial infection that is easily treated, but it can kill a healthy adult through dehydration in as little as 8 hours, and the symptoms are horrifying. In some communities, up to one third of the adults died in a day or two. Terrified, individuals and some entire communities fled the rain forest and began living as mendicants on city streets; some have never returned.

Narrativizing cholera formed a crucial part of the process of coping with this trauma. Narrators sought to articulate what cholera is, where it came from, and why it was killing so many indigenous people. Curers were in a particular bind in this

---

[2]The official death toll compiled by the Regional Epidemiologist of the Ministry of Health and Public Assistance was 12. A survey that I conducted in 1994–95 with Clara Mantini de Briggs, MD, of the entire delta region yielded a count of approximately 500 deaths.

regard. Unable to explain the disease or their inability to treat it, many curers died from cholera after trying to save patients. At the same time, the incredible success of rehydration therapy and antibiotics greatly enhanced the prestige of institutional medicine. Curers used narratives in attempting to prevent the complete delegitimation of their authority.

I collected accounts of the cholera outbreak while it was still raging (November, 1992), as it was abating (June–July, 1993), and when only very sporadic cases were evident (January 1994 and June, 1994–August, 1995). I have recorded three, and in some cases four, accounts of the epidemic from a number of persons, including several curers. I am interested here in how these individuals temporalized the narratives they told at these different points in time. Given the brevity of this essay, I can only make reference to two narratives told by a healer, whom I call Manuel Torres. I had worked with Mr. Torres closely for nearly 5 years when the cholera epidemic began.

The first cases were reported in August, 1992, and I arrived in the delta in November of that year. The peak of the epidemic had just passed, and people were still dying from cholera. Mr. Torres, along with hundreds of other Mariusans, was living in Barrancas, a small city on the edge of the delta. Sitting in a hotel room in nearby Tucupita, Mr. Torres described the epidemic.

(1) 1992.1B, 13 November 1992, Manuel Torres (MT) and Charles Briggs (CB)
1. MT: *Hebu asidaha, hebu asidaha tatuka abanae.*
   A terrible disease, a terrible disease arose over there. [points toward delta]
2. *Tatuka abanae kimia, dokohia mi.*
   Over there arose something that causes diarrhea, vomiting, you see.
3. *No, wabanaka hokokore, hokoi tamatika diana wabaya.*
   No, if a person doesn't die by dawn, s/he dies by noon.
4. CB: *Carajo, uhu!*
   Damn, uuuf!
5. MT: *Anayaha wabae.*
   By the time it gets dark, s/he's dead.
6. CB: *Wabae, ajo!*
   S/he's dead, damn!
7. MT: *Kobenahoro wabae, ha wabae.*
   The Governor died, he was still Governor when he died.
8. CB: *Tai hese.*
   Even him.
9. MT: *Tai hese, tai hese,*
   Even him, even him,
10. *un día araisa wabuae tuatakore.*
    and the next day many others died the same way.

Cholera was initially referred to as *hebu asidaha,* "a terrible disease"; even the expert healers could not divine the "true" or spirit name of the disease. Similarly, Mr. Torres could only spatialize cholera as existing "over there" in the delta—he had no idea where it came from or how it reached the region. Mr. Torres makes this uncertainty explicit several minutes later in the exchange: *Kasabamo naoae? Oko tamaha naminanaha mate!* "Where did it come from? We still don't know this!"

As I have described elsewhere (Briggs, 1992), curers assert that knowledge of *ahotana,* "its origin," constitutes a privileged evidentiary basis for presenting truth claims. A crucial means of imbuing narratives with authority is thus to describe the origin of a phenomenon in an invisible spiritual-cum-geographical realm and then relate, step by step, how it made its way to a particular point in the social world. Lacking any sense of the origin of cholera deprives Mr. Torres of the ability to temporalize his narrative vis-à-vis events that marked the entrance of cholera into the delta or to make any causal assertions as to why it came to the delta and affected Warao communities so severely. As such, Mr. Torres' narrative lacks authority. All of the narratives that I recorded in November, 1992, were framed in precisely this way; even senior men who can assert substantial discursive authority and political power peppered their narratives with *oko naminanaha,* "we don't know," making explicit this lack of authority.

Mr. Torres can only temporalize cholera in terms of the progression of symptoms that it produces in those it infects. Mr. Torres does success in isolating one key event, the death of the "Governor," the man who had led his community for some 30 years. The Governor's death is, however, not sequentialized in a linear fashion but is rather folded back into the broader cycle of people vomiting and having diarrhea and then dying. Mr. Torres' narrative is highly representative of the narratives I recorded in November, 1992—none of the accounts were characterized by more than a rudimentary degree of temporalization in their formal structures and the extent to which experience was objectified in terms of sequential relations between discrete events.

Seven months later, Mr. Torres relates the story of cholera in a rather different fashion:

(1) 1993.4A, 11 June 1993, MT and CB
1. MT: *Tamasabamo karamunae.*
    [The spirits] came to attack from over there. (points to southwest)
2. CB: *Ajo! Sanamatana!*
    Damn! What a catastrophe!
3. MT: *Amaha Wirinoko, Wirinoko ekuya karamunae,*
    The Orinoco River here, they came to attack through the Orinoco,
4.     *tane warubuae ote.*
    that's what they said way over there.

5. CB: *Ote.*
   Way over there.
6. MT: *Dauk<sup>w</sup>aha obonae amahawitu, dauk<sup>w</sup>ahawitu, dauk<sup>w</sup>aha, dauk<sup>w</sup>aha,*
   This very tree gave fruit, this very kind of fruit, fruit, fruit,
7. CB: *dauk<sup>w</sup>aha,*
   fruit
8. MT: *Dauk<sup>w</sup>aha tai Wirinoko eku ho arai nakae,*
   This fruit fell into the waters of the Orinoco,
9. *aisiko hakanae tata,*
   it came swiftly with [the river] over there,
10. *ine mauba.*
    in my dream.
11. CB: *Aaah! Hiauba!*
    Aaah! In your dream!
12. MT: *Mauba, tamasatemo karamunae,*
    In my dream, they came to attack from over there,
13. *amaha karamunae Caroní!*
    they came to attack from Caroní!

Mr. Torres told this narrative to a group of men camped at Hota Kabuka in the delta, where several families were carving dugout canoes. He begins by pointing to the southwest, a region that is purportedly home to some of the most powerful spirits. He then traces the route that cholera took in reaching Warao communities and how it got there, by placing themselves in pieces of fruit and floating downstream.

By asserting that he knows the point of origin of the epidemic, Mr. Torres has made a powerful claim for the authority of his narrative. He is able to relate knowledge of the symptomatology of cholera to the epistemologically privileged discourse of curers. In Line 10, Mr. Torres provides a powerful epistemological frame for the narrative, claiming that it was revealed in a dream—the most authoritative source of evidence. In Line 13, he reveals the name of the "home" of the spirits—Caroní. Knowing the origin of the spirits enables him to name them, and this is the crucial step in learning how to treat cholera victims. Now that he knows the beginning of the cholera story, he can temporalize his narratives systematically, providing sequential formal structures and objectifying the epidemic in terms of discrete events. The narrative continues with a detailed account of how cholera attacked Warao communities, why it sought human victims, and of the pathology of the disease. Mr. Torres' excitement in revealing the origin of the epidemic and the evidentiary basis of his knowledge is conveyed in the excitement he expresses in lines 10–13. Temporalizing the epidemic launches him on the road to presenting an etiological account of why cholera struck Warao communities; by the following January, his cholera narratives contained fully integrated and wide-ranging causal assertions.

## CONCLUSION

According to the perspective I am advocating, deeming sequential organization to be an immanent and criterial dimension of narrative imposes a number of limitations on analysts. First, L&W's definition would lead us to exclude a good deal of discourse from narrative analysis. The accounts that I recorded in the middle of the cholera epidemic would not be considered narratives according to their definition, in that speech is not ordered sequentially through the use of temporal junctures and experience is not objectified in the form of discrete, interrelated events.

More importantly, seeing temporalization as immanent leads us to overlook the importance of studying not simply to what extent a given narrative is temporalized and the mechanisms used in doing so, but the processes through which individuals and communities use temporalization in objectifying and ordering social life. Temporalizing the cholera epidemic played a crucial role in attempting to minimize the devastating long-term effects of the epidemic on indigenous communities by providing a host of different conceptual tools for facing questions regarding why so many people had died and what should be done. This task was particularly important in view of the prevalence of attacks on the legitimacy of cultural identities and practices that were waged against the victims' communities and the severe blow that was dealt to the authority of indigenous healers.

The cholera narratives suggest that variability in the degree to which narratives are temporalized cannot be adequately addressed simply by mapping differences between cultures or communities in terms of narrative syntax, shared orientations regarding storytelling, or ideologies of language. Mr. Torres is a master storyteller, and I have recorded a wide range of different types of sequentially ordered narratives that he has told. Clearly, the structures of feeling and the cognitive horizons associated with lived experience are related in complex ways to vast differences in the extent to which narratives are temporalized. This relationship works in both directions—temporalization not only plays a crucial role in imbuing narratives and narrators with authority but also in shaping their capacity for the social construction of perception, identity, and memory. One question that this essay poses for comparative research is the special importance and complexity with which this relationship is imbued in settings, to use a term proposed by Das (1996) and others, of intense "social suffering."

As the epigraph for this article indicates, Ricoeur (1984) argued that the way we experience temporality is contingent on representing time mimetically in narrative form. Ricoeur predicated the ability to temporalize experience on prior access to "the capacity for identifying action in general by means of its structural features" and "a supplementary competence" in "identifying ... the symbolic mediations of action, or 'symbols'" (1984, p. 54). I think that the equation is more useful if we read it the other way around. The progressive temporalization of the narrative representations of the epidemic that circulated through delta communities constituted a crucial means of objectifying traumatic experiences and resisting the imposition of debilitating identities and images.

As I write, in January of 1997, cholera has been reported in several areas of Venezuela, and cases of what public health authorities are referring to as "severe diarrhea" are emerging in the delta. As death, trauma, and racial stigmatization again threaten delta communities, these narratives are once again being called upon to aid in the struggle for survival and dignity.

## ACKNOWLEDGMENTS

I gratefully acknowledge support from the American Council of Learned Societies, the John Simon Guggenheim Memorial Foundation, the Cultural Anthropology Program of the National Science Foundation, the National Endowment for the Humanities, the Social Sciences Research Council, and the Wenner-Gren Foundation for Anthropological Research, Inc. The research that is reported in this article was conducted jointly with Clara Mantini Briggs, MD.

## REFERENCES

Bauman, R. (1986). *Story, performance, and event: Contextual studies of oral narrative.* Cambridge, England: Cambridge University Press.

Briggs, C. L. (1988). *Competence in performance: The creativity of tradition in Mexican verbal art.* Philadelphia: University of Pennsylvania Press.

Briggs, C. L. (1992). Linguistic ideologies and the naturalization of power in Warao discourse. *Pragmatics, 2,* 387–404.

Culler, J. (1981). *The pursuit of signs.* London: Routledge & Kegan Paul.

Das, V. (1996). Language and body: Transactions in the construction of pain. *Daedalus, 125,* 67–91.

Goffman, E. (1974). *Frame analysis.* New York: Harper & Row.

Goodwin, M. H. (1990). *He-said-she-said: Talk as social organization among Black children.* Bloomington: Indiana University Press.

Heath, S. B. (1983). *Ways with words: Language, life, and work in communities and classrooms.* Cambridge, England: Cambridge University Press.

Labov, W. (1982). Speech actions and reactions in personal narrative. In D. Tannen (Ed.), *Analyzing discourse: Text and talk* (pp. 219–247). Washington, DC: Georgetown University Press.

Labov, W., & Waletzky, J. (this issue). Narrative analysis: Oral versions of personal experience. In J. Helm (Ed.), *Essays on the verbal and visual arts: Proceedings of the 1966 Annual Spring Meeting of the American Ethnological Society* (pp. 12–44). Seattle: University of Washington Press. (Original work published 1967)

Ricoeur, P. (1984). *Time and narrative: Vol. 1* (Kathleen McLaughlin & David Pellauer, Trans.). Chicago: University of Chicago Press.

Toolan, M. J. (1988). *Narrative: A critical lingustics introduction.* London: Routledge.

# Speakers, Listeners, and Speech Events in Issues of Universality

## Courtney B. Cazden
### Harvard Graduate School of Education

Issues of universality in language development continue to be controversial. Child language research, whose present era goes back only about 5 years further than Labov and Waletzky's work, has been criticized for assuming that descriptions based on a limited set of children—usually the children of researchers, their students, or other equally well-educated parents—could be taken as a universal pattern, or at least as a baseline against which to study cross-cultural differences. Although that assumption may not be far wrong in the case of core grammar acquired during the toddler years, the dangers of biased interpretations increase when attention shifts to later acquisition and larger form–function units such as narrative.

In this respect, Labov and Waletzky (1967/this issue; henceforth L&W) and the later version by Labov alone (1972) are noteworthy in two ways. First, Labov's 1972 article, the one most available to many researchers, is based only on Labov's research in south-central Harlem. Thus, unlike research on early grammar, the structural analysis of narratives that has been taken as a putative universal and applied widely to narratives from diverse groups of English and non-English speakers, is derived from an African American corpus—the only instance I know of where this is the case.

However, a structural description of discourse derived from any one speech community is too limited for any assumption of universality. So the second worthy note is that L&W—whose broader corpus included narratives from Labov's earlier research on Martha's Vineyard and elsewhere—implicitly warned against the very use to which their analysis has subsequently been put. Their final sentence suggests that "his view of narrative structure will gain greater significance when materials from radically different cultures are studied in the same way" (this issue). The

---

Requests for reprints should be sent to Courtney B. Cazden, Harvard Graduate School of Education, Cambridge, MA 02138. E-mail: cazdenco@hugse1.harvard.edu

inclusion of that final sentence may have been influenced by the occasion of its oral presentation at a meeting of the American Ethnological Society, a group whose focus is comparative ethnography. However, it still could have been read as an admonition to readers against assuming universality.

Strikingly absent from both L&W and Labov (1972) is any mention of the gender of narrators. Whether gender differences were ignored in the research designs or only in the reporting, readers cannot tell. In either case, these articles should now be read as a product of their times. Thirty years after L&W, gender might be for some researchers the most salient speaker variable of all.

Methodological issues in testing claims of universality involve not only differences among speakers but also differences among speech contexts. For their analysis, L&W combined narratives from "two distinct social contexts": speaking to an interviewer from outside the narrator's primary group and participating in a conversation among group members plus one outsider. It may be the case that such a difference between narrating events did not affect the genre structure that was L&W's focus: "isolating the invariant structural units which are represented by a variety of superficial forms" (this issue). However, it neither detracts from, nor critiques, what L&W accomplished to point out that intragenre variations in the more "superficial forms" we call register variation are also worthy of attention.

A few years ago, Sarah Michaels and I arranged for an interview with an African American fifth-grade girl, whom we called Leona, 4 years after we had recorded her during first grade Sharing Time (ST). In the later research, we created two situations similar to L&W's, but analyzed the resulting narratives separately. We elicited a narrative with a Labov-like prompt: "Tell us about the scariest thing that happened to you" and then asked Leona to retell her narrative about an earache in a story-swapping session with a group of self-selected peers. Thematically, in both versions Leona contrasted the familiar world of home, mother, and food with the hostile institutional world of hospitals, nurses, and medicine as she and her mother traveled between them, first via a "long dark street" and then via a cab that her mother had no money to pay for. There is humor in the telling, but also poignancy when the story is heard as a representative anecdote of societal racism.

Differences between the two versions have been analyzed by Gee (1989), especially for the expressive and performative features Leona added when narrating to her peers. Other differences (detailed in Cazden, 1994) include more variation in how direct speech is introduced to peers; more precise, low-frequency words for the same propositional content to the White interviewer; and differences between the two versions in the content of orienting and evaluative information and in the frequency and function of discourse markers such as "you know" and "right."

Another example of situational variation, here in event structure rather than listeners, appeared in the our earlier ST research. From a corpus of ST narratives spoken in four ethnically mixed classrooms, Cazden, Michaels, and Tabors (1985) found a kind of self-repair that served to clarify information for the listener in a structural form we called "bracketing": the insertion of material, as if in brackets or parentheses, in the middle of an otherwise intact sentence. Here are two examples from Leona's ST narratives, with simplified transcription in which the inserted words are shown in brackets:

[about her grandmother eating too many cakes] ... And she {and we was sleeping} and she went in the room and gobbled 'em up ...

[about her puppy] ... My puppy, he always be following me. He said {my father said} "You can't go" ...

As a subgenre, ST narratives always contain narrative action and usually include some orienting background information as well. Because the expected topic of this situated genre is talk about out-of-school experience in the public forum of the school, orienting information is especially important. However, the genre-like format we found in all our four classrooms constrained the children's solutions to this rhetorical problem. The narratives tend to begin with temporal and spatial location, introduce a key agent, and then get right into the action, typically all in the first sentence, which is spoken with a marked rising intonation. Given this implicit ST convention to get immediately into the action, bracketing seemed to be one strategy diverse children created for inserting further background information as needed.

The analysis thus provides evidence of the influence of the emergent conventions of a recurring narrating event on the microstructure of the narratives told within it, although Cazden et al.'s (1985) original motivation for the analysis of this rhetorical strategy came from more applied concerns. We cited bracketing as evidence of metalinguistic awareness and cognitive work, even on the part of sharers like Leona whose stories their teachers often found hard to follow.

This felicitous convergence of more basic and more applied motivations for discourse analysis also characterizes Labov's research. Structural description of narratives is a contribution to basic linguistics, but the final sentence of his 1972 article speaks directly to applied educational concerns of the era that stimulated federal government funding for his Harlem research: how to improve the education of Black children. Where we asserted evidence of unrecognized cognitive abilities, Labov asserted evidence of unrecognized language proficiency: "Black English vernacular is the vehicle of communication used by some of the most talented and effective speakers of the English language" (1972, p. 396). Sad to say, the same applied educational concerns are alive if not too well today, as evidenced by what one National Public Radio host called the "month-long national shouting match" over Ebonics just as this journal goes to press.

# REFERENCES

Cazden, C. B. (1994). Situational variation in children's language revisited. In D. Biber & E. Finegan (Eds.), *Sociolinguistic perspectives on register* (pp. 277–293). New York: Oxford University Press.

Cazden, C. B., Michaels, S., & Tabors, P. (1985). Spontaneous repairs in Sharing Time narratives: The intersection of metalinguistic awareness, speech event, and narrative style. In S. W. Freedman (Ed.), *The acquisition of written language* (pp. 51–64). Norwood, NJ: Ablex.

Gee, J. P. (1989). Two styles of narrative construction and their linguistic and educational implications. *Discourse Processes, 12,* 287–307.

Labov, W. (1972). The transformation of experience in narrative syntax. In W. Labov (Ed.), *Language in the inner city* (pp. 354–396). Philadelphia: University of Pennsylvania Press.

Labov, W., & Waletzky, J. (this issue). Narrative analysis: Oral versions of personal experience. In J. Helm (Ed.), *Essays on the verbal and visual arts: Proceedings of the 1966 Annual Spring Meeting of the American Ethnological Society* (pp. 12–44). Seattle: University of Washington Press. (Original work published 1967)

# Thematized Echoes

## James Paul Gee
*Hiatt Center, Clark University*

The message I took, years ago, from Labov and Waletzky's (1967/this issue) work on narrative, as well as Labov's related work (e.g., 1972), was rooted more in their examples and analyses than in the specifics of the macrostructure for narrative they propose. The message was this: There is a particular poetic way of using mundane, prosaic language (a way found, in our society, quite often among those who have the least "allegiance" to schools as institutions) that represents a powerful analysis of human experience. It represents, as well, a particularly powerful linguistic capacity and communicative competence at the level of extended discourse. Although such extended discourse often appears monologic, it is, in intent and actual practice, deeply social and dialogic.

Let me give an example, and then say briefly what I take to be the defining characteristics of this use of language, as well as the profound issues to which it gives rise. Following is a story told by a 14-year-old White working-class girl, a girl I will call "Sandra." The story emerged out of a long interview with Sandra (conducted by a female graduate student) about her life and her views on the world. I print the story in lines and stanzas (Gee, 1996).

### STORY: THE RETURN OF THE TABLE

Frame
Stanza 1
1. [Sighs] He's nice.
2. He's, he's, he like he's okay, like
3. I don't know how to explain it.
4. Like, say that you're depressed, he'd just cheer ya up somehow.

---

Requests for reprints should be sent to James Paul Gee, Hiatt Center, Clark University, Worcester, MA 01610. E-mail: jgee@clarku.edu

5. He would, he'd make ya laugh or somethin
6. And you can't stop laughin, it's so funny

## Sub-Story 1: Breaking Things
## Sub-Sub-Story 1: Breaking the Fan

Exposition
<u>Stanza 2</u>
7. Like he does these, like today his mom hit the, she she, he was, he was, he was arguing with his mom,
8. He swears at his mom and stuff like that,
9. He's like that kind of a person
10. And his mom don't care.

<u>Stanza 3</u>
11. He smokes,
12. His mom don't care or nothin,
13. He smokes weed and everything and nobody cares.
14. Cos they can't stop him,
15. He's gonna do it any way
16. Like on house arrest he went out anyway.

## Start of Sub-Sub-Story 1 Proper

<u>Stanza 4 [Started]</u>
17. So they're like so yesterday he was arguing
18. And she held a rake
19. And she went like that to hit him in the back of the butt,

<u>Stanza 5 [Expository Aside]</u>
20. Like she don't hit him,
21. She wouldn't hit him
22. She just taps him with things,
23. She won't actually like actually hit him

<u>Stanza 4 [Continued]</u>
24. She just puts the rake like fool around wit' him,
25. Like go like that,
26. Like he does to her.

Stanza 6
27. Like he was, and like she was holding the rake up like this
28. And he pushed her
29. And the rake toppled over the um, fan.
30. It went kkrrhhh, like that.
31. And he started laughing,

Stanza 7 [Expository Aside]
32. And when he laughs, everybody else laughs
33. Cos the way he laughs is funny,
34. It's like hahahahah!
35. He like laughs like a girl kind of a thing.
36. He's funny.

Stanza 8
37. And then his mother goes, "What are you doing Mike?"
38. And she's like going, "What are you doing? Why are you laughing?"
39. And she goes, "Oh my god it broke, it broke!"
40. And she's gettin all, she's gettin all mad the fan's broken
41. And she trips over the rake,

Stanza 9
42. And she goes into the room
43. And she's like, "Don't laugh, don't laugh,"
44. And he keeps laughin.
45. It's just so funny.

## Sub-Sub-Story 2: Breaking the Table
Exposition

Stanza 10
46. And he'll knock down the table
47. And he'll, like we'll play a game,
48. It's me, Kelly and him and Kelly's boyfriend,
49. It's just kinda fun
50. Cos it's just weird,

Stanza 11
51. We like don't get in trouble,
52. Like he gets blamed for it,

53. Like nothing happens.
54. He don't get punished.

Stanza 12
55. So we always blame him for everything.
56. He don't care,
57. He says, "go ahead, yeah, it doesn't matter."

## Start of Sub-Sub-Story 2 Proper

Stanza 13
58. So we were pulling the table
59. And he was supposed to sit on it, jump on it and sit on it
60. And he didn't,
61. He missed

Stanza 14
62. And the table went blopp! over
63. And it broke.
64. Like it's like a glass patio thing
65. And it went bbchhh! All over everywhere.

Stanza 15
66. He's like, "Oh no!"
67. Well Kel's like, Kelly goes, "What happened, What happened? What did you do now Mike?"
68. He goes, "I broke the table,"
69. She's like "[sigh]", like that.

## Sub-Story 2: Money From Window Falling on Hand

Stanza 16
70. He just got money from his lawyers
71. Because he slit, he slit his wrists last year,
72. Not on purpose,
73. He did it with, like the window fell down on him,

Stanza 17
74. Well, anyway, it came down and sliced his hand like right um here
75. And has a scar there

76. And um, it was bleeding
77. So they had to rush him to the hospital,
78. It wouldn't stop,
79. He had stitches.

Stanza 18
80. And they said that he could sue,
81. And they got five grand.
82. So they just got it two weeks ago
83. So he just bought her new table.

Frame
Stanza 19
84. He's okay.
85. He's, he's nice in a caring,
86. He's like really sweet

Sandra organizes her oral text in terms of "the principle of the echo" (Eliot, 1932), that is, later parts of the text *echo* or mirror earlier ones. This lends—to switch to a visual metaphor—a "Chinese boxes" shape to her text. In Figure 1, the structure of Sandra's oral text is outlined, noting but a few of its most salient echoing features.

Here is a very short and oversimplified analysis of Sandra's text: The whole text is bracketed by a repeated frame, that is: "the boyfriend is nice." The main story is composed of two sub-stories. The first (Sub-Story 1) is about losses caused by the boyfriend accidentally breaking things. The second (Sub-Story 2) is about the boyfriend gaining money because a thing (i.e., a window) has accidentally "broken" him (i.e., injuring his wrists). This inverse accident leads to one of the "lost" things being restored (i.e., the table), yet another sort of *inversion*. Of course, restoration of a lack or loss is a classic narrative-closing device in oral-based cultures (Propp, 1928/1968). The first sub-story (Sub-Story 1) is itself composed of two stories. The first (Sub-Sub-Story 1) is about the breaking of the fan; the second (Sub-Sub-Story 2) is about the breaking of the table.

There are large amounts of parallelism between the two breaking narratives (the fan and the table). Both begin with expository stanzas saying that the boyfriend's actions always go unpunished. These stanzas are followed, in both cases, by "fooling around" involving the boyfriend. Then, in each case, an object falls and makes a noise. The accident leads, in the first case, to the boyfriend being asked: "What are you doing?" and, in the second, to his being asked; "What did you do now?" These questions both go unanswered. The fan story closes with the mother issuing a verbal command to the boyfriend to stop laughing, a command that goes unheeded. The table story closes with the boyfriend's sister issuing no verbal

FRAME:
S1: Boyfriend is nice

STORY: Replacing the table

> SUB-STORY 1: Breaking things
>
>> SUB-SUB-STORY 1: Breaking the fan
>>
>> S2-3:   Exposition: Boyfriend does things, no body cares
>>
>> S4:     Mother fooling around with boyfriend leads to:
>>
>> S6:     Fan falls and makes noise: kkrrhhh
>>         Boyfriend laughs
>>
>> S7:     Boyfriend laughs
>>         Boyfriend makes noise: hahahahah!
>>
>> S8:     Mother asks: "What are you doing Mike?"
>>
>> S9:     Mother tells boyfriend not to laugh
>>         Boyfriend keeps laughing
>
>> SUB-SUB-STORY 2: Breaking the table
>>
>> S10-12:  Exposition: Boyfriend does things, doesn't get in trouble
>>
>> S13:    Boyfriend fooling around with the girls leads to:
>>
>> S14:    Table falls & makes noise: blopp! bbchhh!
>>
>> S15:    Sheena asks "What did you do now, Mike?"
>>         Sheena makes a noise: sigh
>
> SUB-STORY 2: Boyfriend gets money from window falling on his hand

END OF STORY: Boyfriend replaces table ("So he just bought her new table")

FRAME:
S19: Boyfriend is nice

FIGURE 1   Outline of Sandra's story with some echoes noted.

command, but merely an unverbalized sigh. The boyfriend's laughter in the first story is echoed by his sister's sigh in the second.

These two breaking stories are both about accidents involving the boyfriend that lead to loss (fan, table). They are followed by a story (Sub-Story 2) about another accident involving the boyfriend—only this accident is not play, but a serious injury; a person rather than a thing breaks, and the accident leads not to loss, but to gain (money) and restoration (the table). In the fan story, the boyfriend will not heed his mother when she asks him to stop laughing. In the window story, the boyfriend restores the table to the mother without being asked to do so. Such *reversals* and inversions, are, of course, powerful integrative devices. In addition, this sort of parallel structuring lends a certain "equivalence" logic to the text. Different stanzas are equated either through direct similarity or reversals, a looser sort of similarity.

The principle of the echo in Sandra's narrative works to invite the hearer to coconstruct with Sandra a *theme*. It does so in this way: By creating similarities or equivalencies, at a variety of levels, it invites the hearer to construct a theme (or image) that accounts for these similarities, that explains, at a deep level, why these things are similar, what larger issue they subserve. Such themes, of course, emerge out of people's shared cultural knowledge and common experiences, as these are triggered both by "evaluation devices" (Labov & Waletzky 1967; Labov 1972) and "contextualization cues" (Gumperz, 1982).

Based on Sandra's whole interview (see Gee & Crawford, in press), I would suggest that at least one of the important themes underlying Sandra's narrative is this: Sandra rejects or distrusts "authoritative" representation, whether this be authority rooted in adults, factual language, or institutions; in turn, she celebrates language and (inter-)action rooted in spontaneity and affective bonding.

Elsewhere in her interview, Sandra makes it quite clear that in her world disconnections and reversals are salient: between words and deeds, causes and effects, happenings and knowledge about them, and presumed relationships (e.g., between parents and children). She repeatedly tells stories of how things do not connect up in the way one might have expected (e.g., people do not do what they are told or say they will do, they are not punished for misdeeds, and they are blamed for what they did not do).

Further, Sandra makes it clear that she deeply dislikes and distrusts words that are said just because they are true (represent the world as it is) and, in turn, desires and trusts words that are uttered based on how the addressee feels and what she needs. Sandra sees words said only because they are "true" or "facts" backed up by some authority figure (e.g., her sister, her mother, her father, her teacher), as "stupid" and as a way to "ruin" things (e.g., she says that people she cares about give her "the answer I want to hear, that sounds right, with my problem"—and she gives many examples of peers doing this and adults failing to).

In fact, Sandra lives in a rather violent and unpredictable ("chaotic") environment, one in which it takes a great deal of courage and intelligence to survive and flourish. It is an environment, as well, from which one can clearly see that many of the cherished "truths" of government, media, and school are lies. Her narrative take on the world is deeply veridical from where she stands and, at the same time, speaks deeply to the her needs of those of her peers.

Sandra's story looks "topic associating." Though this has been said to a property of African American children's narratives (Michaels, 1981), Sandra is White, with a White peer group. Her story is "Proppian," but it is no folktale. It is literary, but it is not "literature." The properties of Sandra's story are, I would argue, properties of this style of language, not merely of African American school children, Russian folktales, or works of literary art.

This style of language—thematized echoes, we might say—is, I believe (and, rightly or wrongly, I got this idea from Labov and Waletzky) a core property of human sense making. It raises profound issues: Is it universal? How is it differentially realized across cultures and different social groups? Is it attenuated by schools and school-based literacy? How are such "spatial" structures and patterns created "online"? How do the themes of such language both stem from and transform the cultural models of the teller's social groups? How does this form of sense-making relate to others (such as "literature," on the one hand, and "science" on the other)?

There are great many more such questions. It was Labov and Waletzky's work, as well as Labov's related work, together with other work on narrative that I was just beginning to read at the time, that raised these questions for me. Perhaps they were a "theme" that came from a "poetic" juxtaposition of superficially unrelated pieces of work that I just happened to be reading then. After all, I would argue, we not only often talk by thematized echoes, but often read by them as well.

## REFERENCES

Eliot, T. S. (1932). *Selected essays*. New York: Harcourt Brace.
Gee, J. P. (1996). *Social linguistics and literacies: Ideology in discourses* (2nd ed.). London: Taylor & Francis.
Gee, J. P., & Crawford, V. (in press). Two kinds of teenagers: Language, identity, and social class. In D. Alverman, Ed., *Secondary literacy*. Hillsdale, NJ: Lawrence Erlbaum Associates, Inc.
Gumperz, J. J. (1982). *Discourse strategies*. Cambridge, England: Cambridge University Press.
Labov, W. (1972). *Language in the inner city*. Philadelphia: University of Pennsylvania Press.
Labov, W., & Waletzky, J. (this issue). Narrative analysis: Oral versions of personal experience. In J. Helm (Ed.), *Essays on the verbal and visual arts: Proceedings of the 1966 Annual Spring Meeting of the American Ethnological Society* (pp. 12–44). Seattle: University of Washington Press. (Original work published 1967)
Michaels, S. (1981). "Sharing time:" Children's narrative styles and differential access to literacy. *Language in Society, 10,* 423–42.
Propp, V. (1968). *Morphology of the Russian folktale*. Austin: University of Texas Press. (Original work published 1928)

# Beyond Labov and Waletzky: The Antecedents of Narrative Discourse

Catherine E. Snow
*Harvard Graduate School of Education*

Alison Imbens-Bailey
*Infant Child Communication Programs
Arizona State University*

Like other linguistic analyses that emerged in the 1960's, the analysis of narrative by Labov and Waletzky (1967/this issue; henceforth L&W) was remarkable both in its capacity to reorganize people's thinking about the nature of language and in its focus on structure, on the formal properties of language. Thus, it is perhaps not surprising that the primary impact of L&W on researchers in language development has been in organizing our understanding of the sequence with which children's narratives come to display mature structure (e.g., Peterson & McCabe, 1983) and in contributing to our use of narrative as a measure of linguistic and communicative competence (e.g., McCabe & Rollins, 1994).

L&W did not address the question of the function of narratives—the role they play in helping to organize autobiographical memory (Nelson, 1996; Snow, 1991a), in furthering conversational comity (Aston, 1988), in providing a vehicle for thought about problems or difficulties (Bruner, 1986; Miller & Sperry, 1988), in socializing children into membership in their culture (Blum-Kulka, 1997; Grover-Aukrust & Snow, in press; Miller, Potts, Fung, Hoogstra, & Minz, 1990), or in providing contexts for the individuality of the teller to emerge and be supported (Blum-Kulka & Snow, 1992). They did, of course, note the function of evaluation within narrative as expressing the teller's point of view—but without considering the function of the entire narrative from a pragmatic perspective that emphasizes the communicative purpose for which any speech event is undertaken.

---

Requests for reprints should be sent to Catherine E. Snow, Harvard Graduate School of Education, Larsen Hall, Appian Way, Cambridge, MA 02138. E-mail: snowcat@hugse1.harvard.edu

Within a developmental and pragmatic perspective, narratives are not as distinct a form as the full-blown, highly competent, well-articulated narratives presented by L&W might suggest. Narratives grow out of conversations, and young children's narratives are supported conversationally in two senses: their effective telling is supported, and the child as teller is supported in becoming a better narrator. We argue in this article that much of this support focusses on two components of the narrative structure identified by L&W that are most crucial to pragmatic effectiveness and most difficult for the young narrator: orientation and evaluation. Parents, of course, also support the child's telling of events, the core of the narrative, in ways that range from asking leading questions to taking over parts of the telling themselves. However, we argue, with Katherine Nelson (1996), that children's understanding of the organization of events is relatively well developed by the time they can participate in personal narrative conversations, whereas their understanding of the demands for orienting and evaluative information is more restricted. Providing the right kind and amount of orientation and evaluation requires taking the listener's point of view, a capacity that develops after event representation. Thus, these two components of narrative are typically more richly scaffolded for young narrators than is the telling of the events.

We refer to support for providing the right kinds and amount of orientation as *historical support*, that is, support which the adult can provide because of a shared history with the child. The shared history enables the adult to figure out what event the child is referring to, what information needs to be supplied, and what questions to ask to ensure it be supplied. We refer to the adult support for the expression of evaluation as *psychological support*, because it requires taking (and often reinforcing) the child's point of view on the events being told (see Ninio & Snow, 1996, for more detailed discussion of these notions).

To illustrate our view that narratives emerge from conversation both synchronically and diachronically, we present examples of the progression from earliest exchanges about the nonpresent between young children and their parents to exchanges of personal narratives, telling about a nonshared experience of a past event.[1] In particular, we identify some different types of support provided by parents in interaction with their young children as possible sources of orientation and evaluative skills in children's emerging stories about past nonshared events. Conversation between child and parents about events that are partially shared and not very far in the past serves as a supportive context for acquiring the skills needed in narrative discourse.

---

[1] Examples are taken from the New England Corpus (Snow et al., 1996) and the Home-School Study Corpus (Snow, 1991b).

## EARLY CONVERSATIONS ABOUT THE NONPRESENT

Children start out talking about the physical and temporal present, about objects ("dat's a lambie") and events ("uh-oh fall down") in the here-and-now; over 30% of talk observed in children aged 20 to 32 months consists of discussions of a joint focus of attention (Ninio & Snow, 1996; Snow, Pan, Imbens-Bailey, & Herman, 1996). Soon after discussions of the here-and-now emerge at roughly 14 months, discussions start to occur in which parents provide information verbally that children have no direct access to—discussions of topics related to the present and of the nonpresent. However, it takes quite a long time before children participate fully in discussions of nonshared events; such discussions represent less than 5% of all talk observed in children younger than 2 years of age. Discussing events and objects related to the present or recent past events requires the child to decenter from the immediate joint focus and fairly often involves nonshared knowledge. However, these discussions typically refer to events, behaviors, and objects that are related in some fashion to the present and serve to increase the child's encyclopedic knowledge about the properties of things, where they belong, who uses them, how things should behave, and how people feel about them (Imbens-Bailey & Snow, in press).

Historical support was described by Ninio and Snow (1996) as parental use of shared knowledge of past events to enable the child to develop extended discourse. If, however, we expand the notion of historical support to include as well providing knowledge of relevant cultural and physical realities ("lambs say baa, towers fall down when they get too tall"), we can see that early discussions about matters related to the present and about recent past events function to make known to the child norms of behavior and general knowledge—information that will be useful later when the child must evaluate events and actions while telling a personal narrative. In the following exchange with 20-month-old Jamie taken from the New England Corpus, his mother used the towel provided for playing peekaboo as a basis for discussing other uses of towels (M = mother, C = child):[2]

M: Jamie, after you take a bath what does Mommy do?
C: [no response]
M: what does Mommy do?
C: [no response]
M: I put a towel on Jamie just like this.
M: can you put that (= towel) around you?

---

[2]Transcription symbols are based on the CHILDES conventions (MacWhinney, 1991). The following is a key to the transcription symbols used in this article: [//] retrace with correction;[?] uncertain transcription; +/. interruption; unfilled pause; [<], [>] direction of overlapping speech; ["] quotation; <> speech within angled brackets denotes scope of speech affected by a subsequent code.

C: [no response].
M: like this?
C: [no response].
M: put a towel like this around Jamie?
C: [no response].
M: and I rub and rub until you're all dry.

Discussions of events or objects related in some way to the present appear in most cases to be designed to build children's script knowledge, showing them what information they can reasonably expect a listener to have and what orientation material must be provided in later personal narratives. Discussions that go beyond the here-and-now are only possible with children younger than 2 because of parental support of child initiations of these topics (Ninio & Snow, 1996), but as children get older they can begin to make the necessary connections between events in the here-and-now and events related to the present in some manner. For example, 20-month-old Rachel initiates a conversation about a ball, which her mother helps her relate to her memory of televised football. Rachel's mother, with knowledge of American popular culture and of Rachel's television exposure, is able to make sense of her daughter's communicative attempt (New England Corpus):

C: ball.
M: that's a football ball?
C: yes.
M: yeah.
C: people play.
C: [unintelligible] on the tv [unintelligible].
M: people play football on tv?

In the analysis of communicative intentions used by Snow et al. (1996; see also Ninio & Wheeler, 1984), discussing the nonpresent is more removed from the here-and-now than either discussions of topics related to the present or discussions of recently occurring events. No object or event in the immediate context scaffolds the discussions of the nonpresent, so parents often need to provide a great deal of historical support if the discussion is to be successful. The earlier emerging discussions of immediately past events and of topics related to the present typically build on some physical reality (spilled blocks marking that the tower fell down or a picture of a toothbrush as context for discussing the child's toothbrush) that eases the task of making meaning for the young child. They also serve as important precursors to talking about more distant and nonshared experiences by providing information about what topics warrant discussion with others, what aspects of experience should be selected for narrating and which should not.

## EMERGENCE OF TRUE PERSONAL EXPERIENCE NARRATIVES WITH HISTORICAL SUPPORT

True narratives of personal experience most commonly focus on relatively distant, nonshared events, often involving topics that are unrelated to the current discussion, activity, or visible objects. For example, at American dinner tables there is a ritual about telling one's day (Blum-Kulka & Snow, 1992) that emerges once young children begin to attend daycare, preschool, or kindergarten programs. These reports are often among the earliest cases of discussions of nonpresent and nonshared events. They present the child (and the analyst) with some ambiguity about the level of shared knowledge that can be presupposed, given that much of the information conveyed (for example, about what happened at day care) is somewhat scripted and predictable. It is, thus, available at least as a basis for questioning (e.g., "what did you eat for snack?") by adults who have no specific knowledge of the day's events. An example of this comes from the Home-School Study Corpus. The following conversation between 4-year-old Mack and his grandfather is about an event the grandfather had not participated in. He is nonetheless able to support Mack's telling by asking questions to provide historical support (G = Grampa):

G: you like the train ride today?
C: yeah. well um there was a town.
G: town?
C: I liked the town.
G: you went through one town on the way to Boston?
C: one two three four five six <I dunno [= do-'nt know]> [>]
G: <went through> [<] a whole bunch of them?
C: one two three four five six uh five of them. six of them.
G: six of them?
C: uh four of them.
G: yeah?
C: yeah uh seven.
G: did the man come around and get your ticket? hmm?
C: uh +/.
G: you buy it on the train don't you?
M: yeah.
G: did he come around and say <ticket please> ["]?
C: he did-'nt xxx say ticket please.
G: he didn't? <he didn't get> [//] he just come around and took the money?
C: come around!

Mack's grandfather could help Mack tell the story of his train trip because of his geographical and cultural knowledge (he knew the train line and the habits of conductors), and he could elicit this story because of his specific knowledge about the family's plan to take Mack to Boston on the train. Without the historical support he provided, it is unlikely Mack would have been able to tell anything much about this event.

In personal reports like this, the teller often underestimates the need for orientation information by the listener and gets back on track only with the help of clarification questions. We argue, then, that the possibility of effectively conveying the point of a narrative for a preschooler, in anticipation of the listener's questions What? and So what?, rests powerfully on the interactive work done by the listener, through clarification questions and through the inferences the listener can make by sharing general as well as specific, event-related background knowledge with the teller.

By about the age of 5, children are already showing signs of the ability to assess the listener's likely knowledge about the events they narrate. In the following example, also from the Home-School Study Corpus, 5-year-old Brittany questioned her mother's knowledge about Brittany's experiences, revealing her sophisticated understanding of who should know what:

> M: so what'd you do in school today?
> C: nothing. I colored.
> M: you colored?
> C: yeah.
> M: what did you color?
> C: a dinosaur.
> M: a dinosaur.
> C: is that [= tape player?] on?
> M: yep. eat your food.
> <u>Comment:</u> [Mother and child discuss eating food].
> M: what else you do in school today?
> C: I-'m playing with playdough.
> M: oh is that the playdough that you made?
> C: what playdough?
> M: did you make some playdough in school? huh?
> C: when did I tell you this?
> M: no I saw the paper. no you didn't tell me. it was the paper that you brought home. it tells you how to make the playdough.
> C: yeah. that-'is the kind. I-'m full.

## ELABORATION OF THE EVALUATIVE COMPONENT THROUGH PSYCHOLOGICAL SUPPORT

Asking the child to provide or clarify the main point of a story (e.g., "why was she crying?"), providing explicit evaluation (e.g., "Josh is such a clever kid!"), or indicating what stories are worth telling or not (e.g., "that was a great story." vs. "so why are you telling me this?") are all forms of psychological support by which parents signal the need for the child to convey his or her own perspective on the narrated events (McCabe & Peterson, 1991; Peterson & McCabe, 1992).

In the following example, 4-year-old Daniel is able to convey sufficient orientation and event information to make clear who was involved, what happened, when, and where, but it was his mother who provided the evaluation:

C: mama.
M: what hon?
C: Katrina in the six year old class?
M: mmm?
C: she threw up today. last night.
M: yeah? that's terrible.
C: from <orange> [/] orange. from [?] orange.
M: she threw up orange? oh that's disgusting.

## BEYOND LABOV AND WALETZKY

L&W's work was the foundation for our understanding of sequential stages in the development of the capacity to produce narratives of personal experience. Their description of the macrostructure of narratives provided a generation of narrative researchers with the criteria by which to describe growth in narrative abilities. It did not, however, address the mechanism of development of narrative abilities. We have argued that an understanding of how children acquire narrative skills requires reembedding narrative performances in their conversational context, acknowledging the blurry boundaries around narrative talk both in its development and in its conditions of occurrence, and recognizing the work that adults do to help children take the listener's perspective. Taking the listener's perspective requires assessing what listeners are likely to know or not to know about the facts of the story and how they are likely to react to the story, then providing the right amount of information both about the facts and their interpretation. Parents can help children do this effectively because they know so much about their children's lives and psychological reactions. Achieving the level of narrative competence displayed by the narrators quoted in L&W's groundbreaking paper is the product of many years of telling stories collaboratively.

## ACKNOWLEDGMENTS

Catherine Snow acknowledges the support of NIH Grant HD22338 for research on the New England Corpus and the Ford and Spencer Foundations for support of the Home School Study of Language and Literacy Development. Alison Imbens-Bailey acknowledges support during the preparation of this article from U.S. Department of Education Postdoctoral Grant H029D50062 for which M. Jeanne Wilcox is Principal Investigator.

The information contained in this article does not necessarily reflect the views or policies of the Department of Education, and no official endorsement by that department should be inferred.

## REFERENCES

Aston, G. (1988). *Learning comity: An approach to the description and pedagogy of interactive speech.* Bologna, Italy: Ediatrice Clueb.

Bruner, J. (1986). *Actual minds, possible worlds.* Cambridge, MA: Harvard University Press.

Blum-Kulka, S. (1997). *Dinner talk: Cultural patterns of sociability and socialization in family discourse.* Mahwah, NJ: Lawrence Erlbaum Associates, Inc.

Blum-Kulka, S., & Snow, C. E. (1992). Developing autonomy for tellers, tales and telling in family narrative events. *Journal of Narrative and Life History, 2,* 187–217.

Grøver-Aukrust, V. & Snow, C. E. (in press). Narratives and explanations in Norwegian and American mealtime conversations. *Language in Society.*

Imbens-Bailey, A. L., & Snow, C. E. (in press). Making meaning in parent–child interaction. In C. Mandell & A. McCabe (Eds.), *Advances in psychology: The problem of meaning: Cognitive and behavioral approaches.* New York: North-Holland.

Labov, W., & Waletzky, J. (this issue). Narrative analysis: Oral versions of personal experience. In J. Helm (Ed.), *Essays on the verbal and visual arts: Proceedings of the 1966 Annual Spring Meeting of the American Ethnological Society* (pp. 12–44). Seattle: University of Washington Press. (Original work published 1967)

MacWhinney, B. (1991). *The CHILDES project: Computational tools for analyzing talk.* Hillsdale, NJ: Lawrence Erlbaum Associates, Inc.

McCabe, A., & Peterson, C. (1991). Getting the story: A longitudinal study of parental styles in eliciting personal narratives and developing narrative skill. In A. McCabe & C. Peterson (Eds.), *Developing narrative structure* (pp. 217–254). Hillsdale, NJ: Lawrence Erlbaum Associates, Inc.

McCabe, A., & Rollins, P. R. (1994). Assessment of preschool narrative skills. *American Journal of Speech–Language Pathology: A Journal of Clinical Practice, 3,* 45–56.

Miller, P., Potts, R., Fung, H., Hoogstra, C., & Minz, J. (1990). Narrative practices and the social construction of self in childhood. *American Ethnologist, 17,* 292–311.

Miller, P. J., & Sperry, L. L. (1988). Early talk about the past: The origins of conversational stories of personal experience. *Journal of Child Language, 15,* 293–315.

Nelson, K. (1996). *Language in cognitive development: The emergence of the mediated mind.* New York: Cambridge University Press.

Ninio, A., & Snow, C. E. (1996). *Developmental pragmatics.* Boulder, CO: Westview.

Ninio, A., & Wheeler, P. (1984). A manual for classifying verbal communicative acts in mother–infant interaction. In *Working Papers in Developmental Psychology, No. 1.* Jerusalem: The Martin and Vivian Levin Center, Hebrew University.

Peterson, C., & McCabe, A. (1983). *Developmental psycholinguistics: Three ways of looking at a child's narrative.* New York: Plenum.

Peterson, C., & McCabe, A. (1992). Parental styles of narrative elicitation: Effect on children's narrative structure and content. *First Language, 12,* 299–322.

Snow, C. E. (1991a). Building memories: The ontogeny of autobiography. In D. Cicchetti & M. Beeghly (Eds.), *The self in transition: Infancy to childhood* (pp. 213–242). Chicago: University of Chicago Press.

Snow, C. E. (1991b). The theoretical basis for relationships between language and literacy development. *Journal of Research in Childhood Education, 6,* 5–10.

Snow, C. E., Pan, B. A., Imbens-Bailey, A. L., & Herman, J. (1996). Learning how to say what one means: A longitudinal study of children's speech act use. *Social Development, 5,* 56–84.

# Making Sense of the Sense-Making Function of Narrative Evaluation

## Colette Daiute and Katherine Nelson
*City University of New York Graduate Center*

Labov and Waletzky's (1967/this issue; henceforth L&W) narrative analysis scheme gave a prominent place to evaluation as a component of first person narratives and to its function in establishing the meaning of the narrative for the narrator. Subsequent discussion has placed similar emphasis on this aspect of narrative. For example, Bruner (1986) pointed out the significance of the "landscape of consciousness" as the definitive characteristic of narrative, taking it beyond the "landscape of action," the complicating action that L&W viewed as defining. In this commentary, we discuss the nature of evaluation as a sense-making function.

We consider L&W's stated and implied claims about evaluation: (a) evaluation is an isolatable component of narrative discourse, in particular distinguished from referential meaning; (b) evaluation serves an interpretive function, signaling the meaning of the narrative for the narrator; in so doing, (c) evaluation is social because it offers the listener information about the narrator's point of view. More implicitly: (d) evaluation is overtly stated; (e) as "a component" it is unitary, whole; and (f) as a discrete linguistic component, evaluation would develop in a linear progression like syntax and other semantic aspects of language. Based on our research and research by others, we argue for expanding this useful characterization of narrative evaluation. Our analysis of the interaction between structural and sense-making aspects of narrative evaluation suggests that evaluation can serve children as they situate themselves within society, a process that is entwined with the development of narrative discourse.

### SENSE-MAKING FUNCTIONS

L&W contributed to transform linguistic theory into a theory of discourse by distinguishing between the evaluative and referential meaning of narratives. With-

---

Requests for reprints should be sent to Colette Daiute, 43 West 42nd Street, New York, NY 10036. E-mail: cdaiute@email.gc.cuny.edu

out much fanfare, L&W stated, moreover, that evaluation is social as narrators respond to external situations, stimuli, and audiences. By examining the development of young children's oral narratives in home and family contexts and older children's oral and written narratives in school, we have observed that evaluation is iterative; it appears in the narratives of very young children, but it can apparently disappear, and then reappears later in development. This complex history indicates, moreover, that evaluation is an aspect of children's developing awareness of self in relationship to society.

## SCRIPTS AND STORIES: FROM CULTURE TO SELF

Making sense of the world is a major cognitive challenge for children of all ages, essential to meeting basic physical, emotional, and social needs and desires. From the child's perspective, making sense involves figuring out: "What is going on here?" and predicting: "What will happen next?", as such awareness is important to the well-being of all children and even the survival of children in harsh environments. Understanding events in the environment is also relational, motivating the child's question: "Where do I fit?" These orienting cognitive questions embed notions about the important people who influence events in the child's world and about the motivations and intentions of these people, but, because those people and their actions are not abstract, the child must infuse the world as given with personal meaning and an increasing awareness of self as intentional, valuable, and connected to persons and events in her environment.

Discourse experiences provide answers to questions about "What is going on here?" and "How do I fit?" in the form of scripts for familiar routinized activities—the skeletal general action sequences that compose events. The script for an event represents the way things "should be" and the way children, taking their direction from adults come to expect them to be. Thus, scripts incorporate the ways of culture.

Scripts—for getting dressed, having a bath, taking an afternoon walk, or eating lunch—are the stripped down referential core of personal narratives, as L&W conceived them. They are also the developmental starting point of stories. In Bruner's (1990) terms, scripts constitute the "canonical events" against which the unexpected component poses a problem and introduces feeling and thinking (intentionality or meaning) that is the heart of narrative. Scripts, representing *what happens* in general, do not require an internal evaluative component. Stories, however, whether fictional or personal narratives, need a point of view that incorporates an evaluative component implicitly or explicitly. What happened was triumphant or tragic, surprising, gratifying, or disappointing.

There appear to be two important characteristics that differentiate stories from scripts: stories *individuate* the general script by way of the specific noncanonical unexpected happenings and stories *evaluate* happenings within the narrative from the point of view of the narrator. An intriguing hypothesis is that scripts, which are predictable, cultural frames, provide a context in which children learn to individuate and then to evaluate as they narrativize experiences. Consider as a first case the following bedtime narrative by a 23-month-old child (Nelson, 1989).

> *When my sleep/ and and Mormor came / then Mommy coming / then get up time to go home / time to go home / drink p-water (Perrier)/ yesterday did that /Now Emmy sleeping in regular bed*

This typical bedtime monologue by Emily after she was left alone is an example of an individuated variation on everyday routine scripts. Emily recounts a unique one-time occurrence of a scripted event, but there is no overt, and little evidence of covert evaluation. In contrast, consider a production by Emily, again alone at bedtime, from 9 months later at 34 months:

> *Wey <u>bought</u> a baby, cause, the well because, when she, well, we <u>thought</u> it was for Christmas, but when we went to the s-s-store we didn't have our jacket on, but I saw some dolly, and I <u>yelled</u> at my mother and said I want one of those dolly. So after we were finished with the store, we went over to the dolly and she <u>bought</u> me one. so I have one.*

Here the evaluative component is fully integrated into the personal account. Although the bedtime account was individuated from a familiar script, the later story narrative was both individuated and evaluated. The specificity of the event is made clear in the temporality of time and temporal–causal evaluation. However, the evaluation is not brought out as an explicit separate component, but remains implicit in the tone of the recitation. The canonical action is violated, but no point of view was stated explicitly that could provide an evaluation. The narration appears to assume that the listener shares a perspective on the action, that the teller and hearer will make the same sense of it. Although not apparently evaluated, this elaborated "new baby" script does carry an emerging perspective in the use of internal state verbs with individual as well as collective first person pronouns and attributions of order and causal relations.

A further step in this story progression is to take a point of view by recounting a relatively novel story with more explicit evaluative marking. Consider the following example from a boy not yet 5 years old (Applebee, 1978).

> *Once there was a doggy and a <u>little</u> boy. The doggy was <u>pretty silly.</u> He ran away from the <u>little</u> boy and went <u>farther and farther</u> away. The <u>little</u> boy caught the doggy. ... The doggy ran away again. He came near a railroad track. He stepped on it and the train ran over him. <u>But</u> he was still alive. This was <u>big</u> white bull dog and he <u>wanted</u> to go back to his home. When the <u>little</u>*

boy went back home he found the doggy. He was _happy_. *His doggy was still alive.*

In this example, the child has moved beyond the script to make a fictional story with overt evaluative component (italicized), expressing his point of view through his characterization of the main character (e.g., *doggy was pretty silly*). It may be that mastering the cultural genre of story makes the distinctiveness of individuation and evaluation more salient to the child, perhaps providing the basis for further development of both personal narrative and fictional story genres. We present this transition from scripts to stories as a social process in terms of how children use evaluation as a means of communication, as L&W proposed, and argue that, in addition, evaluation serves as a context for development of self through the interpretive force of explicitly stated evaluation.

Next, we explore the relation between scripts and stories as a site for the development of self-concept as children engage in narrative writing.

## STORIES TO SCRIPTS: FROM SELF TO MULTIPLE CULTURES

Considering the use of evaluation in older children reveals that the relation of script-to-story is iterative. As children engage in new cultures, in particular the culture of school, we see the script-to-story progression repeat. Older children, who have already been socialized to the routines and language of their primary cultures, come to know and to enact secondary cultures as they use new rhetorical scripts, also referred to as genres. We have observed that as children master the discourse frames of new genres, their use of explicit evaluation is minimal within that genre, but they eventually express a point of view as they make the genre their own. Evaluation is thus situated rather than absolute. Even after children have acquired the ability to use evaluative devices, there are situations when they may not. We have observed a number of situations where apparent reduction of interpretation in the form of explicit use of evaluation devices is replaced by interpretation of a different, more implicit kind—evaluation that we are calling "cultural" because it involves interpreting the discourse context and selecting the appropriate scripts for self-expression.

Several texts by Shara, an 8-year-old writing a series of articles for the class newspaper illustrate this process (Daiute & Griffin, 1993). When responding to the assignment "Write about what happened when third graders [ ... ] visited the Gardner Museum, and why that was important," Shara offered a text that was her own story of the class trip. She began her story with the classic "who, what, when, where sentence," often taught in relation to journalistic narrative form: "About one

MAKING SENSE OF SENSE-MAKING  211

mouth ago the third and fouth graders went on a field trip to the gardner museeeum." Shara then offered an associatively related set of events with a myriad of evaluative details, as in these few sentences excerpted from the longer narrative:

> *When they got there they <u>saw a lot</u> of broken stauchus. we <u>saw a lot</u> of pichers from <u>famus</u> artist. then are guild gave the tore it was <u>a little bit spcooky</u> <u>because</u> the spirt of miss gardner was on the fouth floor in her will she <u>said</u> that she <u>did not want</u> nobody to go on the fouth floor. we <u>explored</u> the museum there was a piucher called the rape of eropy. It was about a god who trured him selve in to a <u>nice</u> bull <u>because</u> if is wife <u>saw</u> him he would and on the roof there was a <u>big</u> piucher of all the gods.*

Also reflecting her own point of view, Shara ended by reporting on her own personal experience after the class trip.

> *when we came back to the lh school it was time to go home then robins mother fixst my walk man then I went to after school it <u>fun</u> there but im not to talk about that so what when I got to after school I <u>told</u> rosa about my day she <u>said that she wish</u> she was in my class at 5:30 I went home.*

This example illustrates how Shara presented a canonical school event and related rhetorical script—the class trip report—from her own point of view. Shara expressed a point of view through evaluation with qualifying adjectives, internal states, reported speech, causal connections, and intensifiers (selected examples italicized). In addition to specific linguistic devices, Shara offered her perspective on the significance of the events by her use of the personal coda at the end, implying perhaps that Robin's mother fixing her walkman was what was really important about the day. Although evaluation (like spelling, punctuation, and syntax) does not appear to be completely controlled by this young author, the narrative is infused with her point of view and thus more storied than script-like. Nevertheless, Shara faced eventual pressure to move away from this personal style of evaluation.

The progression from evaluated story to referential script is evident in an example written several weeks after Shara's museum report—after Shara had worked with her teacher one-on-one several times. The assignment for the next text was to write about the day in Renaissance Italy (which the class had been studying intensively) when the new doors of the baptistery of Saint Mary of the Flower in Florence were unveiled.

> *The dome of stint marry of the flower **was build** by filippo brunleskey it **took** about ten years he **sarted** to build the dome when he was 24 years old.*
> *filippo **travled** to rome*

*to and **stued** about the coulmes and the archs and the masterpices. When he **came back** he **met** a man named miclanglo he **told** him him about the dome. Filippo **died** but the dome was still build now the dome his still standing in florecs.*
THE END

This text is more like a script, in its straightforward temporal action sequence (in italics) and the paucity of evaluation around these happenings. Notably missing also is the personal coda that Shara had previously used to end many of her texts. As the school year progressed, Shara integrated explicit, personal evaluation with the school narrative script, elaborating upon the bare action sequence script by gradually infusing it with some of the types of evaluation she had used in her earlier storied texts.

This idea that the script-to-story progression repeats embeds the understanding that scripts are cultural constructions; they are not neutral. Scripts implicitly embed beliefs, values, and expectations of the culture. Accounting for cultural points of view in discourse framing is a metalinguistic process and thus may be implicit, whereas personal styles as in stories appear to be marked more explicitly. Of course, cultural discourse practices also shape the nature of specific linguistic devices, but choosing among rhetorical frames, as in Shara's case, involves cultural sense-making. As children mature and engage in diverse contexts, they are required and become able to select among diverse ways of situating and shaping their discourse. Although evaluation may not be explicit in the first phases of older children's use of new rhetorical scripts, children bring to bear an interpretive process all the same. Selecting which rhetorical script to use as the options increase from home scripts to school scripts involves making sense of the discourse context, purpose, audience, and one's own point of view within this cultural complex—interpretive activities within the landscape of consciousness.

This simultaneous dropping of personal evaluation and adopting a new cultural script suggests, we argue, that evaluation functions in at least two ways, representing competing orientations of self–society relationships as constituted in competing interpretive modes. Thus, from early on, evaluation comes into the child's repertoire as a linguistic component available for distinguishing me from not-me. Using different kinds of evaluation later on involves making choices between different kinds of me—as for Shara between the good student me and the personally meaningful me. The role of social interaction in this process of change is integral to the development of evaluation. Cultural and personal evaluation styles together constitute a broader characterization of evaluation as an interpretive function, and further investigation of this relation would be useful in expanding narrative theory and implications of that theory for educational practice.

## THE DEVELOPMENT OF EVALUATIVE ORIENTATION

How do children develop this complex interpretive orientation involving metalinguistic knowledge about interpretive orientations as well as a set of linguistic devices? We propose that the iterative process of script-to-story-to-script involves the construction and interplay of society–self relationships with linguistic and structural features of evaluation. In this sense, the complex evaluative function constitutes human development rather than being simply a distinct linguistic component.

Insights into this development come from the observation that scripts are individual representations of experience, albeit of canonical culturally and socially shared events or discourse genres. Enacted scripts are represented from the child's perspective only. Scripts are thus not dialogic—they are not ordinarily the topic of conversation. Only when children and parents begin talking about memories of personal experiences does the dialogic, and thus the evaluative point of view, enter. In early cases, this evaluative stance is introduced by an adult, as in the following example of a dialogue between a 2-year-old boy and his mother, who were asked to talk about their shared past with family photos on hand as prompts (Engel, 1986; C = child, M = mother):

C: Mommy, the Chrysler building. [ ... ]
M: Yeah, who works in the Chrysler building?
C: Daddy
M: Do you ever go there? [ ... ]
C: We went to ... my Daddy went to work
M: Remember when we went to visit Daddy? Went in the elevator, way way up in the building so we could look down from the big window?
C: big window .M: mmhm
C: ( ) When ... we did go on the big building
M: mmhm, the big building. Was that fun? Would you like to do it again? Sometime.
C: I want to go on the big building.

This excerpt illustrates how the mother's questions guide her child in stating a point of view as they describe their memory of a scene and comment on it. This and similar examples provide support for the assumption that evaluation of what happened emerges between people, as a point of view comes into focus. Notice also how the mother elicits, in particular, the child's feelings as she teaches him to reminisce and to think about his future in terms of past experience.

The dynamic between the interpretive frame of the school-based narrative and the child's personal evaluation is played out in the following interaction between Shara and her teacher as they wrote an entry for the class newspaper together, reporting on the day that Danny, one of the boys in the class, broke his leg. This example illustrates the teacher's attempts to socialize her students to writing the types of narratives that are expected in school—narratives with detailed, factual event sequences organized into structures like paragraphs (T = Teacher, S = Shara).

> T: ... How about, when she got there, Danny was lying on the floor, on the—
> S: with blood.
> T: There was no blood (laughter).
> S: There wasn't.
> T: No.
> S: Oh, shucks.
> ...
> T: was laying, lying not laying, lying on the ground. (typing while talking).
> S: All black and blue.
> T: He wasn't black and blue.
> ....
> T: This is a new paragraph.
> S: Return, Ok.
> T: And then you have to get it indented, tab. Excellent, you remembered that. Now, how do you do that when you're writing your own papers?

Like parents, teachers help children realize their views are particular, but the dialogue often revolves around aspects of subject matter or genre features that children are expected to master rather than about their feelings and desires. Minority students like the African American Shara often use multiple discourses, without the explicit acknowledgment that they are, to some extent, working in a second language or dialect. There are many issues related to the value, ethics, and need for such socialization, but for the purposes of this article, we offer this example to illustrate how scripts and stories—cultural and personal forms of evaluation—interplay with the social interaction context. If the child's world is one that allows for elaboration within different cultural scripts, he or she will not only learn to differentiate a personal point of view within the culture but will also become increasingly skilled at enacting and discussing diverse points of view. As young children begin to challenge familiar scripts at home, older children can learn to do so in school and in the community. Diverse cultural scripts and discourse genres can then become the topic of conversation, given mutual trust to engage in discussion around diversity. Thus, point of view is also made problematic as choices about discourse forms and contexts occur in school and in peer culture as children begin to shape their own identities rather than step into them as prepared by the adults in their culture.

In summary, we argue that to describe the evaluative function as sense-making requires more than characterizing it as a component. In context, evaluation emerges as points of view on an event come into contact in dialogic contexts. In school, children learn to adopt the script-like impersonal frame, and if they have the opportunity to exchange points of view in open and reflective ways, they can infuse diverse cultural scripts with their own personal evaluation.

Through this argument, we propose the following extensions to L&W's original characterization of evaluation. Evaluation is more complex than originally characterized in the following ways: (a) embedded in the social world of discourse, evaluation involves cultural and personal aspects of sense-making; (b) as cultural sense-making, evaluation occurs implicitly to frame narrative discourse in the form of scripts, whereas personal evaluation is more explicit and internal to a particular text; (c) the development of evaluation involves an iterative process (rather than a linear progression), as a context in which children explore relationships between self and society as well as developing particular types of linguistic expertise; and (d) evaluation is varied and situated, rather than absolute or unitary, even though some types of evaluation may be explicit and isolatable within a given text.

These ideas suggest continued theory and research, building upon L&W's original claims, to understand further how children become increasingly engaged with language as an interpretive medium and how their work with discourse engages them in the development of self within community.

## REFERENCES

Applebee, A. (1978). *The child's concept of story.* Chicago: University of Chicago Press.
Bruner, J. (1986). *Actual minds, possible worlds.* Cambridge, MA: Harvard University Press.
Bruner, J. (1990). *Acts of meaning.* Cambridge, MA: Harvard University Press.
Daiute, C., & Griffin, T. M. (1993). The social construction of narrative. In C. Daiute (Ed.), *The development of literacy through social interaction* (pp. 97–120). San Francisco, CA: Jossey-Bass.
Engel, S. (1986). *Learning to reminisce: A developmental study of how young children talk about the past.* Unpublished doctoral dissertation, City University of New York Graduate Center, New York.
Labov, W., & Waletzky, J. (this issue). Narrative analysis: Oral versions of personal experience. In J. Helm (Ed.), *Essays on the verbal and visual arts: Proceedings of the 1966 Annual Spring Meeting of the American Ethnological Society* (pp. 12–44). Seattle: University of Washington Press. (Original work published 1967)
Nelson, K. (1989). *Narratives from the crib.* Cambridge, MA: Harvard University Press.

# The Mutual Construction of Narrative by Mothers and Children: Cross-Cultural Observations

## Jean Berko Gleason and Gigliana Melzi
*Department of Psychology, Boston University*

In this article we expand upon Labov and Waletzky's (1967) discussion of the functions of narrative. These authors referred to referential and evaluative functions: The narrator recapitulates past events and at the same time makes clear to the audience just what the point of the story is, often by describing his or her own feelings about the events. This schema was developed to account for narratives told by a single speaker with particular information to convey, rather than narratives constructed mutually between parents and their young children, who are just learning to describe their experiences in culturally appropriate ways.

Children's earliest spontaneous narratives are typically seen around the age of 2 or 3, but even at that early age, they have long been in conversation with the adults around them, so that what they report is culturally conditioned. In the United States, for instance, parents often ask preschool children to say where they went, whom they saw, what they did; but they are more likely to ask girls to report what someone *said,* than to request this information from boys (Ely, Gleason, Narasimhan, & McCabe, 1995). It is not surprising to learn that with such a history, grown women in our culture are more likely than men to talk about the speech of others and to regard it as important. Initially, parents guide the child's story organization and provide the basic elements of the narrative that they expect to hear. As children develop, they begin to use independently the elements first modeled by the parent; children's narratives are thus a product of their interactions with the adults around them, who provide the framework not just for the narrative, but for children's construction of their world. Our data here are drawn from fieldwork conducted among Gypsies in eastern Hungary (Réger & Gleason, 1991), and from semistruc-

---

Requests for reprints should be sent to Jean Berko Gleason, Department of Psychology, Boston University, 64 Cummington Street, Boston, MA 02215. E-mail: gleason@bu.edu

tured observations among English- and Spanish-speaking mothers and children living in the northeast United States (Melzi, 1997).

## FUNCTIONS OF NARRATIVES IN HUNGARIAN GYPSY COMMUNITIES

Gypsies have their origins in India, and their language is of Indian descent as well. It is not known exactly when they arrived on the European continent, but they have resided in Hungary since at least the early 1400s, where, as elsewhere, they have been subjected to strong pressures to assimilate. Yet they have maintained a strong, cohesive society and a separate identity. Gypsies comprise about 3% of the population of Hungary, and about one third are bilingual speakers of both Hungarian and one of their Romāni dialects. Typically, in a classic diglossic pattern, Romāni is used as an intragroup language and Hungarian is used with outsiders. Literacy is not common in this population.

Narratives serve many functions in an oral culture such as that of the Gypsies: For instance, narratives maintain the history of the community and provide continuity for cultural practices. Storytellers are valued members of society, and there are a number of narrative features particular to storytelling. These include active participation by listeners, who may interrupt the narrator to ask test questions, that is, questions whose answers are already known. This format is particularly common during the narration of stories about Gypsy life in the past.

Narrative also provides a powerful medium of enculturation. Early introduction of children to narrative reflects its importance for Gypsy culture and Gypsy identity. One particular feature of narratives to infants and young children is that they are often used to tell the child explicitly what his or her life will be like. The narrative also includes dialogic improvisation, in which the adult speaks both for herself and for the child. In the following narrative (originally in Romāni), a mother tells her infant son Denesh what life will be like when he grows up and takes horses to the fair:

> All right, all right! My son is leaving, isn't he, my son? "Where are you going, Denesh?" "To the great fair. We are driving the horses." ... "How many horses are you driving, Denesh?" "Two or three!" .... "What will you do with them, Denesh?" "Well, I love small colts! Then I will go and harness them to the cart and pick up many small children and I'll drive." ... My big son will drive the horses. (Réger & Gleason, 1991, p. 607)

Here, the function of the narrative is as a blueprint of expectations for the future; the Gypsy child learns the explicit expectations of his society through these interactive stories.

## LATINO MOTHERS AND CHILDREN

Thus, the form and content of narratives is shaped by the world view or folk psychology of a culture. Even subtle subcultural differences are reflected in the elicitation styles of parents, and, consequently, in the narrative style learned by children. We have seen this in a comparison of storytelling among Latino and Anglo American children living in the United States.

In this study 31 working-class mothers were asked to engage in a conversation with their preschoolers and to talk with them about past personal experiences, some of which had been shared with the parent and some of which were unshared. About half of the mothers were Spanish-speaking immigrants from Central America (from El Salvador, Honduras, and Guatemala), and the others were native speakers of English, predominantly from Irish American backgrounds.

The Anglo and Latino mothers were quite similar in their elicitation styles when they asked the child to talk about a past event that they had shared, for instance a trip to the park. In these shared narratives, both groups of mothers scaffolded their children's story construction through the use of well-placed questions, statements, and interjections. For instance, mothers in both groups often began with memory questions ("Remember the time that we ... ") or with linguistic prompts ("Tell me about the wedding ... ").

Major differences between these two groups of mothers emerged when they talked about unshared events. The narrative interactions that follow are between two 4-year-old girls and their mothers, talking about an unshared experience. These interactions illustrate some of the differences that were frequently observed in the larger sample (C = child, M = mother).

<u>Juanita and Isabel</u>
1. C: es que ... es que estoy hablando del cumpleaños de Julie.
   *is that ... is that I'm talking about Julie's birthday.*
2. M: ah ok entonces, Juanita, platíqueme del cumpleaños de Julie.
   *oh ok then talk to me about Julie's birthday.*
3. C: del cumpleaños de Julie... yo ... me +//.
   *about Julie's birthday ... I ... I was +//.*
4. C: **mire usted** ... yo pensé que usted se había ido con mi papi y me había dejado con **la Julie**.
   *look there ... I thought that you had left with daddy and that you had left me with the Julie.*
5. M: aja.
   mhmm.
6. C: la hija de **la Julie**.
   *(with) the daughter of the Julie.*
7. C: con la hija de la... de la... de la ...

>     *with the daughter of the ... of the ... of the...*
> 8. M: **de la comadre Rosibel?**
>     *of our buddy Rosibel?*
> 9. C: ... de la comadre Rosibel.
>     *... of our buddy Rosibel.*
> 10. M: sí?
>     *really?*
> 11. C: y yo pensé que usted me había dejado ese día.
>     *and I thought you had left me that day.*
> 12. M: sí?
>     *really?*
> 13. C: mhmm.
> 14. M: mhmm.
> 15. M: ok.

Bridgie and Margaret:
 1. M: so um how was school yesterday?
 2. C: I didn't have no school.
 3. M: yeah we had ... you had school yesterday.
 4. C: uhuh ... today.
 5. M: today there's no school.
 6. C: shh! (as if it were a secret).
 7. M: how was school yesterday?
 8. M: did you play in the park?
 9. C: mhmm.
10. M: did someone bump you on the head?
11. M: who bumped you on the head?
12. C: Derek.
13. M: Derek?
14. M: what happened?
15. C: I was going to ran into his leg and um he hit me.
16. M: yeah?
17. M: with what?
18. M: what did he hit you with?
19. C: his leg.
20. M: his leg?
21. M: did it hurt?
22. C: mhmm.
23. M: yeah.
24. M: are you ok?
25. C: I was crying.
26. M: you were crying?

| | | |
|---|---|---|
| 27. M: | did somebody give you hugs and kisses? | |
| 28. C: | my daddy. | |
| 29. M: | your daddy? | |
| 30. M: | yeah? | |
| 31. M: | oh. | |
| 32. M: | where did he hit you ... in the head? | |
| 33. C: | mhmm. | |
| 34. M: | how does it ... feel today? | |
| 35. C: | good. | |
| 36. M: | yeah? | |
| 37. M: | it's all better? | |
| 38. C: | O. | |
| 39. M: | good. | |

In the interaction between Juanita and Isabel, the mother takes a rather passive role, allowing the child to direct the conversation and transmit information. She encourages her child to speak by using back-channeling devices, such as *aja* or *sí?*, and helps her retrieve information when the child is clearly searching for it (e.g., the name *Rosibel*), but she does not provide the elements or themes of the narrative. In this Latino interaction, we get the sense that mother and child are chatting, as Isabel says: "Platíqueme de ... " (*Chat with me about ...* ).

There is no apparent goal that mother and child are working toward except the social one of talking and sharing experiences. In addition, the conversation takes on a "gossipy tone" through Juanita's use of certain linguistic devices (highlighted in Turns 4, 6, and 8). For example, the use of a definite article such as *la* or *el* in front of a person's name is not part of standard dialect. It is often used to mark gossip or teasing in Latino communities.

Margaret, the Anglo American mother, by contrast, takes a more active role. She directs the conversation toward the goal of creating a classically structured narrative that is sequentially ordered around a climactic, main episode. She begins with questions about the time and place the main event occurred (yesterday, school); she follows with questions about the main event, or what could be considered the high-point of the story (getting hit on the head). She then concludes by asking Bridgie to evaluate the experience by talking about her feelings. Finally, the mother elicits the coda of the story: She brings the child back to the present by asking her how she feels today, (all better).

The cross-cultural differences in the mothers' styles of elicitation vary with the mothers' interpretations of the narrative task, and these interpretations reflect parental values found elsewhere in the culture (Melzi, 1997). Cross-cultural research on socialization has shown that whereas Latino mothers place a high value on social behavior and interpersonal relationships, Anglo American mothers tend to be more didactic, stressing independence and development of skills (Harwood,

Wilson, & Schulze, 1995). In responding to our request that they converse with their children, the Latino mothers focused on the social or interpersonal aspect of the task and appeared to be chatting with their children, with no expectation that the child produce a structured story. The Anglo American mothers focused more on the didactic aspect of the task, having a preconceived idea of what the child should produce.

## CONCLUSION

Labov and Waletzky provided us with a powerful insight into the nature of narrative. As they so accurately noted, the narrative allows the speaker to recount an experience and to tell an audience the personal meaning of that experience. Narrative structure is not, however, innate. Children acquire their ways of seeing the world and of interpreting events through interaction with the adults in their culture; here we have tried to show some of the cross-cultural differences in narrative that were revealed when we examined parent–child interaction among Latino, Anglo, and Gypsy families. Narrative can interpret the past and structure the present. It can also predict the future: As one Gypsy mother sang to her baby: "Sleep little baby sleep. When you grow up you will love many women, and leave them."

## REFERENCES

Ely, R., Gleason, J. B., Narasimhan, B., & McCabe, A. (1995). Family talk about talk: Mothers lead the way. *Discourse Processes, 19,* 201–218.

Harwood, R. L., Wilson, S. P., & Schulze, P. A. (1995, March). *Culture and class influences on Anglo and Puerto Rican mothers' long-term socialization goals and perceptions of child behavior.* Paper presented at the meeting of the Society for Research in Child Development, Indianapolis, IN.

Labov, W., & Waletzky, J. (this issue). Narrative analysis: Oral versions of personal experience. In J. Helm (Ed.), *Essays on the verbal and visual arts: Proceedings of the 1966 Annual Spring Meeting of the American Ethnological Society* (pp. 12–44). Seattle: University of Washington Press. (Original work published 1967)

Melzi, G. (1997). *Developing narrative voice: Conversations between Latino mothers and their preschool children.* Unpublished doctoral dissertation, Boston University, Boston.

Réger, Z., & Gleason, J. B. (1991) Romāni child directed speech and children's language among Gypsies in Hungary. *Language in Society, 20,* 601–617.

# Frog Stories From Four-Year-Olds: Individual Differences in the Expression of Referential and Evaluative Content

### Erika Hoff-Ginsberg
*Department of Psychology, Florida Atlantic University*

Narrative, according to Labov and Waletzky (1967/this issue; henceforth L&W), is "one method of recapitulating past experience by matching a verbal sequence of clauses to the sequence of events which actually occurred" (p. 20). However, the fundamental insight of L&W's paper is that a narrative that is only a recounting of past experience is not much of a narrative. Normally, narratives not only recapitulate a sequence of events, they also communicate the attitude of the narrator toward those events. That attitude, which narrators express by attributing thoughts and feelings to the participants in the events and by explicitly evaluating the events themselves, is what gives a narrative meaning. L&W labeled the recounting component of narrative its *referential content* and the component that reveals the attitude of the narrator its *evaluative content*.

This distinction between two components of narrative immediately raises questions for the developmental psychologist interested in narrative competence: How is the development of referential competence related to the development of evaluative competence—are they the same thing or are they separate, albeit contemporaneous, developments? Relatedly, what are the antecedents of these narrative skills, and do these skills have common antecedents, or do they depend on different prerequisite competencies or experiences?

I became interested in these questions in the course of pursuing a longitudinal study of language development in children from two different socioeconomic strata (SES). I had previously found that individual differences at 2 years in lexical

---

Requests for reprints should be sent to Erika Hoff-Ginsberg, Division of Science, College of Liberal Arts, 2912 College Avenue, Davie, FL 33314–7714. E-mail: ehoff@acc.fau.edu

development, grammatical development, and the development of conversational skill were related to the children's SES and birth order (Hoff-Ginsberg, 1997). I was interested in whether these factors also explained differences in the children's narrative skills at the age of 4½. Previous work on the development of referential and evaluative competencies in normal and in atypical populations provided coding systems for assessing children's narratives (Bamberg & Damrad-Frye, 1991; Berman, 1988; Reilly, Klima, & Bellugi, 1990), but there had not been previous investigations of individual differences in these competencies. The goals of my investigation were (a) to describe the range of variation in narrative competence within a typically developing sample of 4½-year-olds, (b) to ask how variation in referential and evaluative competence were related to each other, and (c) to search for sources of individual differences in children's SES, birth order, and gender.

## METHOD

### Participants

The children in this study were 40 monolingual English-speaking children living in the midwestern United States. All were within 2 weeks of their 4½-year-old birthday. Twenty came from high-SES homes in which both parents were college educated; 20 came from mid-SES homes in which both parents were high school educated. There were approximately equal numbers of first born and later born children and of boys and girls. (Additional detail on the background of these children is available in Hoff-Ginsberg, 1991, 1997.)

### Procedure

Narratives were elicited from each child by a female examiner who was familiar to the child and who visited each child at home. The children were shown the wordless picture book, *Frog, Where Are You?* by Mercer Mayer (1969). They first viewed the book silently with the examiner and then were asked to "tell the story." The children's stories were audiotaped and later transcribed.

### Measures

To assess the referential content of the children's "frog stories" we used Berman's (1988) coding system, which analyzes the plot of this story as containing six different essential, plot-advancing elements. The number of these plot elements mentioned was counted, yielding a score between 0 and 6 for each narrative.

To assess the evaluative content of the children's frog stories, we used a coding system developed by Reilly et al. (1990), based on L&W. The total frequency was counted for two kinds of evaluative or enhancing statements:

1. *Affective enhancers* such as expressions of emotional states ("he was mad"), sound effects ("splash"), and emphatic markers such as repetition ("and he looked and looked and looked").
2. *Social cognitive enhancers* such as expressions of the mental states of characters and mention of things not in the book but relevant to the motivation of the characters ("the frog wasn't there").

The length of each narrative was also measured—both in number of utterances and number of verb phrases. An utterance was defined as a grammatical sentence—or less, if pause and intonation contour indicated an utterance boundary. In long sequences of clauses conjoined with *and*, each clause was counted as an utterance.

## RESULTS

### Range of Individual Variation

There was substantial variability among the 40 children in terms of the length, the referential content, and the evaluative content of their stories. These data are presented in Table 1.

### Components of Individual Variation

Correlations were calculated between the measures of the referential and evaluative content to assess the relation between these two components of narrative quality. Because the measures of evaluative content were total frequencies of each category of enhancing statement, those measures were corrected for story length, as measured in verb phrases (VP). The intercorrelations among referential content (i.e., number of plot elements mentioned), evaluative content (i.e., number of affective enhancers/VP and number of cognitive enhancers/VP) and story length in utterances are presented in Table 2.

Three out of the six correlations calculated were statistically significant. Narratives that included more of the referential content of the story also were richer in affective and cognitive enhancers (as measured by density per verb phrase). The magnitude of these correlations indicates that approximately 10% of the variance in referential and evaluative content is shared. Put another way, although the referentially more complete narratives did tend to be the narratives that were also

### TABLE 1
### Range of Individual Variation in the Length and Content of Narratives

| Measure | Range |
|---|---|
| Length | 14–96 utterances |
|  | 0–82 verb phrases |
| Referential content | 0–6 plot elements mentioned |
| Evaluative content | 0–17 affective enhancers produced |
|  | 0–30 cognitive enhancers produced |

### TABLE 2
### Intercorrelations Among Measures of Children's Narratives

| Measure | 1 | 2 | 3 |
|---|---|---|---|
| 1. Length (in utterances) | | | |
| 2. Number of plot lines | .194 | | |
| 3. Affective enhancers/VP | .235 | .346** | |
| 4. Cognitive enhancers/VP | .165 | .279* | .313* |

*Note.* VP = verb phrases.
$*p < .05$, one-tailed. $**p < .01$, one-tailed.

richer in evaluative content, there was still substantial variation in evaluative content at a single level of referential completeness. None of the measures of referential or evaluative content was significantly related to narrative length, measured in utterances.

### Antecedents of Individual Variation

Analyses of SES, birth order, and gender revealed no significant associations with the referential content, the evaluative content, or the length of children's narratives.

## DISCUSSION

Our preliminary exploration of the referential and evaluative content of 4½-year-olds' frog stories yielded three main findings:

1. Within a typically developing group of children, all within 1 month of each other in age, there is enormous variability in the quality of the narratives they produce—both in terms of referential content and in terms of evaluative content.

2. About 10% of the variance in referential and evaluative content is shared, leaving 90% of variability in each unrelated to variability in the other.
3. This variability among typically developing 4½-year-olds in the quality of the narratives they produce is unrelated to their SES (within a relatively narrow range of SES), unrelated to their birth order, and unrelated to gender.

The conclusion these findings suggest is that there is variance in children's narrative development to explain, and we do not yet know how to explain it. Furthermore, the finding that story length was unrelated to quality in terms of content and that referential content and evaluative content were only moderately related to each other suggests that there may be separable prerequisites to producing extended discourse (measured here as story length), to telling a referentially complete story (measured here as number of plot elements mentioned), and to telling a story in which the attribution of mental states to the participants and the evaluation of the events gives the story meaning. Thirty years after its publication, L&W's description of the multiple components of adults' narratives remains a provocative call for researchers interested in narrative development.

## ACKNOWLEDGMENTS

An earlier version of this work was presented as a poster at the 1996 meetings of the International Society for the Study of Behavioral Development, Quebec City, Canada. This research was supported by NICHD Grant HD20936 and by a Spencer Foundation Small Grant to Erika Hoff-Ginsberg. I am grateful to Joyce Corsica, Sheri Reget, and Sheila Juers for their work in coding.

## REFERENCES

Bamberg, M., & Damrad-Frye, R. (1991). On the ability to provide evaluative comments: Further explorations of children's narrative competencies. *Journal of Child Language, 18,* 689–710.

Berman, R. A. (1988). On the ability to relate events in narrative. *Discourse Processes, 11,* 469–497.

Hoff-Ginsberg, E. (1991). Mother–child conversation in different social classes and communicative settings. *Child Development, 62,* 782–296.

Hoff-Ginsberg, E. (1997). *Differences in maternal speech and early language development associated with birth order and socioeconomic status: Implications for theories and for children.* Manuscript in preparation.

Labov, W., & Waletzky, J. (this issue). Narrative analysis: Oral versions of personal experience. In J. Helm (Ed.), *Essays on the verbal and visual arts: Proceedings of the 1966 Annual Spring Meeting of the American Ethnological Society* (pp. 12–44). Seattle: University of Washington Press. (Original work published 1967)

Mayer, M. (1969). *Frog, where are you?* New York: Dial.

Reilly, J., Klima, E. S., & Bellugi, U. (1990). Once more with feeling: Affect and language in atypical populations. *Development and Psychopathology, 2,* 367–391.

# How to Read the Work of Child Authors: A Tribute to Labov and Waletzky

### Susan Engel
*Department of Psychology, Bennington College*

When I first read Labov and Waletzky's article (1967/this issue) as a graduate student, I was thrilled. Here were researchers who showed that spoken stories had a linguistic structure replete with significance. They showed that these stories did something, psychologically speaking, for the people who told them and listened to them. The other thing that impressed me was their articulation of the vital yet still mysterious connection between the formal characteristics of accomplished narratives (great novels for instance) and the kinds of stories that unfold between ordinary people in everyday situations.

Much of my work has focused on identifying the emergence of narrative processes during the first 3 years of a child's life. What are those emerging narratives like, and what functions do they serve? When and how does narrative structure begin to shape our thoughts and interactions? I have found that still another developmental mystery lies in the transition between the informal and often fragmented narratives that occur between 2- to 6-year-olds and the adults and friends they talk with, and the more formal, often written, narratives of school-age children. These stories are not novels, nor the treasured oral histories of a community, and yet they do reflect cultural norms. They are often more fully or conventionally formed than those of younger narrative speakers. What should we make of these first attempts at nonconversational stories? Are they a stepping stone between the narrative germs embedded in the talk of parents and their toddlers and the novels of an adult writer?

In this article I will share one story with you and suggest some of the ways it might be analyzed. I chose it for three reasons, and I will take a moment to explain the reasons because they embody my thesis for this article.

---

Requests for reprints should be sent to Susan Engel, Department of Psychology, Bennington College, RD 2, Box 178A, Great Barrington, MA 01230. E-mail = sengel@williams.edu

First of all, as you will see, the story is surprising and gripping. As Feldman (Feldman & Kalmar, in press) and her colleagues pointed out so articulately, in our effort to gain scientific clarity, it is essential not to forget that, at heart, stories must be aesthetically dense and filled with the human drama that makes them worth studying in the first place. Feldman and her colleagues use published stories that are writerly, rather than the often dull and arid stories psychologists construct as stimuli to use in their studies. This is as important for the stories we elicit as it is for those we read or show to our subjects. Labov and Waletzky demonstrated the importance of the dramatic substance of narratives by asking people to tell stories of situations in which they faced danger. My strong hunch is that when researchers opt for using simplified generic stories for the purpose of experimental control and clarity, they lose much hope of illuminating the phenomena that led them to narrative research in the first place. By the same token, when looking at the stories people produce, we need to take the drama and aesthetic of the work as seriously as we do the logic or conventional well-formedness of the story.

The second reason for using this particular story is that it shows that meaning drives structure. The emotional force of what the author is trying to convey underlies the literary devices that are employed. This is particularly relevant when you are talking about a child author, who, as I have claimed elsewhere (Engel, 1995) reinvents stylistic techniques in order to serve her communicative, ideational, and emotional purposes.

The third reason for using this story is that it shows that, for young as well as adult authors, the line between fiction and autobiography is a wavery one at best and that the evaluation that may be explicit in a self-proclaimed autobiographical work is often powerful, but none the less hidden, in the drama of an autobiographical worked disguised as fiction. I hope each of these points will become clearer as I discuss the story itself.

The story was written by a White, middle-class, 9-year-old girl named Ella. She lives with her mother, father, and a younger sister named Justine, in a rural area 100 miles east of New York City. Though written during the school day, it was not in response to any particular assignment. Her parents have both visited countries at war, but no one in the family has been to Vietnam. Though filled with the usual dramas of childhood, Ella has led a fairly protected life. As you will see, these details of her life are important in figuring out what to make of her story. The spelling has been corrected in transcription.

> *I am Ella from Vietnam. I am in the war. The Americans are attacking us Vietnamese people. I am spying on my sister who is from the U.S. She is in the army too. Sergeant Knuckles is sending me in. Oh I have two Americans on my tail. Good I killed them. Here is a medical Doctor taking care of some of our hurt people. It is very dangerous. I just got a foot away from my sister who is known as one of the best fighters in America she is also my evilest*

*sister. I am so glad to be in my tent once again. And to be writing my Mom and Dad a letter. Just so you know my sister would never write a letter to Mom and Dad only I would. Except she would if it was mean.*

> *Dear Mom and Dad*
> *I miss you very much, and I know that you worry about me but there is nothing to worry about because with Sargent Knuckle by my side I will never even have to worry. I love you.*
> *Signed*
> *Ella*

*There goes a gun shot. I better track down my sister. Wake up Knuckle, wake up. But he wasn't there, he left a note saying he was by the pond so I ran over there as fast as I could. And there he was laying down dead. Oh no he couldn't be dead. But he was. It is the army so I have to leave him and track down my sister. O.K. back to my journey. I hear my sister. I will find her. But first write a letter to my Mom and Dad.*

> *Dear Mom and Dad,*
> *Sargent Knuckle died by don't worry I will be fine.*
> *I love you.*
> *Love Ella*

*I am tracking my sister down there she is. I am Justine, my sister is Ella and I just shot her now she is dead.*

> *Dear Mom and Dad*
> *I just killed Ella so too bad. I know when you get this letter you will cry your sorry little butts off but too bad. I hate you.*
> *From Justine*

One might begin by identifying the basic elements of this story—the external landscape:

A Vietnamese girl is in the war and writing to her parents.
She is protected by a good and strong man, Sargent Knuckles.
Her sister is her enemy.
The protector, Knuckles, is killed.
The Vietnamese girl continues to write to her parents.
She has a confrontation with her enemy sister.
She is killed by the sister.
The sister gets her revenge.

At the most basic level this story meets narrative criteria. It has a protagonist, action, a theme, and a problem that gets resolved. This simple analysis also shows that this 9-year-old author employs multidetermined narrative devices. What do I mean? The letter writing is both part of the action (the external landscape) and a literary device that expresses the internal landscape of the story, the conflict between two sisters.

Let me try to say this another way. The theme of the story concerns sibling rivalry (in its most epic proportions). However, there is more. The story also explores the dilemma of how it is that two people can be totally opposed and yet still both have points of view. This is a fundamental psychological problem for all of us: How is it two people can experience the same event so differently and yet simultaneously? In Ella's story this theme is not only conveyed through the facts and events of the story (two sisters on opposite sides of a war, fighting one another) but it is also conveyed through the literary structure itself: letters that switch in narrative voice. The structure serves to express or explore the theme, but also creates the dramatic tension of the story. Ella has invented a narrative form that expresses her emotional and cognitive meanings.

Among her other literary devices, the young author employs three kinds of narrative shifts to create emotional impact on her reader and to develop the themes of her story. In the second paragraph, in which Knuckles is killed, the narrative switches from running commentary to past tense four times. The author switches between narrative description and epistolary form five times. Finally, at the end there is a dramatic switch in narrative voice from Ella to Justine. In addition to these narrative shifts there are two styles of narration in the story: action ("there are two Americans on my tail") and characterization ("my sister would never write a letter to my parents"). Among the other things these shifts achieve, they create constant tension in the relationship between narrator and reader. This technique can be seen in its most brilliant form in the work of Herman Melville (Bruner, 1996).

Stylistically and emotionally, this story is jam-packed. That is the point: the two often go together. If we are ever to understand how the earliest conversational stories do and don't lead to written stories and literature, we need to keep one eye on the connections between the formal and logical characteristics and the emotional and aesthetic force of stories. The most fruitful stories to study are not the neatest but the messiest (complex) ones.

What and where in this story is the comment or evaluation that Labov and Waletzky told us is an essential characteristic of a narrative? How should the reader take it? Well, like most good stories it is dense with significance. At the most obvious level it is a story of intense sibling rivalry. It also reminds us that the most intimate and commonplace emotions are often more effectively rendered for a listener when they are played out in an exotic dramatic setting (for this storyteller and her listeners, fighters in Vietnam are one such dramatic setting). The comment is contained within the denouement of this story. As Labov and Waletsky pointed out, the comment or evaluation tells you what to make of the story and gives significance to the temporal description of action. As E. M. Forster (1927) wrote in *Aspects of the Novel*, temporal sequence on its own does not a story make:

> When we isolate the story like this from the nobler aspects through which it moves, and hold it out on the forceps,—wriggling and interminable, the naked worm of time—it presents an appearance that is both unlovely and dull. (p. 28)

In order to understand a cryptic or embedded comment, the analyst must also be a genuine reader, ready to interpret. My interpretation of the comment is that evil is stronger than good, and heroes suffer.

The evaluation in this story is not presented as a directive, nor is it contained in any one sentence. The comment cannot be isolated and lifted out of the text per se, but instead can only be discovered through the act of interpretation. This is the case with most good writing. The evaluation is embedded within the narrative and is experienced over time by a reader or listener.

This last point brings me to one of the most interesting and underdeveloped avenues of further exploration. Labov and Waletzky laid out the importance of understanding that stories serve social purposes and that they must be interpreted in the context of their social functions. Coming at this from a different angle, Austin's (1962) and Searle's (1970) work can be extended to show that not only words do things, stories do things as well. In fact, a story can be understood in terms of its illocutionary and its perlocutionary effect.

Miller's work on children's conversational stories in family settings shows that when children tells stories they not only revive whatever emotion they felt at the time of a given event, they evoke emotions in their listeners (Miller, Mintz, Hoogstra, Fong, & Potts, 1992). The structure of a text (spoken or written) can be unearthed and identified, but a story's effect on a listener also has a great deal to tell us. We learn not only about the listener, but about the story and its author as well. Take Ella's story for example. Another way to take the story would be to analyze its effect on a listener. In other words, analyze the narrative structure through the listeners' ears. What do other children hear when they hear a story like this? How does their representation differ from that of the adult listener? Just as we question the use of knowledge about an author in interpreting a particular novel, we might ask the same of young children's stories. How does knowledge of the child affect our reading of her story? In all of these questions, the idea that stories are a form of social interaction is fundamental.

In sum, Ella's story reminds us that young children invent literary devices in the service of conveying important material. Children need to talk and write about things that matter to them. Death, jealousy, greed, love, and passion are as vital to a child's story as they are to the works of adult authors. In order to do empirical and theoretical justice to the richness of children's narratives, we have got to get hold of the stories they most want to tell and the audiences to whom they most want to tell them.

Labov and Waletzky argued that we needed to find the lines of continuity between the casual and spontaneous stories people tell one another in every day settings and the stories that are preserved, in writing or orally, as exemplars of a community or culture. In the last 15 years or so, it has become apparent that of equally consuming interest are the lines that connect the first fragments of stories shared by some toddlers and their parents, the written and spoken stories of the ordinary adult, and the revered stories of accomplished authors or tellers.

## REFERENCES

Austin, J. L. (1962). *How to do things with words.* New York: Oxford University Press.

Bruner, J. (1996). Unpublished lecture to the Colloquium on Legal Interpretation and the Theory of Practice, New York University School of Law, New York.

Engel, S. (1995). *The stories children tell.* New York: Freeman.

Feldman, C., & Kalmar, D. (in press). Autobiography and fiction as modes of thought. In D. Olson & N. Torrence (Eds), *Modes of thoughts: Explorations in culture and cognition.* Cambridge, England: Cambridge University Press.

Forster, E. M. (1927). *Aspects of the novel.* New York: Harcourt Brace.

Labov, W., & Waletzky, J. (this issue). Narrative analysis: Oral versions of personal experience. In J. Helm (Ed.), *Essays on the verbal and visual arts: Proceedings of the 1966 Annual Spring Meeting of the American Ethnological Society* (pp. 12–44). Seattle: University of Washington Press. (Original work published 1967)

Miller, P., Mintz, J., Hoogstra, L., Fong, H., & Potts, R. (1992) The narrated self: Young children's construction of self in relation to others in conversational stories of personal experience. *Merrill–Palmer Quarterly, 38*, 45–67.

Searle, J. (1970). *Speech acts.* Cambridge, England: Cambridge University Press.

# Narrative Theory and Narrative Development: The Labovian Impact

### Ruth A. Berman
*Department of Linguistics, Tel Aviv University*

It is a pleasure for me to join in honoring the contribution of William Labov to the emergence of narrative as a field of study for linguists. In personal terms, this homage takes me back over 30 years, when we shared graduate classes at Columbia University, and Bill interviewed me for his sociolinguistic research on pronunciation. Academically, Labov and Waletzky's (1967/this issue; henceforth L&W) seminal work on oral narratives has exerted a profound influence on my thinking about the relation between narrative theory and narrative development, a field I came to almost by accident some 10 years ago, when Dan Slobin and I decided to embed our study of the development of temporality in different languages in the discourse context of the picture-storybook, *Frog, Where Are You?* (Bamberg, 1987; Berman & Slobin, 1994). Since then, Labov's ideas on the nature of narrative discourse have been at the core of much of my work, as well as that of my students and colleagues.

One major reason for this impact is suggested right at the outset of L&W's pioneering paper. They start by explicitly stating that "the analysis will be *formal*" and "the analysis is *functional*." Analysis of linguistic form–narrative function interrelations was a crucial motivation for our study of how children and adults relate the events presented in a picture storybook in different languages. This orientation to narrative analysis is at the core of my own work on narrative development in Hebrew, as summed up in Berman (1995), concerning: tense–aspect and connectivity (Berman, 1988), null subjects (Berman, 1990), verbalized perspectives on a scene (Berman, 1993), uses of the form *and* (Berman, 1996a), expression of "setting" elements—L&W's "orientation"—(Berman, 1996b), reference to characters in a picture-series (Berman & Katzenberger, in press), and narrative clause-linkage in different languages (Berman, 1997).

---

Requests for reprints should be sent to Ruth Berman, Department of Linguistics, Tel Aviv University, Gilman Building, Ramat Aviv, Tel Aviv 69978, Israel. E-mail: rberman@post.tau.ac.il

The form–function approach to narrative analysis pioneered by L&W has clearly proved broadly generalizable. It has been effectively extended from personal-experience accounts to other narrative genres and elicitation settings, from Black English to other languages, and from older children and adults to preschoolers. This article starts with a survey of the developmental research inspired by Labov's work, specifically in the domain of *evaluation,* ending with a suggestion for how narrative theory might be adapted to characterize the course of narrative development.

## STUDIES OF NARRATIVE DEVELOPMENT

Labov's ideas have had a crucial impact on a range of studies on children's developing narrative abilities. Foremost among these is the "high-point" analysis applied in Peterson & McCabe's (1983) large-scale study of children's personal-experience narratives. Other studies have shown that the ability to relate to a high-point and to proceed with formulating a resolution and sometimes a coda, too, has proved to be an important criterion of children's narrative abilities in different contexts and elicitation settings. The topic focused on here is the role of what L&W was the first to identify as evaluative elements in narrative discourse.

Labov (1972) explicitly noted the developmental relevance of narrative evaluation as follows: "An unexpected result of the comparison [of evaluative elements] across age levels [preadolescents aged 9 to 13 years, adolescents aged 14 to 19, and adults] is that the use of many syntactic devices for evaluation does not develop until late in life, rising geometrically from preadolescents to adolescents to adults" (p. 355). This echoes a central theme of the work of Dan Slobin and our colleagues (cf. Berman & Slobin, 1994) on the development of narrative form–function relations, as well as in the analyses of Maya Hickmann (Hickmann, 1995) in regard to the expression of reference: Many linguistic forms are early to emerge, but the ability to deploy a full range of rhetorical options, and to integrate them appropriately to meet a range of narrative functions, has a long developmental history, often lasting through to adulthood. Furthermore, the challenge implied by Labov's developmental observation has been taken up in a range of studies on the role of evaluation in developing narrative abilities among children from as young as 2 years old (Miller & Sperry, 1988).

Taking Labov's ideas as a starting point, researchers on children's narratives have devised various schemes for analyzing evaluative elements at different developmental phases. In the course of their high-point analysis of personal-experience accounts from children aged 3 to 10 years, Peterson and McCabe (1983) isolated 21 types of evaluation, reorganized here into seven groups: (a) *Interactive elements:* attention-getters like "Listen to this" and expression of narrator affect like "I hate people like that"; (b) *Prosodic devices:* for example, onomatopoeia, emphatic stress, vowel elongation; (c) *Rhetorical devices:* for example, exclamation, repetition, similes, and other metaphors; (d) *Lexical devices:* for example, intensifiers (including "gratuitous terms" like *very, just, really*) and evaluative modifiers like *ugly, exciting, accidentally;* (e) *Irrealis modality:* for example, expression of hopes, desires, and intentions, of hypotheses and inferences, and negation; (f) *Causal elements:* motivations for character's actions and results of narrative events; and (g) *Internal states:* cognitive and affective states attributed to the protagonist(s). They found clear developmental differences in how much children favored some types of evaluators, for example, gratuitous terms and stressors. Although overall incidence of evaluation did not change with age, older children used a larger variety of such devices (p. 59).

Narrative evaluation has also been analyzed for the "frog story" picture book narratives. Building on Labov's (1972) distinction between external and internal evaluation, Bamberg and Damrad-Frye (1991) identified five lexical categories of "evaluative commentary" for stories told by 5-year-old, 9-year-old, and adult speakers of American English: (a) *Frames of mind:* reference to affective or cognitive states, for example, *scared, thinking;* (b) *Character speech:* direct or reported speech quoting from or attributed to characters in the story; (c) *Hedges:* distancing devices that lessen narrator commitment to a proposition, for example, *kind of, probably;* (d) *Negative qualifiers:* for example, *not, un-* ; and (e) *Causal connectors:* items that relate two or more clauses causally, for example, *because, so.* They found that adults used significantly more evaluative devices than 5- and 9-year-olds and the latter more than younger children. Only 9-year-olds and adults made wide use of reference to frames of mind (similar to the Berman & Slobin, 1994, English and Hebrew frog story texts; pp. 73–82), but for the children this was typically confined to a local level, whereas among adults evaluative devices served a global narrative function.

Reilly (1992) added paralinguistic dimensions to her analysis of frog stories told by other groups of American English-speaking children aged 3 to 11 years, identifying six types of "affective expression": (a) *Characterization or quoted speech:* narrator speaks in the role of a character; (b) *Evaluative comments:* affective and cognitive states and character traits attributed to a character; (c) *Facial expression:* for example, a smile or frown; (d) *Gestures:* relating to a particular utterance; (e) *Prosodic features:* pitch, length, volume, and voice quality; and (f) *Lexical-phonological stress.* Reilly found a clear advance with age in reliance on explicitly linguistic devices for expression of affect and other evaluative elements. Bamberg and Reilly (1996) proposed a synthesis between these two descriptive frameworks, with evaluative comments, including narrator attribution of emotions or mental states to the characters and evaluation of the character's actions from the narrator's point of view. They found that even young children use affective expressions, but with age this ability undergoes reconstruction from a local to a global level of organization; ultimately reference to emotions and the expression of affect serve "to orient the audience in a more integrated fashion toward the story and its narrator as a unit" (Bamberg & Reilly, p. 335).

These findings combine to show that the ability to flesh out narrative events with evaluative commentary develops with age both qualitatively and quantitatively. As Labov (1972) indicated, adolescents and adults are better able to deploy a variety of syntactic and other linguistic devices for evaluation. Developmental research further shows that, with time, children acquire the cognitive ability to adopt a narrator stance, which includes both attributing motivations to characters and expressing their own attitudes to and evaluation of the events described in their narrations. Moreover, these developments are consistent across different elicitation procedures. For example, Katzenberger's (1994) analysis of texts produced by 4- to 6-year-olds, 10-year-olds, and adults based on short picture series revealed that only the adults provided some elements of evaluation. In longer texts, however, older children as well as adults embed their evaluative comments within a hierarchically organized, global "action structure," rather than confining them to the linear, local level of narrative organization (Berman, 1995; Shen & Berman, 1996).

Another group of largely unpublished studies revealed that evaluation provides an important criterion of children's storytelling abilities not only across time but across populations. One such factor is cultural background. For example, Küntay and Nakamura's (1993) analysis of frog story texts in Turkish and Japanese revealed that children in these cultures avoided making explicit reference to the psychological or mental states of the characters. This contrasts with the findings of Bamberg and Damrad-Frye (1991) and of Berman and Slobin (1994) for the category of frames of mind in the frog story narratives of English- and Hebrew-speaking children. The Küntay and Nakamura study also suggested gender differences, with girls seeming to become more engaged in the task, producing longer, more elaborate stories. This is confirmed by findings of Hebrew-language studies. Ten-year-olds and adults asked to make up a story about "a dream that came true" revealed no significant sex differences for overall amount of evaluation, but they did differ in type of evaluation: Girls and women referred to more characters, and they used significantly more intensifiers and affective expressions than the boys and men, but not more reference to nonaffective cognitive states. An analysis of stories written by 4th-graders about an imaginary trip showed that the girls' stories were three times longer on the average than those of the boys, and they contained a much higher proportion of evaluative elements and a wider variety of such elements. Other studies indicate that use of evaluative devices also differentiates between the stories produced by children from different socioeconomic backgrounds.

These studies suggested that narrative abilities could be extended to compare not only developmental phases, but also genders, text types, and populations of different sociocultural background across three interrelated dimensions: (a) *overall narrative structure:* the narrative components defined by L&W as abstract, orientation, complicating action, result or resolution, and coda; (b) *narrative quality:* storytelling skills defined by amount, type, and location of evaluative elements;

and (c) *narrative syntax:* forms of linguistic expression used in producing a coherent and cohesive text.

## A PROPOSAL FOR INTEGRATING EVALUATION WITH NARRATIVE STRUCTURE AND CONTENT

The studies reviewed in the previous section indicate that researchers have expressed a need for refining categories of evaluation beyond Labov's original insights. My proposal in this connection is twofold: first, to distinguish between evaluative form and function by a tripartite distinction between linguistic form, semantic content, and narrative function; and second, to divide narrative components into three types of elements: eventive, attitudinal-evaluative, and factual-informative.

### Categories of Evaluation

A problem common to the various classifications of kinds of evaluative elements is their tendency to confuse form–function criteria. Thus Reinhart (1984, 1995) rightly notes that Labov's criteria are syntactic-structural rather than semantic-contentive. Her proposals suggest the need for a clear distinction between linguistic form, semantic content, and narrative or textual functions. In my interpretations, "form" refers to linguistic and paralinguistic devices used to express semantic content and to perform narrative functions, the full range of what Berman and Slobin (1994) defined as "expressive options." Linguistic devices include affixes and clitics, closed and open class lexical items, set expressions, syntactic constructions (e.g., relative clauses, passive voice), and syntactic operations (e.g., word order changes, elision). Paralinguistic devices include facial expressions, gestures, and prosodic elements such as stress and intonation. The heading of form would thus cover Labov's (1972) four subtypes of internal evaluation, Peterson and McCabe's (1983) prosodic and rhetorical devices, Bamberg and Damrad-Frye's (1991) character speech and negative qualifiers, and Reilly's (1992) six types of devices for affective expression. *Semantic content* refers to the referential import of these different forms and includes: stative predicates versus activities and events, with internal states subdivided into affect, cognition, and perception; physical attributes *(tall, purple)* and internal states *(hungry, tired)* as well as traditionally evaluative descriptions *(nice, helpful);* comparisons between objects and events; modality, and other classes of irrealis reference like negation or generic aspect; and semantic categories of predicate modification such as causatives, manner, and degree. *Narrative* or *Discourse functions* refer to the purposes fulfilled by forms that carry these different meanings in a given text along several interrelated dimensions.

These include rhetorical functions in expressing relations between parts of a text; story-embedded functions in attributing qualities, motivations, states of mind and feeling to the characters and situations in the narrative; and communicative functions in expressing the narrator's stance and attitude to the characters and events in the story and relating explicitly to the audience.

Some classes of expression will cut across categories. For example, repetition seems an important evaluative device, one which subsumes formal linguistic repetition of identical elements, syntactic parallelism, and semantic correspondences. Reinhart (1995) noted all of these as important means of fleshing out the narrative skeleton in both literary texts and personal experience accounts. Analysis of frog story texts of different age groups shows that repetition follows a distinct developmental path: Initially it marks online disfluencies or local-level intensification; later it has the role of a global-level rhetorical device (Berman, 1987). Detailed analysis of evaluative elements along these different dimensions is beyond the scope of this article, but noting these distinctions should serve to highlight the complex array of factors involved in narrative evaluation.

### Elements of Narrative Structure and Content

Reinhart (1984, 1995) proposed a further elaboration of the Labovian distinction between narrative-referential clauses and evaluative elements. For her, both informative background and Labov's (1972) evaluative elements constitute the nonnarrative, atemporal material that creates the background elements of a narrative text. Evaluation gives a story its "meaning" by specifying the status of the information conveyed in the story and defining how the story is to be interpreted, whereas narrative or referential elements simply convey a sequence of events. Along these lines, I propose the following tripartite analysis of narrative texts.

1. Narrative clauses: Sequential elements or eventives correspond to Labov's referential clauses and describe events in temporally ordered clauses;
2. Evaluative elements: Interpretive elements or "attitudinals" reflect the narrator's perspective on and subjective interpretation of events;
3. Informative elements: Descriptive elements or "factuals" provide information about the external or physical circumstances in which events take place.

The label *eventive* focuses on the dynamic facet of Labov's narrative elements. These eventive elements are typically expressed propositionally in clauses, each of which constitutes a distinct, unified prediction (Berman & Slobin, 1994, pp. 6, 660–663), and they share certain properties across narrative genres. First, they represent the chain of events that constitute the story's "plotline" (Berman & Slobin, 1994, pp. 44–51) and serve to report what happens as the story unfolds. Second, these propositions are related by ties of temporal sequentiality and follow one another along the time axis, in an order that corresponds to how the events occurred. Narrative elements are thus bound by the constraint of temporal ordering and so meet Reinhart's (1984) criterion of "narrativity" or temporal continuity for foreground material. Third, the other, nonnarrative elements are mainly stative rather than dynamic or active, related by ties of nohtemporal contingencies such as cause, purpose, or concession and by nonsequential temporal relations like simultaneity, in which events cooccur in time, or retrospection, wherein clause-sequence is counter to order of events.

Evaluative elements, in contrast, present the narrator's interpretation of these events. They include the narrators' subjective commentary on their attitude towards the events they are reporting and on how they assume the protagonists relate to these events in terms of the motivations, emotions, and mental states that narrators attribute to these protagonists.

Factives are informative or descriptive elements that differ from both sequential eventives and evaluative attitudinals. They provide additional factual information about the characters and circumstances within which events take place and as such are included partly under the heading of evaluation in Labov's analyses. They take account of Reinhart's proposal for a distinct category of informative background, which together with evaluative material constitute what she defined as the background component of narrative texts. Informative elements describe physical or material attributes of the characters and locative or temporal properties of events. Like evaluative material, they do not add new events to the plotline chain of events; unlike evaluation, these descriptive elements are factual, rather than inferential or attitudinal. They occur most typically in the setting or orientation openings to narratives, and they include the when, where, and who (but not the why) of any narrative. Developmentally motivated analyses of very young children (Peterson, 1990) and among older children and adults (Berman, 1996b) show that these elements emerge relatively late.

In sum, narrative clauses constitute the action structure in which events are sequentially organized from the initial enabling event through to its resolution (Giora & Shen, 1994); evaluative elements reflect the perspective of the narrator and of the characters on events; and informative or descriptive elements take into account what the addressee might want to know or needs to know. This three-way division of narrative elements allows us to construct an integrated framework for analyzing narrative structure and its development, incorporating two distinct dimensions: the different constituents of narrative structure as proposed by various structural analyses since the 1970s (e.g, Mandler, 1982; Rumelhart, 1975; Shen, 1989) and how these are realized in different categories of narrative content, as first proposed by Labov (1972) and extended here. This framework is set out here (a plus in parentheses "(+)" stands for optional elements, and a slash "/" stands for elements that may but need not cooccur, indicating that particular structural components either must or may be expressed by one or more of these three categories):

| Constituents of Narrative Structure | Categories of Narrative Content |
| --- | --- |
| Orientation [=setting] | Information (+ Evaluation) |
| Initiating Event | Narrative Clause/s |
| Episode(s) [=attempts; complicating action] | Narrative Clause/s (+Eval/Info) |
| Resolution [=outcome] | Narrative Clause/s (+Eval/Info) |
| Coda [=wrap-up] | Eval (+Info) |

In developmental perspective, each of the three narrative functions noted here reflects specific types of cognitive abilities: (a) knowledge of sequentiality—for the construction of temporally ordered narrative clauses and developing action structure; (b) consideration of audience knowledge—in order to provide listeners with necessary background information and descriptive elements; and (c) the ability to give expression to narrator and character perspective—fleshing out the narrative with evaluative interpretation. That is, in acquiring narrative knowledge, children need to gain command of the structural elements that make up the plotline events and actions, and they need to learn to embed these events and actions in a network of informative description and evaluative commentary as part of telling a "good" story (Reilly, 1992). Second, in producing a narrative text, children must not only do what Bruner (1986) defined as constructing two landscapes simultaneously—both "a landscape of action," in which the constituents are the arguments of action and a "landscape of consciousness," relating to what those involved in the action know, think, or feel (p. 14). They must also, and simultaneously, integrate all the diverse facets of narrative structure and narrative content in realtime, online processing. Ultimately, they need to integrate the use of appropriate linguistic forms to meet the three narrative functions of eventivity, interpretation, and informativeness. The task of mapping various linguistic forms to a given discourse function and concurrently employing these same linguistic forms to meet a range of discourse functions constitutes a heavy cognitive load for children, and so the integration of linguistic form–discourse function is a lengthy process.

The challenge to research on narrative development emerging from Labov's ideas on narrative theory is to characterize how these different abilities interact and realign across time among children of different ages and from different sociocultural and linguistic backgrounds.

## ACKNOWLEDGMENTS

I am grateful to Yeshayahu "Shayke" Shen for his helpful comments, and to Judy Reilly for her important input on narrative development. Errors and inadequacies are mine alone.

## REFERENCES

Bamberg, M. (1987). *The acquisition of narrative: Learning to use language*. Berlin: Mouton.
Bamberg, M., & Damrad-Frye, R. (1991). On the ability to provide evaluative comments: Further of children's narrative competencies. *Journal of Child Language, 18,* 689–710.
Bamberg, M., & Reilly, J. S. (1996). Emotion, narrative, and affect: How children discover the between what to say and how to say it. In D. Slobin, J. Gerhardt, A. Kyratzis, & J. Guo (Eds.), *Social interaction, social context, and language* (pp. 329–342). Mahwah: NJ: Lawrence Erlbaum Associates, Inc.
Berman, R. A. (1987). *Repetition and recurrence in the Hebrew "frog story."* Unpublished manuscript, University of California, Berkeley.
Berman, R. A. (1988). On the ability to relate events in narrative. *Discourse Processes, 11,* 469–497.
Berman, R. A. (1990). Acquiring an (S)VO language: Subjectless sentences in children's Hebrew. *Linguistics, 28,* 1135–1166.
Berman, R. A. (1993). The development of language use: Expressing perspectives on a scene. In E. Dromi (Ed.), *Language and cognition: A developmental perspective* (pp. 172–201). Norwood, NJ: Ablex.
Berman, R. A. (1995). Narrative competence and storytelling performance: How children tell stories in different contexts. *Journal of Narrative and Life History, 5,* 285–313.
Berman, R. A. (1996a). Form and function in developing narrative skills. In D. Slobin, J. Gerhardt, A. Kyratzis, & J. Guo (Eds.), *Social interaction, social context, and language* (pp. 343–367). Mahwah, NJ: Lawrence Erlbaum Associates, Inc.
Berman, R. A. (1996b, July). *Setting the narrative scene: How children begin to tell a story.* Plenary Lecture, VIIth International Association for the Study of Child Language, Istanbul, Turkey.
Berman, R. A. (1997). Typological perspectives on connectivity. In Z. Penner & N. Dittmar (Eds.), *Erst- und Zweitsprachenerwerb* [First and second language acquisition]. Bern, Germany: Peter Lang Ag.
Berman, R. A., & Katzenberger, I. (in press). Cognitive and linguistic factors in the development of picture-series narration. In A. G. Ramat & M. Chini (Eds.), *Organization of learners' texts: SILTA.*
Berman, R. A., & Slobin, D. I. (1994). *Relating events in narrative: A crosslinguistic developmental study.* Hillsdale, NJ: Lawrence Erlbaum Associates, Inc.
Bruner, J. (1986). *Actual minds, possible worlds.* Cambridge, MA: Harvard University Press.
Giora, R., & Shen, Y. (1994). Degrees of narrativity and strategies of semantic reduction. *Poetics, 22,* 447–458.
Hickmann, M. (1995). Discourse organization and the development of reference to person, space, and time. In P. Fletcher & B. MacWhinney (Eds.), *The handbook of child language* (pp. 194–218). Oxford, England: Basil Blackwell.

Katzenberger, I. (1994). *Hayexolet lesaper sipur al pi sidrat tmunot: Hebetim kognitiviyim, leshoniyim vehitpatxutiyim* [Cognitive, linguistic, and developmental factors in the narration of picture-series]. Unpublished doctoral dissertation, Tel Aviv University, Tel Aviv, Israel.

Küntay, A., & Nakamura, K. (1993, July). Evaluative strategies in monological Japanese and Turkish narratives. Paper given at VIth International Congress for the Study of Child Language, Trieste, Italy.

Labov, W. (1972). *Language in the inner city.* Philadelphia: University of Pennsylvania Press.

Labov, W., & Waletzky, J. (this issue). Narrative analysis: Oral versions of personal experience. In J. Helm (Ed.), *Essays on the verbal and visual arts: Proceedings of the 1966 Annual Spring Meeting of the American Ethnological Society* (pp. 12–44). Seattle: University of Washington Press. (Original work published 1967)

Mandler, J. (1982). Some uses and abuses of a story grammar. *Discourse Processes, 5,* 305–318.

Miller, P. J., & Sperry, L.L. (1988). Early talk about the past: Origins of conversational stories of personal experience. *Journal of Child Language, 15,* 293–315.

Peterson, C. (1990). The who, when, and where of early narratives. *Journal of Child Language, 17,* 433–455.

Peterson, C., & McCabe, A. (1983). *Developmental psycholinguistics: Three ways of looking at a narrative.* New York: Plenum.

Reilly, J. S. (1992). How to tell a good story: The intersect of language and affect in children's narratives. *Journal of Narrative and Life History, 2,* 355–377.

Reinhart, T. (1984). Principles of gestalt perception in the temporal organization of narrative texts. *Linguistics, 22,* 779–809.

Reinhart, T. (1995). Mi-tekst le-mashma'ut: Emtsa'ey haha'araxa [From text to meaning: Strategies of evaluation]. In Y. Shen (Ed.), *Hebetim kognitiviyim shel mivne hanarativ* (pp. 4–37). Tel Aviv, Israel: Tel Aviv University, The Porter Institute.

Rumelhart, D. E. (1975). Notes on a schema for stories. In D. G. Bobrow & A. Collins (Eds.), *Representation and understanding: Studies in cognitive science.* New York: Academic.

Shen, Y. (1989). The X-Bar grammar for stories: Story grammar revisited. *Text, 9,* 415–467.

Shen, Y., & Berman, R. A. (1996). Me-ha'irua habobed lemivne hape'ula: Shlabim behitpatxut hanaravit [From isolated event to action structure: Phases in narrative development]. In Y. Shimron (Ed.), *Psycholinguistic studies in Hebrew: Language acquisition, reading, and writing.* Jerusalem: Magness.

# Narrative Units and the Temporal Organization of Ordinary Discourse

### Björn Wiemer
*Department of Linguistics, Universität Konstanz*

In their famous paper, Labov and Waletzky (1967/this issue; henceforth L&W) coined the term *narrative units* (sentences), which "recapitulate experience in the same order as the original events." Beforehand, they made it clear that "narrative will be considered as one verbal technique for recapitulating experience, in particular, a technique of constructing narrative units which match the temporal sequence of that experience." Since that time, discussions have not stopped as to defining what counts as narrative discourse and what is but an artificial "surrogate" of it. L&W formed the basis for investigations into narratives of "ordinary life" (cf. Gülich & Quasthoff, 1985, for an overview). However, it seems that, first, narrative discourse is a gradable phenomenon that also pertains to more "artificial" genres like renarrations of picture stories, in which the plot to be related is already given, as well as to (pretended or real) personal letters and similar kinds of written communication. Units of narrative sentences are not dependent on factors like involvement,[1] because they are inherent in any coherent piece of monologic discourse. Secondly, the temporal structure of narrative-like discourse, as belonging to its referential level, demands further scrutiny with regard to specific classes of linguistic paradigms and lexemes.

In this article I want to show how L&W's definition of narrative unit fits into some recent work on the temporal organization of narratives or narrative-like discourse (both written and oral) in Polish and German. For this purpose I wish to give a very brief summary of some empirical results that cast light on aspects of narratives that have remained rather unnoticed, though they, by and large, corroborate L&W's findings.[2]

---

Requests for reprints should be sent to Björn Wiemer, Universität Konstanz, FG Sprachwissenschaft-Slavistik, Postfach 55 60, D 179, D-78457 Konstanz, Germany. E-mail: bjoern.wiemer@uni-konstanz.de

[1] For this term see Tannen, 1982.
[2] The data derive from my own research (Wiemer, 1997a). A shortened English version is Wiemer (1997b).

## FOUR KINDS OF CHRONOLOGY FACTORS

First of all, let us consider which are the most relevant factors of temporal organization in any piece of discourse that may be called coherent. According to Lehmann (1989; Lehmann & Hamburger Studiengruppe, 1993), four types of chronology factors should be distinguished:

1. *Lexical chronology:* explicit lexical means such as adverbials, particles, conjunctions; hereafter they will be called *connectors*.
2. *Actional chronology:* characteristics of verb morphology indicating tense and actionality. Actionality may be grammaticalized as aspect (e.g., in Polish or Russian) or remain implicit as Aktionsarten and so forth (for example, German *essen* vs. *aufessen*, English *to eat* vs. *to eat up*). In any case, the interaction of finite verbs on the textual level conditions their behavior as markers of taxical relations ("before," "after," "parallel to") or, in other words, their potential of indicating a *sequence* of events (see Example 1), a *parallelism* of states or durative actions (see Example 2), or an *incidence* of an event on the background of a durative action or a state (see Example 3):

Example 1
 a. Der Fäller schlug mit der Axt zu. Der Baum fiel zu Boden.
 b. Drwal przyłożył siekierę. Drzewo padło na ziemię.
English: The lumberjack chopped the tree with an axe. The tree fell to the ground.

Example 2
 a. Als wir uns der Stadt näherten, goß es in Strömen.
 b. Kiedy zbliżaliśmy się do miasta, lało jak z cebry.
English: As we were approaching the city, it was raining heavily.

Example 3
 a. Als wir im Zimmer saßen, flog [auf einmal] ein Vogel gegen die Scheibe.
 b. Gdy siedzieliśmy w pokoju, [nagle] ptak uderzył o szybę.
English: While we were sitting in the room, [suddenly] a bird flew into the window.

3. *Natural chronology:* knowledge about the normal order of events. This comprises all sorts of frame-like encyclopedic knowledge (scripts, etc.) relevant for the taxical conceptualizing of events, but also actualized knowledge deriving from the previous linguistic context.
4. *Iconic chronology:* takes part in any case when the order of propositions (i.e., their predicates) is in accordance with the real order of the narrated events.

It is easy to see that iconic chronology lies at the bottom of what L&W called narrative units. Iconic chronology is related to natural chronology in the same way as L&W's narrative clauses to the *semantic interpretation* and the *operational displacement set*.[3] The interaction of iconic and natural chronology can be shown by permutating the relative order of the two clauses in Example 1:

Example 4
  a. Der Baum fiel zu Boden. Der Fäller schlug mit der Axt zu.
  b. Drzewo padło na ziemię. Drwal przyłożył siekierę.
English: The tree fell to the ground. The lumberjack chopped the tree with an axe.

Because both sentence pairs (Examples 1 and 4) can be ascribed a semantic interpretation, only the relative order between them determines the understanding (other conditions remaining equal). Lexical indicators of chronological order may be used to override iconic relations. They can even reorder defaults arising from grammatical aspect (as in Polish and Russian) or from mere lexical defaults (as in German).[4] However, they may also strengthen actional chronology as, for example, in Example 3, in which the sudden event occurring on some durative background can be underlined by expressions like those in brackets (German *auf einmal* and Polish *nagle*). All four chronology types can, thus, interact as sources of redundancy in the temporal organization. It is now an empirical question how far such redundancies are really exploited.

## ACTIONAL VERSUS LEXICAL CHRONOLOGY

In this respect, one should wonder whether Polish (or Russian), being an "aspect language," more often does without explicit lexical markers of temporal sequence than German. A comparison of Polish and German data demonstrates that such an expectation is only partly confirmed by linguistic reality. Polish and German pupils (aged 10–12 and 17–19 years respectively) were given the task of renarrating two short picture stories. The calculated amount of adverbial sequencers relative to the sum total of clauses (propositions) in the obtained oral discourses was for the Polish pupils 3.84% (10–12 years) and 3.81% (17–19 years) respectively and for the German ones 31.81% (10–12 years) and 19.93% (17–19 years) respectively. Such an outcome clearly corroborates these expectations.

We must nonetheless account for the fact that the chosen picture stories forced the informants to accentuate sequentiality of actions. The same pupils were also asked to write a letter from an (imagined) stay during their holidays. These letters had to be addressed to a close person (parents, sister, friend, etc.). What was related

---
[3] See the definition of narrative clause and displacement set in L&W.
[4] These are sometimes labeled under "lexical aspect" (e.g., Smith, 1986).

in them were to not so much stories about non-iterative event chains, but rather accounts of sequences of habitual actions or descriptions. As a consequence, the percentages of all kinds of temporal adverbials (relative to the sum total of clauses) tended to converge: In comparison to the renarrations they became more frequent in the Polish letters (11.13% and 6.12% respectively) and much less frequent in the German ones (14.69% and 10.31% respectively).

From this we can conclude that the relative weight of different chronology factors (here: actional vs. lexical chronology) is conditioned by the preconceived conceptual structure of the underlying "plot." In fact, features of verbal morphology may not always be a decisive "tool" in ordinary discourse, because they are made use of only to a low degree. Thus, L&W's distinction between narratives proper and their "alternatives" (p. 20) proves to be relevant even if applied to the interaction of actional and lexical chronology.

## INCIDENCE AND SUBORDINATION

Among the three taxical situation types introduced previously, incidence is by far the least frequent one. Very rarely can one find clear examples as in Example 5. Hypotactically organized "paradigm examples" of incidence, which are often cited for Polish (or Russian), occurred only very scarcely. More often than not the actional potential of imperfective verbs specifying the background versus perfective verbs denoting the foreground can only be induced from paratactically organized sentences—and mostly due to the additional use of adverbial connectors (Example 6):

Example 5
( ... ) wie wir so genüßlich auf den Luftmatratzen *umherschwammen* und *uns sonnten, sahen* (= erblickten) wir *auf einmal* 3 Haie. ( ... )
English: When/As we *were enjoying floating* on our mattresses and *were suntanning*, we *suddenly* saw (= noticed) three sharks.

Example 6
(about some underwater adventures) ( ... ) Raz *zaatakowała* mnie kałamornica, *akurat przepływałem* między skałami—to *było* jej terytorium. Szalona, chciała mnie chyba zjeść, ale zawiązałem jej odnoża w "węzeł gordyjski". ( ... )
English: On one occasion an octopus *attacked* me, I *was just swimming* through (some) rocks. This *was* its territory. Furious, it must have wanted to eat me. But I tied its arms together.

What about Polish adverbial participles (gerunds)? They could have replaced temporal clauses, but they actually did not. They were used even more scarcely than temporal connectors and, more so, if exploited, in a prevailing number of cases they did not explicate truly taxical relations. The temporal interpretation in any case remained left open to the mutual semantic interpretability of the involved verb forms, irrespectively of their finite versus nonfinite status or the absence versus presence of lexical connectors. Therefore, in excluding syntactic embedding from the definition of narrative, L&W (p. 20) made explicit important facts about highly pervasive "ordinary" ways of relating form to function, which are preserved even if more "sophisticated" ways of linguistic structuring are exploited.

## PREVALENCE OF ICONIC CHRONOLOGY

All of what has been said gives strong support to the validity of L&W's central claims and results. These brought to the fore the relation between iconic and natural chronology, less so between actional and lexical chronology. Data from other research and taken from other languages confirm that neither paratactic connectors nor temporal conjunctions, if used at all, have been exploited to annul iconic chronology, that is, L&W's notion of narrative unit. In all groups, more than 90% of all clauses strongly followed iconic chronology, the succession of propositions has been in accordance with natural chronology, and no explicit factors of actional chronology (verb morphology and verb defaults) or lexical chronology (connectors) would even have been necessary to specify the order of events. They are thus mostly redundant.

## CONCLUDING EVALUATION

In conclusion, I want to point at a very central demand stimulated by L&W that has by no means lost its relevance. Their main concern was directed towards an "understanding of ( ... ) the simplest and most fundamental narrative structures" (this issue). In their paper they continued by splitting up these structures into a referential and an evaluative level. Here I have to tried to show that much of what belongs to the referential level appears already preconceived pragmatically by iconic relations between the plot of the story and the order of clauses. Thus, the "natural order of events" most often need not be explicated by any other means of temporal ordering. Many means that have been considered to contribute to the temporal structure in fact should better be studied as "tools" enhancing thematic coherence—no more and no less. This observation holds not only with regard to narratives of vicarious experience, but also with respect to more artificial kinds of narration. For a linguist, it now becomes tempting to tighten a cooperation between L&W's still fruitful approach with more recent theories of iconicity in language and literature. Also, it should be a desirable task to be pursued by linguists in the near future to investigate more thoroughly and reliably the interaction of all the four chronology factors mentioned in this article. For they can supply a powerful explanatory tool for synchronic and diachronic typology.

## REFERENCES

Gülich, E., & Quasthoff, U. (1985). Narrative analysis. In T. A. van Dijk (Ed.), *Handbook of discourse analysis, Vol. II: Dimensions of discourse* (pp. 169–197). New York: Academic.

Labov, W., & Waletzky, J. (this issue). Narrative analysis: Oral versions of personal experience. In J. Helm (Ed.), *Essays on the verbal and visual arts: Proceedings of the 1966 Annual Spring Meeting of the American Ethnological Society* (pp. 12–44). Seattle: University of Washington Press. (Original work published 1967)

Lehmann, V. (1989). Chronologische Funktionen des Aspekts im Sprachvergleich Russisch–Deutsch. [Chronological functions of aspect in comparing Russian and German]. *Linguistische Arbeitsberichte, 70,* 58–65.

Lehmann, V., & Hamburger Studiengruppe. (1993). Interaktion chronologischer Faktoren beim Verstehen von Erzähltexten. [Interaction of chronological factors in the perception of narrative texts]. In S. Kempgen (Ed.), *Slavistische Linguistik 1992* (pp. 157–195). München, Germany: Sagner.

Smith, C. (1986). A Speaker-based approach to aspect. *Linguistics and Philosophy, 9*(1), 97–115.

Tannen, D. (1982). Oral and literate strategies in spoken and written narratives. *Language, 58*(1), 1–21.

Wiemer, B. (1997a). *Diskursreferenz im Polnischen und Deutschen (aufgezeigt an der Rede ein- und zweisprachiger Schüler)* [Discourse reference in Polish and German (illustrated on speech of mono- and bilingual pupils)]. München, Germany: Sagner.

Wiemer, B. (1997b). *Displaced speech—Systematic account and acquisitional background (illustrated by Polish and German).* Working Paper of the Fachgruppe Sprachwissenschaft 83. Konstanz, Germany: University of Konstanz.

# Extending Labov and Waletzky

Carole Peterson
*Department of Psychology, Memorial University of Newfoundland*

Allyssa McCabe
*Department of Psychology, University of Massachusetts, Lowell*

The article by Labov and Waletzky (1967/this issue; henceforth L&W) is one of the clearest examples we know that shows that the impact of a paper is not necessarily related to where it is published. When we were applying L&W's approach to our own corpus of data, both of our copies of this manuscript mysteriously disappeared on more than one occasion. Not surprisingly, local college libraries had no copy of the book edited by June Helm. Consequently, on at least two occasions we called the father of one of us (who conveniently lived in Seattle) and asked him to trundle off to the University of Washington library in Seattle in order to get another copy for us.

One of us, Peterson, first encountered L&W's paper while a doctoral student many years ago. At the time, work on child communication was dominated by Piaget's theoretical descriptions of egocentrism in young children and research on children's communicative skills was sparse. After all, according to Piaget, preoperational children were so egocentric that real communication hardly existed. Instead, studies documenting various deficiencies in young children's communicative skills abounded. One of the major paradigms used at the time was the referential communication task in which a child was supposed to describe nonsense forms to a listener such that the latter could unambiguously identify them. Nonsense figures were used because otherwise the child could succeed by just saying: "it's the dog." Researchers felt at the time that in order to study communication, it was crucial to simplify the task to its basic essentials; somehow, describing nonsense figures in an invented, somewhat bizarre task for mysterious reasons (mysterious

---

Requests for reprints should be sent to Carole Peterson, Psychology Department, Memorial University of Newfoundland, St. John's, Newfoundland, Canada A1B 3X9. E-mail: carole@play.psych.mun.ca

at least to the child) was supposed to do this. However, it was hard for us to think of a communication task that had less ecological validity, although it is undoubtedly the case that all methods of research compromise ecological validity to some degree. What child had to do anything comparable in real life? Furthermore, the referential communication paradigm missed the richness and complexity of the everyday communication that seemed to be taking place whenever one visited a preschool.

L&W formulated an analytic approach for studying narrative that, as it were, illuminated the "communicative gold" by which we were all surrounded. Their approach was highly appealing for a number of reasons. It took as its subject everyday talk, and in particular, talk that was produced in ecologically valid ways. Everyone talks about the past events in their lives that have significance for them, and such narratives were now the subject matter to be studied. L&W articulated a structure that characterized narratives, one that was unique among other such approaches that emerged at about the same time in that it featured emotion as central to (personal) narration. Every narrative has an emotional point, they claimed, a reason for being told, and this point appears in the narrative through evaluation.

At this time, the two authors had the good fortune to begin a long and fruitful collaboration with each other. Although we admired the approach to narrative analysis proposed by L&W as well as their work with adolescents, we wondered about how they applied it to children's narratives. In their original article (this issue) they noted that: "we find that orientation sections are typically lacking in narratives of children and less verbal adults whose narratives fail in other ways to carry out referential functions, e.g., to preserve temporal sequence."

We felt that L&W's description of the narrative skills of children was an underestimation of their skills. The narrative task given to some of the children in L&W was to describe the plot of a TV show such as The Man from U.N.C.L.E., and the children's accounts were not only very confusing, but lacking in the structural organization, especially evaluation, that L&W saw as so important. However, as we found, the task given to young children is of key importance: Children who are totally confusing when recounting TV or movie plots can give clear accounts of some of their own personal experiences. In this respect, then, Labov's later writings (e.g., Labov, 1972) were better in theory than his own actual developmental practice had been (also described in Labov, 1972, p. 367): "The social situation is the most powerful determinant of verbal behavior and ... an adult must enter into the right social relation with a child if he wants to find out what a child can do. This is just what many teachers cannot do," he wrote (p. 212), and he was right about that. The authors of this article found that if you get to know children and tell them stories about your own personal experience while ensuring that they do not feel self-conscious about talking to you (e.g., have them do art projects or play cards), children will tell highly evaluated stories from a very early age.

A developmental approach for studying children's narratives was essential, and our first task was to collect hundreds of narratives from children across a wide age range (4–9 years). We then attempted to induce a developmental pattern. Such age-related progressions in structure were found; furthermore, we found surprisingly competent narrative structure in children who were quite young (Peterson & McCabe, 1983). Children as young as early elementary-school age were able to provide narratives that were well-structured according to L&W's proposal. Although these narratives were not as long and elaborated as the narratives provided by adult subjects, they were well-structured nonetheless. We found more primitive precursors in younger children. Consider the following personal narrative from a girl aged 3 years, 4 months, in which her evaluation is italicized. She was by no means the best narrator in our sample (McCabe & Peterson, 1991, pp. 247–248; I = interviewer, L = Leah):

I: So you were hiding on your mommy, were you
L: Yeah.
I: What happened?
L: Um, ah, She looked in the neighborhood and she looked everywhere. *She thought I was killed and she thought a man had stealed me.*
I: Somebody had stealed you. She thought somebody had stealed you?
L: Yeah, *but I didn't, cause I was hiding that.*
I: You were hiding behind that, were you?
L: Cause, cause I didn't know that she was getting, she said, "Leah, get your shorts" and then I was lying down, *then, then she couldn't find me.* Then that's what, and then, and then, then I came out.
I: You did?
L: But they find me, but I was saying, *"No, I don't want to go in there. I don't want to go in there,"* (said loudly). I was shouting, *so* she smacked me. And then I was in my shorts, I was hiding under there and *Mommy didn't know where I are so that's what she did, see. And she didn't know where I was, where, so I was over hiding in that chair,* but it was raining out first, *cause I was crying.* Then I went in there *to hide. Then I was hiding under there* and then, then, and then she gave me a smack on the hand and *she thought that somebody had stealing me,* and then, and then ...
I: She thought somebody was stealing you.
L: Yeah, but *but I thought I was going down the street with M. and J.*
I: Mmm.
L: *So I wasn't. I was hiding under there.*

Note that in addition to telling a well-developed genuine narrative here, the child's performance was relatively independent of the interviewer, who mostly echoed the child's remarks as per our typical interviewing procedure.

We pored over L&W as we developed our own coding manual based very much on their ideas. The more we studied their work, the more we became concerned with their practice of classifying types of propositions in a mutually exclusive way. They classified clauses as representing events (either complicating or resolving, depending upon their relation to the high point or crisis point of the narrative), or orientation, or evaluation, or codas. Orienting the listener to the context of their story as well as telling them about the events that occurred fulfill the referential function of a narrative, whereas evaluation informs the listener about why the narrative is told, what the point is, and why it is important. According to L&W, evaluation was concentrated at the high point and in effect defined it. Our concern was that we found evaluation in particular (and to a lesser extent orientation as well) everywhere in a narrative, not just in those clauses that are classified as evaluative. A judicious choice of words, an addition of a particular adjective or adverb, a dependent clause or prepositional phrase—all can and did carry evaluative information. In fact, we found that although only 15% of children's narrative clauses were wholly devoted to evaluation, an additional, impressive 35% of their clauses had embedded evaluation in them (Peterson & McCabe, 1983). Thus, narrative analysis needs to find ways to deal with all of this embedded evaluation. Similarly, we found orientation embedded in numerous other clauses (e.g., "We drove up North *at the end of May,*" in which the final clause is an orientative addition to a clause that would be simply classified as a complicating action using L&W's original system). To miss such embedded orientation would be to miss children's impressive competence in this area (Menig-Peterson & McCabe, 1978).

We have also found it easier to obtain acceptable reliability estimates by breaking L&W's types of evaluation (clarified in Labov, 1972) into more discreet categories and by adding some additional types we found in the children's narratives. Our maintenance of 21 different types of evaluation was confirmed by statistical analysis; those different types of evaluation did not correlate significantly with each other (except for phonological stress and phonological elongation), nor did any major factor emerge from a principal components analysis (Peterson & McCabe, 1983).

Not only did we add and subdivide L&W's evaluative devices, we rethought one in particular. Although L&W argued that reported speech served as embedded evaluation, Peterson and McCabe (1983) argued that in children's narratives reported speech was often more a kind of complicating action than it was any sort of evaluation. Sometimes, in fact, it was the only kind of action to be found in a narrative. Had we counted it as evaluation, we would have had to reject the discourse as a narrative because we followed Labov's (1972) strict requirement of two temporal clauses in a sequence that recapitulated a sequence of events in the real world. Ely and McCabe (1993) revised this revision further: They took the position that reported speech should be treated as another distinct constituent of narration. Thus, there are six, not five, constituents of narrative: (a) orientation, (b) complication (later complicating action), (c) evaluation, (d) resolution, (e) codas and other appendages or boundary markers such as abstracts, and (f) reported speech. True, orientation and evaluation and sometimes actions are embedded within reported speech (e.g., "She said he had caught [complicating action] an enormous [evaluation] striped bass last fall [orientation]") but that is the point we made earlier.

Other avenues suggested by this work begged for exploration. How did children knit together their sentences with a tissue of connectives? How did this knitting change over time? We turned to studying children's use of connectives in their narratives and how this usage changed with age. As part of this exploration we found that connectives fulfilled both semantic and pragmatic functions within a narrative. Thus, children used connectives in more complex ways than we had at first supposed, ways that were profitably differentiated using Labov's (1972) categories; specifically, children are much more likely to connect sentences in an action sequence with connectives such as *and* than they are when they shift from telling some action to giving a background, orientative comment (Peterson & McCabe, 1991a, 1991b).

Going in a different direction, how did parents play a role in teaching their children narrative skills? Did they teach narration through scaffolding, as proposed by Vygotsky (1986)? Did all parents emphasize narrative components equally? These too were questions that piqued our curiosity. We found that the questioning techniques used by parents in fact were related to the narrative skills of their children. Children whose parents extended each narrative topic told long, complex narratives, whereas children whose parents constantly switched from topic to topic produced shorter, relatively impoverished narratives (McCabe & Peterson, 1991). The impact of parents' interviewing style revealed another way in which Labov's analysis was useful: Parents emphasize different Labovian components in their interviewing practices with their children, and the children come to echo these different preferences. Thus, parents who emphasized orienting context in their scaffolding had children who later incorporated more orienting context in their stand-alone narratives when they got older (Peterson & McCabe, 1994), whereas parents who emphasized action (complication and resolution) had children who told more classic narratives in Labovian terms (Peterson & McCabe, 1992).

If parents within one culture exhibit differential preferences for Labovian components, McCabe and her colleagues hypothesized that perhaps cultures also diverge along similar lines. For example, Minami and McCabe (1995) found that Japanese mothers pay more attention (e.g., the Japanese equivalent of "unhuh"), request description less frequently, and evaluate what their children narrate less frequently than English-speaking mothers. Over time, this kind of differential emphasis of Labovian components should manifest itself in children's narrative structure.

L&W foreshadowed this cultural work when they suggested that one needed to closely correlate the narrator's social characteristics with the structure of their narratives and that effective communication must consider class and ethnic differences. Nevertheless, many investigators have been seduced into considering one structure as the template that underlies all well-structured narratives. This is true not only for those applying L&W's approach but also those whose work is informed by different approaches, for example, story grammar and its emphasis on goals.

Currently, a number of investigators are documenting cultural differences in what is considered to be a well-structured narrative. McCabe and her colleagues used the same interviewing procedure outlined previously (and more fully described in Peterson & McCabe, 1983) with children from various cultures; full participants of the children's culture used translations of that procedure and the analysis adapted from L&W. Table 1 (adapted from McCabe, 1996) summarizes the ways we found cultures to differentially emphasize the basic components.

Although African American and European North American children tell the kind of classic narrative about one single experience that L&W described (largely on the basis of interviewing African American adolescents and men), it should also be clear that in all cultures investigated—except the European North American—children prefer to synthesize several real-life experiences in their narratives. Table 1 also demonstrates that European North American children evaluate less and stress action sequences more than all other cultures examined. African American children focus less on description than other groups, whereas Latino children focus the most on this component. Also of importance is the fact that 49% of the personal narratives my colleagues collected from Spanish-speaking children contained no clear sequence of two actions; yet these narratives felt like good narratives. McCabe and her colleagues were forced to reexamine the most basic—previously unchallenged—aspect of what we had taken from Labov's approach, namely his requirement that there be a minimal sequence of two actions to call discourse narrative.

TABLE 1
Some Major Formal Dimensions of Cultural Variation in Oral Personal Experiences of 7-Year-Olds

| | | | Latino | | |
| --- | --- | --- | --- | --- | --- |
| Percentage of Comments That Are | African American | Japanese American | English Dominant | Spanish Dominant | European/ North American |
| Evaluation | 28 | 24 | 29 | 34 | 15 |
| Actions | 48 | 49 | 36 | 30 | 57 |
| Description | 15 | 27 | 28 | 28 | 23 |
| Boundary markers | 8 | — | 7 | 9 | 4 |
| Sequencing of actions | Yes, in 74% of narratives | Yes—% not available | Yes, in 63% of narratives | Yes, in 51% of narratives | Yes, in 100% of narratives |

*Note.* Adapted from McCabe (1996). All groups typically had multiple experiences per narrative except European/North American children, who typically had single experiences.

We decided that even though there were not always two events to be found in a lengthy discourse, we would accept such narratives as the following (from a 7-year-old El Salvadorean girl) on their own terms:

> Well I went in the hospital, in the Mass General Hospital—there where my Uncle Roberto works. That he has two children who are not twins but who are only two children because first Robertico was born, who is named after his dad, and then Christopher was born ... But my Uncle Roberto have a dog who is one of those German ones, who is already two months old. And now, because the mom's name is Butterfly. She is with a man whose name is, who is my Uncle whose name is Juan. And by chance he gave him that dog. But look that dog, he bites Alex because he runs and bites much. HERE he bit him, and he bites him even in the face and here in the arms.

Events leading up to and from her stay in the hospital are not the ones she chooses to talk about. Instead Carmen preferred to fill us in on her family connections to the hospital, and even the family connections of her dog.

In short, for over 20 years we have fruitfully applied L&W's approach to a variety of different sets of personal narratives. This article focusses on the major ways we have extended that work. We have found ourselves questioning and extending every one of L&W's basic assumptions. However, only a myopic scholar would fail to see that those extensions would not have been possible without their original analysis. Furthermore, it is a remarkably flexible approach that can prove useful and command respect even when its most basic assumptions are not only challenged, but changed. Words like *seminal* and *ground breaking* come to mind, but, though applicable, they are far too trite. Instead, we conclude with a simple expression of gratitude.

## REFERENCES

Ely, R., & McCabe, A. (1993). Remembered voices. *Journal of Child Language, 20,* 671–696.

Labov, W. (1972). *Language in the inner city: Studies in the Black English vernacular.* Philadelphia: University of Pennsylvania Press.

Labov, W., & Waletzky, J. (this issue). Narrative analysis: Oral versions of personal experience. In J. Helm (Ed.), *Essays on the verbal and visual arts: Proceedings of the 1966 Annual Spring Meeting of the American Ethnological Society* (pp. 12–44). Seattle: University of Washington Press. (Original work published 1967)

McCabe, A. (1996). *Chameleon readers: Teaching children to appreciate all kinds of good stories.* New York: McGraw-Hill.

McCabe, A., & Peterson, C. (1991). Getting the story: A longitudinal study of parental styles in eliciting oral personal narratives and developing narrative skill. In A. McCabe & C. Peterson (Eds.), *Developing narrative structure* (pp. 217–253). Hillsdale, NJ: Lawrence Erlbaum Associates, Inc.

Menig-Peterson, C., & McCabe, A. (1978) Children's orientation of a listener to the context of their narratives. *Developmental Psychology, 74,* 582–592.

Minami, M., & McCabe, A. (1995). Rice balls versus bear hunts: Japanese and Caucasian family narrative patterns. *Journal of Child Language, 22,* 423–446.

Peterson, C., & McCabe, A. (1983). *Developmental psycholinguistics: Three ways of looking at a child's narrative.* New York: Plenum.

Peterson, C., & McCabe, A. (1991a). Linking children's connective use and narrative structure. In A. McCabe & C. Peterson (Eds.), *Developing narrative structure* (pp. 29–53). Hillsdale, NJ: Lawrence Erlbaum Associates, Inc.

Peterson, C., & McCabe, A. (1991b). On the threshold of the storyrealm: Semantic versus pragmatic use of connectives in narratives. *Merrill–Palmer Quarterly, 37,* 445–464.

Peterson, C., & McCabe, A. (1992). Parental styles of narrative elicitation: Effect on children's narrative structure and content. *First Language, 12,* 299–321.

Peterson, C., & McCabe, A. (1994). A social interactionist account of developing decontextualized narrative skill. *Developmental Psychology, 30,* 937–948.

Vygotsky, L. (1986). *Thought and language.* Cambridge, MA: MIT Press.

# Some Observations on Narratives by Aphasics and Their Contributions to Narrative Theory

## Hanna K. Ulatowska and Gloria Streit Olness
*Callier Center for Communication Disorders*
*University of Texas at Dallas*

This article addresses the degree to which the field of narrative analysis has provided an account of the relation between sentence-level and discourse-level phenomena in narratives, specifically, the impact of surface linguistic structures on linear and hierarchical aspects of narratives. The reference database for this discussion is narratives produced by aphasics, that is, persons with loss or disruption of language following central nervous system damage. Because aphasics are typically impaired in their morphological, lexical, and syntactic skills; because they endure these losses at various levels of severity; and because many of them maintain the ability to attempt narrative production and comprehension tasks due to largely intact cognitive skills, they allow us to investigate the relative roles of morphological, lexical, and syntactic skills in successful production and comprehension of narratives.

Major conclusions drawn from this evidence are twofold. First, the linear aspects of narratives can be produced successfully with restricted morphological and syntactic support. However, a paucity of sentence-level surface devices is associated with an impoverishment of the hierarchical aspects of narratives, for example, highlighting information, emphasizing and evaluating details, providing nontemporal transitions, organizing complex narratives, and so forth. Theoretical implications for the field of narrative analysis are discussed.

---

Requests for reprints should be sent to Hanna K. Ulatowska, University of Texas at Dallas, UTD/Callier Center, 1966 Inwood Road, Dallas, TX 75235. E-mail: hanna@utdallas.edu

## LINEAR AND HIERARCHICAL CHARACTERISTICS OF NARRATIVES

As seen in the seminal work by Labov and Waletzky (1967/this issue; henceforth L&W), narratives display both linear and hierarchical characteristics. L&W emphasized the linear quality of narratives in that a "strict temporal sequence" of events expressed in narrative clauses is the "defining characteristic of narrative" and establishes the narrative's referential function. Narratives also display hierarchical characteristics. L&W proposed that speakers highlight certain information through use of evaluation and that the absence of these evaluations results in a narrative that "lacks significance" and "has no point." Speakers highlight certain events or information as being more prominent in a hierarchy of relative importance to convey a point to a listener. It is important to note that such an emphasis is largely semantic in nature, as L&W noted: "The fundamental definition of evaluation must be semantic, although its implications are structural."

Subsequent work on narratives also emphasizes both linear and hierarchical characteristics of narratives. For instance, Longacre (1983) emphasized the temporal nature of narratives as a discourse genre. With respect to hierarchical information, van Dijk's (1980) macrostructure model was fundamentally a hierarchical model of relations drawn between and among propositions in a narrative. Longacre (1981) discussed the means by which a continuum of verb and clause structures acts as a tool to highlight information associated with the "peak" or climax of a narrative. Finally, the models of story grammarians (e.g., Rumelhart, 1975; Yekovich & Thorndyke, 1981), although they are now outdated, were largely hierarchical in nature, clumping groups of propositions into structural categories.

A significant aspect of the distinction between temporal and hierarchical characteristics of narratives is that they can be differentiated in part by the surface linguistic devices used for each function. As noted by L&W, and later expanded in linguistic approaches (e.g., Longacre, 1981), morphological forms marking tense and aspect, as well as differential use of independent versus dependent clauses, embedding, and so forth are key means of distinguishing referential and evaluative clauses in narratives. It is this relation between sentential and discourse phenomena in narratives which is the primary focus of this article.

Several specific questions are addressed: To what degree are the linear and hierarchical characteristics of narratives dependent upon morphology, lexicon, and syntax? Can these functions of narratives still be performed without a full complement of surface linguistic devices? In narratives for which the linear or hierarchical characteristics are compromised by a decreased range of surface linguistic tools, are the narratives produced still narratives, or do they become another entity? The answer to these questions reflects on the theoretical role of morphological, lexical, and syntactic surface forms on narrative discourse productions, as well as the qualities that make narratives truly narratives.

## LINEAR AND HIERARCHICAL ASPECTS OF NARRATIVES IN APHASIA

To what degree are narratives compromised by the morphological, lexical, and syntactic deficits of aphasics? With respect to the linear aspects of narratives, the sequence of clauses in narratives produced by aphasics closely matches the chronological sequence of events. This serves to maintain the temporal coherence of the narratives, despite a reduction and impairment of surface structure markers of temporality, such as grammatical morphemes signaling tense and aspect in verbs and temporal connectors. Aphasics compensate for this by a concatenation of clauses with narrative heads. There is an adherence to prototypical narratives with a strictly linear progression of events, expressed via simple concatenation of propositions and use of conjunctions *and* and *then*. Such narratives are usually successful in conveying the main event sequence, and appear narrative-like. This would support the premise of L&W that temporality expressed through the sequence of narrative heads constitutes the backbone of the narrative. It also suggests that this skill is not so much dependent on surface linguistic devices as it is on cognitive sequencing; it is likely that surface devices are secondary or redundant for purposes of expressing linear aspects of narratives, at least in simple narratives. Thus, it would appear that when the linear aspect of narratives is being considered, cognitive approaches to narrative analysis (e.g., van Dijk's, 1980, macrostructure model) are not necessarily negligent in their lack of attention to surface linguistic devices.

However, data from aphasics would suggest that surface linguistic devices are quite critical for highlighting narrative information in a hierarchical fashion. First, dependence of aphasics on concatenation and simplification of sentential structure (i.e., reduced syntactic embedding) guards against deviations from the main narrative line (Ulatowska, Freedman-Stern, Doyel, Macaluso-Haynes, & North, 1983; Ulatowska, North, & Macaluso-Haynes, 1981). Thus, the narratives do not mark the difference between foregrounded and backgrounded information. Secondly, connectors such as adverbials and subordinating conjunctions, which signal relations of conditionality, causality, and consequence between larger portions of narratives, are largely missing. Associated with this are difficulties with departures from prototypical narratives, for example, attempts to provide nontemporal transitions between segments of a narrative or attempts to transition between a narrative and another discourse genre, such as expository discourse. Thirdly, aphasics display a loss of temporal features within the verbs themselves, as well as the aforementioned reduction in the range of morphemes marking tense and aspect. For instance, verbs such as *last* and *continue* are frequently replaced by verbs such as *to be,* and verbs are often not marked for tense and aspect (Ulatowska & Sadowska, 1989, 1992). Because changes in surface features, including verb form, are often used to mark the climax of a narrative (Longacre, 1981), aphasic narratives often display a flattening of the plot line, peaks that are poorly marked, and a flow of events that is often uneven. Such a flattening may lead to a reduced ability to express main points or highlighted information in the narrative (Robinson, 1981). Finally, aphasic narratives often display a reduction in the amount of narrative evaluation. This may be associated with the linguistic complexity and variety of structural devices needed to produce evaluations, as Labov (1972) described in detail, as well as the aforementioned difficulty in providing nontemporal transitions.

It is interesting to note that these surface linguistic deficits do not affect aphasics' ability to derive hierarchical information in narrative comprehension, but primarily their ability to express it. Although aphasics are able to identify main points from narratives relatively better than details (Brookshire & Nicholas, 1993), their ability to express the gist of a narrative in the form of a theme is often deficient because they do not have the necessary syntactic and lexical skills to express the rich, dense relations between the narrative events in a succinct fashion (Ulatowska & Chapman, 1994).

Thus, although aphasics are able to produce temporally simple narratives, they are impoverished in their ability to depart from this chronological arrangement of narrated events. In addition, they are unable to mark salience of specific information within a narrative. A restricted range of surface linguistic devices markedly reduces the ability of aphasics to express hierarchical information in narratives, which is evidence for the intimate balance between surface linguistic devices and expression of highlighted information in narratives.

## CLOSING COMMENTS

We would suggest that although data from aphasic narratives highlights the importance of surface linguistic devices for the hierarchical organization of narratives, the field of narrative analysis has not yet adequately addressed the relation between sentence-level surface devices and narrative discourse. To our knowledge, there is no unified model of their interdependence. Historically, those models that have focused on linguistic skills (e.g., Labov, 1972; Longacre, 1981) look largely at different types of evaluation, marking of climax, highlighting of information, and so forth in isolation, without equal attention to their relation to the overall macrostructure of the narrative. At the same time, those models that consider higher levels of narrative organization (e.g., van Dijk, 1980) provide little information on the relation between these macrostructures and the linguistic devices that are used to support them. Thus, although we have evidence from aphasia research to indicate that the presence or absence of certain surface linguistic devices affects the quality of narratives, we have no systematic framework to explain this interaction in detail.

To close, we now present some of the interactions that could be included in such a model, were it to be developed. Again, we draw our evidence from aphasic narratives. Consider, for instance, the following narrative produced by an aphasic (Ulatowska et al., 1983). The speaker is telling the story of a car accident that happened on a snorkeling trip to a lake called Possum Kingdom.

> Going to Possum Kingdom.
> Almost there.
> Other guy was drunk.
> Head on collision.
> And Mike S was driving.
> And me passenger.
> Head on collision.
> And would've died.
> Some guy stopped along the road.
> And put snorkel in my throat.
> And would've died.
> And other guy went insane.
> and [sic] that's it. (p. 333)

This narrative, like other narratives produced by aphasics, is characterized by poor sentence grammar, while still maintaining good conceptual organization. With respect to surface linguistic features, note that there is extensive concatenation of propositions, several sentences lack a verb, and there is limited complex verb morphology. The primary means of evaluation in this text is repetition, for example, "head on collision," whereas other syntactic and lexical means of evaluation are lacking. However, the temporal order of the events is clearly stated, reflecting the speaker's cognitive ability to express the event coherently. Moreover, the coda, "and that's it," acts as a ritualized termination of the temporal sequence.

A theoretical account of such a narrative would need to minimally consider some key interactions. First, do cognitive temporal organization of expressed events and the temporal information conveyed in surface linguistic devices provide distinct information or redundant information about the temporal order of events? Obviously, a simple narrative can be produced with little or no tense marking on verbs and few complex connectors, via simple concatenation, but does this mean that the sequence of expressed events is the only information that contributes to the linear aspect of narratives? What kinds of narratives (e.g., complex narratives that stray from a linear organization or narratives embedded in other discourse types) depend more closely on surface linguistic markers of temporality? In what contexts do the surface linguistic devices become critical for encoding the linear characteristics of a narrative, and how do they function in the overall development of the narrative?

Secondly, what are the relative roles of various means of evaluation, and what is the dependence of each type of evaluation upon surface linguistic devices? For example, repetition of a proposition (as seen in the preceding sample narrative) requires minimal linguistic skills. Is it as effective, or more effective, than other types of evaluation when speakers attempt to express a point with a narrative? What types of combinations of evaluations highlight information more effectively, and which of these depend upon surface linguistic devices?

In summary, relations between linguistic means of expressing temporality and salience must minimally be considered in any model of the relation between surface linguistic devices and discourse organization. In addition, such a model would also need to consider the interaction of these devices with degree of narrative complexity. The field of narrative analysis currently lacks models that address these complex, interactive issues. We hope that this data from aphasia research might in some small measure provide insights that allow us to advance our global understanding of narrative production.

## REFERENCES

Brookshire, R. H., & Nicholas, L. E. (1993). Comprehension of narrative discourse by aphasic listeners. In H. H. Brownell & Y. Joanette (Eds.), *Narrative discourse in neurologically impaired and normal aging adults* (pp. 151–170). San Diego, CA: Singular.

Labov, W. (1972). *Language in the inner city: Studies in the Black English vernacular.* Philadelphia: University of Pennsylvania Press.

Labov, W., & Waletzky, J. (this issue). Narrative analysis: Oral versions of personal experience. In J. Helm (Ed.), *Essays on the verbal and visual arts: Proceedings of the 1966 Annual Spring Meeting of the American Ethnological Society* (pp. 12–44). Seattle: University of Washington Press. (Original work published 1967)

Longacre, R. E. (1981). A spectrum and profile approach to discourse analysis. *Text, 1,* 337–359.

Longacre, R. E. (1983). *The grammar of discourse.* New York: Plenum.

Robinson, J. A. (1981). Personal narratives reconsidered. *Journal of American Folklore, 94,* 58–85.

Rumelhart, D. E. (1975). Notes on a schema for stories. In D. G. Bobrow & A. M. Collins (Eds.), *Representation and understanding* (pp. 211–236). New York: Academic.

Ulatowska, H. K., & Chapman, S. B. (1994). Discourse macrostructure in aphasia. In R. L. Bloom, L. K. Obler, S. De Santi, & J. S. Ehrlich (Eds.), *Discourse analysis and applications: Studies in adult clinical populations* (pp. 29–46). Hillsdale, NJ: Lawrence Erlbaum Associates, Inc.

Ulatowska, H. K., Freedman-Stern, R., Doyel, A. W., Macaluso-Haynes, S., & North, A. J. (1983). Production of narrative discourse in aphasia. *Brain and Language, 19,* 317–334.

Ulatowska, H. K., North, A. J., & Macaluso-Haynes, S. (1981). Production of narrative and procedural discourse in aphasia. *Brain and Language, 13,* 345–371.

Ulatowska, H. K., & Sadowska, M. (1989). Discourse and agrammatism. *Polish Psychological Bulletin, 20,* 127–138.

Ulatowska, H. K., & Sadowska, M. (1992). Some observations on aphasic texts. In S. J. Hwang, & W. R. Merrifield (Eds.), *Language in context: Essays for Robert E. Longacre* (pp. 51–66). Arlington, TX: The Summer Institute of Linguistics and the University of Texas at Arlington.

van Dijk, T. A. (1980). *Macrostructures: An interdisciplinary study of global structures in discourse, interaction, and cognition.* Hillsdale, NJ: Lawrence Erlbaum Associates, Inc.

Yekovich, F. R., & Thorndyke, P. W. (1981). An evaluation of alternative functional models of narrative schemata. *Journal of Verbal Learning and Verbal Behavior, 20,* 454–469.

# The Role of Narrative in the Study of Language and Aging

### Anne R. Bower
*Polisher Research Institute, Philadelphia Geriatric Center*

In this discussion, I consider the relevance of Labov and Waletzky's (1967/this issue; henceforth L&W) structural model for oral *narrative* analysis for the study of language and aging. At present, two important bands of research contribute to our understanding of language and aging, namely a developmental research paradigm (DRP) and a sociolinguistic research paradigm (SRP). As it has in many other areas of social scientific inquiry, L&W's model has been adopted and applied by researchers working in both developmental and sociolinguistic paradigms. Because so much of the research in both paradigms relies particularly on elderly speakers' narratives, it is prudent to consider how the verbal productions designated as narratives are identified and utilized in each research paradigm and the extent to which these definitions affect conclusions about linguistic capability.

Both DRP and SRP rely heavily on discourse units designated as narrative to identify and assess a variety of cognitive, linguistic, and communicative skills in elderly speakers. However, they arrive at strikingly different conclusions about elderly speakers' linguistic and communicative capabilities. Findings from the DRP point to elders' decreased capabilities in articulating complex syntactic structures, reduced control over event structure conceptualization, and reduced pragmatic skills. Within this paradigm, elders' linguistic and communicative capabilities are widely conceptualized in terms of decline, decrement, and deterioration at worst, or maintenance, at best. The metaphor of decline is so entrenched in this band of research that it has been characterized by British social psychologists concerned with aging and language as "the decrement model" (Coupland, Coupland, & Giles 1991). In contrast, sociolinguistic studies of elders' speech show linguistic and communicative capabilities that are far from deteriorating or reduced. SRP reports

---

Requests for reprints should be sent to Anne R. Bower, Philadelphia Geriatric Center, 5301 Old York Road, Philadelphia, PA 19141.

sustained or increased complexity in syntactic structures, increased manipulation of event structures and other narrative related concepts, and evidence of skillful pragmatic management of the narrative speech situation.

How are we to interpret these contrasting findings? Which research paradigm promises a more accurate assessment and clearer understanding of our elders' speech capabilities? In my view, this is a pressing question because, at present, the DRP dominates research in language and aging, and with it, the negative decrement model prevails. The view that advancing years are likely to bring linguistic deterioration and decline significantly influences the clinical development of diagnostic protocols that purport to identify and assess the degree of decline or maintenance of an elder's linguistic and communicative capabilities. In the discussion to follow, I contend that L&W's model for isolating, identifying, and analyzing oral narrative, applied within the context of culturally sensitive sociolinguistic practice, offers the opportunity for a sharper assessment of elderly speakers' linguistic and communicative capabilities than that produced in the DRP.

## NARRATIVE IN THE DRP

DRP researchers have developed a variety of verbal tasks intended to reveal the individual's linguistic ability to report and evaluate a sequence of events. For example, directed story comprehension and story retelling exercises require subjects to listen to a prose passage read by an interviewer and then to retell the story. The subject may be asked to retell the story again several times at different intervals (North, Ulatowska, Macaluso-Haynes, & Bell, 1986; Obler, 1980). In directed story generating exercises, the subject is shown a single picture of a cohort "salient" theme, for example, a Norman Rockwell Americana illustration or the illustration of a child taking a cookie out of a jar, and is then asked to tell a story about the scene (North et al., 1986; Ulatowska & Chapman, 1991). Another exercise requires the subject to organize a set of illustrations of forest animals engaged in various activities into an order about which the subject then tells a story (Ulatowska & Chapman, 1991). Story generating exercises designated as *spontaneous* require respondents to talk with researchers about everyday topics of personal interest to the subject (Kemper, Rash, Kynette, & Norman, 1990; Pratt & Robbins, 1991). The subject may be requested to draw on personal experience for a story, to recount a familiar fairy tale or fable, or to describe an everyday procedure (Ripich, 1991).

The speech situations in which these verbal productions are elicited are typically clinical, and the experimental nature of the verbal tasks at hand is well-recognized and oriented to by both respondent and experimenter. In uneven attempts to broaden the representative quality of the speech generated in the experimental setting, a few studies have altered the structure of the interview situation. For example, Hutchinson and Jensen (1980) introduced a longitudinal element by utilizing language data from multiple sessions with the same respondent, rather than relying on a single interview. Pratt and Robins (1991) designed small group interactions in which to conduct their storytelling and other language exercises, although they positioned their spontaneous story-generating exercises between formal story recall tasks and word list readings. There is ample evidence to suggest that such speech situations produce formal, highly monitored speech styles (Labov, 1972, 1984; Milroy, 1987; Trudgill, 1983), and whether such speech situations produce representative pictures of the linguistic and communicative capabilities of the elderly respondents has been questioned (Bower, 1992).

These verbal tasks produce a variety of speech events, such as formal recitations, constructed accounts, anecdotes, reminiscences, life history fragments, familiar fairy tales, fables, and personal experience narratives. Yet, irrespective of their content and structure or the speech situations in which they were elicited, DRP researchers are very likely to gloss these verbal productions as "stories" or narratives.

These verbal productions are typically mined for information about elders' command of complex syntactic structures, capabilities in event structure conceptualization, and control of pragmatic skills. However, for the purpose of this discussion about narrative, we focus only on event structure conceptualization. Because story complexity and production are regarded as directly reflective of both cognitive and pragmatic capabilities (Ripich, 1991; Santi & Obler, 1991; Ulatowska & Chapman, 1991), the structural complexity of the narrative draws considerable attention. For example, in directed storytelling and retelling exercises, the focus tends to be on the elder's ability to "correctly" repeat or paraphrase the key propositions as designated in advance by the experiment designers. Here, elderly speakers are found to have greater difficulty in such paraphrasing than younger speakers and to be more likely than younger speakers to produce elaborate, indefinite paraphrases and nonmeaningful fillers (Emery, 1986; Obler, 1980). DRP studies construe such strategies, which may create the impression of the rambling verbosity often associated with elderly speakers, as elders' efforts to create the appearance of conceptual and pragmatic ability (Gold, Andres, Arbuckle, & Schwartzman, 1988; Walker, Roberts, & Hedrick, 1988).

For spontaneous stories, a number of schemas are employed in identifying narrative structure. Stein and Glenn's (1979) episode analysis, Sutton-Smith's (1978) hierarchical structure, Peterson and McCabe's (1983) "high point" approach, adapted in fact from L&W's format, and "story grammar" models culled from a variety of discourse processing studies (Fayol & Lemaire, 1993; Mandl, Stein, & Trabasso, 1984) figure prominently. However the individual researcher formulates and defines the story structure, it is not uncommon to encounter a sharp bias in favor of perceived length, topical relevance, and structural completeness. Stories that lack the "correct" complement of structural parts may be referred to as "fragments of experience" (Bokus, 1992), as "underdeveloped" (Pratt & Robins,

1991), "inadequate" (Ripich, 1991), or "impoverished" (Peterson & McCabe, 1983). As a consequence, the elderly speaker's cognitive, linguistic, or communicative competence may be questioned.

Elders who do produce lengthy, transparently topical stories that include all or most of the structural parts the researcher has identified as necessary for a complete story are less likely to be judged cognitively impaired than elders who do not. Yet, because both structural completeness criteria and researchers' judgments vary, even stories that overtly adhere to task-related topic or that have elaborate event structures are not necessarily assured a completeness judgment. Although some researchers may regard these stories as "well-ordered sequences" (Peterson & McCabe, 1983), using another schema, they may be designated "rambling" or "verbose" (Gold et al., 1988).

In sum, the overall picture, as reported, is gloomy, although the variety of verbal productions and testing situations used in DRP research make findings difficult to integrate and frequently contradictory. Cognitive deficiency, rather than experiment design, the testing situation's inherent stylistic constraints, or the applicability of the story schema, is readily offered as the explanation for the elderly speakers' production of story structures that do not meet the researcher's completeness criteria.

## ELDERS' NARRATIVES AND L&W'S MODEL

Although the language of elderly members of the speech community has always figured prominently in dialectological and sociolinguistic research, studies dealing exclusively with elderly speakers' linguistic and communicative capabilities are still underrepresented in sociolinguistic literature (but see Guy & Boyd, 1990; Sankoff & Lessard, 1975). However, the few discourse studies that are available are informed by sociolinguistic data collection methods and apply L&W's analytic format to elders' discourse. From these, a considerably different picture of elders' linguistic and communicative capabilities emerges. For the purposes of this discussion, two recent sociolinguistic studies of elderly speakers' personal narratives will serve to illustrate the differences in approach between the two bands of research. These are Labov and Auger's (1993) study of syntactic complexity in elders' narratives and Bower's (in press) study of expressive style in elderly men's narratives.

The discourse data used in these two studies differ strikingly from that used by DRP researchers in the way they were collected and in the approach to conceptualizing and utilizing personal narrative. In contrast to the DRP's clinical or experimental settings, the discourse that produced the narratives used in these two studies occurred in speech situations that approximated or overlapped with the speakers' normal, family interaction patterns. In some cases, the respondent and the interviewer only were present at the interview. In other cases, the respondent's family members were present at various times during the interview. The recording sessions themselves were long, typically 3- to 5-hour, tape-recorded conversations. Further, the speakers involved in these studies had participated in interview sessions prior to the conversation that produced the narratives used in the study.

In contrast to the stories that serve in DRP research, the oral narratives used in these two sociolinguistic studies were not generated by a sequence of pictures, an assigned topic, or a recall exercise. Rather, they reflected the synthesized, autobiographical experience of the elderly speakers. In some cases, the narratives were offered in response to interviewer queries within the speech setting described previously. Typically, however, the narratives were initiated by the elderly speakers themselves as illustrations of points, as evidence for arguments, and as reports of experience that related to the ongoing, jointly constructed topic development. In short, the narratives used in the sociolinguistic studies cited here represent a point on the stylistic continuum at a distant remove from the stories produced in the artificial, experimental settings of the DRP. Not surprisingly, the analysis of narratives collected under these circumstances offers a strikingly different picture of the elderly speakers' linguistic and communicative capabilities. Let us turn now to the substance of those findings.

Labov and Auger addressed the issue of syntactic complexity in a longitudinal study of two elderly Italian American speakers' personal narratives. Applying L&W's model, Labov and Auger identified and analyzed nine personal narratives in the tape-recorded conversations at Time 1 with the speakers when they were 66 and 71 years old. These were compared with the same narratives told by the same speakers 17 years later at Time 2, when they were 83 and 87 years old. The interviews were conducted by the original interviewer (also 17 years older), in the same kitchen and living room in South Philadelphia, using the same interview schedule, and replicating the topical sequence in which the narratives had emerged in Time 1. Consistent with the practice of DRP researchers, Labov and Auger adopted the presence of subordinating and left-branching syntactic structures as indicators of syntactic complexity in the narrative. As mentioned earlier, a key finding in DRP research has been that elders' ability to produce and command syntactically complex structures decreases with advancing years. However, Labov and Auger's clause-by-clause examination of each narrative revealed no differences in syntactic complexity between Time 1 and Time 2 narratives. Rather, Labov and Auger identified an increase in subordination and left branching structures (p. 124). Further, the evaluative structure, which reveals the significance of the recounted events, notably increased in syntactic complexity in both speakers' Time 2 narratives. For these octogenarians at least, their narrative syntax is more complex than it was in their late 60s and early 70s.

Although a Time 1 and Time 2 comparison of the narratives' event structures was not an aim of Labov and Auger's study, a comparative review of the temporal sequence of events reveals no deletions or alterations in event sequencing and no evidence of the fillers and "meaningless paraphrases" that clinicians are likely to report in their story data. The event structures of their stories are unchanged, and the increased complexity of the evaluative component suggests that, if anything, these narratives are even better told 17 years later than they were previously. The narratives of these elders clearly does not show linguistic or communicative deterioration.

Bower's study of the bereavement narratives from elderly Irish American widowers broadened the focus from clause-level syntax to the identification of patterns in the speakers' organization of referential and evaluative material. Applying L&W's model, Bower identified and analyzed 34 personal narratives in the tape-recorded discussions of 9 elderly (70 years +) Irish American widowers speaking at length about the death of their long-term spouse. Two distinctive styles characterized these ethnic widowers' narrative accounts of their personal experience of their wife's death. In some of the narratives, for example, referential material dominated. The narratives recounted the spouse's death in extraordinarily terse, even minimalistic syntax. Factual details were the focus, and no evaluative material was present in the narratives. Others of the narratives, in contrast, were characterized by sequences of syntactically complex clauses that were topically unrelated to preceding clauses. Evaluative material appeared throughout the narratives in structural positions that fragmented and interrupted the complicating action sequences (the event structures), making them difficult to follow. The overall impression was one of verbosity.

Bower problematized the interpretation of these two distinctive patterns in the narratives' organization by considering four explanatory models, two of which are germane to this discussion: the cognitive deficiency explanation (consistent with the DRP) and the sociocultural explanation (consistent with the SRP).

As mentioned earlier, DRP research conceptualizes narrative in terms of structural completeness and relevance to the story-generating task rather than to any external, speech community related norms and values. Bower argued that if these bereavement narratives were considered as spontaneous stories and were analyzed according to the parameters adopted by the DRP, the following conclusions would be likely: With regard to the minimalist narratives, the elderly narrators' ability to construct syntactically complex and elaborated sentences was clearly failing. They could only produce a narrative that followed the chronology of events in the simplest of syntax. In the narratives that seemed to be fragmented and verbose, the syntactically complex, "empty" sentences reflected the elaborated but meaningless style typical of elderly speakers who offered more talk in order to compensate for their declining linguistic capabilities. From the DRP perspective on spontaneous narrative, these death narratives' distinctive structural contours would be interpreted as evidence of structural deficiency. At best, this deficiency would be attributed to the "normal" loss of linguistic and communicative function due to aging. At worst, the structural deficiencies would be construed as indicative of cognitive deficit or impairment.

In contrast to the DRP interpretation, a socioculturally sensitive interpretation of the widowers' narratives that takes into account the speakers' values and attitudes about what can and cannot be said in personal narrative yields a strikingly different assessment of these narratives' structure. For example, Bower contended that although Irish Americans are properly recognized for their verbal acuity and vigor, it is not a speech community that readily speaks about its personal emotions—either in private or in public. Anthropological, sociological, and psychological studies attest to the paucity of individual revelations about inner state and personal feeling in the private, therapeutic, and public discourse of Irish Americans (Glassie, 1982; McGoldrick, 1982; Scheper-Hughes, 1979; Zborowski, 1969). Taken in this context, the minimalist, factual, nonevaluative focus of some of these narratives could be regarded as culturally appropriate verbal behavior rather than as an indication of linguistic deterioration. For these elderly Irish Americans, it was culturally inappropriate to express their emotional reaction to their wife's death. As a result, expressions of emotion did not make their way into the narrative and the narrative appeared to lack evaluative material. Further, Bower pointed out, that if we reconsider the narratives that appeared to be structurally fragmented or verbose in light of this Irish American cultural value of nonexpressivity, we arrive at an additional insight. The rambling discourse that appeared to intrude on the story line did, in fact, bracket tentative, personal statements by the narrator about his inner state at the time of bereavement. Rather than constituting evidence for cognitive impairment, this ostensible rambling served the very important function of linguistically distancing the speaker from a perilous, norm-violating statement of emotion. Bower contested a likely DRP assessment that these elders were suffering from age-related deterioration of their linguistic and communicative abilities. Rather, the structural organization of these narratives reflected culturally appropriate presentations of experience that demonstrated the elderly speakers' full command over and participation in the speech norms and values of their community.

## CONCLUSION

Incontestably, personal narrative represents a valuable source of insight into the linguistic and communicative competence of the elderly speaker. How such narratives are elicited and analyzed becomes the critical issue. In my view, L&W's conceptualization of oral narrative, and the interview context closely associated with it, offers, at present, the most value-neutral and empirically productive framework for approaching the study of language and aging. L&W's model offers a descriptive focus on the narrative consistent with its structuralist-functionalist inception. Its clause-based, line-by-line format permits microexamination of the speaker's actual words and builds from this as its starting point. Its identification of an overall five-part structure permits us to isolate, identify, and compare speakers' conceptual organization of their experience. The referential and evaluative functions of oral narrative outlined by L&W's model offer a semantic starting point for description that is extraordinarily sensitive to cultural values and norms.

Further, narrative analysis is closely associated with the context of the narrative's elicitation. Indeed, the elicitation of oral narrative of personal experience has become a hallmark of sociolinguistic fieldwork methodology. Sociolinguistic methodology seeks to move the interview situation toward a speech situation that more closely approximates the ordinary speaking situations of the respondent. Whether or not this methodology succeeds in this effort is controversial (Milroy, 1987; Wolfson, 1982). Nonetheless, most would agree that recounting personal experience in the sociolinguistic interview setting not only catalyzes the interaction toward less formality but also represents a by-product of the decreasing formality of the situation.

The two sociolinguistic studies reviewed here draw heavily on the resources of this model, to good effect. As Labov and Auger's (1993) study indicated, the speech our elders produce as they engage in recounting the personal experiences that have become part of their biography, in settings that closely approximate their ordinary interactional milieu, reveals a full, even artful, command of complex syntactic structures in narrative that contrasts markedly with DRP reports of reduced capabilities in this regard. Bower's study invoked both structural and functional dimensions of L&W's model in attributing sociocultural meaning to the presence and absence of evaluative structures in the narratives of the ethnic elders. Despite their advanced years, age is not the only defining feature of elders' language use. They have lived their lives as members of a speech communities, and there is no reason to assume that they cease to respond to or invoke the cultural norms that influence language and verbal behavior such as narrative simply because they become aged, impaired, or isolated from their life-long, primary social networks. Consequently, it is very difficult to envision any narrative analysis that does not incorporate knowledge of the speaker's cultural values and attitudes about how a story must be told and what may or may not be said in a personal narrative. This view contrasts sharply with the DRP's view, which mandates a priori completeness and relevance criteria in assessing the elder's command over narrative structure.

There is no question that the effects of physiological aging on linguistic and communicative language use must and should be examined, but we must remember that language itself is not a purely physiological function. It is socially constituted and regulated to so thorough an extent that it is impossible to rely on research findings that do not build culturally sensitive social context into the language gathering methods. If, as Coupland et al. (1991) suggested, biological aging cannot be addressed apart from the social context of aging, then this is emphatically true for the study of linguistic aging.

# REFERENCES

Bokus, B. (1992). Peer co-narration: Changes in the structure of preschoolers' participation. *Journal of Narrative and Life History, 2,* 253–276.
Bower, A. (1992, November). Observing the speech of the elderly. In *Conceputalizing language in the study of aging.* Symposium conducted at the 45th Annual Meeting of the Gerontological Society of America (P. Saunders, Chair), Washington, DC.
Bower, A. (in press). Evaluation in the bereavement narratives of elderly Irish-American widowers. In H. Hamilton (Ed.), *Old age and language: Multidisciplinary perspectives.* New York: Garland.
Coupland, N., Coupland, J., & Giles, H. (1991). *Language, society and the elderly.* Oxford, England: Basil Blackwell.
Emery, O. (1986). Linguistic decrement in normal aging. In *Language and Communication, 6,* 47–64.
Fayol, M., & Lemaire, P. (1993). Levels of approach to discourse. In H. Brownell & Y. Joanette (Eds.), *Narrative discourse in neurologically impaired and normal aging adults* (pp. 2–21). San Diego, CA: Singular.
Glassie, H. (1982). *Passing the time in Ballymenone.* Philadelphia: University of Pennsylvania Press.
Gold, D., Andres, D., Arbuckle, T., & Schwartzman, A. (1988). Measurement and correlates of verbosity in elderly people. *Journal of Gerontology: Psychological Sciences, 43,* 27–33.
Guy, G., & Boyd, S. (1990). The development of a morphological class. *Language Variation and Change, 2,* 1–18.
Hutchinson, J., & Jensen, M. (1980). A pragmatic evaluation of discourse communication in normal and senile elderly in a nursing home. In L. Obler & M. Albert (Eds.), *Language and communication in the elderly* (pp. 59–73). Lexington, MA: Lexington.
Kemper, S., Rash, S., Kynette, D., & Norman, S. (1990). Telling stories: The structure of adults' narratives. *European Journal of Cognitive Psychology, 2,* 205–228.
Labov, W. (1972). *Sociolinguistic patterns.* Philadelphia: University of Pennsylvania Press.
Labov, W. (1984). Field methods of the project on linguistic change and variation. In J. Baugh & J. Sherzer (Eds.), *Language in use* (pp. 28–53). Englewood Cliffs, NJ: Prentice-Hall.
Labov, W., & Auger, J. (1993). The effect of normal aging on discourse: A sociolinguistic approach. In H. Brownell & Y. Joanette (Eds.), *Discourse in neurologically impaired and normal aging adults* (pp. 115–133). San Diego, CA: Singular.
Labov, W., & Waletzky, J. (this issue). Narrative analysis: Oral versions of personal experience. In J. Helm (Ed.), *Essays on the verbal and visual arts: Proceedings of the 1966 Annual Spring Meeting of the American Ethnological Society* (pp. 12–44). Seattle: University of Washington Press. (Original work published 1967)
Mandl, H., Stein, N., & Trabasso, T. (1984). *Learning and comprehension of text.* Hillsdale, NJ: Lawrence Erlbaum Associates, Inc.
McGoldrick, M. (1982). Irish families. In M. McGoldrick, J. Pearce, & J. Giordano (Eds.), *Ethnicity in family therapy* (pp. 310–339). New York: Guilford.
Milroy, L. (1987). *Observing and analyzing natural language: A critical account of sociolinguistic method.* Oxford, England: Basil Blackwell.
North, A., Ulatowska, H., Macaluso-Haynes, S., & Bell, H. (1986). Discourse performance in older adults. *International Journal of Aging and Human Development, 23,* 267–283.
Obler, L. (1980). Narrative discourse style in the elderly. In L. Obler & M. Albert (Eds.), *Language and communication in the elderly: Clinical, therapeutic and experimental issues* (pp. 75–90). Lexington, MA: Lexington Books.
Peterson, C., & McCabe, A. (1983). *Developmental psycholinguistics.* New York: Plenum.
Pratt, M., & Robins, S. (1991). That's the way it was: Age differences in the structure and quality of adults' personal narratives. *Discourse Processes, 14,* 73–85.

Ripich, D. (1991). Differential diagnosis and assessment. In R. Lubinski (Ed.), *Dementia and communication* (pp. 188–215). Philadelphia: B.C. Decker.

Sankoff, D., & Lessard, R. (1975). Vocabulary richness: A sociolinguistic analysis. *Science, 19,* 689–690.

Santi, S., & Obler, L. (1991). Methodological issues in research on aging and language. In D. Ripich (Ed.), *Handbook of geriatric communication disorders* (pp. 333–347). Austin, TX: Pro-ed.

Scheper-Hughes, N. (1979). *Saints, scholars and schizophrenics: Mental illness in rural Ireland.* Berkeley: University of California Press.

Stein, N., & Glenn, C. (1979). An analysis of story comprehension in elementary school children. In R. Freedle (Ed.), *New directions in discourse processing* (pp. 53–120). Norwood, NJ: Ablex.

Sutton-Smith, B. (1978). *The folkstories of children.* Philadelphia: University of Pennsylvania Press.

Trudgill, P. (1983). *Sociolinguistics* (2nd ed.). Harmondsworth, England: Penguin.

Ulatowska, H., & Chapman, S. (1991). Discourse studies. In R. Lubinski (Ed.), *Dementia and communication* (pp. 115–132). Philadelphia: B.C. Decker.

Walker, V., Roberts, P., & Hedrick, D. (1988). Linguistic analysis of the discourse narratives of young and aged women. *Folia Phoniatica, 40,* 58–64.

Wolfson, N. (1982). *CHP: The conversational historic present in American English narrative.* Dordrecht, The Netherlands: Foris.

Zborowski, M. (1969). *People in pain.* San Francisco: Jossey-Bass.

# Micro-Units and Macro-Units in Text Theory and in Investigations of Left- and Right-Brain-Damaged Patients

### Wolfgang U. Dressler
*Institut für Sprachwissenschaft, Universität Wien*

### Heinz Karl Stark
*Institut für Hirnkreislaufforschung, Ludwig Boltzmann Gesellschaft, Wien*

Labov and Waletzky's (1967/this issue; henceforth L&W) methodology both in its original form and in its later refinements (cf. Labov, 1972; Labov & Fenshel, 1977) has had a great impact on our textlinguistic and neurolinguistic research in Vienna (at first only within the Department of Linguistics of the University of Vienna) since the mid-70s (first pertinent publication only in Dressler, 1980). However, both for text- and neurolinguistic reasons it became necessary to successively introduce modifications of L&W's concepts. These revisions are the focus of our contribution to this issue.

Let us start with purely textlinguistic reasons for modifications. L&W's "analytical framework for the analysis of oral versions of personal experience in English" (p. 3) had no basis in either text theory or narrative theory, not to speak of textlinguistic theory, which emerged only after 1967. For adherents and protagonists of text linguistics (cf. Beaugrande & Dressler, 1981; Dressler, 1972, 1989; Stark & Stark, 1991) it proved necessary to integrate this framework into a textlinguistic theory. The ensuing modifications concerned above all the following concepts:

1. The smallest units of L&W's framework are, on the expression side, the clause and, on the content side, the proposition (cf. Labov, 1972, sections 8 and 9; Labov & Fenshel, 1977, p. 51). In our own research, we have used propositions in the semantic sense, but counted them when they were formally expressed by clauses

---

Requests for reprints should be sent to Wolfgang U. Dressler, Institut für Sprachwissenschaft, Universität Wien, Berggasse 11, A-1090 Wien, Austria. E-mail: ulli@ling.univie.ac.at

or similar units. Furthermore, we added the following constitutive property of the formal expression of each proposition: It must have its own field of communicative dynamism, that is, (within the framework of functional sentence perspective of the Prague school of linguistics) it must have a theme (topic) and rheme (focus) of its own with a hierarchy of communicative information values (cf. Firbas, 1992). As a result, drastically backgrounded secondary (subordinate) clauses, which have no communicative dynamism of their own, are not counted as separate propositions but attached to the proposition of the (main) clause they are subordinated to. This is in agreement with L&W's practice, as for instance in their Example 6 $_1j_0$:

Example 1
(1) *they thought I was just trying to catch up because I was going on or slowing down* (1967, p. 24)

We disagree, however, with their separation of participles as separate clauses or propositions, as in their Example 6 $_2c_{16}$ *racing,* because such a participle does not have a separate field of communicative dynamism.

2. L&W (1967/this issue) considered the congruence of event line and story line as the primary sequence, from which more complicated sequences should be derived (cf. Labov, 1972, pp. 359–360 and 375–393). This descriptive principle can be better thought of, as suggested in Dressler's (1989, 1996) textsemiotic preference theory, as an instance of the ordo naturalis, that is, the iconic (diagrammatic) relation of the sequence of propositions with the temporal sequence of perceived and cognitively ordered event units.

3. With regard to L&W's macrostructural units (cf. Labov, 1972, pp. 362–375; henceforth: *macro-units*) of complication and resolution, in longer narratives it was necessary to segment each of them into episodes (following van Dijk, 1980, p. 141) in order to account for the macro- and microstructure of these macro-units. These lower-order macro-units (i.e., episodes) belong either to the obligatory foreground of the story or to the optional background that adds descriptive or explanatory detail.

4. Finally, we would like to mention that empirical work with Austrian German oral and written narratives of both brain-damaged patients and normal controls showed that L&W's macro-unit "evaluation" (cf. Labov, 1972, pp. 370–375) hardly ever occurred as a separate unit at the surface level of texts. Rather, it appeared in a dispersed format, usually only in the form of evaluative aspects of parts of propositions belonging to other macro-units, for instance as evaluative words, particles, conjunctions, and, more generally, in the stylistic choice among alternatives (cf. Labov's, 1972, and Polanyi's, 1985, notion of evaluation structure of discourse).

Our subsequent neurolinguistic work (Dressler, 1980, 1983; Dressler & Pléh, 1988; Dressler et al., in press; Stark, Bruck, & Stark, 1988; Stark & Stark, 1991) focused mainly on the analysis of (predominantly oral) reproductions of narrative texts. Emphasis has been on comparing reproductions of brain-damaged patients and of normal controls with the original narratives. L&W's macro-units and propositions (as *micro-units*) functioned as our units of analysis. In our comparative analysis, we were particularly interested in the question of which macro- and micro-units are completely or partially preserved or omitted by patients (of various types and degree of severity of impairments) when compared with the normal controls. These investigations have led us to introduce two further modifications to L&W's framework, which we also consider highly relevant:

5. Elaborating on L&W's distinction between the obligatory macro-units complication, resolution, evaluation and the optional macro-units orientation and coda, we attempted to gradually differentiate the informative value of macro-units and of propositions within macro-units for the gist of the narrative. In doing this we used, first of all, concepts of communicative dynamism (and of functional sentence perspective) of the Prague School (cf. Firbas, 1992) and of the text-constitutive standard of informativity of Beaugrande and Dressler (1982). Because L&W's "narrative clauses" belong to the event line and thus to the narrative skeleton of a story which tends to be foregrounded, they have a greater chance to be regarded as the set of most or more informative and thus as essential propositions rather than nonnarrative, "free" clauses.

One result of these investigations has been that Broca's aphasics and global aphasics omit only the least informative units; the latter ones, of course, only if they are able to produce narratives at all (cf. Dressler, 1980; Dressler & Pléh, 1988; Dressler et al., 1977; Stark et al., 1988; Stark & Stark, 1991). On the contrary, Wernicke's aphasics, severe anomic (amnestic) aphasics, and many right-brain-damaged patients even expanded less informative propositions with made-up confabulations.

Let us illustrate this point with an example of the immediate oral recall situation. The German original is given here in an English glossing (/ signalling macro-units):

Example 2
1. Mary and Peter were walking in the downtown area./
2. Both of them stopped in front of a shop,/
3. and she admired a dress in the shop-window./
4. Suddenly she recalled that she owed him money,
5. looked sadly into her purse,
6. and paid him back the amount with a sigh.
7. Now she was broke again./
8. Next morning, her door-bell rang.
9. Peter was standing there with a package in his hands.
10. It was the dress./
11. He had noticed,
12. that she wanted this dress,
13. but had no money to buy it.

For example, a female Broca's aphasic, H.R. (mildly disturbed, over 10 years post onset), omitted only the uninformative parts of Propositions 1 and 8 and the last, backgrounded macro-unit (Propositions 11–13).

6. In our investigations, which culminated in the comparison of left- and right-brain-damaged patients (cf. Dressler et al., in press), we focussed on text pragmatics as a domain in which right-brain-damaged patients, in contrast to aphasics, are usually considered to have major problems (cf. Joanette & Brownell, 1989). The area most relevant to the neurolinguistic integration of L&W's framework has proved to be the area of pragmatic inferences (cf. van de Velde, 1981, 1992). For example, relatively uninformative propositions, as opposed to highly informative ones, can be easily inferred from the cotext and thus easily dropped both in reproductions of narratives and in productions of (narrative) picture stories. More important, most sequences of propositions can only be interpreted as cohesive and coherent, if the interpreter (either hearer or analyst) makes inferences that bridge "cognitive gaps" between propositions (cf. Labov, 1972, pp. 359–362).

Finally right-brain-damaged patients and Wernicke's (sensory) aphasics often produce confabulations, that is, they make inferences that are provoked by the cotext or context (cf. McCarthy & Warrington, 1990, p. 313; Parkin & Leng, 1993, p. 56), but go far beyond inferences drawn by unimpaired subjects. For example, a male right-brain-damaged patient, W.K. (moderately to mildly impaired, 3 years post onset), produced the following two subsequent confabulations when recalling the story given in our Example 2:

Example 3
a. *Die Maria äussert den den Wunsch—über den Kauf eines Kleides*
"The Mary utters the the wish—about buying a dress"
b. (Because she was already in financial difficulties with respect to Peter) *machte sie den Anschein, als ob sie sich das überlegen würde.*
"she appeared, as if she would reconsider it (sc. a))"

In conclusion, we assert the persistent impact of L&W's pioneering work in their original paper in 1967. Our textlinguistic and neurolinguistic studies confirm the potential, inherent in their work, of being expanded and employed in areas and approaches they may have not originally considered possible. Moreover, certain aspects of our subsequent textlinguistic and pragmatic modelling made explicit what was already implicit in their own study.

## REFERENCES

Beaugrande, R. A. de, & Dressler, W. U. (1981). *Introduction to text linguistics.* London: Longman.
Dressler, W. U. (1972). *Einführung in die Textlinguistik* [Introduction to textlinguistics]. Tübingen, Germany: Niemeyer.

Dressler, W. U. (1980). Disturbi linguistici del riassunto nell'afasia [Linguistic impairments of story recall]. *Acta Phoniatrica Latina, 2*, 19–22.
Dressler, W. U. (1983). Textlinguistik unter Berücksichtigung der Patholinguistik [Textlinguistics with an emphasis on pathological linguistics]. In W. Kühlwein (Ed.), *Texte in Sprachwissenschaft, Sprachunterricht, Sprachtherapie* (pp. 15–23). Tübingen, Germany: Narr.
Dressler, W. U. (1989). *Semiotische Parameter einer textlinguistischen Natürlichkeitstheorie* [Semiotic parameters of a textlinguistic theory of naturalness]. Vienna: Verlag der Österreichischen Akademie der Wissenschaften.
Dressler, W. U. (1996). Parallelism between natural textlinguistics and other components of natural linguistics. *Sprachtypologie und Universalienforschung, 49*, 295–311.
Dressler, W. U., & Pléh, Cs. (1988). On text disturbances in aphasia. In W. U. Dressler & J. A. Stark (Eds.), *Linguistic analyses of aphasic language* (pp. 151–178). New York: Springer-Verlag.
Dressler, W. U., Stark, H. K., Vassilakou, M., Rauchensteiner, D., Tošic, J., Weitzenauer, S., Wasner, P., Hirsch, A., Pons, C., Stark, J., & Brunner, G. (in press). Textpragmatic impairments of figure–ground distinction in right-brain-damaged stroke patients compared with aphasics and healthy controls. *Journal of Pragmatics*.
Firbas, J. (1992). *Functional sentence perspective in written and spoken communication*. Cambridge, England: Cambridge University Press.
Joanette, Y., & Brownell, H. H. (Eds.). (1989). *Discourse ability and brain damage*. New York: Springer-Verlag.
Labov, W. (1972). *Language in the inner city*. Philadelphia: University of Pennsylvania Press.
Labov, W., & Fenshel, D. (1977). *Therapeutic discourse*. New York: Academic.
Labov, W., & Waletzky, J. (this issue). Narrative analysis: Oral versions of personal experience. In J. Helm (Ed.), *Essays on the verbal and visual arts: Proceedings of the 1966 Annual Spring Meeting of the American Ethnological Society* (pp. 12–44). Seattle: University of Washington Press. (Original work published 1967)
McCarthy, R. A., & Warrington, E. A. (1990). *Cognitive neuropsychology*. San Diego, CA: Academic.
Parkin, A. J., & Leng, N. R. C. (1993). *Neuropsychology of the amnesic syndrome*. Hillsdale, NJ: Lawrence Erlbaum Associates, Inc.
Polanyi, L. (1985). *Telling the American story: A structural and cultural analysis of conversational storytelling*. Norwood, NJ: Ablex.
Stark, H. K., Bruck, J., & Stark, J. A. (1988). Verbal and nonverbal aspects of text production in aphasia. In E. Scherzer, R. Simon, & J. Stark (Eds.), *Proceedings of the first European conference on aphasiology* (pp. 121–129). Vienna: Allgemeine Unfallversicherungsanstalt.
Stark, J. A., & Stark, H.K. (1991). Störungen der Textverarbeitung bei Aphasie [Disturbances in text processing in aphasics]. In G. Blanken (Ed.), *Einführung in die linguistische Aphasiologie* (pp. 231–285). Freiburg, Germany: HochschulVerlag.
van de Velde, R. (1981). *Interpretation, Kohärenz und Inferenz* [Interpretation, coherence, and inference]. Hamburg, Germany: Buske.
van de Velde, R. (1992). *Text and thinking*. Berlin, Germany: de Gruyter.
van Dijk, T. A. (1980). *Textwissenschaft* [The science of texts]. Tübingen, Germany: Niemeyer.

# Narrative: Experience, Memory, Folklore

### Charlotte Linde
*Institute for Research on Learning and Stanford University*

## UPWARDS AND ONWARDS FROM THE SENTENCE

I remember reading Labov and Waletzky (1967/this issue; henceforth L&W) as a graduate student: It was enormously liberating, allowing the young linguist to move out from the sentence to the much larger world of discourse, language in action, rather than sentences pinned to the page. This was the paper that extended the boundaries of linguistic analysis beyond the sentence level, by showing that the risky and messy level of discourse could be studied with the same tools of analysis that worked at the then-legitimate levels of the phoneme, the morpheme, or the sentence. (Earlier efforts to bring discourse analysis into linguistics, such as Harris, 1963, attempted to work up from the sentence to construct the level of discourse, rather than starting by recognizing a higher level unit, like the narrative, and working down from there to the sentence level, as L&W did.)

I experienced L&W as liberating because it gave a foundation for studying language in "use." Social life is not transacted in sentences or even in speech acts. It happens in the exchange and negotiation of discourse units: narratives, primarily, then descriptions, explanations, plans, and so forth.

It was a startling experience to go back and reread L&W carefully after at least 25 years of considering it one of the central texts that have formed my thinking. What was surprising in the rereading is to see how formally constrained L&W actually is, how much of the paper is concerned with developing formal definitions of the structure of narrative.

Elsewhere, I have critiqued the virtues and limits of the structural approach to discourse (Linde, 1997). A structural account is necessary to allow us to identify units, to understand their parts, and to specify their dimensions of variation. However, it can not provide tools for understanding the use of discourse, or to put

---

Requests for reprints should be sent to Charlotte Linde, 66 Willow Place, Menlo Park, CA 94025. E-mail: charlotte_linde@irl.org

it in Labov's terms, to understand why anyone says anything. To approach this problem, an account of discourse must also include a description of the wider set of social practices within which discourses must be understood.

Clearly, there were attempts at formalization in L&W that did not prove to be fruitful, for example, the attempt to define the parts of the narrative strictly formally, by displacement sets. This does not appear to have led to major advances in our understanding of discourse, either within narrative studies or by extension to other discourse units.

What did prove extremely fruitful, for my research and many others, was the identification of the parts of the narrative: abstract, orientation, narrative clause, evaluation, and coda, defined partially formally, partially semantically, and partially by their function within the narrative. Evaluation, the component of narrative structure that defies a purely formal definition, is exactly the locus of the most important social and communicative action.

## TRANSITIONAL NATURE OF THE NARRATIVE OF PERSONAL EXPERIENCE

I now turn to specific issues in L&W that have been important for my past and current thinking, in particular the distinction between personal narrative and more collective forms such as folktale or myth. Although drawing on earlier structuralist work in folklore, L&W defined the narrative of personal experience as a form distinguished from "complex long-standing literary or oral traditions," such as myths, folk tales, legends, histories, epics, toasts, and sagas. The narratives that L&W analyzed were defined as not "the products of expert storytellers that have been retold many times, but the original productions of a representative sample of the population."

This definition needs a lot of unpacking. Viewing narrative as an "original production" almost suggests that it comes bubbling up from the unconscious, or that it is created fresh, for the first time, on the spot. (Note that this was a general issue for this era of linguistics. A parallel claim was Chomsky's insistence, contra the behaviorists, that sentences are generated by a creative process, rather than learned and repeated.) Although some of the narratives in L&W may be told for the first and only time, such as accounts of television cartoons, others show signs of having been told many times before. These are the artful, polished narratives of significant or life-threatening events, such as the story of the outraged husband (Narrative 1) or the brothers' knife fight (Narrative 3). Yet, the repeated tales are still distinguishable from traditional narratives, which belong to a group, rather than primarily to an individual teller.

What has been enormously fruitful, in my work, is to examine narratives that fall between the two ends of the continuum of originality. These are personal narratives that are told and retold, or nonpersonal narratives, part of a group's repertoire, that become part of the speaker's personal repertoire.

## Narrative and Memory

One type of personal narrative that is told and retold is the narrative that forms a part of the speaker's life story. I have defined the life story (Linde, 1993) as a discontinuous unit that consists of all the stories and associated discourse units, such as explanations and chronicles, and the connections between them, told by an individual during the course of his or her lifetime, that satisfy the following two criteria: (a) The stories and associated discourse units contained in the life story have as their primary evaluation a point about the speaker, not a general point about the way the world is, and (b) the stories and associated discourse units have extended reportability. That is, they are tellable and are told and retold over the course of a long period of time.

The life story is thus comprised exactly of the most significant narratives of a speaker's life, which are told and retold, reinterpreted and reshaped for different situations. These narratives are not memorized and replayed like a recorded tape, but rather exhibit the expected features of recipient design. Speakers find and then partially stabilize effective ways of describing events and evaluating their meaning, which they change somewhat to suit a particular audience, or more rarely, radically alter as their understanding of events and meanings changes.

## Narrative and Memory in Institutions

A speaker's life story is held not only by the speaker, but by family, friends, and people who participate in the speaker's life. Such close associates can have storytelling rights to critique the speaker's stories, correcting facts, interpretations, and evaluations. Life stories are thus a means for socially transacting an individual's memory. Further, others who do not "have" such rights by their position may take them, as in the case of gossip about an absent person (Goodwin, 1990).

Once we broaden the notion of memory from an individually based, cognitive phenomenon to a social phenomenon, we may also ask about the memory of groups and institutions. (In this article, I use the term *institution* to describe any group that persists over time, at any level of reified or official structuring. Thus, I include as an institution a corporation, a gang, a family, and a regular Tuesday night poker game.) Clearly such entities remember. They remember with file cabinets, procedures, bureaucratic forms, photo albums, tattoos, memorial statuary, and so forth. However, most particularly they remember with narratives. Such narratives may be official stories, for example, an authorized biography of the founder of a corporation. However, they also include oral stories, both official and nonofficial. Stories are told all the time, by everyone, for a variety of purposes.

In understanding their role in institutional memory, the first problem is how to tell that a given story forms part of the institutional memory. That is, stories may be told once or twice, or many times, but only by the people who were participants in the events. The key moment for the development of institutional memory comes when a story is told by someone who was not a participant in the event. A person telling a story about an event relevant to an institution that happened at which she was not present is telling a story that is part of the institutional memory, a story she must have heard from someone else. Nonparticipant stories offer a chance to understand the informal channels by which the institutional memory is reproduced.

Let me tell a story about a story, to illustrate how nonparticipant narratives work within an institution's memory. When the director of the Institute for Research on Learning (IRL) first assumed that post, he had to preside almost immediately at meetings in which it was necessary for him to tell the story of the origin of IRL, in the presence of IRL members who had been there at the founding, or at least much longer than he had. At first, he handled this awkward discourse obligation by telling the story with strong evidential markers of nonparticipation: "I've only been on board for three weeks, but I've been told that … ". These evidentials marked his somewhat delicate membership position: He was the director, and hence the person who should properly tell the story, but he was also a newcomer, who did not know it as well as his subordinates. Over the course of time, as he has become more and more centrally a member of the Institute and its history, he has come to tell the story with no marking of how he came to know it. Although the story is told in the third person, it is told vividly, with a camera's eye view, including details of motivation, direct quotations, and so forth. Furthermore, other IRL employees' versions of the story have been changed by the way he tells it, even those employees who were present at the original events. Over the years, the director's account of the business reasons for the founding of institute has affected, differentially, the accounts of many of the researchers who previously concentrated only on intellectual reasons.

In Linde (1996) I showed how nonparticipant narratives are shaped by the teller's identity as a member or nonmember of the group whose story is being told and by the teller's position within the group as a person who does or does not have storytelling rights to that story. The linguistic manipulation of identity includes speakers' use of point-of-view markers such as evidentials of knowing and not knowing, indicators of subjectivity such as attribution or nonattribution to others of feelings, judgments, motives, direct evaluations, and realistic versus formulaic retellings.

Institutions appear to have an implicational hierarchy of the narratives they will maintain. The most common are origin stories. That is, if an institution has only one narrative that everyone in it knows, that will be an origin story (Vansina, 1985). In organizations, this is often a story of a charismatic founder, whether it is Howard

Hughes at Hughes Aircraft, or Mrs. Stanford at Stanford University.[1] Mendoza-Denton (1997), in work with Latina gang members, showed that although they do not maintain a rich institutional memory, most members do know the story of how the two major gangs came into being through a fight over a pair of sneakers. For families, depending on where the family draws its boundaries, the origin story may be the account of how Mommy and Daddy met, a story which many Americans can recount (Silberstein, 1982; Stone 1988). Or it may be the story of how the family came to the United States, or moved to California, or made or lost its money.

Returning to the range of stories an institution may maintain, if there is a second story, it is likely to be a story of an averted disaster or a turning point for the institution. Additional narratives may be accounts of successes, additional noteworthy characters, and so forth.

As this hierarchy suggests, it appears that different institutions may work their pasts in very different ways. Some institutions make strong and frequent use of their past, telling and retelling their stories to induct new members into their history and to interpret new activities and directions as in fundamental agreement with founding principles. Other institutions may make little use of narratives of their past. Even institutions of the same type differ. For example, the major insurance company that forms one site for my studies of narrative in institutional memory works its past very intensely. One might think that this was obvious for an insurance company: It is an inherently conservative organization, because its job is to conserve both its own and its policy holders' assets. However, insurance companies differ in how they work their pasts. A simple comparison shows this. My company includes pointers to its history, with photo of its founder and high points of its development on its Web page. Other comparable companies do not mention history in their Web pages. In the academic domain, Mrs. Stanford, the founder of Stanford University is intensely present at Stanford. There is a statue of her, her vision for the university is cited in editorials in the student newspaper, and, as a student informed me, the university shuttle bus system is named after her favorite mare, Marguerite. In contrast, the founder of Hunter College was for me as an undergraduate, a bearded and dusty oil painting in the main lobby with no name or story attached.

In addition to these historical narratives, institutions also support what I call *paradigmatic narratives*. For example, in the case of the insurance company I have studied, there is a paradigmatic narrative that gives an account of the trajectory of

---

[1] There is a class of organizational folktales, similar to origin stories, that attach to founders or salient leaders. Thus, Martin, Feldman, Hatch, & Sitkins (1983) described a number of stories that are told in a variety of workplaces as having uniquely happened to their founder. For example, one of these is the tale of the president of a large organization being asked by a receptionist to show identification. These stories are told to indicate the kind of values the organization claims to embody. In the case of Thomas J. Watson at IBM, he complied with the regulation, in the case of Charles Revson at Revlon, he fired the receptionist.

an ideal sales agent career: this includes how he was recruited, his activities in early years, how he achieved his success, and so forth. (I use "he" because this account is definitely gendered. One issue the company is now facing is that recently recruited women agents do not find this paradigmatic narrative useful for their construction of their own stories.) The paradigmatic narrative is distinguished from a myth or folktale, because the full paradigmatic narrative is never told on any given occasion. Rather, pieces of it are told as possibilities. Thus, a manager recruiting a possible new agent might cite the beginning part of the story: "You'll work hard for the first seven years or so, and then you can start to reap the rewards." Further, the paradigmatic narrative gives salience to the telling of stories of individual agents' careers. Thus when a manager tells a story about old George down the street, the relevance of this story is as an instance that approximates to the ideal agent career. As Goffman pointed out, it is the task of a narrator to justify taking up air time by making the story the story of Everyman, what any reasonable person would do in similar circumstances. The paradigmatic narrative represents the work of an entire institution to create such relevance for particular narratives.

Both paradigmatic narratives and the actual official narratives told within an institution strongly constrain the other narratives that may be told within the institution. The narrative of a speaker's own career within an institution is shaped both by the founder's story and by the paradigmatic narratives. A speaker's narrative may either be coherent with the founding and paradigmatic narratives or may contest them, but is always told against the background of these familiar and authoritative accounts. In particular, it is evaluations that are constrained. For example, in the life insurance company I have studied, the story of the founder is presented as the tale of a midwestern farmer, famed for his probity and honesty in business, who shaped the company in his image. This means that any agent telling his (or more recently, her) story can not present it as a story of risk-taking, high-stakes entrepreneurship. Although a story of business risk-taking often is positively evaluated within other business organizations, even within other types of insurance companies, in this company the founder's story presents and constrains what may be evaluated as appropriate business actions, and it is reliability and long-term conservatism that receive positive evaluations.

These studies of narrative in institutions begin to move the study of narrative back to its roots in the study of folklore. They show that narratives in groups and institutions are not solely individual productions, but rather are constrained by the narratives that have a long-term life within the institution, as well as by the practices and occasions on which narrative are told. Recent work in folklore has shifted emphasis from the analysis of the structure of folktales and the description of the full tale stock of a given community to descriptions of actual performances of folktales and how they are used within a wider description of social practices (Bauman, 1992; Foley, 1995).

In particular, considering occasions for narration allows us to ask how, when, and why certain narratives are told. (Dégh, 1989, discussed the ways in which traditional village storytelling in Hungary was dependent on certain occasions for gathering, such as communal work sessions or wakes. However, this analysis does not find a link between specific occasions and particular folktales.) Institutions have occasions that permit the telling of certain narratives. Other potential narratives, the unspeakables, are often difficult to speak because there is no sanctioned public occasion for them. Table 1 indicates types of occasions for narrative remembering in institutions, divided by those that are specifically designed for remembering, and those that allow remembering as a part of some other activity, but do not require narration.

To take one example, officially marked anniversaries of an event, whether the founding of a corporation, a marriage, or an invasion, call for the recounting of the story of that original event. In contrast, the annual meeting of a corporation allows for, but is not necessarily organized around, retelling particular stories. Institutional problems may form the occasion for old-timers to recount how similar problems were solved in the past or what previous problems a currently problematic policy was designed to solve. Certain sites, like historical museums or memorial statues or displays, are designed to represent or elicit certain stories. Sites of notable events may allow for the retelling of those events, although they are not specifically designed for memory: "That's the cave where Luigi and his men hid out from the government when … " (Levi, 1963.) Basso (1996) described the extensive use that the Western Apache make of places and place names as occasions for stories that function as moral instruction in how to behave. Traditional observances like the Passover Seder are specifically designed for the recounting and updating of centrally important stories. Noteworthy nomenclature allows a hearer to request the account of what something means or how it came to be. For example, the term *GO's*

TABLE 1
Occasions for Narrative Remembering

|  | *Designed for Remembering* | *Used for Remembering* |
|---|---|---|
| Time | | |
| Regular occurrences | Anniversaries | Annual meetings |
| Occasional | Retirement parties, roasts, audits, inductions, wakes | Arrival of a traveling bard, coronations, institutional problems |
| Place | Museums, memorial displays, photo albums | Sites of events |
| Artifacts | Memorial artifacts, designed displays | Artifacts accidentally preserved |
| Practices | Traditional observances | Nomenclature |

(Gentil Organisateurs) for the staff of Club Med is said to go back to the earliest founding when conditions were Spartan, and the staff had to be exceedingly "gentil" to deal with the complaints of customers.

This account of occasions begins to show the ecology of narratives in institutions. Thus, the study of narrative is able to move from the purely structural issues of the form of narrative, to the consideration of the use of narrative in the constitution of social life, and the construction of institutional memory.

## ACKNOWLEDGMENTS

I thank my colleagues at the Institute for Research on Learning who have worked with me on the insurance study and have been valued and delightful collaborators in both data collection and analysis: Christopher Darrouzet, Joe Harding, Nancy Lawrence, and Charline Poirier. I also thank Helga Wild and Christopher Darrouzet again, for sharing interview data from another project, as well as their help with the analysis. I am also grateful to many others for discussions and comments at various points in this work: Susan Anderson, Bill Clancey, Michael Bamberg, Geof Bowker, Penny Eckert, Margaret Graham, James Greeno, Norma Mendoza-Denton, Sigrid Mueller, Leigh Star, Etienne Wenger, and Ruth Wodak. This entire article, I hope, expresses my debt to William Labov.

## REFERENCES

Basso, K. H. (1996). *Wisdom sits in places: Landscape and language among the Western Apache.* Albuquerque: University of New Mexico Press.
Bauman, R. (1992). "Folklore" and "performance": In R. Bauman (Ed.), *Folklore, cultural performances and popular entertainments: A communications centered handbook* (pp. 29–49). Oxford, England: Oxford University Press.
Chomsky, N. (1959). Review of Skinner's *Verbal behavior. Language, 35,* 26–58.
Dégh, L. (1989). *Folktales and society: Story-telling.* Bloomington: Indiana University Press.
Foley, J. M. (1995). *The singer of tales in performance.* Bloomington: Indiana University Press.
Goffman, E. Footing. In *Forms of talk* (pp. 124–157). Philadelphia: University of Pennsylvania Press.
Goodwin, M. H. (1990). *He-said-she-said: Talk as social organization among Black children.* Bloomington: Indiana University Press.
Harris, Z. (1963). *Discourse analysis reprints.* The Hague, Netherlands: Mouton.
Labov, W., & Waletzky, J. (this issue). Narrative analysis: Oral versions of personal experience. In J. Helm (Ed.), *Essays on the verbal and visual arts: Proceedings of the 1966 Annual Spring Meeting of the American Ethnological Society* (pp. 12–44). Seattle: University of Washington Press. (Original work published 1967)
Levi, C. (1963). *Christ stopped at Eboli: The story of a year.* New York: Farrar, Straus.
Linde, C. (1993). *Life stories: The creation of coherence.* Oxford, England: Oxford University Press.

Linde, C. (1996). Whose story is this?: Point of view variation and group identity. In J. Arnold, R. Blake, B. Davidson, S. Schwenter, & J. Solomon (Eds.), *Oral narrative sociolinguistic variation: Data, theory and analysis.* Stanford, CA: CSLI.

Linde, C. (1997). Discourse analysis, structuralism and social practice. In J. Baugh, C. Feagin, G. Guy, & D. Schiffrin (Eds.), *Towards a social science of language: A Festschrift for William Labov.* Amsterdam: Benjamins.

Martin, J., Feldman, M. S., Hatch, M. J., & Sitkin, S. (1983). The uniqueness paradox in organizational stories. *Administrative Science Quarterly, 28,* 438–453.

Mendoza-Denton, N. (1997). *Chicana/Mexicana identity and linguistic variation: An ethnographic and sociolinguistic study of gang affiliation in an urban high school.* Stanford, CA: Stanford University, Department of Linguistics.

Silberstein, S. (1982). Textbuilding and personal style in oral courtship narrative. Ann Arbor: University of Michigan, Department of Linguistics.

Stone, E. (1988). *Black sheep and kissing cousins: How our family stories shape us.* New York: Times Books, Random House.

Vansina, J. (1985). *Oral tradition as history.* Madison: University of Wisconsin Press.

# Narrative Explanations: Accounting for Past Experience in Interviews

### Jenny Cook-Gumperz
*University of California, Santa Barbara*

### John J. Gumperz
*University of California, Berkeley*

In this article we focus on the strategic use of narrative as a resource for getting the business of bureaucratic explanation done in face-to-face interviews. Our data consists of extracts from selection interviews recorded in situ in the British Midlands and involves both British and Pakistani workers applying for paid traineeships in a Government-sponsored further education program. Candidates in these sessions are assessed in part by their ability to demonstrate an understanding of the work they will do and so help to make a case for their selection. Through a narrative recounting of their past accomplishments, they project a view of an institutionally typified self as a potential actor and show how this self can enter into institutional participation.

At first glance it may appear that our materials are different from how *narratives* are usually understood in the literature on personal narratives (Linde, 1993; Polanyi, 1989). They are not freely produced but occur in the context of an interview situation in which what the candidate says is orchestrated to a large extent by the interviewer's questions, questions that successful interview candidates must be able to use in their explanation. Moreover, although we use the term projection, the more usual understanding of narratives as projections of the self in which the narrator embarks on a path to self-presentation as a processes of self-discovery does not apply (Ochs & Capps, 1996). Rather, in the institutionally constrained interview context, the mode of presentation the narrator chooses must project an institutional self that will reflect some knowledge of what it takes to be seen as an acceptable

---

Requests for reprints should be sent to Jenny Cook-Gumperz, Department of Education, University of California, Santa Barbara, CA. E-mail: gumperz@education.ucsb.edu

candidate. The issues we deal with in this analysis turn on the fact that although these interview narratives are in a way jointly constructed, candidates vary in their ability to recognize the cues provided for them and thus to convey an institutional self.

We feel justified in using the term narrative because these explanatory accounts show the essential structural characteristics of narratives as set up by Labov and Waletzky in 1967 (this issue; henceforth L&W). Their paper constituted the first linguistic treatment of the basic parameters of informal storytelling in as much as they pointed out that everyday narratives have a normative organization such that the structure is developed through an entailed set of thematic sequences that are temporally ordered. They further stressed that temporal sequencing is realized via specific linguistic forms in the clause structure. A key assumption deriving from this model is that speakers and hearers depend on recognizing the linguistic and conversational expectations the sequential paradigm sets up and would regard deviation from the sequential ordering, or lack of critical development of a section, as a sign of an imperfect narrative (Labov, 1981). It is essential to this argument that the content of a narrative makes a point, that is to say, a narrative must be worth telling as such, and its point is revealed both in the sequential ordering and in the evaluative sequences the narrator inserts. It is as if narrators must remind both themselves and the audience of the significance of each new piece of information both for the over-arching purpose of the narrative and for the immediate context of the story.

Although L&W dealt exclusively with instances in which the narrators solve the problem of the local organization of the story by themselves, more recent work by folklorists and others highlights the interactive construction of narratives in cultural traditions ranging from Hawaiian "talk story" to Samoan speechmaking (Duranti & Brenneis, 1986). Such interactively conjoint storytelling leaves room for different ways of reaching the point of a story. The audience's involvement is a way of gauging what is important in the narrative detail, and this can provide for more circuitous routes to the evaluative point; moreover, more than one point may be involved. It is in the conjoint telling of stories that we see how narrative organization does not just depend on discourse structure, but narrativity is realized through cognitive expectations about the ordering and sequencing of information with both linguistic and conversational consequences.

In what follows, we discuss three extracts from interviews in which candidates are expected to rely on narrative accounts to reconstruct past experiences as constituents of explanation, justifying their suitability for a training program. Narratives are given as explanatory accounts such that the interviewee must represent past actions as providing grounds for their current situation as well as warrants for any future action.[1] Here we want to focus on the cognitive work that

---

[1]Cook-Gumperz and Gumperz (1996) discussed the use of narratives in difficult face-to-face interviews such as educational assessments.

narrative does in guiding the interview process. Narratives with their temporal account of human actions and their built-in evaluation of the consequences of these actions, become the means by which this is done. Thus, the narrative serves both to create ordering in the interview such that after its occurrence a final evaluation and coda is required. Until a narrative explanation is provided, the interview as such cannot be brought to a satisfactory conclusion. Secondly, the narrative creates a shared background in terms of which the candidate's statements can be understood. To be successful in the interview, the candidate must build on this shared understanding of how the institutional requirements can be demonstrated as fitting a particular person, such that this person can project an institutionally typified self.

In the interviews that follow with native (NE) and non-native English (NNE) speakers, we can see that in spite of the continued miscuing in the NNE interviews, the interviewer persists in attempting to find a way of beginning the narrative and thus moving through this stage to the conclusion of the interview. If the narrative does not happen, then an ending, which must stand in the way of an evaluation to all that has gone before, cannot take place. If, as in Interviews 2 and 3, the interviewee provides all the information, but not in the expected temporally sequenced narrative form, the ending is not seen as satisfactory.

In each case the narrative is specifically elicited by the questioning of the interviewer, who also then becomes the audience for the account. In this way, the explanation is part of a coconstructed sequence in which initially the interviewer sets up the premises or orientation; thereafter, the interviewee becomes the center of the interaction as they take over their narrative turn. The interviewer's questioning can be seen as providing the grounds for the interviewee to demonstrate institutionally appropriate experiences through which the institutional self becomes apparent as a temporally ordered narrative explanation. In our analysis we show that what occurs is that, although the NE speaker interactively constructs a narrative, the NNE speakers do not recognize the interviewer's questions as providing the grounds for what could be incorporated into an institutionally satisfactory explanation. Although the two NNE speakers offer larger amounts of specific information at the outset of the interview, the expected temporally sequenced narrative does not follow. In all three examples the interviewer asks lexically similar questions at the outset and at key points through the interview but as the two NNE interviews take a different course, these questions become embedded in a different set of contextual presuppositions and so evoke a different response.

Extract 1: Native–Native
72. T: alright, ... ok, ... .alright, Henry?
73. H: yeah. now, Mark, eh you've chosen as your training in trades,
74.      motor vehicle repair and maintenance, ... ehm, ... curious choice.
75.      really ... .ehm ... in the light of your past experience.
76. M: hmmm,

| | | |
|---|---|---|
| 77. | T: | you've worked for Hyser limited, from ah November. seventy- |
| 78. | | eight,.. until August eighty-one. |
| 79. | M: | yep. |
| 80. | H: | yeah? I would have thought that perhaps you ... would have, |
| 81. | | given more thought to ... .contractor's plant repair and, |
| 82. | | maintenance. |
| 83. | M: | Well, |
| 84. | T: | Rather than motor vehicles? |
| 85. | M: | Well what it were is, when I first left school, ... I started |
| 86. | | the motor vehicle course at Atkinton College, |
| 87. | H: | yeah? |
| 88. | M: | So I ... made it this way to doing motor vehicles at college. |
| 89. | | now I've got the practical side, in the motor vehicle. so I |
| 90. | | would expect, you know,..it would open my- I could put- I could |
| 91. | | put the skill center. |
| 92. | H: | The practical side, |
| 93. | M: | Yeah |
| 94. | H: | Of motor vehicles |
| 95. | M: | Yeah. |

*(several turns of additional questioning omitted)*

| | | |
|---|---|---|
| 106. | H: | You know, what you've already started, |
| 107. | | you've ... .had what ... what on ... four years. |
| 108. | M: | four years, |
| 109. | H: | of time in, ... yeah |
| 110. | M: | Well, |
| 111. | H: | Doing, |
| 112. | | that type of thing? |
| 113. | M: | Yeah. .Well I'm,..you know, I didn't- I- |
| 114. | | didn't think about it. oh, what it were is, *the main thing were |
| 115. | | I were doing the ... motor vehicle course, |
| 116. | H: | Yeah? |
| 117. | M: | And that being, ... when I take- ... finish the exams this summer, |
| 118. | | being qualified mechanic ... .I don't hm ... I don't know.. m ... |
| 119. | | as much on the practical side, of the maintenance on ... cars ... |
| 120. | | and that type of thing. |
| 121. | H: | ... So you've been doing the theory side. |
| 122. | M: | ... yeah, at the m- |
| 123. | H: | at tech college. |
| 124. | M: | at college, yeah. |
| 125. | H: | but just on motor-. |
| 126. | | vehicles. |
| 127. | M: | Yeah |

140. M: ehh I've not done TOO much, NO.
141. H: *No/ *What sort of thing HAVE you done?

The extract begins with a negotiation phase (72–84) in which the participants exchange information until it seems that a satisfactory starting point is reached and the interviewee launches into the explanation (85–91). In the orientation section, the interviewer does most of the talking while the interviewee responds with back channel signals like *hmm, yep,* and *well* with rising final intonation contour, designed to leave the exchange open. He is apparently looking for what is wanted until he recognizes the need to begin his narrative. With Line 84, what is at issue becomes clear: the choice of motor vehicle repair versus plant maintenance. In L&W's terms the abstract–orientation phase of the narrative has been coconstructed. The interviewee then provides a temporally organized account of how he came to make his choice. Starting with school-leaving, he goes on to his part-time technical college course, followed by work experience (85–91). Then, after some further questioning by the interviewer (H), Mark (the interviewee) returns to his account and ends in an evaluative sequence that the interviewer reformulates in Lines 121 and 123, again coconstructing the evaluation: "you have been doing the theory side" .... "but just on motor vehicles." This implicates that he has not yet done the theory of plant repair nor the practical motor repair course. Although the NE interview takes up a total of 69 turns, the NNE interviews reproduced next are considerably shorter, because the initial negotiation of a theme-setting or orientation phase is aborted.

Extract 2: Non-Native 1
 99. T: Alright.ok. ... Henry?
100. H: Alright Habez. your choice.. for ... a training course,
101.    is motor vehicle repair and maintenance. is that right?
102. Hb: Yeah.
103. H: Yeah? Could you tell me please, ... what made you make that-
104.    choice?
105. Hb: Make me? ... well I had done this course before three months.
107. H: Yeah.
108. Hb: So:: ... I am still interested in that course.
109. H: Yeah.
110. Hb: So I would like to improve ... this course, in skills center/
111. H: Yeah/ and what ... the ... course that you did before,
112.    what sorts of things did you do on that course? On motor vehicles?
113. Hb: .Uh I can't remember all things when I haven't got that paper.
114.    which is- I have done .... this-
115. H: Could you not/ tell me in your own words, some of the things
116.    that you did while you were on that particular course?

117. Hb: Well I'll tell you, but I can't remember ALL things/
118. H: No/ I'm not expecting you to remember all the things, I'm
119. just expecting you to remember SOME of the things.

Extract 3: Non-Native 2
101. T: that's the main comment.]
102. H: (pause, sigh) alright, abdul. so … ..WHY have you … picked …
103. motor vehicles, as your choice of training?
104. A: I feel I like this/and also: one of my friend got his own
105. garage here.
106. H: yeah.
107. A: so it will easy to- .. for me to get a job … one of these.
108. ..days … . for he promised me, if I .. I got … got training,
109. from skill center. so it would be-
110. H: for WHAT … you said that you LIKE … this sort of thing.
111. what makes you so sure that you'll like … . motor vehicles?
112. you, just like motor cars? ..Or do you like … eh do you do
113. any of your own repairs, etc? Have you got a motor car of
114. Your own?
115. A: no. I got one./
116. H: ehm.. do you do any of your own repairs?
117. A: yeah. won't start. no matter how come. I always try to do.
118. myself/
119. H: What sort of things do you do?
120. A: Well, I've done brake shoes. brakes … . I think so.
121. Do service myself, you know,
122. H: hm./
123. A: I think.
124. H: Do the services yourself.
125. A: Yeah.
126. H: This is including the engine?
127. A: … Well, not … completely it-.. change oil,
128. H: ..No/When we're talking,
129. about the engine, I'm talking about the actual services done.
130. I'm not talking about any major repairs … ehm but.. simple
131. things, like changing plugs, changing points, setting points.
132. A: Yeah. that's-
133. H: etc, etc.
134. A: What I do myself. yeah.
135. H: ehm.. could you tell me one of the important things, you did, or?

In all three extracts the interviewer follows up the opening exchanges with a similar question asking the candidate to justify his choice of course program. However, the response in the two NNE interviews are different from the first, in that the interviewees reply immediately with statements of their own personal preferences. The pattern of turn exchange established with the first candidate, wherein the interviewer made suggestive comments and the candidate relied on back channel cues, is reversed. As a consequence, the NNE candidates receive much less information and are given fewer cues on which they can build their narrative account. If we take the NE interview as modeling the interviewer's discourse expectations, then some indications of the problems in the NNE interviews become apparent. It seems that neither participant is able to negotiate an acceptable beginning for the explanatory account that will answer the "stock" interview question: "Why do you want to do X?" When the interviewer attempts to elicit more detailed justifications, the candidate replies with statements of personal preferences along with factual detail, but the expected temporally sequenced narrative is not given.

Based on previous research with similar materials, we assume the candidates on their part expected the interviewer to provide more explicit information concerning such matters as necessary qualifications, job possibilities, requirements, and so forth, which they then expected to ratify with a very brief comment.[2] Usually such facts are set down in the written materials that the candidates have received, so they remain unsaid. However, to be asked a direct question immediately goes counter to candidates' discourse expectations, and when the interviewer repeats his questions as in Extract 2 (105), and Extract 3 (110–113), and once more tries to elicit an explanation, he still only receives statements of preference or fact. It is as if neither candidate can find a way of moving into the temporally sequenced narrative account. All the information necessary to the narrative may have been given, but it is not presented in the expected form. Had the information in Extract 3 (104–105) been temporally sequenced, then, although occurring too soon in the interview, a narrative account would have begun. For example, the statement "and also one of my friend he got his own garage here" (104) could have been phrased as a beginning narrative: "When I was working with my friend, who 's got his own garage here, I ... .", projecting a possible temporal and causative connection between the friend and the decision to apply for a course in motor vehicle repair. In this case, the account would be recognized as a narrative explanation.

The differences between the first and the second two interviews can be substantiated further by examining the first person pronoun used in key parts of responses

---

[2] See Gumperz and Roberts (1991).

to the interviewer's questioning. In Extract 1 (85—) the *I* by the way it is embedded in the narrative account reflects the institutionalized *I:* It refers to selected details of the candidates life, typical of any career path leading to a training or educational institution. In Extracts 2 and 3, by contrast, the candidates respond with "I feel I will like it" and "I am still interested in that course." In both cases, the positioning of their remarks not as evaluations but as initial statements in the orientation phase, before any narrative explanation has been given, makes the pronominals appear as projecting a personal self and therefore not as presenting someone who understands the institutional requirements of the traineeship.

In sum, the narrative explanation becomes the locus of the projection of an institutional self. For the institutionalized *I* to be developed, a narrative must be told that selects details from a person's life for a telling that transforms the personal *I* into an account that meets specific institutional requirements. These requirements are made manifest through the coconstructed initial phases of the narrative presentation, and in this way a satisfactory explanation is produced.

## REFERENCES

Cook-Gumperz, J., & Gumperz, J. J. (1996). Treacherous words: Gender and power in academic assessment. *Folia Linguistica, 30*(3–4), 167–188.

Duranti, A., & Brenneis, D. (1986). The audience as co-author. *Text, 6,* 239–247.

Gumperz, J., & Roberts, C. (1991). Understanding in intercultural encounters. In J. Blomeart & J. Vershuren (Eds.), *The pragmatics of intercultural and international communication* (pp. 51–90). Amsterdam: Benjamins.

Labov, W. (1981). Speech actions and reactions in personal narrative. In D. Tannen (Ed.), *Analyzing discourse: Text and talk* (pp. 219–247). Washington, DC: Georgetown University Press.

Labov, W., & Waletzky, J. (this issue). Narrative analysis: Oral versions of personal experience. In J. Helm (Ed.), *Essays on the verbal and visual arts: Proceedings of the 1966 Annual Spring Meeting of the American Ethnological Society* (pp. 12–44). Seattle: University of Washington Press. (Original work published 1967)

Linde, C. (1993). *Life stories: The creation of coherence.* New York: Oxford University Press.

Ochs, E., & Capps, L. (1996). Narrating the self. *Annual Review of Anthropology, 25,* 19–43.

Polanyi, L. (1989). *Telling the American story: A structural and cultural analysis of conversational story-telling.* Cambridge, MA: MIT Press.

# Construing Experience: Some Story Genres

### J. R. Martin
*Department of Linguistics, University of Sydney*

### G. A. Plum
*Department of Linguistics, Macquarie University*

## FIRST CONTACT

As far as we can recall, we first drew on Labov and Waletzky (1967/this issue; henceforth L&W) in the late 1970s when we were beginning to develop genre theory within the general framework of systemic functional linguistics (SFL). Our main sources for thinking about generic structure at the time were Mitchell (1957/1975), the classic Firthian study of buying and selling in a Moroccan marketplace, and Hasan (1977), a seminal SFL paper that focussed on appointment making. Our aim was to develop a social model of genre that generalized across these and other text types (Christie & Martin, 1997; Eggins & Martin, 1997; Martin, 1985/ 1989, 1992; Ventola, 1987), and we appreciated having L&W's work to draw on.

Over the years, their work had a continuing influence on the development of this model, especially with respect to two strands of the research. One strand was community based and oriented to mapping the repertoire of genres through which people enact their lives. Plum (1988, in press) in particular was intrigued by the possibility of developing a sociolinguistic interview that was specifically designed to "elicit" genres, including narratives. The other strand was school based (Rothery, 1990) and concerned with mapping the repertoire of genres used by students to succeed in school and to redistribute control of these to students who were not accessing them (Hasan & Williams, 1985/1996; Martin, 1993). Here we were concerned with deconstructing the kinds of narrative students were expected to write and critique (Rothery & Macken, 1991). In both strands, the role of evaluation, flagged by L&W as construing the point of narrative, became more and more crucial.

## STORIES IN THE COMMUNITY

As noted previously, Plum's sociolinguistic interview was designed to prompt a range of genres, including narratives; he interviewed 50 members of the "dog fancy"—the community of people who breed and show dogs. Working with reference to the school-based research outlined here (see following), Plum was looking for a range of narratives, alongside the "narrative of personal experience" genre outlined by L&W. Certainly narratives of the type they describe were collected:

Abstract
They're very gentle [Staffordshire bull-terriers]. For arguments sake, like the big boy is an example.

Orientation
We walked through the middle of Fairfield, back when he was about two years old. And there was a fellow in the middle of the street, whacking his little boy. The boy was about four or five years old and he was whacking the daylights out of him. And I thought to meself, "Poor little bugger," you know.

Complication
And as I walked past, the dog went "whack" and grabbed the bloke on the hand. Never broke the skin or anything; just grabbed him on the hand.

Evaluation
I said, "I'm sorry, mate." I says, "It's you smacking the kid; he doesn't like you smack kids." He said, "I'm not smacking the kid." So I pat the dog on the nose; I said, "Let go, let go." I says, "Come on. Sorry, mate, forget it." He said, "I'm not going to smack the kid, don't worry."

Resolution
And as I walked away, the dog kept walking and all he was doing was walking and looking back at the bloke to make sure he wasn't going to touch the kid again.

Coda
He just sensed that it was unnecessary because the bloke was ... Like smacking a kid is smacking a kid, but when you whack the living daylights out of him, it's a different sort of thing. (Plum, 1988, in press, Vol. II:213)

The structure (Abstract) ^ Orientation ^ Complication ^ Evaluation ^ Resolution ^ (Coda) was postulated by L&W (1967/this issue, p. 38) as prototypical of the "complex normal form" of the narrative of personal experience, and Plum found that this structure accounted satisfactorily for 15% of the 134 narrative-type texts elicited in response to four questions aimed at such genres. However, in the vast majority of texts the "crisis" stage of Complication → Evaluation → Resolution—the middle stage of a beginning → middle → end structure—represented neither a crisis, considered the hallmark of a narrative (Sacks, 1972), nor could it be said to comprise the stages Complication, Evaluation, and Resolution. Instead, he found that many texts were organized in quite different ways around a sequence of events to make a point about them, with the positioning and nature of the evaluative language central to a reclassification of narrative genres. On the other hand, Abstract, Orientation, and Coda offered entirely satisfactory accounts of the beginning and end stages of these texts.

Three text types were posited as agnate with the canonical narrative of personal experience, namely, *recount, anecdote* and *exemplum:*

Recounts deal with a sequence of events that are presented by the teller as unfolding unproblematically—irrespective of how unusual, dangerous, tragic, and so forth, they might have been—in a Record of Events. The typical structure of a recount is (Orientation) → Record of Events → (Reorientation), with the Reorientation being both Coda-like, returning the story to the here and now, and Resolution-like, finishing off with a flourish what is potentially an interminable sequence of events, thus making it "tellable" in the terms of Labov (1972) by inventing its own point. Significantly, recounts don't have anything comparable to L&W's suspension of action through evaluation—their evaluative comments being realized prosodically—because they are not about restoring a disturbed equilibrium.

Anecdotes are accounts of a remarkable event, the point of which is to invite a listener to share a reaction—a laugh, a groan, a tear, and so forth, as appropriate. They negotiate solidarity by offering an affectual response to an extraordinary event for the listener or reader to share. The typical structure of an anecdote is (Orientation) → Remarkable Event → Reaction → (Coda), with the Reaction, that is, the aimed-at and shared affectual response, often being linguistically recoded by the narrator through reiteration of a key aspect of the Remarkable Event in order to emphasize its remarkable nature.

Exemplums share a judgment about a noteworthy incident, rather than an emotional response to a remarkable event as in the anecdote. The listener is positioned to approve or disapprove of the conduct of a story's protagonists, and in this respect the exemplum is related to other moralizing genres such as the parable, fable, gossip (and certain "thematic narratives" that project a "message"; Cranny-Francis, 1996; Martin, 1996). The typical structure of an exemplum is (Orientation) ^ Incident ^ Interpretation ^ (Coda), with the tellable events of the story downgraded to a mere incident whose only function is to serve as the raw material for the making of a point that lies totally outside the text.

A synopsis of the staging of these three genres, in relation to the narrative of personal experience, is outlined in Table 1. The comment column captures the positioning and nature of the all important evaluative language.

Looking over some of Labov's data, one can't help wondering whether stories told as anecdotes and exemplums were inadvertently recontextualized by Labov as narratives of personal experience as a result of his interviewing technique—which involved keeping people talking unself-consciously with a view to gathering data on phonological and morphological change in progress (rather than storytelling per se). Consider for example the following text from Labov (1966, pp. 71–72):

WL: What happened to you? [following an affirmative response to WL's "danger of death" question]
I: The school I go to is Food and Maritime—that's maritime training—and I was up in the masthead, and the wind started blowing. I had a rope secured around me to keep me from falling—but the rope parted, and I was just hanging there by my fingernails. I never prayed to God so fast and so hard in my life.
WL: What happened?
I: Well, I came out all right ... Well, the guys came up and they got me.
WL: How long were you up there?
I: About ten minutes.
WL: I can see you're still sweating, thinking about it.
I: Yeh, I came down, I couldn't hold a pencil in my hand, I couldn't touch nothin'. I was shakin' like a leaf. Sometimes I get scared thinkin' about it ... but ... uh ... well, it's training.

As rendered here, one might well analyze the text as a narrative of personal experience:

TABLE 1
Comparative Staging Across Four Story Genres

| Genres | Staging | | | | |
|---|---|---|---|---|---|
| | Open | Experience | Comment | Experience | Close |
| Recount | (Orientation) | Record of events | [Prosodic] | — | (Reorientation) |
| Anecdote | (Orientation) | Remarkable event | Reaction | — | (Coda) |
| Exemplum | (Orientation) | Incident | Interpretation | — | (Coda) |
| Narrative | (Orientation) | Complication | Evaluation | Resolution | (Coda) |

Orientation
The school I go to is Food and Maritime—that's maritime training—and I was up in the masthead, and the wind started blowing.

Complication
I had a rope secured around me to keep me from falling—but the rope parted, and I was just hanging there by my fingernails.

Evaluation
I never prayed to God so fast and so hard in my life.

Resolution
... I came out all right ... the guys came up and they got me.

Coda
(WL: I can see you're still sweating, thinking about it.)
Yeh, I came down, I couldn't hold a pencil in my hand, I couldn't touch nothin'. I was shakin' like a leaf. Sometimes I get scared thinkin' about it ... but ... uh ... well, it's training.

Without Labov's interventions the narrator may well have stopped after making the point that he'd never been so scared in his life. The narrator obviously survived to tell the tale, so an explicit resolution stage is not really required, and the story may well have been intended as an anecdote:

Orientation
The school I go to is Food and Maritime—that's maritime training—and I was up in the masthead, and the wind started blowing.

Remarkable Event
I had a rope secured around me to keep me from falling—but the rope parted, and I was just hanging there by my fingernails.

Reaction
I never prayed to God so fast and so hard in my life.

L&W point to the significance of the evaluation in the creation of other types of narrative when they say that "perhaps the most frequent variant [of the narrative of personal experience] is the case where the evaluation ends the resolution: jokes, ghost stories and surprise endings take this" (p. 37). This is again noted by Labov (1982) in the context of two "fight" narratives in which "the evaluation section is placed at the end of the narrative, and merged with the final action or *resolution*"

(p. 226). However, neither paper discusses this structure, indicative of an agnate narrative genre.

## STORIES IN SCHOOL

Our early school research focussed on writing in primary schools, particularly in response to the process writing and whole language programs imported from the United States. We observed (Martin & Rothery, 1984; Rothery, 1996) that the most common of the narrative genres written, and the only genre that one could expect all students to have written by the end of primary school, was *observation*, with recount being the second most common. Observation, with a typical structure of (Orientation) ^ Event Description ^ Comment, states what happened as a single event—collapsing a series of temporally sequenced events into one—and how that event affected the narrator, whereas the recount focusses on telling what happened.

Observation is not only commonly found in the primary school but also in the community, with a very significant difference in frequency between the writing of young children and the storytelling of adults: Whereas observations constituted 57% (1020/1789) of all story texts in the primary school study, they only constituted 18% (24/134) of all narrative texts produced in response to narrative questions in Plum's study. On distributional if not functional grounds, observation must be considered one of the narrative genres.

The recount genre is one that thrives in writing pedagogies in which models of a range of genres are not provided and teacher intervention is proscribed. Here's a typical example, following up a class trip to the zoo (Droga, 1990).

Orientation
One day I went to the zoo ...

Record of events
... and I saw Rhinoceros I moved to a Hippopotamus I touched him and he is hand and he is big and so I went on and I saw the tiger and this man was feeding him it was eating it up Mum tod me mv on and next came then a gorilla. I had a baby gorilla. My mum tod me to move on. I saw a watch. It was 5 ock.

We also observed that these primary school recounts were remarkably devoid of evaluation. They tended towards flat factual records of experience, and in this respect they were unlike spoken story genres, including spoken recounts, which tend to have a prosody of evaluation running through them. In some secondary English classrooms, the genre reappears in journal and diary writing. These recounts tend to be heavily evaluated, in response to progressive English teachers' concern with surveilling the personal voice of their students. In the following text, the 15-year-old student deploys this evaluation in opposition to the surveillance of her teacher, to the delight of her peers—and carried on this resistance for most of the year.

Record of Events (& ongoing evaluation)
Fucken Hell man, who the hell told you I liked doing this kind of shit. On Saturday I saw Brian and Brendon and his Girlfriend at Waterloo, I was waiting to catch the bloody bus, anyway they started talking to me so that killed alot of time. Anyway I had to go to the Laundromat Yesterday and I saw my ex-boyfriend man he looks fucken ugly god knows what I went out with him, he looks like a fucken dickhead.
ANY WAYS HE WAS
so ugly only a blind woman would go out with him. I ran into this elderly man that lived down one of my old streets and because I had a bag of clothes the stupid cunt said to us are you running away from home which is bull-shit because the sooner that I got home the happier I would have been. Then my ex-boyfriend comes up which makes it even worse and he starts calling this old cunt a cradle snatching little ass-hole. I mean as if its any of his business, and like this is totally humiliating cause I mean everybody and I mean everybody tried to see who the hell was making all the fucken noise and yes there I was trying to hide my face as soon as possible ...

We found anecdotes and exemplums to be extremely rare. By the end of primary school and into secondary, story writing comes under the influence of the print and electronic media. The challenge for us here had to do with whether Labov and Waletzky's narrative structure could be usefully generalized to the longer written texts that students are expected to write and critique in secondary English classrooms. L&W's narrative structure was used in some materials; Rothery (1994) introduced it alongside some of the alternative story structures reviewed previously. Over time, however, it seemed to us that the notion of complicating action would have to be elaborated to account for the complex pattern of recursive disruptions in longer narratives (Hasan, 1989), and it seemed that a more sophisticated framework for considering evaluation was required (Martin, in press-a, in press-b).

One of the perils of introducing explicit teaching of generic structure, including narrative structure, into the curriculum was driven home to us in some otherwise competent materials produced by the (Australian) Northern Territory Department of Education. Acting without the participation of the relevant functional linguists in Darwin, the following text was used to model L&W's narrative of personal experience structure:

### The Orphan Child

Long ago, at a place called Kabbari, a group of people had gathered. An orphan child said he was hungry.

His brother said, "I will go and hunt goanna for you to eat." And off he went.

One of the group gave the orphan some cooked roots of a waterlily to eat. He had never eaten this type of waterlily before. He ate it. He cried for more. There was no more. His cries became louder and louder.

Far out to sea, the serpent heard the child crying. She swam towards the sound, stopping every now and then to listen to make sure she was headed the right way.

Nothing the people could do made the orphan stop crying. On and on he cried.

When the serpent reached the land, she swam under the land, towards the sound. The people tried everything to get the orphan to stop crying. Still the orphan cried.

Suddenly the fire went out as the ground became wet. The people who were sleeping felt cold as the wetness touched their skins. The people knew the serpent had reached them and they were afraid.

The ground became wetter and colder. The serpent burst through the ground and swallowed all the people, every one. She made sure she swallowed the crying orphan first. At this moment the orphan's older brother returned with a goanna on his back. The serpent swallowed him too. Later, the serpent spat everyone out and they turned into rock forms.

This is the origin of the landforms you can see at Kabbari today. High on the escarpment stands the rock figure of the older brother holding a goanna on his back. Way below to his right, is the little rock of the orphan. Behind the orphan child are all the rock forms of the people. Further around is the serpent whose face can be seen clearly in the escarpment. (Northern Territory Department of Education, 1993)

We do not attempt a detailed analysis here as we are not specialists in Australian Aboriginal culture, from which the story has been recontextualized. However, it is obvious from the way the story ends that its function in that culture has to do with the history of land, which is, of course, closely tied up with people's custodial relation to that land. The story has not been told to make a point about an individual overcoming adversity; rather, it uses different kinds of language and structure to encode a fragment of Aboriginal law that bears critically on issues of native title and land ownership. It is salutary to note that one cannot emphasize or repeat often enough in certain contexts the cultural specificity of genres and the dangers of borrowing a text from one culture to illustrate a functional structure from another—however user-friendly to the "other" one wants materials to appear.

## CODA

No doubt our close encounters with L&W will continue for some time. Our research underscores the importance of thinking carefully about how narratives are collected and the significance of data collection dedicated specifically to genre research. In the short term, we hope to extend our work on evaluation and more complex event structures, in order to enhance L&W's insight into the significance of the interaction of events with evaluation in narrative. Our feeling is that this kind of work is best pursued in a highly theorized framework (such as SFL), which models language and social context and the dialectic between the two as explicitly as possible—with a view to building rich accounts of narrative and other genres, comparable to the functional descriptions of English grammar provided by Halliday (1994) and Matthiessen (1995) and used as the basis for our analyses.

## REFERENCES

Christie, F., & Martin, J. R. (Eds.). (1997). *Genres and institutions: Social processes in the workplace and school* (Open Linguistics Series). London: Cassell.

Cranny-Francis, A. (1996). Technology and/or weapon: The disciplines of reading in the Secondary English classroom. In R. Hasan & G. Williams (Eds.), *Literacy in society* (pp. 172–190). London: Longman.

Droga, L. (1990). *The recount genre* (Language and Social Power Project). Sydney, Australia: Metropolitan East Disadvantaged Schools Program.

Eggins, S., & Martin, J. R. (1997). Genres and registers of discourse. In T. A. van Dijk (Ed.), *Discourse: A multidisciplinary introduction* (pp. 230–256). London: Sage.

Halliday, M. A. K. (1994). *An introduction to functional grammar* (2nd ed.). London: Edward Arnold.

Hasan, R. (1977). Text in the systemic-functional model. In W. Dressler (Ed.), *Current trends in textlinguistics* (pp. 226–246). Berlin, Germany: Walter de Gruyter.

Hasan, R. (1989). *Linguistics, language and verbal art.* London: Oxford University Press. (Original work published 1985 by Deakin University Press, Geelong, Victoria, Australia)

Hasan, R., & Williams, G. (Eds.). (1996). *Literacy in society* (Open University Series). London: Longman.

Labov, W. (1966). *The social stratification of English in New York City.* Washington, DC: Center for Applied Linguistics.

Labov, W. (1972). The transformation of experience in narrative syntax. In W. Labov (Ed.), *Language in the inner city: Studies in the black English vernacular* (pp. 354–396). Philadelphia: University of Pennsylvania Press.

Labov, W. (1982). Speech actions and reactions in personal narrative. In D. Tannen (Ed.), *Analyzing discourse: Text and talk* (pp. 219–247). Washington, DC: Georgetown University Press.

Labov, W., & Waletzky, J. (this issue). Narrative analysis: Oral versions of personal experience. In J. Helm (Ed.), *Essays on the verbal and visual arts: Proceedings of the 1966 Annual Spring Meeting of the American Ethnological Society* (pp. 12–44). Seattle: University of Washington Press. (Original work published 1967)

Martin, J. R. (1989). *Factual writing: Exploring and challenging social reality.* London: Oxford University Press. (Original work published 1985 by Deakin University Press, Geelong, Victoria, Australia)

Martin, J. R. (1992). *English text: System and structure.* Amsterdam: Benjamins.
Martin, J. R. (1993). Genre and literacy—Modelling context in educational linguistics. *Annual Review of Applied Linguistics, 13,* 141–172.
Martin, J. R. (1996). Evaluating disruption: Symbolising theme in junior secondary narrative. In R. Hasan & G. Williams (Eds.), *Literacy in society* (pp. 124–171). London: Longman.
Martin, J. R. (in press-a). Inter-feeling: Gender, class, appraisal in *Educating Rita.* In S. Hunston & G. Thompson (Eds.), *Evaluation in text.* London: Oxford University Press.
Martin, J. R. (in press-b). Register and genre: Modelling social context in functional linguistics—narrative genres. In E. Pedro (Ed.), *Social discourse analysis.* Lisbon, Portugal: Portuguese Linguistics Association.
Martin, J. R., & Rothery, J. (1984). *Choice of genre in a suburban primary school.* Paper presented at Annual Conference of the Applied Linguistics Association of Australia, Alice Springs, Northern Territory.
Matthiessen, C. M. I. M. (1995). *Lexicogrammatical cartography: English systems.* Tokyo: International Language Sciences Publishers.
Mitchell, T. F. (1957). The language of buying and selling in Cyrenaica: A situational statement. *Hesperis, 26,* 31–71. (Reprinted in T. F. Mitchell, 1975, *Prinicples of neo-Firthian logic.* London: Longman.)
Northern Territory Department of Education. (1993). *Getting going with games: Narrative genre.* Darwin, Northern Territories, Australia: Author.
Plum, G. A. (1988). *Text and contextual conditioning in spoken English: A genre-based approach.* Unpublished doctoral dissertation, Department of Linguistics, University of Sydney.
Plum, G. A. (in press). Text and contextual conditioning in spoken English: A genre-based approach.*Monographs in systemic linguistics.* Nottingham, England: University of Nottingham, Department of English Studies.
Rothery, J. (1990). *Story writing in primary school: Assessing narrative type genres.* Unpublished doctoral dissertation, Department of Linguistics, University of Sydney, Australia.
Rothery, J. (1994). *Exploring literacy in school English (Write it Right resources for literacy and learning).* Sydney, Australia: Metropolitan East Disadvantaged Schools Program.
Rothery, J. (1996). Making changes: Developing an educational linguistics. In R. Hasan & G. Williams (Eds.), *Literacy in society* (pp. 86–123). London: Longman.
Rothery, J., & Macken, M. (1991). *Developing critical literacy: An analysis of the writing task in a year 10 reference test.* Sydney, Australia: Metropolitan East Disadvantaged Schools Program.
Sacks, H. (1972). On the analyzability of stories by children. In J. J. Gumperz & D. Hymes (Eds.), *Directions in the ethnography of communication* (pp. 325–345). New York: Holt, Rinehart & Winston.
Ventola, E. (1987). *The structure of social interaction: A systemic approach to the semiotics of service encounters* (Open Linguistics Series). London: Pinter.

# Labov's Model of Narrative Analysis as an Emerging Study in Discourse

## Martha Shiro
*Harvard Graduate School of Education and Universidad Central de Venezuela*

Storytelling is a frequent and effective way of communicating in everyday spoken interaction as well as in written forms. However, the study of narratives from a linguistic perspective stems from a recent, though prolific, endeavor. In this area of research, Labov's work on narratives, initiated more than 30 years ago, has been influential in many ways. His major contribution, one that permeates all his studies and has broadened the scope of linguistics, is his view of language as social behavior. At a time when linguistic studies focused mainly on isolating language from its use and therefore, from its social context, Labov postulated that there cannot be "a successful linguistic theory or practice which is not social" (Labov, 1972b, p. xix). In his search for a "socially realistic linguistics" he set out to explain linguistic variation by taking into account features of social context. Thus, he successfully explained phonological variation (formerly thought to vary freely) in speakers of different regions and social classes (Labov, 1972b).

Labov's studies on narrative discourse seem to have a different purpose. Rather than highlighting differences due to social factors, Labov and Waletzky's (1967/this issue; henceforth L&W) model of narrative analysis helped highlight equivalences, that is, similarities between social classes. This change in perspective can be attributed to two underlying purposes that Labov had in mind when studying narratives. One is to prove his major theoretical point that "a very large part of sentence grammar is dependent on and arises from rules of social interaction, social conventions, and abstract discourse processes" (Linde & Labov, 1975, p. 938). The other underlying motivating force is to disprove "the hypothesis of language deprivation," which posits that low socioeconomic status speakers suffer from some kind of "linguistic disadvantage." In the study on inner city adolescents, L&W (see also Labov, 1972a) demonstrated that Black English speakers in urban areas tell stories just as skillfully as sophisticated middle-class storytellers do.

In this article I review Labov's approach to narrative analysis, placing it in the framework of research in discourse analysis. In 1967, the year L&W published their seminal paper, there was practically no research in the area of discourse. Narratives were studied mostly in the area of literary analysis (e.g., Barthes, 1966; Propp, 1928/1958) and there was little concern for structure beyond the sentence in language studies (but see Harris, 1952).

From a sociolinguistic perspective, Labov's interest in spontaneous spoken language naturally led him to study different forms of connected speech: narrative, ritual insults, and therapeutic discourse. His studies of the vernacular and of Black English, together with his concern in disproving the "language deprivation" hypothesis led him to propose an analytic model that would detect narrative skills not springing from the syntactic well-formedness of sentences. Thus, the analytic model found in L&W and, later, in Labov (1972a), is of a functional type. It relates discourse function to form, which was an innovative way of looking at language. In this way, Labov's analysis embraces the two presently prevailing views of discourse, as Schiffrin (1994, p. 23) defines them: discourse as language use and discourse as language above the sentence.

Labov defined narratives as "one method of recapitulating past experience by matching a verbal sequence of clauses to the sequence of events which (it is inferred) actually occurred" (Labov, 1972a, pp. 359–360.). Two major narrative functions were described: *referential* and *expressive*.

The referential function is informative and consists basically of a temporal sequence of narrative events, expressed by clauses that are labeled *restricted* because they cannot be moved within the narrative without losing the coherence of the story or telling a different story.[1] A list of all *narrative clauses* represents the temporal sequence and, consequently, the skeleton of the story. Labov (1972a, p. 376) described the structure of narrative clauses as having a simple phrase structure, containing a verb of action in the past tense.

The expressive function, on the other hand, is evaluative and is defined as "that part of the narrative that reveals the attitude of the narrator towards the narrative by emphasizing the relative importance of some narrative units as compared to others" (L&W, p. 32). Evaluative clauses can usually be moved within the narrative text without destroying its coherence, and thus, they are labeled *free* clauses. Evaluative expressions are classified as follows (Labov, 1972a, p. 371):

---

[1] Compare, for example: A. She got married and had a child. B. She had a child and got married. Changing the order of the events changes the story.

1. *Intensifiers,* which strengthen the sequence of narrative events, such as: gestures accompanied by deixis, expressive phonology (e.g., vowel lengthening, onomatopoeia), quantifiers, repetitions, ritual utterances.
2. *Comparators,* which compare events that did occur with those that did not occur, such as: negatives, comparatives, superlatives, metaphors, similes, questions, imperatives, clauses containing modals or futures.
3. *Correlatives,* which bring together two events that actually occurred, can be realized as progressives or appended participles.
4. *Explicatives,* expansions of the narrative clauses, achieved by qualifications that can be causal or contrastive.

This summary shows Labov's view of how narrative function is related to linguistic form, or, more precisely, to the structure of the clause.

The overall structure of a fully formed narrative consists of the following elements (Labov, 1972a, p. 363): (a) *Abstract,* one or two clauses at the beginning summarizing the whole story; (b) *Orientation,* which identifies the time, place, persons, or situation; (c) *Complicating Action,* narrative clauses comprising the sequence of events; (d) *Evaluation,* giving the point of the story; (e) *Resolution,* the part that follows evaluation; and (f) *Coda,* an ending that brings the listener back to the present.

Thus, in Labov's analysis of narratives as connected speech, recurring structural patterns are revealed in the textual organization.

Labov's attempt to explain the relation between form and function, as seen in the previous description of his model of narrative analysis, was successful in the sense that the functional categories can be easily identified and quantified. However, many of the categories, although functionally defined, use formal criteria for identification. Furthermore, form and function are seen as having a one-to-one relation. Any (independent) clause in a narrative fulfills either a referential or an expressive function. Other studies (e.g., Schiffrin, 1994) show, however, that an utterance can have multiple functions in discourse, an assumption that does not seem to fit with the Labovian model.

The most interesting, but also the most problematic, analytic category is related to Labov's concept of evaluation. Labov emphasized the idea that the speaker's subjectivity permeates narrative discourse, giving it its raison d'être. Defining evaluative language, in formal or in functional terms, is a complicated task. Labov mixed both in his definition. Evaluation is functionally defined as language used to suspend the action in the story, but formal criteria such as progressives, futures, or modals are used to identify the different types of evaluation. Moreover, the term evaluation is used to label all the expressions in the narrative that suspend the action, irrespective of their function in the story, and it is also used to label the structural component that precedes resolution (i.e., the *high point,* Peterson & McCabe, 1983). This ambiguity in the definition of the term complicates the concept even more.

Nonetheless, Labov's view of evaluation is a very interesting one. Its relation to the speaker's subjectivity and construction of narrative point of view may be exploited to delve into the relation between language and ideology or to detect social and cultural differences. All these concerns were neglected in Labov's narrative analysis, given that his priority was to emphasize similarities rather than differences in narrative production.[2]

Labov's (1972a) study also included a section on the development of evaluative syntax with age (pp. 393–396), implying, most accurately, that the use of evaluation is the narrative ability that takes longer to develop. He found that teenagers (ages 13–16) used almost three times more evaluative expressions than preadolescents (ages 10–12, p. 391). Other studies (e.g., Peterson & McCabe, 1983) indicated that children (ages 4–9) do not show major changes in the percentage of evaluative expressions. However, recent research suggests that children show development in how they distribute evaluative expressions within the narrative structure (Bamberg & Damrad-Frye, 1991), indicating that this is an ability whose development cannot be detected in terms of frequency of occurrence, but should also be analyzed in functional terms, that is, the role they play in the narrative discourse. Labov's developmental findings constituted a pioneering contribution to studies of language acquisition, again at a time when the major concern of developmental studies was the acquisition of grammar, vocabulary, or phonology.[3]

Labov's work focused on language use and, therefore, he found that only "reportable" events are included in narratives. However, he did not pursue this issue sufficiently to detect what makes an event "reportable" in different cultural context. Labov highlighted the importance of the prompts that elicit the narratives, stressing the importance of the situational context and the relationship between interlocutors (Labov, 1981). The implication is that Black English Vernacular speakers in his sample tell the most skillful stories in the appropriate situation, but fail to do so in school, where the context is perceived as inappropriate.

Labov's model of narrative analysis is meant to describe recounts of personal experience. However, this model cannot be applied to personal narratives having more than one episode, because its underlying assumption is that personal experience narratives consist of one episode only. Certainly, a great number of stories told in spontaneous conversations tend to have only one episode, but the scope of the analysis is limited if it cannot account for multiple episode narratives. This constraint does not help in the identification of the boundaries of a narrative in the ongoing discourse. No criteria were offered to determine whether two contiguous episodes should be treated as one or two narratives.

---

[2] Lavandera (1988) argued that the lack of interest in relating discourse to social and ideological issues is typical of Anglo Saxon discourse analysis.

[3] A series of studies on the acquisition of discourse appeared later in 1977 (Ervin-Tripp & Mitchell-Kernan, 1977).

Another drawback of this model is that it excludes accounts in which events are not reported in the sequence they occurred, classifying them as nonnarrative texts. In what other category should they be placed? How does this criterion apply to fantasy stories whose relation with "reality" is less straightforward than personal narratives?

Although Labov (1972a) only focused on narratives of personal experience, he briefly mentioned that vicarious narratives are less evaluated than narratives of personal experience a hypothesis that does not seem to be confirmed by studies comparing these two narrative genres (Shiro, 1997). Nevertheless, a line of research can emerge from these comments, comparing vicarious and nonvicarious narratives and detecting their variations in terms of age and social class.

In sum, Labov's narrative analysis documents that, independent of whether the narrator is a speaker of a highly prestigious or a more stigmatized language variety, storytelling can be very effective. Although the cultural differences in which the narratives become communicatively effective were largely ignored, his analytic model raises interesting issues about language in general and narratives in particular. A major issue is the relation between discourse function and grammatical form. The conclusion that the sentence is not an independent, self-sufficient unit, and that in many cases grammatical structure is determined by decisions taken at the level of discourse organization. is very valid. Furthermore, Labov discussed, although in less detail, the relation between text and context, analyzing the role of prompts and speaker–hearer relationships in narrative production. Finally, his view of evaluation, though fraught with controversy, has generated a great deal of research that needs to be further pursued.

## REFERENCES

Bamberg, M., & Damrad-Frye, R. (1991). On the ability to provide evaluative comments: Further explorations of children's narrative competencies. *Journal of Child Language, 18,* 689–710.

Barthes, R. (1966). Introduction a l'analyse structurale des récit [An introduction to the structural analysis of narratives]. In R. Barthes, W. Kayser, W. C. Booth, P. Hamon (Eds.), *Poétique du récit* (pp. 7–57). Paris: Éditions du Seuil.

Ervin-Tripp, S., & Mitchell-Kernan, C. (1977). *Child discourse.* New York: Academic.

Harris, Z. (1952). Discourse analysis. *Language, 28,* 1–30.

Labov, W. (1970). The logic of non-standard English. In J. Alatis (Ed.), *Linguistics and the teaching of standard English to speakers of other languages: Georgetown University Round Table* (pp. 1–43). Washington, DC: Georgetown University Press.

Labov, W. (1972a). *Language in the inner city.* Philadelphia: University of Pennsylvania Press.

Labov, W. (1972b). *Sociolinguistic patterns.* Oxford, England: Basil Blackwell.

Labov, W. (1981). Speech actions and reactions in personal narratives. In D. Tannen (Ed.), *Analyzing discourse: Text and talk: Georgetown University Round Table* (pp. 219–247). Washington, DC: Georgetown University Press.

Labov, W., & Waletzky, J. (this issue). Narrative analysis: Oral versions of personal experience. In J. Helm (Ed.), *Essays on the verbal and visual arts: Proceedings of the 1966 Annual Spring Meeting*

of the American Ethnological Society (pp. 12–44). Seattle: University of Washington Press. (Original work published 1967)

Lavandera, B. (1988). The study of language in its socio-cultural context. In F. Newmeyer (Ed.), *Linguistics: The Cambridge survey* (Vol. IV, pp. 1–13). Cambridge, England: Cambridge University Press.

Linde, C., & Labov, W. (1975). Spatial networks as a site for the study of language and thought. *Language, 51,* 924–939.

Peterson C., & McCabe, A. (1983). *Developmental psycholinguistics.* New York: Plenum.

Propp, V. (1958). *Morphology of the folktale.* Bloomington, IN: Indiana University Press. (Original work published 1928)

Schiffrin, D. (1994). *Approaches to discourse.* Oxford, England: Basil Blackwell.

Shiro, M. (1997). *Getting your story across: A discourse analysis approach to evaluative stance in Venezuelan children's narratives.* Paper presented at the VIIth International Child Language Congress, Istanbul, Turkey.

# Social Characteristics and Self-Expression in Narrative

### Barbara Johnstone
*Department of English, Carnegie Mellon University*

The work described in "Narrative Analysis" was part of a project aimed at describing the rich linguistic repertoires of African American and Hispanic children, then thought by educators to be nonverbal. It was also part of Labov's career-long project of coming to understand the underlying mechanisms of language change.[1] To accomplish these goals, it was necessary for Labov and Waletzky (1967/this issue) to consider how social facts and linguistic facts were related. As they put it: "The ultimate aims of our work will require close correlations of the narrator's [sic] social characteristics with the structure of their narratives" (p. 5). In "Narrative Analysis" Labov and Waletzky developed an abstract deep-structure characterization of the structural and functional parts of personal-experience narrative that could be used in studying such correlations.

Sociolinguists have continued to try to link "social characteristics" of narrators with characteristics of their narratives.[2] Undertaken beginning in the 1970s, when it began to be acceptable in linguistics to specialize in discourse, and published mainly in the 1980s, this work expanded in many directions. To list only a fraction: there are studies of personal-experience narrative by Americans and non-Americans (e.g., Chafe, 1980); African Americans (Etter-Lewis, 1993; Heath, 1983) and

---

Requests for reprints should be sent to Barbara Johnstone, Department of English, Carnegie Mellon University, Pittsburgh, PA 15213–3890. E-mail: bj4@andrew.cmu.edu

[1] It is of course dangerous to rely on speculations about authorial intent. People who commit words to paper may not know what they mean, the words may not really be theirs, privileged interpretations of the words may silence other interpretations. On the other hand, though, it is courteous and practical to take seriously what people say as having some bearing on something true, and Labov and Waletzky were as explicit about their intentions as could be.

[2] Although most subsequent work on personal-experience narrative by sociolinguists has not been explicitly in service of the study of language change, most has, implicitly or explicitly, in part or wholly, had the goal of displaying and describing a kind of verbal skill that is devalued and hence often unheard in the Western educational and high-cultural tradition.

Hispanic Americans (McLeod-Porter, 1991); New Yorkers (Polanyi, 1985), Midwesterners (Johnstone, 1990) and Texans (Bauman, 1986); women (Riessman, 1988) and men; older people (Brewer, 1994) and younger people (Cook-Gumperz & Green, 1984; Shuman, 1986).

None of these studies, and none that I know of since, has ever challenged the existence of personal-experience narrative. This is surprising, and it underscores Labov's amazing perceptiveness. In an era in which familiar analytical and explanatory concepts are regularly critiqued and regularly found, with justification, to be subtly ethnocentric or oppressive, it has not been suggested, for example, that personal-experience narrative is really just something Western people do, or a way of managing to find some people wanting. In fact, telling about personal experiences seems to be something all humans do, even if not all in the same way—a point made by psychologists like Jerome Bruner (1986) and Roy Schafer (1981), among others.

The idea that speakers have social characteristics has not fared so well, however. After supposing for many years that individuals' behavior could be explained in terms of facts about them that they brought to interactions, many sociolinguists are now interested in the processes that give rise to categorizations like "male" and "female," "African American," and "White" in the first place and in the ways people make strategic use of such categories as they create and express selves and others and relationships among selves and others. This is not the place to review this literature, most of which is not focussed on personal-experience narrative in any case; a very short list, including only people working in the variationist sociolinguistic tradition, would include Eckert and McConnell-Ginet (1992) and many of the papers in Hall and Bucholtz (1995) on the creation and expression of gender, Rampton (1995) on the creation and expression of ethnicity, and Johnstone (1996a) and Johnstone and Bean (1997) on the creation and expression of individuality. (Some of this work draws on that of LePage & Tabouret-Keller, 1985) What I do instead is to illustrate with one example what can be gained from thinking about sociolinguistic variation in narrative as a resource for self-expression rather than as the result of preexisting social facts about speakers.

Linda Davis is a White woman in her 20s from a very small town in East Texas. She is a country-western singer and occasional songwriter with an increasingly successful career who now lives in Nashville in between concert tours. She is married to her manager and has a school-age daughter. This transcribed extract comes from an interview with her by my coworker Judith Mattson Bean (see Johnstone and Bean, 1997, for a description of the whole project), during which Bean asked Davis about how her being from Texas had been perceived in Nashville when she first moved there.

> Davis:... when I first got there, I worked uh at a s- rest- a restaurant at a uh, recording [Iŋ] studio. And I was answering [In] the phone and stuff, but also recording [Iŋ] so my [may] music is what took me there and I had a reason

to go, I felt like [layk]. It was more than just, "Well I think I'll [al] move to Nashville." It was it was a little more substance than that; however, those associations have long since passed, but, and new ones have taken their place, but it got me there anyway. But when I [ay] uh, uh ... 'bout, four years into being [Iŋ] there, I got a job at the hotel playing [Iŋ] piano and singing [Iŋ]. And you get so many, oh, all over the country, all over the world, people that come and stay and so, w- we had a lot of Japanese or Oriental people that stayed at at our, the hotel, the Sheraton, because there were a lot of companies they owned and they came in, so *they* were quite [kwayt] interested in my [may], uh you know, the way I talked [towkt] and stuff, and, they'd always want to hear "Tennessee Waltz" and "The Green Green *Glass* of Home,"
Bean: /Yeah
Davis: /they called [kald] it. *They even wrote me a note on a napkin wanting to [wow'ndə] hear the "Green Green Glass" — they spelled /it "glass" — "of Home." It was so funny,* =
Bean: /((laughs))                                  =It is. ((laughing))
Davis: *and I I mean I'd [ad] sing it every [evər] time [tam] you know and they always put a dollar in my [ma] jar [jowr] so I'd [ad] sing it twice [twas] if they wanted [wownəd] me to. ((laughing voice))*

The list of demographic facts about her would lead us to expect, among other things, that Davis might sound Southern and rural, and indeed she does. She invariably pronounces the vowel in words like *talk* or *want* as a diphthong, [ow];[3] she answers yes–no questions with "Yes, ma'am" or "No, ma'am;" she greets a stranger more effusively than a New Yorker would greet a long-lost friend; and she talks about the fundamentalist Baptist faith that organizes her life and explains her world. Her speech is also variable in some of the ways one would expect an East Texan's speech to be: /ay/ before voiceless obstruents is sometimes monophthongized as [a], *-ing* is sometimes pronounced /In/, she is sometimes very folksy-sounding in style.

An account in the traditional sociolinguistic mode of how Davis sounds would leave it at that,[4] or perhaps, following the lead of James and Lesley Milroy (J. Milroy, 1987; L. Milroy, 1992) take the further step of correlating the degree of variability in Davis's speech with the number and nature of her social ties with people in the community she comes from. In either case, because the goal would be to relate facts about how Davis talks with facts about her that continue to be true throughout her talk (her region, gender, age, income, social network, and so on),

---

[3] The only exception is when the following consonant is /l/, as in *call*; because this /l/ is vocalized, the vowel is not preconsonantal in this environment the way it is in the other words.

[4] In fact, "discourse-level" features of talk such as greeting behavior, forms of address, and ways of creating coherence are not usually examined in variationist studies, partly because they are very difficult to describe in quantifiable ways.

the ebb and flow of variability in the course of this interaction would not be examined.

If we do focus on the ebb and flow of variability, we can see how Davis uses it as a resource in constructing and expressing her personal identity. In the short excerpt we are examining, Davis begins with scene-setting orientation ("I was answering the phone and stuff," "I got a job at the hotel," "We had a lot of Japanese or Oriental people"), then moves into the anecdote about the "Green Green Glass of Home."[5] As she does this, she displays two aspects of her personality. In the first part of the excerpt Davis uses relatively standard-sounding speech to present herself as a thoughtful person (in implicit contrast to the stereotypical rural naive hoping to be discovered in Nashville). Her diction is sometimes elevated ("it was a little more substance than that"; "those associations have long since passed, but, and new ones have taken their place"), and she chooses the more standard-sounding phonological variants, [Iŋ] for -*ing* and [ay] for /ay/, at a higher rate. (Her choices for these two variables are 80% standard-sounding and 20% rural-sounding in this part of the extract; see Johnstone [1996b] for an explanation of how I calculated these numbers.) In the second part of the extract (italicized in the transcript), Davis shows that she is also still a country girl. Her speech becomes more rural sounding both in the ways I focussed on (for the two phonological variables I looked at, her choices here were the more rural-sounding ones 100% of the time) and in other ways, as she pronounces "wanting to" as *[wow'ndə]*, "every" as *[evɛr]*.

There are several reasons for this shift. For one thing, as Labov has pointed out (1972, pp. 92–94), people become less self-conscious and hence more "vernacular" as they narrate more emotional experiences. (This is why eliciting danger-of-death stories is part of the variationist's interview protocol.) It is thus not surprising that Davis's speech should become more rural-sounding as she moves from orientation to narration and evaluation (even though this is hardly a danger-of-death story). However, does she become less self-conscious or just conscious of herself in a different way? Like all the other public women we have interviewed, Davis thought of this interview not just as a favor to a couple of professors but as a potential source of publicity, an opportunity to underscore the ways she typifies a successful country-western artist and the things that make her unique.[6] She was being called on to perform, and I don't think she stopped performing just when the story got interesting. Instead, she used the resources of sociolinguistic variation to show that

---

[5] Because this anecdote is about something that used to happen repeatedly (Davis claims), it is not exactly the kind of personal-experience narrative Labov and Waletzky were describing. However, it has the same general structure. The joke is, of course, that the country-western standard in question is really called "The Green, Green *Grass* of Home."

[6] We were careful to point out to the women we talked to that we were not going to be writing for the general public and that academic publishing is a very slow process. However, as a result of a university press release, the project has attracted a fair amount of media attention in Texas. It turns out that our interviewees were smarter than we were about the publicity it might generate.

she had two crucial characteristics for country music success: a calculating head and a country heart. To do this, she created and expressed first an intelligent, thoughtful, relatively standard-sounding self, then a warm, accepting rural-sounding one. She used the linguistic resources she had—including rural-sounding speech—not just in automatic display of who she already was but to make a claim about who she thought she was and how she wanted others to see her.

The same could be said, and shown, about how people make use of other sorts of linguistic resources, ways of sounding associated with gender, class, ethnicity, or age. To say that Davis sounds the way she does because of her social characteristics (e.g., because she is from a small town in East Texas) is accurate to a point, but it fails to address the underlying reasons why Davis talks the way she does from moment to moment, reasons that have to do with self-expression in the context of choice among various linguistic and cultural resources.

## REFERENCES

Bauman, R. (1986). *Story, performance, and event: Contextual studies of oral narrative.* Cambridge, England: Cambridge University Press.
Brewer, J. (1994). Affirming the past and confirming humanness: Repetition in the discourse of elderly adults. In B. Johnstone (Ed.), *Repetition in discourse: Interdisciplinary perspectives* (pp. 230–239). Norwood, NJ: Ablex.
Bruner, J. (1986). *Actual minds, possible worlds.* Cambridge, MA: Harvard University Press.
Chafe, W. (Ed.). (1980). *The pear stories: Cognitive, cultural, and linguistic aspects of narrative production.* Norwood, NJ: Ablex.
Cook-Gumperz, J., & Green, J. L. (1984). A sense of story: Influences on children's storytelling ability. In D. Tannen (Ed.), *Coherence in spoken and written discourse* (pp. 201–218). Norwood, NJ: Ablex.
Eckert, P., & McConnell-Ginet, S. (1992). Think practically and look locally: Language and gender as community-based practice. *Annual Review of Anthropology, 21,* 461–490.
Etter-Lewis, G. (1993). *My soul is my own: Oral narratives of African American women in the professions.* New York: Routledge.
Hall, K., & Bucholtz, M. (Eds.) (1995). *Gender articulated: Language and the socially constructed self.* New York: Routledge.
Heath, S. B. (1983). *Ways with words: Language, life, and work in communities and classrooms.* Cambridge, England: Cambridge University Press.
Johnstone, B. (1990). *Stories, community, and place: Narratives from middle America.* Bloomington: Indiana University Press.
Johnstone, B. (1996a). *The linguistic individual: Self-expression in language and linguistics.* New York: Oxford University Press.
Johnstone, B. (1996b, October). *Rural speech forms as symbolic resources in contemporary Texas.* Paper presented at the 25th conference on New Ways of Analyzing Variations in English, Las Vegas, NV.
Johnstone, B., & Bean, J. M. (1997). Self-expression and linguistic variation. *Language in Society, 26,* 221–246.
Labov, W. (1972). *Sociolinguistic patterns.* Philadelphia: University of Pennsylvania Press.
Labov, W., & Waletzky, J. (this issue). Narrative analysis: Oral versions of personal experience. In J. Helm (Ed.), *Essays on the verbal and visual arts: Proceedings of the 1966 Annual Spring Meeting*

*of the American Ethnological Society* (pp. 12–44). Seattle: University of Washington Press. (Original work published 1967)

LePage, R. B., & Tabouret-Keller, A. (1985). *Acts of identity: Creole-based approaches to language and ethnicity.* Cambridge, England: Cambridge University Press.

McLeod-Porter, D. (1991). *Gender, ethnicity, and narrative: A linguistic and rhetorical analysis of adolescents' personal experience stories.* Unpublished doctoral dissertation, Texas A&M University, College Station.

Milroy, J. (1992). *Linguistic variation and change.* Oxford, England: Blackwell.

Milroy, L. (1987). *Language and social networks* (2nd ed.) Oxford, England: Blackwell.

Polanyi, L. (1985). *Telling the American story: A structural and cultural analysis of conversational storytelling.* Norwood, NJ: Ablex.

Rampton, B. (1995). *Crossing: Language and ethnicity among adolescents.* London: Longman

Riessman, K. C. (1988). Worlds of difference: Contrasting experience in marriage and narrative style. In A. D. Todd & S. Fisher (Eds.), *Gender and discourse: The power of talk* (pp. 151–173). Norwood NJ: Ablex.

Schafer, R. (1981). Narration in the psychoanalytic dialogue. In W. J. T. Mitchell (Ed.), *On narrative* (pp. 25–49). Chicago: University of Chicago Press.

Shuman, A. (1986). *Storytelling rights: The uses of oral and written texts by urban adolescents.* Cambridge, England: Cambridge University Press.

# Literary Texts and the Violation of Narrative Norms

## Susan Ehrlich
*Department of Languages, Literatures and Linguistics, York University*

Of increasing interest in text linguistics and discourse analysis is the identification of linguistic properties of narrative texts responsible for their temporal organization. Indeed, many discourse analysts, beginning with Labov and Waletzky (1967/this issue; henceforth L&W), have argued that a defining characteristic of narrative discourse is its temporal organization. For L&W, a narrative is defined as "any sequence of clauses which contains at least one temporal juncture." That is, minimally a narrative must contain one sequence of clauses that refers to events that are temporally ordered with respect to each other, clauses that cannot be interchanged without a "change in the temporal sequence of the original semantic interpretation." For example, the sequence of clauses: "I punched this boy/and he punched me" contains *temporal juncture* because its temporal interpretation will be altered if the order of the clauses is reversed: "This boy punched me/and I punched him." Put another way, then, L&W proposed that a defining characteristic of narrative is the existence of a partial matching between the temporal order of events in the real or a fictional world and their order of presentation in a text.

More recent work in discourse semantics (e.g., Dry, 1983; Dowty, 1986) has attempted to isolate the linguistic properties of clauses that create what L&W have termed temporal juncture. Because temporal juncture depends on the sequential interpretation of clauses (otherwise, a change in the order of clauses will not alter their temporal interpretation), clauses that exhibit temporal juncture will designate events that create the perception of time movement within some narrative world. For Dry (1983), it is predicates that refer to the initial and final endpoints of situations that function to push the reference time of a narrative forward. The effect is illustrated in Example 1:

---

Requests for reprints should be sent to Susan Ehrlich, Department of Languages, Literatures, and Linguistics, York University, 4700 Keele Street, North York, Ontario, Canada M3J 1P3. E-mail: sehrlich@yorku.ca.

Example 1
Fred walked into the room. The janitor *sat down* on the couch.

Example 2
Fred walked into the room. The janitor *was sitting down* on the couch.

In Example 1 the event represented by the predicate *sat down* is interpreted as occurring later than the time of Fred's walking into the room. Because the simple past tense in English refers to the endpoint of a situation, the second sentence of Example 1 moves the reference time of the narrative forward. When the same predicate occurs in the past progressive (which refers to a point that is not a situation's endpoint) as in Example 2, its event is interpreted as contemporaneous or overlapping with the previous sentence's event. Thus, the second sentence of Example 2 does not have the effect of pushing the reference time of the narrative forward. In L&W's terms, the two clauses in Example 2 do not exhibit temporal juncture because a change in their order does not result in a change in temporal interpretation.

The aspectual alternation between the simple past and past progressive in English interacts with predicate-type to the extent that only *events* (i.e., situations with natural endpoints), and not *states* (i.e., situations without natural endpoints), in the simple past tense will create new reference points on the narrative time line. Using Vendler's (1967) taxonomy of predicate-types, Dry (1983) categorized both *achievements* and *accomplishments* as events and both *activities* and *statives* as states. Within this system, achievements are defined as situations with a punctual occurrence having a natural endpoint (e.g., reaching the top, blinking). Accomplishments also have natural endpoints but are situations of greater duration than achievements (e.g., building a house, typing a letter). Activities (e.g., running, swimming) and statives are classified as states rather than events because neither have natural endpoints, only arbitrary ones. Statives are different from activities in that there is no energy required to maintain them (e.g., knowing someone, being short, owning a car). The effect of predicate-type on the movement of narrative time is illustrated in Example 3 and 4:

Example 3
Fred walked into the room. Susan *got up* from her chair.
Example 4
Fred walked into the room. Susan *sat* in her chair.

Because the second sentence of Example 3 contains the achievement predicate, *got up*, it refers to the endpoint of this situation and therefore is interpreted as denoting an event that occurs later than the previous sentence's event. By contrast, the second sentence of Example 4 contains an activity predicate (i.e., a situation without a natural endpoint) and thus the state denoted by this predicate is interpreted as overlapping with the previous sentence's event; the reference time of the narrative does not move time forward.

On the basis of examples such as 1 through 4, Dry made the following generalization: English main clause achievement and accomplishment predicates (i.e., event predicates) in simple past tense will serve to propel the reference time of a narrative forward. In the following passage, for example, from D. H. Lawrence's *Sons and Lovers* (1913/1971), the underlined predicates (all achievements and accomplishments in the simple past tense) designate time-line events that function to move the reference time of the narrative forward.

Example 5
Mrs. Morel *looked down* at him. She had dreaded this baby like a catastrophe, because of her feelings for her husband. And now she *felt* strangely towards the infant. Her heart was heavy because of the child, almost as if it were unhealthy, or malformed. Yet it seemed quite well ... .

"He looks as if he was thinking about something—quite sorrowful," *said* Mrs. Kirk. Suddenly, looking at him, the heavy feeling at the mother's heart *melted into* passionate grief. She *bowed* over him, and a few tears *shook* swiftly *out* of her very heart. The baby *lifted* his fingers.

"My lamb!" she *cried* softly.

And at that moment she *felt,* in some far inner place of her soul, that she and her husband were guilty.

The baby was looking up at her. It had blue eyes like her own but its look was heavy, steady, as if it had realized something that had stunned some points of its soul. (p. 50)

Several sentences in the initial paragraph of this passage do not contain achievement and accomplishment predicates in simple past tense and thus do not move time forward. Rather, they represent states that obtain both before and after the time-line events of the narrative (e.g., "Her heart was heavy because of the child ... , Yet it seemed quite well ... .") or activities that occurred before the events of the narrative present (e.g., "She had dreaded this baby like a catastrophe ... "). Likewise, the final paragraph of the passage contains an event in the past progressive (i.e., *was looking*) and a stative (i.e., *had blue eyes*) that are interpreted as simultaneous with the previously mentioned time-line event. From this example, we see that Dry (1983) has provided the linguistic criteria for distinguishing between L&W's notion of narrative versus nonnarrative clauses.

## TEMPORAL ORGANIZATION OF COMPLEX NARRATIVES

In my own work (e.g., Ehrlich, 1990, 1995), I have attempted to provide linguistic descriptions of literary narratives with complex temporal organizations. The utility of L&W's framework to these descriptions has been in its delineation of the narrative norms of the most fundamental of narrative structures. As Fleischman (1991) pointed out, it is not the case that narratives never violate conventions of narrativity; rather, she argued, it is precisely because narrative norms are operative that their violations have the stylistic and rhetorical effects they do.

> That is, the fact that artificial narratives, in particular, exhibit such features as flashbacks, prolepses, or other violations of chronology, or repeat the same events more than once ... ; the fact that certain texts foreground description rather than events ... the fact that narratives commonly exhibit these marked features does not invalidate the notion of a narrative norm or prototype. To the contrary, without a norm—understood as a set of unmarked values for particular properties—the marked values could not produce the effects they do. (Fleischman, 1991, p. 79)

In what follows, I demonstrate that the violation of certain narrative norms described previously is crucial to the particular rhetorical and stylistic effects produced. More specifically, I am interested in the *incoherence* that results when narrative events understood as being over or completed within a narrative world are repeated. Such repetition undermines the narrative convention of iconicity, referred to earlier, whereby the representation of narrative events parallels their occurrence in the depicted world. That is, an event that occurs once in the narrative world is narrated several times (i.e., repeated) in the narrative text. What is noteworthy about the repetitions I exemplify here (see following) is that they do not represent the events as being anterior to the narrative present, even though the initial mention of the event indicates (through the simple past tense and achievement or accomplishment predicate-type) that the event is completed. Dry (1983, p. 34) applied the terms *given* and *new,* ordinarily used in relation to the representation of noun phrases within a discourse, to the representation of events within a discourse. For Dry: "in the case of time movement, what is to be judged given or new is the information that a certain event occurred, or a certain state came into being." Consider, for example, the constructed discourse in Example 6:

Example 6
Mary finally finished her manuscript. Having finished this substantial piece of work, she felt free to move on to her long-neglected domestic tasks.

Although the first sentence of this discourse conveys (through the simple past tense and accomplishment predicate-type) that its event is complete within the narrative world, the repetition of the event in a participial construction represents it as given information (i.e., as having already taken place within the narrative world). That is, the second representation of the event as given is coherent with the first mention, which represents the event as having been completed. By contrast, the examples I discuss next are temporally incoherent to the extent that the repeated events are represented as new information (i.e., as occurring for the first time in the narrative world), even though their initial mention has established the events as given information.

Consider the following examples from Virginia Woolf's fictional prose.

Example 7
"Oh, Mr. Tansley," she *said,* "do take me to the Lighthouse with you. I should so love it."

She was telling lies he could see. She *was saying* what she did not mean to annoy him, for some reason. She was laughing at him (Woolf, 1927/1964, *To the Lighthouse,* pp. 99–100)

Example 8
Now it was time to move and as a woman gathers her things together, her cloak, her gloves, her opera-glasses and gets up to go out of the theatre into the street, she rose from the sofa and *went* to Peter.

And it was awfully strange, he thought, how she still had the power as she came tinkling, rustling, still had the power as she *came across* the room, to make the moon which he detested, rise at Bourton on the terrace in the summer sky. (Woolf, 1925/1964, *Mrs. Dalloway,* p. 55)

Example 9
"No going to the Lighthouse, James," he *said* as he stood by the window, speaking awkwardly but trying in deference to Mrs. Ramsay to soften his voice into some semblance of geniality at least ... .

This going to the Lighthouse was a passion of his, she saw, and then as if her husband had not said enough with his caustic saying that it would not be fine tomorrow, this odious little man *went and rubbed* it in all over again. (*To the Lighthouse,* p. 18)

In each of these passages, the first underlined predicate serves to move the reference time of the narrative forward; that is, each of the predicates is in the simple past tense and is either an achievement or an accomplishment. In Dry's terms, the designated events become given information within the discourse because it is communicated through their tense and predicate-type that they have occurred in the narrative world. The subsequent mentions of these events, however, do not represent them as given information, (i.e., as anterior to the narrative present), but rather as new information (i.e., as occurring for the first time in the narrative world). The superficial temporal incoherence evident in these passages, then, represents a violation of the narrative norm of iconicity, a violation that I am claiming is the source of a particular stylistic and rhetorical effect.

## STYLISTIC EFFECT: SHIFTS IN POINT OF VIEW

In order to describe the function of the repetitions exemplified previously, it is helpful to consider Genette's (1980) distinction between "who sees" within a narrative and "who speaks." It is not necessarily the case that the consciousness whose point of view orients the events and descriptions of a narrative (i.e., who sees) is also the formal voice (i.e., who speaks) within a narrative. Indeed, in much of Virginia Woolf's prose the subjective impressions of characters emerge even though the act of telling the narrative is performed by a narrator who is distinct from the characters and occurs at a point in time after the narrated events. Auerbach (1968, p. 536) characterized Woolf's style as a multipersonal representation of consciousness: "The essential characteristic of the technique represented by Virginia Woolf is that we are given not merely one person whose consciousness (that is, the impressions it receives) is rendered but many persons, with frequent shifts from one to another." Thus, not only is there sometimes a disjunction between the formal speaker of the text (i.e., the narrator) and the point of view through which the narrative is mediated in Woolf's prose, there are also frequent shifts in the source consciousness perceiving the events and descriptions of the narrative. My claim is that the temporal incoherence resulting from the presentation of given narrative events as new can be resolved if the repetition of the event is interpreted as conveying a different perspective or point of view on the event. That is, the representation of the second mention of the event as new within the narrative world is coherent if the event is indeed interpreted as occurring for the first time, but from the point of view of a different source consciousness. A visual analogy is perhaps useful at this point. If narrative events are repeated within a film, one strategy for making sense of such repetition is to attribute their second occurrence to a new character or consciousness. Thus, the repetition of completed events within a narrative can result in a superficial temporal incoherence that, in its resolution, can function to create a new vantage point from which given events are interpreted.

Consider Example 7. It initially represents Lily Briscoe's (the referent of *she*) speech act as an accomplishment predicate in simple past tense. Thus, the speech act becomes given information within the discourse. The second mention of the speech act, however, in the past progressive represents the event as ongoing. As a way of imposing coherence on what seems to be temporally incoherent, I am claiming that the reader interprets the second mention of the speech act as filtered through a different source consciousness. That is, although from one point of view the speech act is completed within the narrative world, from a different point of view (i.e., Mr. Tansley's) the act is ongoing and simultaneous with thoughts about Lily Briscoe's true feelings.

Examples 8 and 9 are slightly different from 7 in that the repetition is not exact repetition: different predicates designate the second mention of the narrative events in question. In Example 8, Mrs. Dalloway's travelling across the room is first represented by the accomplishment predicate, *go to,* in simple past tense *(went to Peter)* and then by the accomplishment predicate, *come across,* in simple past tense *(she came across the room).* Again, I am claiming that the temporal incoherence that results from presenting a given narrative event *(went to Peter)* as new *(she came across the room)* can be resolved if the second mention of the event is interpreted as conveying a different perspective on the event. Put another way, the second mention of the event is new within the discourse from the perspective of a new or different source consciousness. In Example 9, the point of view shifts from the narrator (a relatively objective vantage point) to Peter. Likewise, in Example 9 the point of view shifts from the narrator to Mrs. Ramsay. Like Example 8, the passage in 9 represents given information as new with the repetition of a speech act designated by an accomplishment predicate in simple past tense *(went and rubbed it in).* Rather than interpreting the second mention of the event as incoherent with the first, I am claiming that readers impose a shift in point of view on the second mention of the event and impute it to a new source consciousness, that of Mrs. Ramsay.

Hrushovski (1982), in a general discussion of strategies or procedures for imposing coherence on superficially incoherent texts, cited "imposing a shift of speaker" as one such strategy. He provided the following example:

Example 10
He opened the door. A few pieces of clothing were strewn about. He caught the fish in his net. (Hrushovski, 1982, p. 162)

Although the first two sentences in Example 10 are not connected by any formal or logical means, they are readily interpreted as coherent if we assume that readers draw inferences about doors being entrances to rooms and rooms often containing clothes. According to Hrushovski, it is more difficult to interpret the third sentence of Example 10 as coherent with previous discourse, because fish are not normally caught with nets in rooms. At least two strategies can be used to restore coherence to this passage. A metaphorical interpretation is possible whereby the third sentence could be understood nonliterally, for example, as a man entering a room and catching a thief. Alternatively, Hrushovski claimed, a shift of speaker can be imposed upon the passage such that the sentence is interpreted as the man's thoughts (i.e., as a shift in point of view) as he enters the room. In a similar way, I am suggesting that the repetition of narrative events in the passages from Woolf's prose functions (along with other linguistic features) to introduce a different point of view into the discourse. Rather than interpreting the repeated events as incoherent with the representation of the original event, they are interpreted as events occurring for the first time (i.e., in the narrative present) but from the point of view of a different source consciousness. Thus, the superficial temporal incoherence that results from the repetition of completed events within the narrative world (representation of given events as new) can be resolved if the repeated events are imputed to a different consciousness. This shift in point of view, of course, relies crucially on the similarity involved in repetition. The introduction of a new narrative event into the discourse would not necessarily invoke a shift in perspective; it is the repeating of given events that helps to create a new perspective on them.

## CONCLUSION

A crucial point of L&W's work concerns the relation between complex narratives and more fundamental narrative structures: "In our opinion, it will not be possible to make very much progress in the analysis and understanding of these complex narratives until the simplest and most fundamental narrative structures are analyzed in direct connection with their originating functions" (this issue). Following Fleischman (1990, 1991), I have demonstrated the way that complex narratives may exploit some of the narrative norms identified by L&W for particular rhetorical effects. Although L&W's framework accounts for narratives with a single temporal axis, narratives such as those exemplified here are organized around multiple time axes. Like Picasso paintings that depict a "figure" simultaneously from multiple viewpoints, these narratives represent the same event from multiple vantage points. In the same way that Picasso developed formal techniques for the "unconventional" representation of figures, so Woolf has exploited narrative norms in her multipersonal representation of consciousness.

## REFERENCES

Auerbach, E. (1968). *Mimesis.* Princeton, NJ: Princeton University Press.
Dowty, D. (1986). The effects of aspectual class on the temporal structure of discourse: Semantics or pragmatics? *Linguistics and Philosophy, 9,* 37–61.
Dry, H. (1983). The movement of narrative time. *Journal of Literary Semantics, 12,* 19–53.
Ehrlich, S. (1990). *Point of view: A linguistic analysis of literary style.* London: Routledge.
Ehrlich, S. (1995). Narrative iconicity and repetition in oral and literary narratives. In P. Verdonk & J. J. Weber (Eds.), *Twentieth-century fiction: From text to context* (pp. 78–95). London: Routledge.
Fleischman, S. (1990). *Tense and narrativity.* Austin: University of Texas Press.
Fleischman, S. (1991). Toward a theory of tense-aspect in narrative discourse. In J. Gvozdanovic, T. Janssen, & O. Dahl (Eds.), *The function of tense in texts* (pp. 75–97). Amsterdam: North Holland.
Genette, G. (1980). *Narrative discourse.* Ithaca, NY: Cornell University Press.

Hrushovski, B. (1982). Integrational semantics. In H. Byrnes (Ed.), *Contemporary perceptions of language: Interdisciplinary dimensions* (pp. 156–190). Washington, DC: Georgetown University Press.
Labov, W., & Waletzky, J. (this issue). Narrative analysis: Oral versions of personal experience. In J. Helm (Ed.), *Essays on the verbal and visual arts: Proceedings of the 1966 Annual Spring Meeting of the American Ethnological Society* (pp. 12–44). Seattle: University of Washington Press. (Original work published 1967)
Lawrence, D. H. (1971). *Sons and lovers.* Harmondsworth, England: Penguin. (Original work published 1913)
Vendler, Z. (1967). *Linguistics in philosophy.* Ithaca, NY: Cornell University Press.
Woolf, V. (1964). *Mrs. Dalloway.* Harmondsworth, England: Penguin. (Original work published 1925)
Woolf, V. (1964). *To the lighthouse.* Harmondsworth, England: Penguin. (Original work published 1927)

# "He Lived to Tell the Tale"

### Rom Harré
*Linacre College, Oxford, England, and
Department of Psychology, Georgetown University*

Only the other day a lone yachtsman was rescued from his capsized boat in the Southern Ocean, having spent 4 days inside the hull. A few weeks ago a lone adventurer, setting out to cross the Antarctic continent alone, was forced to abandon his venture through ill health. Each had a good tale to tell. Each told a tale from a possible repertoire of many tales that adventurers tell. How was what they did related to what they said? I do not mean in the naive sense of whether what they said was true, but how was the possibility of the telling of an adventure related to the plan to undertake it? This question raises one of the deepest issues in our attempts to study the relations of language and life.

Social psychology has altered the focus of its research effort somewhat these days, from a study of the effects of isolated "treatments" on what people do, to the analysis of extended episodes of interaction. Perhaps in this new frame the beginnings of an answer to the question posed to the linguist by the tie between narratives and lives can be found. The question then arises of what is it that explains the structure of such episodes. However, before that question can be answered it is necessary to choose among a myriad of possibilities, a working "ontology." By that I mean a characterization of the basic elements into which episodes are to be analyzed. Furthermore, our everyday knowledge of how life goes includes some such idea as the role or standing that people have in different episodes.

However, where does language come into this program? Linguistic matters come into prominence in three ways, at least. First of all, much of human social interaction is conducted linguistically, and indeed there is an increasing trend towards purely linguistic interactions as media of communication develop. Second, conversations are a useful working model or analogue for more complex interactions, in which other modes of conduct than the verbal play a part. Third, there is the fascinating

---

Requests for reprints should be sent to Rom Harré, Linacre College, Oxford OX1 3JA, England. E-mail: harrew@guvax.acc.georgetown.edu or rom.harre@linacre.ox.ac.uk.

matter of *lived* and *told narratives,* raised by our reflections on adventurers and their travellers' tales. By that I mean the idea that the way we live, when studied in microscopic detail, seems to reveal patterns of living that reproduce well-known stories (Bruner, 1986). At the same time, human beings, wherever we encounter them, are busy recounting bits of their lives as stories. What is the relation between these "narratives"? To illustrate the sort of thing I mean, here is a vignette from my own life. I was asked to play in the little orchestra in Blackfriars chapel, the Dominican house in Oxford, for the Christmas Day mass. I noticed that as I agreed I thought of how I would tell my friend Robinson about it. Here I work for the Jesuits and play for the Dominicans. Living and telling go together.

In this short article I reflect on the relation between lived and told narratives. Acting with others involves not only one's interactional skills, but also the standing one has in this or that episode vis-à-vis the others. As Goffman (1981) put it: What sort of footing do I have with these people in these circumstances? More recently, this aspect of interaction has come to be called one's *position* (Davies & Harré, 1990). However, positions, as clusters of rights and obligations to act in certain ways, are linked with the significance of one's actions as social acts. What one is seen to be doing or heard to be saying is made more or less determinate by the position in which one is located, either by the conventions that define the episode as of a certain type, say a doctoral defence, or the more ephemeral positionings into which we move and are moved in everyday interactions. Finally, both positions and acts are tied in with the story line or narrative that is unfolding in the episode. Analysis of real examples shows not only that mutual positionings shift and modulate, but that a pattern of actions may support more than one sequence of acts, the social meanings of what has been said and done. So there is always likely to be more than one story line unfolding, more than one narrative being lived.

The telling of tales is more readily researchable than the living of lives. So perhaps the point of departure for the investigation of lived narratives ought to be the told narrative that precedes, accompanies, or recounts an episode. As we have argued in proposing analyses of environmental discourses (Brockmeier, Harré, & Mühlhäusler, 1997), there are not only different degrees of detail to which one can attend, but several useful ways of decomposing a narrative. For example, one can look on a story as a *Bildungsroman,* in which there is a pattern of episodes through which character is developed. Or one can use Propp's system (Propp, 1968), which reveals a finer grain pattern than the broad outline of the *Bildungsroman*. For example, the hero, when seemingly in the power of an irresistible and malevolent force, is provided, unexpectedly, with a useful weapon or resource, and so on. What is the nature of the narrative conventions that are so revealed?

To push that question further we can ask about how the general treatment of structures—and episodes are structures—could be applied in the case of narrative. Structures are patterns of elements standing in certain relations, at least some of which must be reasonably invariant under at least some transformations. To analyze a structure one chooses a certain ontology, set of elements, and relations. Of course, anything in this world may and probably does have many different structures, each of which is made available to an observer by choice of analytical schema. Some structures come into being through time—the diachronic—and some exist all at one time—the synchronic. Episodes are, necessarily, diachronic. However, how do we account for any of the many possible structures that some method of analysis reveals?

There are at least two possibilities. There may be a preexisting template, for instance a script or handbook which lays down, as a set of instructions, what is to be done by each participant and what their actions mean. Of course, it hardly needs saying that predetermined constraints on meaning are by no means wholly effective, there being huge latitude for eccentric, recalcitrant, and so on interpretations, as idiosyncratic as some may be. Nevertheless, in a fuzzy sort of way, templates do constrain actors, certainly at the level of actions and to some extent at the level of acts. When a student of narrative, be it told or lived, writes down an analysis using such a system as Propp's functions, the explanatory mode is implicitly the template. However, it may also be that there is no over-all schema, or narrative convention, that expresses a full-blown story line. This may be because the story line is very general (as it might be in improvised theater). "Nurse and patient" is a prominent story line in family life, both lived and told, but its implementation is capable of indefinite variation in detail. However, more interestingly it may be because what happens next is predetermined to some degree by what has happened before, but only over a short time span. In ethnomethodology this was called the "adjacency pair." A well-structured episode, which everyone finds satisfying and which no one wants to call into question or undertake remedial revisions, may have no more powerful a structuring underpinning than sequences of adjacency pairs. Looking for a larger scale structure may simply be hunting the snark.

The methodological payoff of the foregoing is the idea that the form of the explicit told narrative, the account, is a guide to the implicit form of the lived narrative, the episode. However, as in many cases in which techniques or insights drawn from linguistics and literary studies are transposed to psychology, we must be on our guard against promiscuous causal hypothesizing. The account makes the episode intelligible and in some measure may succeed in making it warranted to the audience in play. However, it must be remembered that any slicing of life into episodes is driven by some project or other and that the claims to have revealed this or that structure are relative to the positions adopted, assigned, or ascribed to the participants. For any episode there are, in principle, many possible accounts. The question for the psychologist is how accounting facilitates living, not what causes the pattern revealed by the account. Nothing may cause it.

The double entendre in the title of this article was meant to draw our attention to the interplay of lived and told narratives. Finally, in the light of the multiplicity of possible story lines that any episode could realize, the fit between lives and narratives may be itself an artifact, that is, contrived. The story I tell may not have been the story I tried to live.

## REFERENCES

Brockmeier, J., Harré, R., & Mühlhäusler, P. (1997). *Greenspeak.* Unpublished manuscript.
Bruner, J. S. (1986). *Actual minds, possible worlds.* Cambridge, MA: Harvard University Press.
Davies, B., & Harré, R. (1990). Positioning: The social construction of selves. *Journal for the Theory of Social Behaviour, 20,* 43–63.
Goffman, E. (1981). *Forms of talk.* Philadelphia: University of Philadelphia Press.
Labov, W., & Waletzky, J. (this issue). Narrative analysis: Oral versions of personal experience. In J. Helm (Ed.), *Essays on the verbal and visual arts: Proceedings of the 1966 Annual Spring Meeting of the American Ethnological Society* (pp. 12–44). Seattle: University of Washington Press. (Original work published 1967)
Propp, V. (1968). *Morphology of the folk tale.* Austin: University of Texas Press.

# Positioning Between Structure and Performance

### Michael G. W. Bamberg
*Department of Psychology, Clark University*

## TEMPORALITY AND EVALUATION

There are two possible interpretations of what the term *narrative* implies in Labov and Waletzky's original 1967 (this issue; henceforth L&W) framework in terms of how narrative is linked to *personal experience* in particular and to sense-making in general. The first, more simplistic reading implies that narratives—particularly those of personal experience—are representations of something that once happened and what this past happening meant (or "now" means) to the narrator. The second, more indirect reading requires the act of telling—or "representing" at a particular occasion in the form of a particular story—to intervene, so to speak, between the actual experience and the story. It was the first reading of L&W that originally fascinated me and lured me into exploring narratives as a window to people's experiences. However, in the course of having worked with narratives over the last two decades, I have moved more and more to adopt the second reading.

Other contributors to this issue have commented in one or another way on this tension between a traditional, structural approach and a more performance-based, pragmatic approach to narrative and narrative analysis. Whereas the first takes its starting point from what was said (and the way it was said) and works toward why it was said, that is, its meaning, the second focuses more strongly on how it was performed as the main index for what the narrative as an act of instantiation means to the performer. It also should be noted that within this second reading the audience is much more of a factor that impinges on the shape of the narrative and its performance. What actually is being said is one of the many different performance features in what the speaker aims to achieve in the act of narrating.

---

Requests for reprints should be sent to Michael Bamberg, Department of Psychology, Clark University, Worcester, MA 01610–1477. E-mail: mbamberg@clarku.edu.

L&W's analytical suggestion to start with the identification of *narrative clauses,* that is, with "matching a verbal sequence of clauses to the sequence of events which actually occurred" (this issue), and then take the *free clauses* as an index for the narrator's evaluative stance, appears to give prominence to form over function, inasmuch as it seems common sensible that one has to first identify the sequence of temporal events before one can assess the seemingly more subjective criteria that led to an evaluative stance on those events. Thus, the events present somewhat of an "objective" basis, without which an evaluative stance could not be rationally claimed and upheld. Temporality, which later in the 70s became a fascinating topic for all kinds of cross-linguistic comparisons, seemed to form a solid basis upon which formal linguistic systems and systems in use (as in narratives) could be explored.

Without being able to follow up on the history of these hopes and their demise (and some recent transports [in state] to new hopes in the exploration of the relation between language and space), I attempt here to outline an approach to evaluation that picks up on L&W's original suggestions; however, one that is more in line with their functionalist orientation, treating temporality as one among many other performance features that all ultimately are in the service of discursive purposes and the formations of local identities.

## NARRATIVE POSITIONING

Although the notion of *positioning* was originally not developed exclusively for the analysis of narrating as an interactive activity, it nevertheless attempted to employ strategically the notion of plots and story lines. Building on Hollway (1984), Davies and Harré (1990) defined positioning as a discursive practice "whereby selves are located in conversations as observably and intersubjectively coherent participants in jointly produced story lines" (p. 48). Thus, in conversations—due to the intrinsic social force of conversing—people position themselves in relation to one another in ways that traditionally have been defined as *roles.* More importantly, in doing so, people "produce" one another (and themselves) situationally as "social beings."

Although this approach explicitly addresses the analysis of language under the heading of how people attend to one another in interactional settings, and although traditional narrative analysis along the lines suggested by L&W addresses the analysis of what the language is referentially "about," namely sequentially ordered (past) events and their evaluations, we have attempted to apply the notion of positioning more productively to the analysis of storytelling (see Bamberg, 1996a, 1996b, 1997; Crawford, 1996; Talbot, Bibace, Bokhour, & Bamberg, 1997) in order to link these two approaches. For this purpose, we considered the process of positioning to take place at three different *levels* that are formulated in the following as three different positioning questions:

1. *How are the characters positioned in relation to one another within the reported events?* At this level, we attempt to analyze how characters within the story world are constructed in terms of, for example, protagonists and antagonists or as perpetrators and victims. More concretely, this type of analysis aims at the linguistic means that do the job of marking one person as, for example: (a) the agent who is in control while the action is inflicted upon the other; or (b) as the central character who is helplessly at the mercy of outside (quasi "natural") forces or who is rewarded by luck, fate, or personal qualities (such as bravery, nobility, or simply "character").

2. *How does the speaker position him- or herself to the audience?* At this level, we seek to analyze the linguistic means that are characteristic for the particular discourse mode that is being employed. Does, for instance, the narrator attempt to instruct the listener in terms of what to do in face of adversary conditions or does the narrator engage in making excuses for his actions and in attributing blame to others?

3. *How do narrators position themselves to themselves?* How is language employed to make claims that the narrator holds to be true and relevant above and beyond the local conversational situation? In other words, we hold that the linguistic devices employed in narrating point to more than the content (or what the narrative is "about") and the interlocutor. In constructing the content and one's audience in terms of role participants, the narrator transcends the question of: "How do I want to be understood by you, the audience?" and constructs a (local) answer to the question: "Who am I?" Simultaneously, however, we must caution that any attempted answer to this question is not one that necessarily holds across contexts, but rather is a project of limited range.

## Positioning: Three Examples

*Children's accounts of emotion situations.* As a first example of how the positioning approach to narratives was put to use, let me offer two illustrations from my ongoing studies of children's accounts of emotion events. When asked to give an account of a situation when "you made someone else angry," a 6-year-old answered: "It was a couple of years ago, when I took the crab away from my brother, then I stuck my fist out, and he ran into it and got a bloody nose." Typical for this answer is the positioning of the *I* as an agent who nevertheless does not have full control over the outcome of his actions and consequently cannot be held responsible. The narrator positions the *I* in such a way that the event described is characteristic of the event type "accident." The *other,* here his brother, is positioned vis-à-vis the *I* as somewhat agentive: If he hadn't moved himself into the fist, this situation would not have occurred.

In contrast to the linguistic devices employed for this type of scenario, accounts of situations when "I once was angry" typically position the *other* as being a highly individuated and often unjust agent, whose actions are targeted willfully at the *I*, construing the relationship between the two characters as one of perpetrator and victim: "When my sister slapped me across the face, just because she didn't let me in her room, and I wanted to play a game, but she didn't let me, and she slapped me across the face."

The two different types of linguistic strategies can clearly be differentiated in terms of the syntactic constructions that are employed (see for more details Bamberg, 1996a, 1996b, 1997). However, these different syntactic construction types are argued to be pragmatically organized by the discursive purpose for which they are employed: whereas constructions used for the construal of the first type of positioning serve the purpose of saving face, the strategies employed for the second positioning serve to elicit empathy and align the audience in a moral stance with the *I* against the *other*.

*Teenager's accounts of their sexual identity.* Crawford (1996) prepared a detailed analysis of all three positioning levels in two different narrative accounts of the same experience, both given by the same 13-year-old girl. The experience involved being away from home and spending an excessive amount of time on the phone. The first account takes place in a classroom context and is given to a female acquaintance of the same age:

Narrative 1
We were talking on the phone from the hotel ... to this kid John ... for three hours, and the phone bill came up to fifteen dollars, for one night, my Mom was like wicked mad at us. (Crawford, 1996, p. 45)

At another occasion, the same situation is presented to her best friend (female) and two overhearing boys, again in the classroom:

Narrative 2
When I was in Connecticut this weekend, my friends, we were stayin for competition, right, and they met this boy, right, so they called him out from the hotel, and he was having phone sex with one of my friends, you know how they have phone sex, right, like, aw, you're wearing this, oh baby, you look so fine, you know, and all, they're having phone sex, I was sittin there, I was cracking up, I was like "no sir." (Crawford, 1996, pp. 59–60)

In her analysis, Crawford first delineated the positioning devices used to set up the *we* versus *my Mom* in the first narrative, resulting in a typical teenage alignment against an adult world, in harmony with the peer-group values. By contrast, Narrative 2 employs a rather different positioning strategy: Firstly, the descriptions of the agentive characters are different (*we* vs. *they; they* made the call, whereas in Narrative 1, *we* used the phone); secondly, *this kid John,* who was the recipient of the call in Narrative 1, is positioned agentively as *having phone sex* in Narrative 2; and thirdly, *I,* who is not mentioned in Narrative 1, is singled out and positioned as nonagentive (sitting) and explicitly distancing herself from what is happening. In addition to positioning the characters distinctly, the narrator (in a number of free clauses in the middle of Narrative 2) seeks to position herself to her audience as an expert on the topic of phone sex (Positioning Level 2).

In sum, the linguistic devices employed in the two narratives result: (a) in different positioning of the characters in the narrative event (the situation described) and (b) in two rather different relationships between the narrator and her two different audiences. Furthermore, Crawford demonstrated that the differences in these two positioning strategies resulted in two different moral positions and identity claims, both of them interactively and locally achieved. The first can best be described as a claim with regard to her position as a young person in conflict with the adult world of telephone bills and responsibilities, the second as a young person who is knowledgeable about topics concerning boys and sexuality. Both claims are made against the background of existing moral orders that are being tested out and questioned in the narrative discourse conducted with the audience. In other words, the two claims as to how the narrator wants to be understood as a person (who she "is") are explorations that could be modified in the subsequent course of the conversation. The narrator's implicit claim in the second narrative that "she is not that kind of girl" is clearly maintained, but "open to negotiation" (see Crawford, 1996, for an elaboration on this point).

*Women's accounts of their pregnancies.* In my third example, we (Talbot, Bibace, Bokhour, & Bamberg, 1997) attempted to distill the identity claims in an even more direct way. We analyzed narrative interviews of two pregnant women who had been diagnosed previously "at risk" due to a history of gestational diabetes, thereby, in case of a further pregnancy, placing themselves as well as their fetus at risk. By performing a discursive analysis of these women's positioning strategies, we hoped to be able to reveal their claims as to who they are and how they made sense of their situation in comparison with the master narrative of the normal course of pregnancy and birth giving.

Our analysis started with a detailed analysis of how the two interviewees positioned themselves as characters within the depicted situations as they relate to their family members, friends, and neighbors, but mainly in their relationships with their physicians. From there, moving to Positioning Level 2, we analyzed their positioning strategies with the interviewer (and behind her a more generalized [female] audience). Let me skip a detailed account of the linguistic constructions employed by both interviewees and move straight to a summary of their claims as to how they seem to understand themselves—at least in this conversation—in light of their claims as to who they are and how they want to be understood.

Mary, the first interviewee, views herself as a self-reliant person, who is better equipped than anyone to devise a program of self-care that will meet her individual needs and ensure the health and safety of herself and her unborn baby. Her complaint regarding doctors is that they fail to respect the soundness of her judgment and the efficacy of her agency. Her identity claim as a self-reliant individual lends her authority as she advises others to claim self-reliance for themselves. She constructs her own identity by asserting that she herself is unusual and that ways of understanding pregnancy that may apply to others often are not useful to her in her efforts to cope with the adversarial challenges of a difficult pregnancy.

Sue—the other interviewee—attributes the notion of pregnancy that she disputes not to medical authorities, but to the majority of the general public, whom she portrays as uninformed. Her critique of this popular view of pregnancy is in a sense more radical than Mary's, for Sue is asserting not only that this widespread version bears no resemblance to her pregnancy, but that it fails to take into consideration the truth that complications are a common experience for many pregnant women. Bearing witness to this diversity of experience among expectant mothers, she concludes that the concept of normality embodied in the standard pregnancy narrative is in need of revision. When doctors appear in her account, they are depicted not as opponents but as benign and knowledgeable allies who help her to arrive at a more realistic appreciation of pregnancy as a potentially perilous undertaking. Far from constructing herself as asserting her power to control the outcome of events in her pregnancy, Sue insists that uncertainty is ineluctably a part of the process and that no expectant mother can eliminate pregnancy's inherent risks or dispel its mysteries. Sue constructs herself as a realist, whose authority is grounded in openness to points of view beside her own and in her realistic acceptance of the limitations to her own control. In other words, she grounds her lack of power and self-control in a position of authoritative realism.

## POSITIONING AND EVALUATION

The three examples of positioning analysis were meant to outline how this type of analysis proceeds. Although children at the age of 6 years do not seem to be able to make far-reaching claims with regard to their identity that enable us to analyze their narratives for positioning at Level 3, their choices of linguistic constructions to position themselves as characters in reported personal experiences reflect clearly the ability to construct scenarios in light of discursive purposes such as attributing blame or saving face. Our analysis of the two reportings of the same event in the 13-year-old adolescent's narratives highlighted positioning at Level 2. Here the construction of the narrator–audience relationship by use of linguistic constructions was foregrounded. Although both narratives referred to the same event, the language used marked two different positioning vis-à-vis the two audiences: Both entailed claims regarding "what kind of girl I am," though both claims are thoroughly grounded in the here-and-now of the conversational setting. The identity claims (Level 3) may best be understood as situationally instantiated and put up for negotiation. Our positioning analysis of Mary and Sue focused more strongly on the linguistic means employed to construct identity claims relevant for Positioning Level 3. Although these claims are nevertheless locally tied to the interview situation, they bespeak a discourse type that searches across past events (of personal experience) for evidence to make claims of a more decontextual sort. In our article (Talbot et al., 1997) we attempted to sort these discourses in relation to preexisting master discourses on the topic of pregnancy and moral identity; that is, we asked the question: Where did these discourses come from and how did they achieve their coherence and persuasive powers?

Turning back to the question of how this type of positioning analysis compares with L&W's original notion of evaluation, it should be noted that in my proposal narrative is defined considerably more broadly than in L&W: The discursive situation and the discursive purpose are as central as the semantic (temporal) organization of the narrative. In this sense, the analysis of positioning is an attempt to unite the pragmatics of narrating with the linguistic (structural) analysis à la L&W into one that emphasizes more strongly issues such as "the assignment of praise and blame" (Labov, this issue) and "viewpoint" as central to the emergence of structure and meaning in narratives.

In line with Labov's general acclaim of the analysis of language use, I hold that the analysis of positioning is basically a linguistic analysis, one, however, that takes linguistic (and extralinguistic) devices as performance features (or as "contextualization cues"; see Cook-Gumperz & Gumperz, this issue) that index how narrators want to be understood. "Temporally ordering" and "stepping out of the flow of events" are two options in the repertoire of speakers. Other contributors to this issue have pointed to other devices that figure centrally in their analyses, and Labov's own contribution clearly points in the same direction. Positioning analysis may possibly best be understood as granting more centrality to the speaker's active engagement in the construction process of narratives.

At the same time, the proposed type of analysis points up that any attempt to assemble and analyze performance features as put to use for discursive purposes needs to acquire a multiplicity of potential functions. Although the "what's-the-point-question" seems to be particularly legitimate, a story may often serve more than one purpose: Above its very referential and informative function, it may entertain, be a piece of moral advice, extend an offer to become more intimate, seek audience alignment for the purpose of joint revenge, and serve as a claim as to "who I really am"—and all this at the same time. In addition, these functions are not only achieved with narratives that position the self as one of the central actors. They are also used in narratives about (third) persons other than the self—fictional or nonfictional, and they similarly apply to generic *others* as central characters. Thus, although narrative analysis traditionally tends to privilege narratives of personal experience as providing some special access to experience and "the person," narratives as acts of narrating in general lay themselves open to the same kind of positioning analysis.

## REFERENCES

Bamberg, M. (1996a). Emotion talk(s): The role of perspective in the construction of emotions. In S. Niemeier & R. Dirven (Eds.), *The language of emotions* (pp. 209–225). Amsterdam: John Benjamins.

Bamberg, M. (1996b). Perspective and agency in the construal of narrative events. In D. Stringfellow, E. Cahana-Amitay, E. Hughes, & A. Zukowski (Eds.), *Proceedings of the 20th Annual Boston Conference on Language Development, Vol. 1* (pp. 30–39). Somerville, MA: Cascadilla.

Bamberg, M. (1997). Language, concepts, and emotions. The role of language in the construction of emotions. *Language Sciences, 19,* 309–340.

Crawford, V. (1996). *Identity construction in conversational narratives.* Unpublished masters thesis, Clark University, Department of Psychology, Worcester, MA.

Davies, B., & Harré. (1990). Positioning: The social construction of selves. *Journal for the Theory of Social Behaviour, 20,* 43–63.

Hollway, W. (1984). Gender difference and the production of subjectivity. In J. Henriqes, W. Hollway, C. Urwin, C. Venn, & V. Walkerdine (Eds.), *Changing the subject: Psychology, social regulation and subjectivity* (pp. 227–263). London: Methuen.

Labov, W., & Waletzky, J. (this issue). Narrative analysis: Oral versions of personal experience. In J. Helm (Ed.), *Essays on the verbal and visual arts: Proceedings of the 1966 Annual Spring Meeting of the American Ethnological Society* (pp. 12–44). Seattle: University of Washington Press. (Original work published 1967)

Talbot, J., Bibace, R., Bokhour, B., & Bamberg, M. (1997). Affirmation and resistance of dominant discourses: The rhetorical construction of pregnancy. *Journal of Narrative and Life History, 6,* 225–251.

# When Sentences Are Not Enough: Narrative Data and Cultural Identity

## Alison Imbens-Bailey
*University of California, Los Angeles*

One of the most compelling motivations William Labov (1972) gave for the decision he and Joshua Waletzky made in 1967 (Labov & Waletzky, this issue; henceforth L&W) to undertake their analysis of narratives of personal experience was a concern that a study of the internal structure of Black English Vernacular—its grammar and sound system—would not be able to explain why Black youth were failing in school, rather, it would take an understanding of the vernacular culture itself and analysis of the communicative competencies required to be an effective user of Black English Vernacular. What began as a method of generating casual and, as near as possible, spontaneous speech samples for analyses beyond the levels of syntax and semantics, grew to become a bedrock of narrative analysis across many social science disciplines.

In recognizing that analyzing single sentences was not sufficient for finding an explanation of the diversity of linguistic skills across a range of ages, social classes, and ethnicities, L&W made a number of important contributions to the social sciences in general and to sociolinguistics and education in particular. Two major contributions are considered here: L&W's introduction of an interview method that has since been widely adopted in the social science arena to answer a variety of research questions, and their recognition of a close link between language and cultural identity.

L&W collected narratives during 600 interviews with Anglo, Hispanic, and African Americans ranging in age from just 10 years to 72 years. Their technique for generating narratives of personal experience would prove essential for undertaking the later study of Black English Vernacular (Labov, 1972). When stand-

---

Requests for reprints should be sent to Alison Imbens-Bailey, Department of Education, Moore Hall, Box 951521, University of California, Los Angeles, 405 Hilgard Avenue, Los Angeles, CA 90095–1521. E-mail: aimbens@ucla.edu

ardized tests, trails, and screenings reported the failure of minority youth to succeed in school, rather than accept the predominant deficit theory of their day that placed the blame for failure on inadequate cognitive abilities in minority children, L&W turned to narrative as an alternative method that could be used for measuring linguistic skills beyond the level of the sentence. The narrative data collected and analyzed would not only serve to better capture the linguistic abilities of the youth L&W worked with in Central Harlem, but also helped to embed their linguistic analysis within the Black and Puerto Rican youth cultures.

## NARRATIVE AS SOCIAL SCIENCE RESEARCH TOOL

In 1967 L&W demonstrated the successful use of narratives of personal experience as a technique for generating a large body of data on the verbal skills of children and adults of various social classes and ethnic groups. They asked their study participants to respond to conversationally embedded queries such as, "Were you ever in a situation where you thought you were in serious danger of getting killed?" or "Were you ever in a fight with someone bigger than you?" A simple affirmative response (e.g., "Yes") was almost guaranteed to be followed by further elaboration in the form of a personal narrative. L&W had successfully tapped into a basic tenet of human communication. A bold claim of being in danger of being killed or fighting an overwhelming opponent had to be justified by the claimant or they would remain in violation of the "cooperative principles" of conversation. Specifically, they would renege on the maxim of "quality" that requires the speaker to be fully informative (Grice, 1975).

By asking participants in their studies to respond to such prompts for retelling personal experiences, L&W were able to elicit samples of casual speech that were far less affected by the typical constraints of face-to-face interviews. In face-to-face interviews, the researcher often has a fixed interview schedule and the explicit question-and-answer format may lead the study participants to pay more attention to their own responses.

Since L&W's early studies of narratives of personal experience, many researchers have adopted these techniques by which to generate extended discourse for various types of structural and content analyses in a variety of fields, for example, education, clinical psychology, developmental psychology, and linguistics. Data in the form of narratives of personal experience have been found to offer the researcher many advantages, including the opportunity to uncover topics and themes important to study participants that would have remained unknown and consequently unanalyzed by the researcher using a fixed interview schedule to gather data (Mishler, 1986). The opportunity to analyze formal features in personal narratives is also proving a fruitful alternative to either content analysis or psychometric scales in the fields of anthropology and psychology (e.g., Angrosino,

1995; Veroff, Chadiha, Leber, & Sutherland, 1993). Analysis of the formal features of a narrative has the advantage of being less affected by study participants. It is unlikely that participants are consciously manipulating the formal elements of their narratives (for example, their use of personal pronouns or the number and types of conjunctive forms they use), even as they may manipulate the content of their responses to what they perceive a researcher wants to hear.

Narratives (at least good ones) are by their very nature self-contained (Cortazzi, 1993). L&W, in their analytic approach to describing the overall structure of personal narratives, posit five components or sections that in combination comprise the referential and evaluative features of narrative. The orientation component of narrative provides the listener with necessary background information to answer the questions "Who is involved?", "Where is the action set?", and "When is this happening?". This component of personal narratives provides the researcher with another advantage, as Cortazzi (1993) highlighted in his own study of British school teachers' narratives of their professional lives:

> Teachers motivated by the narrative process will provide enough background on the classroom context for a recipient to interpret their narratives. This means there will be sufficient context for a visiting researcher/teacher who is unfamiliar with the teller's school to understand the point [the evaluative component]. This is important methodologically since a large number of teachers could be interviewed to elicit narratives without the necessity of observing classrooms or of gathering additional background information. (pp. 54–55)

In research on the development of ethnic identities with Armenian American preadolescents and adolescents, I generated samples of extended discourse by eliciting narratives of personal experiences with the Armenian and mainstream American communities (Imbens-Bailey, 1995, 1996). The use of personal narratives in this study of ethnic identity was a deliberate attempt to replace the methodologies of previous studies, which had relied primarily on participants completing attitudinal scales or levels of agreement with researcher-generated statements (e.g., Lambert, 1987; Phinney, 1989). A major drawback of these previous methods is that they do not enable participants to qualify their response with contextual material. For example, an English-speaking Canadian child may conceivably agree with a researcher's statement that French Canadians are unfriendly, but will be unable to convey to the researcher that this is their experience only in certain circumstances, such as when French Canadians are addressed in English and not French.

In addition to the advantages already identified by others and outlined earlier, I considered the elicitation of personal narratives to be an important alternative method to using open-ended questions in interviews with preteens. Using traditional interview methods with children, I found that many questions about ethnicity were too abstract for 8- and 9-year-olds. Children often interpreted interview questions literally, as in the following example from an open-ended question-and-answer session with 8-year-old Aram, a bilingual. The interviewer was intending to get some idea of the range of activities that Aram participated in throughout his day using his skills as a speaker of both English and Armenian (I = interviewer, A = Aram):

> I: Which parts of the day do you speak Armenian and which parts of the day do you speak English?
> A: I don't know.
> I: You don't know? Okay.
> A: I don't bring my watch [to school].

Giving narratives about actual events offered young children a more concrete way of talking about issues related to their ethnicity. In contrast to this failed open-ended question, consider the response 9-year-old Peggy gives to the prompt to tell a narrative about her first day in an Armenian–English bilingual school (P = Peggy):

> I: Can you tell me what happened on your first day at school here?
> P: I was in the kindergarten.
> I: Mmhm.
> P: And I was crying the whole day. Like, I was nervous. I didn't know any English. It was hard for me. And, like, a couple of days later, my mom, she just left me without me, my knowing. And I ran out the door with her. But Mrs. S [name of teacher] wouldn't let me. She took me back. For a full day I kept crying.

However, even presenting children with a prompt for a personal narrative can prove somewhat problematic when children respond with a minimal "Yes" and provide no further response, violating the principles of cooperation for conversational exchange. Peterson and McCabe (1983; McCabe, 1992) extended L&W's elicitation technique in a manner that helps to overcome this pragmatic naivete on the part of young study participants. Peterson and McCabe practiced the art of *giving-a-story-to-get-a-story,* which they pointed out more closely approximates the exchange of narratives in natural, spontaneous conversation. This technique serves to model for the child or novice study participant what is expected of them by the researcher. It also helps to break down the barriers that often exist between interviewer and interviewee by conveying that in the context of stories about personal experiences there are no right and wrong answers to the interviewer's prompts. In response to a story by the researcher, study participants can then more readily reciprocate with their own story.

## NARRATIVE AND CULTURAL IDENTITY

In his iteration of the advantages of using personal narratives in social science research, Labov (1972) argued for the quality of data produced by the elicitation techniques he and Waletzky followed. They found their study participants to be "deeply involved in rehearsing or even reliving events in the past." (Labov, 1972, p. 354). This aspect of personal narratives has been taken up by researchers in the field of psychology. In addition to the methodological advantages of analyzing narrative data outlined previously, the very fact that narratives of personal experience get the narrator involved in the recreation of lived events both emotionally and cognitively can provide the psychologist with a window into the mental life of the narrator. The evaluative function of personal narratives that was emphasized in L&W's approach to narrative analysis is the linguistic expression of the narrator's perspective on the narrated events.

L&W's own analytic work focused on internal structures to examine the logic and function of personal narratives. Other research on narrative has, however, extended this approach to include, for example, the study of stories as socializing agents (e.g., Heath, 1983; Miller, Potts, Fung, Hoogstra, & Minz, 1990) and as evidence of cognitive competencies and processes (e.g., Bruner, 1990; Case & McKough, 1990; Lewis, 1994). Analysis of personal narratives was chosen for my own study of ethnic identity not only for it's methodological advantages, but because of increasing research on personal narratives that shows their relation to the development of self-identity (e.g., Polkingholme, 1991; Snow, 1991). Personal narratives are shaped by the context in which individuals develop (Miller et al., 1990), and analysis of narratives about ethnicity was felt to provide insights into the way children growing up in an Armenian American community orient themselves towards the Armenian ethnic group.

The generation of narratives of personal experiences with the Armenian community allowed me to operationalize ethnic identity as something children are "doing" rather than as something children are "being." That is, children were asked to relate what they do that makes them a member of the Armenian community, rather than simply label themselves as Armenian. A label may mean different things to different children and is not as readily interpretable as stories about actual participation. Once narratives about participation had been generated, a number of analyses could be conducted, including identifying the frequency and type of linguistic markers of affinity, namely pronominal self-reference, and assessing attitudes towards narrated events provided in the evaluative component of the narratives. In fact, considering a narrative in its entirety as a singular speech act, the evaluative component of a personal narrative made it possible to identify the type of speech being performed by the narrator. For example, whether a narrative functioned to justify certain actions with the Armenian community or stated beliefs about Armenian and mainstream Americans.

Results of this study of ethnic identity suggested that knowledge of Armenian was related to how much children used first person singular versus first person plural pronouns in their stories of Armenian cultural events, as well as to their attitude toward the Armenian and mainstream cultures, controlling for factors such as parental attitudes, generation of immigration, and degree of formal schooling in Armenian. Children most proficient in Armenian language skills told stories in which they participated jointly in activities with other Armenian Americans. These children also evaluated their personal experiences in a more positive manner. Children less proficient in Armenian language skills were no more negative about their experiences, rather, they rarely evaluated the events in the stories they told or conveyed neutral affect about their activities with the Armenian community.

For the analysis of pronominal preference, a context in which children's talk about their own activities and others would not be constrained was essential. Narratives of personal experience provided this context. In a direct question-and-answer situation children's responses would have been largely confined to self-reference in the singular form (e.g., "Are you a member of Armenian Scouts?" "Yes, I am a member of Armenian scouts"). By giving children the opportunity to create a narrative about their involvement in activities such as plays produced by cultural clubs or bazaars and festivals organized by church groups, the children were free to choose pronominal forms with which to reference their activities (e.g., the prompt "Tell me about one time you were at Armenian scouts" could be responded to with "I went to downtown to a memorial for the Armenian holocaust," or "We, went to a summer camp with Armenian children from all over the country") in a manner that was hypothesized to be a reflection of children's degree of affinity with the members of their ethnic community. Similarly, only the contextual detail embedded in the children's narratives provided information on who and what was connected to the children's evaluations of the narrated events. It would have been far more difficult if not impossible a priori to elicit information about all the different types of people and activities for which children felt close affinity or held positive attitudes.

Without the pioneering efforts of L&W for identifying key structural and functional components of personal narratives, it is unlikely that narrative analysis as a measure of linguistic and communicative sophistication would have reached the level of popularity it enjoys today. Just as unlikely is the possibility that narrative would have become a vital tool in the social science researcher's procedural kitbag without L&W's insight into the evaluative component of narratives of personal experience. This component allows us a window onto the workings and development of the human mind. Witness as testament to L&W's own ground-breaking application of narrative analysis for explaining ties between language, literacy, and cultural identity among African American and Puerto Rican youth, the debate, nearly 30 years later, taking place in the Oakland, California school district over the status of Black English, once again referred to as Ebonics, and whether it currently plays a role in the school failure of urban minority children ("Voice of Inner City Streets," 1996).

## ACKNOWLEDGMENTS

This article was prepared while I was a postdoctoral fellow at Arizona State University.

I acknowledge the support of postdoctoral training from U.S. Department of Education Grant H029D50062, for which M. Jeanne Wilcox is Principal Investigator. The information contained in this article does not necessarily reflect the views or policies of the U.S. Department of Education and no official endorsement by that Department should be inferred.

I also thank Allyssa McCabe and Guido Imbens for helpful comments and suggestions.

## REFERENCES

Angrosino, M. V. (1995). Metaphors of ethnic identity: Projective life history narratives of Trinidadians of Indian descent. *Journal of Narrative and Life History, 5,* 125–146.

Bruner, J. (1990). *Acts of meaning.* Cambridge, MA: Harvard University Press.

Case, R., & McKough, A. (1990). Schooling and the development of central conceptual knowledge structures: An example from the domain of children's narrative. *International Journal of Education, 13,* 835–855.

Cortazzi, M. (1993). *Narrative analysis.* London: Falmer.

Grice, H. P. (1975). Logic and conversation. In P. Cole & J. L. Morgan (Eds.), *Syntax and semantics, 3: Speech acts* (pp. 41–58). New York: Academic.

Heath, S. B. (1983) *Way with words: Language, life and work in communities and classrooms.* Cambridge, England: Cambridge University Press.

Imbens-Bailey, A. (1995). *Oral proficiency and literacy in an ancestral language: Implications for ethnic identity.* Unpublished doctoral dissertation, Harvard University, Cambridge, MA.

Imbens-Bailey, A. (1996). Ancestral language acquisition: Implications for aspects of ethnic identity among Armenian-American children and adolescents. *Journal of Language and Social Psychology, 15,* 422–443.

Labov, W. (1972). *Language in the inner city: Studies in the Black English Vernacular.* Philadelphia: University of Pennsylvania Press.

Labov, W., & Waletzky, J. (this issue). Narrative analysis: Oral versions of personal experience. In J. Helm (Ed.), *Essays on the verbal and visual arts: Proceedings of the 1966 Annual Spring Meeting of the American Ethnological Society* (pp. 12–44). Seattle: University of Washington Press. (Original work published 1967)

Lambert, W. E. (1987). The effects of bilingual and bicultural experiences on children's attitudes and social perspectives. In P. Homel, M. Palij, & D. Aaronson (Eds.), *Childhood bilingualism: Aspects of linguistic, cognitive and social development* (pp. 197–221). Hillsdale, NJ: Lawrence Erlbaum Associates, Inc.

Lewis, C. (1994). Episodes, events, and narratives in the child's understanding of mind. In C. Lewis & P. Mitchell (Eds.), *Children's early understanding of mind* (pp. 457–480). Hove, UK: Lawrence Erlbaum Associates, Inc.

McCabe, A. (1992). *Language games to play with your child: Enhancing communication from infancy through late childhood.* New York: Insight Books

Miller, P. J., Potts, R., Fung, H., Hoogstra, L., & Minz, J. (1990). Narrative practices and the social construction of self in childhood. *American Ethnologist, 17,* 292–311.

Mishler, E. G. (1986). *Research interviewing.* Cambridge, MA: Harvard University Press.

Peterson, C., & McCabe, A. (1983). *Developmental psycholinguistics: Three ways of looking at a child's narrative.* New York: Plenum.

Phinney, J. S. (1989). Stages of ethnic identity development in minority group adolescents. *Journal of Early Adolescence, 9,* 34–49.

Polkinghorne, D. (1991). Narrative and self-concept. *Journal of Narrative and Life History, 1,* 135–153.

Snow, C. E. (1991). Building memories: The ontogeny of autobiography. In D. Cicchetti & M. Beeghly (Eds.), *The self in transition: Infancy to childhood* (pp. 213–242). Chicago: University of Chicago Press.

Veroff, J., Chadiha, L., Leber, D., & Sutherland, L. (1993). Affects and interactions in newlyweds' narratives: Black and White couples compared. *Journal of Narrative and Life History, 3,* 361–390.

Voice of inner city streets is defended and criticized. (1996, December 30). *The New York Times,* p. A9.

# Everything *Including* Talk and Why You Hafta Listen

## Richard Ely
### Department of Psychology, Boston University

In celebrating the 30th anniversary of the publication of Labov and Waletzky's (1967/this issue; henceforth L&W) treatise on narratives of personal experience, I will describe how their paper influenced my own work on personal narratives. In their description of what has come to be known as *high point analysis*, L&W identified two features of narratives, reported speech and self-aggrandizement, that have been the focus of several recent research projects. These two aspects of narratives are represented in the title of this article, the words of which are drawn loosely from two of the narratives in the corpus analyzed by L&W. *Everything Including Talk* refers to reported speech. *Why You Hafta Listen* relates broadly to the concept of evaluation and in this article is related specifically to both reported speech as a form of evaluation as well as to the concept of self-aggrandizement.

The article begins with a summary of findings from a number of studies of reported speech that I and my colleagues have published over the last several years. I then move on to describe some of our current work that focuses on narrative self-presentation.

## EVERYTHING *INCLUDING* TALK ...

The second narrative in the corpus of 14 narratives presented in L&W's paper began with the following statement: "I had dogs that could do *everything but talk*" (this issue, emphasis added). The narrator introduces his story about one of his dogs by implying that many of his dogs possessed extraordinary (and almost human-like) qualities. The one exception was an ability that many consider the most uniquely human—the ability to communicate through language. A number of lines later, the

---

Requests for reprints should be sent to Department of Psychology, Boston University, 64 Cummington Street, Boston, MA 02215. E-mail: rely@bu.edu.

narrator makes a second similar statement about talk (" ... but as I say he could do everything but talk"). Thereafter, the narrator quotes the speech of himself and the speech of others a total of six times, a frequency exceeded by only one other narrative in the corpus. This attention to language, and specifically the representation of talk in narratives, was identified by L&W as one form of narrative evaluation, as one way the narrator could express to the listener his or her attitude toward the situation being recounted. Reported speech, or talk about past talk, has been a focus of a number of studies that I and my colleagues have conducted over the past several years.

L&W (1967/this issue) described narratives as verbal recapitulations of experience. The narrator strings together a series of narrative units whose sequence matches temporally the sequence of the original event. This conceptualization emphasizes the referential or "what happened" aspect of narratives. In addition to telling what happened, the narrator must also identify a point of view toward the events being described in order to engage the listener. In the absence of this evaluation, listeners are likely to adopt a "so what" stance (Labov, 1972), reflecting their disinterest or lack of involvement. Thus, evaluation and reference are the two key elements in L&W's functional approach to narrative analysis.

The original L&W paper served as an important resource for Peterson and McCabe's (1983) study of children's personal narratives. They utilized high point analysis as one of several ways of analyzing the structure of the narratives in their corpus. They, like Labov (1972), treated reported speech primarily as one form of embedded evaluation, that is, as evaluation that lies within the narrative frame and preserves the narrative's dramatic continuity. In narratives of personal experience, in which the narrator is portrayed as one of the storyworld characters, the narrator can quote his or her own speech. Self-quotation is seen as a more primitive or less developed form of evaluation and contrasts with the more sophisticated and more highly embedded form of evaluation embodied in the citation of the speech of a neutral observer (Labov, 1972, pp. 372–373). It is also important to point out that L&W (this issue) recognized that evaluation and reference could be joined (or "fused") in a single clause. Thus, reported speech could represent both the what happened as well as a sense of why what happened matters.

As might be expected in a paper laying out a broad theoretical approach, L&W's treatment of reported speech was brief. Nevertheless, given that reported speech in personal narratives is a form of revoicing (Bakhtin, 1986) that is loosely analogous to what language researchers do when they record, transcribe, and analyze speech, we felt it deserved greater attention. In addition, a review of the literature revealed little empirical work on the use of reported speech in both children's (Ely & McCabe, 1993) and adults' narratives (Ely, Gleason, Narasimhan, & McCabe, 1995).

Our general approach toward analyzing reported speech involved identifying and coding each occurrence of reported speech in the data. Coding included categorizing the form of reported speech as either direct, indirect, or narratized speech. Direct speech purports to represent (or demonstrate) what was originally said and in written transcription is marked by quotation marks ("I said, 'You git back there and get that duck!'").[1] Indirect speech is usually marked by the use of a speech verb (e.g., say, tell) and a nominal or infinitive clause and affords the listener a reasonably clear sense of the form of the original utterance ("And I told him to cut it out"). Narratized speech represents a summary description of a speech event ("I talked him out of pulling the trigger") or merely states that a speech event took place. In addition to coding for form, we also coded each instance of reported speech for speech acts (e.g., assertives, directives, expressives) based on the narrator's characterization of the reported utterance. Finally, we noted the identity of the reported speaker (e.g., the self or another child or adult).

Our first study (Ely & McCabe, 1993) utilized the Peterson and McCabe (1983) corpus of personal narratives from working-class children between the ages of 4 and 9 years. Reported speech was found in more than half the children's narratives and was found to increase dramatically with age. Direct speech was the most common form of reported speech, as is also true of the nearly 50 instances of reported speech in the L&W corpus. Children quoted themselves far more frequently than they quoted others. The high frequency of self-quotation in young children's narratives supports the developmental claim implied in Labov's (1972) comment that quoting the speech of the self is a less sophisticated form of embedded evaluation than quoting the speech of others. Further support for this view comes from a second study in which the reported speech of parents and children was analyzed (Ely et al., 1995). In this study, children again quoted themselves far more frequently than any other category of speaker. However, in contrast to children, the adults (the mothers and fathers) quoted other adults more frequently than themselves or any other category of speaker.

In terms of speech acts, nearly three quarters of children's quotations were coded as directives or assertives, with directives alone accounting for more than 40% the total (Ely & McCabe, 1993). A somewhat similar pattern was also found in the use of quotations by adults (Ely et al., 1995). Expressives, speech acts that express the speaker's feelings and are dependent on the speaker's sincerity, were infrequent across both studies. Although this finding might seem to refute the notion that reported speech is a vehicle for evaluation, it is important to note that in reported speech reference and evaluation are often fused. An example of this phenomenon can be seen in Narrative 8 in L&W's corpus. In this narrative, the narrator reports how he was approached by a sailor who says "gimme a cigarette." By choosing to voice the demand in direct speech, the narrator forcefully conveys the sailor's sense of entitlement, a sense that is important in order to fully appreciate the seriousness

---

[1]These and the following two examples come from the L&W corpus.

or degree of danger conveyed in the narrative. Consider how differently the listener might experience the same scene if it were reported more generally, either in indirect speech ("he told me to give him a cigarette") or in narratized speech ("he demanded a cigarette"). This is but one example of how seamlessly reference and evaluation can be blended in the narrator's use of reported speech.

In addition to the work already described, we conducted one study that suggested how individual differences in narrative style might be acquired (Ely et al., 1996). This longitudinal study analyzed parent–child conversations about past events in a small sample of families. Monthly recordings of parents' elicitations of personal narratives from their children (ages 2 to 4) were analyzed. In addition, the children were interviewed by an experimenter, who sought to elicit narratives in a supportive but nondirective manner (McCabe & Peterson, 1991; Peterson & McCabe, 1983). We looked at the degree to which parents exposed their children to talk about speech itself and the frequency with which parents prompted their children to report past speech (e.g., "What did you say to me all the way home in the car yesterday?"). When we examined whether there was a relation between parents' focus on talk and children's later use of quotations in the narratives elicited by the experimenter (at age 5 years), we found a positive and statistically significant correlation between the two variables. We interpreted this finding as evidence that early parental input may influence children's later narrative practice (Peterson & McCabe, 1992).

This finding, focusing on individual differences, may be instructive when looking more broadly at group and cultural differences in narrative form. For example, across all our studies, we found consistent gender differences, with females using reported speech more frequently than males. In our longitudinal study we found that girls were prompted to talk about past talk more frequently than were boys (Ely et al., 1996). It is my sense that the gender differences in reported speech found in our work may be another example of the kinds of group and cultural differences in the prevalence of particular forms of evaluation that Labov (1972, p. 395) has already documented. Identifying these and other differences (and the origins of these differences) across diverse language communities and cultures is an important ongoing task for narrative researchers (McCabe, 1996; Michaels, 1981).

## … AND WHY YOU HAFTA LISTEN

And I told him to cut it out.
Course kids, you know—he don't *hafta listen* to me.

In the first part of this article, I described how reported speech is one of the reasons a listener may feel compelled to listen. A more important reason why the listener may fell compelled to listen to a narrative is that the narrator, in many circumstances, is trying to portray himself or herself in the best possible light. L&W (this issue) described this process as self-aggrandizement, and it is certainly true that most of the narratives of personal experience contained in their corpus reflect this goal. However, a broader claim is contained in the notion that good narratives depict events that are out of the ordinary and hence are "reportable" (Labov, 1972), whether or not those events depict the narrator or other storyworld participants positively or negatively.

The view that personal narratives are important vehicles for self-presentation is a perspective that has guided our current project. Narrative as a form of personal identity or narrative as an approach to adult personality has been the focus of much recent work by a number of theorists and researchers (Brewer, 1986; Bruner, 1990; McAdams, 1993; Neisser, 1988; Singer & Salovey, 1993; Tomkins, 1987; see also articles in the special issue of this journal edited by Singer & Sarbin, 1995). This same perspective has also been applied to children's narratives (Feeny & Eder, 1995; Fivush, 1994; McCabe, 1991, 1996; Miller, Mintz, Hoogstra, Fung, & Potts, 1992; Snow, 1990; Sperry & Sperry, 1995).

Our own ongoing project builds on this body of work (Ely, Melzi, Hadge, & McCabe, in press). For example, we recently examined children's personal narratives for the presence of themes of *agency* and *communion*, two basic and orthogonal modalities of human life (Bakan, 1966; McAdams, 1988). Agency refers to a sense of mastery, dominance, and independence from others; communion refers to a sense of integration, connection, and submission to a larger whole. We hypothesized that the presence of these two themes in personal narratives, especially themes of agency, would contribute in an important way to the sense that the events described are eminently reportable.

In our analysis of the Peterson and McCabe (1983) corpus, we found that themes of agency were relatively pervasive in children's narratives and were more common than were themes of communion. In addition, the frequency with which themes of agency were included in children's personal narratives increased with age. Themes of agency included descriptions of acting bravely, engaging in dynamic physical action, or displaying physical or psychological strength. We interpreted these results as suggesting that most children (and especially the older children in the sample) recognized that narratives, in order to be stories worth telling, inevitably depict important aspects of human life. Their inclusion makes for a good narrative. Their absence is likely to lead to a chronicle or travelogue, texts that are unlikely to make the audience feel that they have to listen.

In our upcoming work, we are exploring the feasibility of coding the negative or binary opposite poles of agency and communion: passivity and dissociation (Wiggins, 1991). For example, a child's citation of fear or weakness in a personal narrative is potentially as revealing as citations of bravery and strength. The former statements mark the lack of agency as relevant to the child's view of the self or as relevant to the child's conceptualization of others. Preliminary analyses suggest that themes of passivity, particularly weakness, are especially frequent in young children's narratives. Thus, it is possible that self-aggrandizement represents a developmental milestone that comes after an earlier period during which self-deprecation or self-disparagement figure more prominently.[2] This hypothesis, along with many others that lie latent in L&W's paper, is an example of the rich intellectual legacy this work has left to the field of narrative studies.

## REFERENCES

Bakan, D. (1966). *The duality of human existence: An essay on psychology and religion.* Chicago: Rand McNally.
Bakhtin, M. M. (1986). *Speech genres and other late essays.* Austin: University of Texas Press.
Brewer, W. F. (1986). What is autobiographical memory? In D. C. Rubin (Ed.), *Autobiographical memory* (pp. 25–49). New York: Cambridge University Press.
Bruner, J. (1990). *Acts of meaning.* Cambridge, MA: Harvard University Press.
Ely, R., Gleason, J. B., & McCabe, A. (1996). "Why didn't you talk to your mommy, honey?": Gender differences in talk about past talk. *Research on Language and Social Interaction, 20,* 7–25.
Ely, R., Gleason, J. B., Narasimhan, B., & McCabe, A. (1995). Family talk about talk: Mothers lead the way. *Discourse Processes, 19,* 201–218.
Ely, R., & McCabe, A. (1993). Remembered voices. *Journal of Child Language, 20,* 671–696.
Ely, R., Melzi, G., Hadge, L., & McCabe. (in press). Being brave, being nice: Themes of agency and communion in children's narratives. *Journal of Personality.*
Feeny, N. C., & Eder, R. A. (1995, March). *The relation between narrative content and self-concept.* Paper presented at the Biennial Meeting of the Society for Research in Child Development, Indianapolis, IN.
Fivush, R. (1994). Constructing narrative, emotion, and self in parent–child conversations about the past. In U. Neisser & R. Fivush (Eds.), *The remembering self: Construction and accuracy in the self-narrative* (pp. 136–157). New York: Cambridge University Press.
Labov, W. (1972). *Language in the inner city.* Philadelphia: University of Pennsylvania Press.
Labov, W., & Waletzky, J. (this issue). Narrative analysis: Oral versions of personal experience. In J. Helm (Ed.), *Essays on the verbal and visual arts: Proceedings of the 1966 Annual Spring Meeting of the American Ethnological Society* (pp. 12–44). Seattle: University of Washington Press. (Original work published 1967)
McAdams, D. P. (1988). *Power, intimacy, and the life story: Personological inquiries into identity.* New York: Guilford.
McAdams, D. P. (1993). *The stories we live by: Personal myths and the making of the self.* New York: William Morrow.
McCabe, A. (1991). Preface: Structure as a way of understanding. In A. McCabe & C. Peterson (Eds.), *Developing narrative structure* (pp. ix–xvii). Hillsdale, NJ: Lawrence Erlbaum Associates, Inc.
McCabe, A. (Ed.). (1996). *Chameleon readers: Teaching children to appreciate all kinds of good stories.* New York: McGraw-Hill.

---

[2]It is interesting to note that the L&W corpus was drawn from working-class subjects who were 10 years of age and older. In contrast, the subjects in the Peterson and McCabe (1983) corpus, though also working class, were children between the ages of 4 and 9 years.

McCabe, A., & Peterson, C. (1991). Getting the story: A longitudinal study of parental styles in eliciting narratives and developing narrative skill. In A. McCabe & C. Peterson (Eds.), *Developing narrative structure* (pp. 217–253). Hillsdale, NJ: Lawrence Erlbaum Associates, Inc.

Michaels, S. (1981). "Sharing time": Children's narrative styles and differential access to literacy. *Language in Society, 10,* 423–442.

Miller, P. J., Mintz, J., Hoogstra, L., Fung, H., & Potts, R. (1992). The narrated self: Young children's construction of self in relation to others in conversational stories of personal experience. *Merrill–Palmer Quarterly, 38,* 45–67.

Neisser, U. (1988). Five kinds of self-knowledge. *Philosophical Psychology, 1,* 35–59.

Peterson, C., & McCabe, A. (1983). *Developmental psycholinguistics: Three ways of looking at a child's narrative.* New York: Plenum.

Peterson, C., & McCabe, A. (1992). Parental styles of narrative elicitation: Effect on children's narrative structure and content. *First Language, 12,* 299–321.

Singer, J. A., & Salovey, P. (1993). *The remembered self: Emotion and memory in personality.* New York: Free Press.

Singer, J. A., & Sarbin, T. R. (Eds.). (1995). Narrative construction of emotional life [Special issue]. *Journal of Narrative and Life History, 5*(3).

Snow, C. E. (1990). Building memories: The ontogeny of autobiography. In D. Cicchetti & M. Beeghly (Eds.), *The self in transition* (pp. 213–242). Chicago: University of Chicago Press.

Sperry, L. L., & Sperry, D. E. (1995). Young children's presentations of self in conversational narration. In L. L Sperry & P. A. Smiley (Eds.), *New directions for child development: 69. Exploring young children's concepts of self and other through conversation* (pp. 47–60). San Francisco: Jossey-Bass.

Tomkins, S. S. (1987). Script theory. In J. Aronoff, A. I. Rabin, & R. A. Zucker (Eds.), *The emergence of personality* (pp. 147–216). New York: Springer.

Wiggins, J. S. (1991). Agency and communion as conceptual coordinates for the understanding and measurement of interpersonal behavior. In D. Cicchetti & W. Grove (Eds.), *Thinking clearly about psychology: Essays in honor of Paul Everett Meehl* (pp. 89–113). Minneapolis: University of Minnesota Press.

# Talking With the Dead: Self-Construction as Dialogue

### Ingrid E. Josephs
*Institute of Psychology, Otto-von-Guericke-University, Magdeburg, Germany*

The first notion to get rid of is that memory is primarily or literally reduplicative, or reproductive.  .... It is with remembering as it is with the stroke in a skilled game. We may fancy that we are repeating a series of movements learned a long time before from a textbook or from a teacher. But motion study shows that in fact we build up the stroke afresh on a basis of the immediately preceding balance of postures and the momentary needs of the game. Every time we make it, it has its own characteristics. (Bartlett, 1932/1995, p. 204)

When the narrator pretends to remember how, exactly, the wind was blowing at seven o'clock in the evening, twenty-one years ago, why do I not smile? I assume it. But I have to confess, that I do not remember anything, whatever happened, like a witness in court, or a narrator pretends to remember. I do never know how it was. I know it differently, not as a story, but as future. As a possibility. (Frisch,[1] 1960/1983, p. 8)

## ONCE UPON A TIME—LABOV AND WALETZKY'S UNDERSTANDING OF NARRATIVE

Once upon a time, or more exactly 30 years ago, Labov and Waletzky (1967/this issue) presented a detailed structural, formal analysis of oral narratives of personal experience. *Narrative* is defined as "one method of recapitulating past experience by matching a verbal sequence of clauses to the sequence of events that actually occurred" (p. 12). The basic unit of the narrative is the narrative clause whose "order cannot be changed without changing the inferred sequence of events in the original semantic interpretation" (p. 14). Thus, their definition is grounded in temporal

---

Requests for reprints should be sent to Ingrid E. Josephs, Institute of Psychology,Otto-von-Guericke-University, Am Varenholt 42, D-44797 Bochum, Germany. E-mail: ingrid.josephs@gse-w.uni-magdeburg.de

[1]All quotations of Frisch as well as the titles of his books and dramas are translated by me.

connections among successive clauses; flashbacks, evaluative comments, or descriptions of character and setting are excluded from the "primary sequence," which makes up the core narrative. They are not, however, excluded from the full story in which they serve other functions, for example, orienting the listener to time, place, and character or evaluating the meaning of the story. The authors stressed especially this latter function: A narrative without evaluation "lacks significance: it has no point." Furthermore, "many narratives are designed to place the narrator in the most favorable possible light: a function which we may call self-aggrandizement."

Summarizing, a past experience, which is up to that moment regarded as "unstoried," is said to be narrated if the temporal structure of reality is mirrored in the story—which itself also serves an important function with regard to the self-presentation of the storyteller. Real experiences, story as a mirror, the storyteller as a self-presenter ... Is this the only story of a story?

## ONCE UPON A TIME—MAX FRISCH'S COUNTER-STORY

Once upon a time, or more exactly 30 years ago, the writer Max Frisch, who had dedicated his literary oeuvre to a topic psychologists would call "storied identity," added to his story on stories an important drama, namely: "Biography—A Game" (Frisch, 1995). The main protagonist, Hannes Kürmann, a professor of ethology, had the choice to relive his past once again on stage, that is, to decide for a new life story or biography. "You have the allowance, Mr. Kürmann, to start again wherever you want, and to choose again ... " (p. 649), says the stage director. Kürmann believes in this "free choice" of one's story:

> I refuse to believe that our biography, mine or yours, or somebody else's could not end differently. Entirely differently. I only need to behave one single time in a different way—and I will not become a professor, but go to prison, for example, for three years ... . (p. 650)

Contrary to these insights, however, Kürmann repeats his former life choices on stage. Thus, Kürmann can choose nothing but himself, "his" biography. Once we have decided for "our" story we cannot escape, or at least we do not—our story then becomes our reality, our identity, our prison.

In Frisch's (1964) brilliant novel *My Name be Gantenbein,* Gantenbein, the inventor of different as-if identities, who "tries stories on like clothes" (p. 20) states:

> I am sitting in a bar, in the afternoon, that's why I am alone with the barman who tells me his life. Why? He does it and I listen, while drinking or smoking; I am waiting for

somebody, I read the newspaper. That's the way it was! he says, while washing up the glasses. A true story. I believe it! I say. He dries the clean glasses. Yes, he repeats, that's the way it was! I drink—I think: A man made an experience, and now he looks for the story for his experience ... one cannot live with an experience which remains without a story, it seems ... . (pp. 8–11)

Frisch—though in a different way than Labov and Waletzky—also differentiates story from experience. According to Frisch (1960/1983, pp. 8–11) the experience calls for the story and even needs the story in order to express itself. The experience invents its cause, so to speak, and that's why it invents a past, a "once upon a time." The story, the narrative, is not a voluntary act to frame and recapitulate past experiences, but it is a necessity to make life "readable." Once the story has been chosen, it becomes a fact, an inescapable reality. According to Frisch, a "real" story in the past tense is always an invention (and a deception) that does not admit to be an invention; it is an outline backwards: I do not know how it was, but I can imagine how it would be if I had to repeat it again. Past experience, in this sense, is a prediction. This is an insight the barman, Labov and Waletzky, and most of us in our "normal" everyday lives do not easily share.

## FROM NARRATIVE TO DIALOGUE: A DIALOGICAL CONCEPTUALIZATION OF THE SELF

The relation between self, experience, and story is a topic that is, of course, not an unknown land for psychologists either (see, e.g., Bruner, 1990; Polkinghorne, 1988). Instead of being regarded as a means for self-presentation (Labov & Waletzky, 1967), the story or the narrative can rather be viewed as a "necessary" means to "construct" one's self. This notion is grounded in James's (1890) and Mead's (e.g., 1913) self theories, especially in their *I–Me* differentiation. According to Sarbin (1986) and others, the *I*—as the storyteller—tells stories about the character, namely the *Me*. With the advent of the reception of Bakhtin's polyphonic novel (e.g., 1981), the idea of multiple authors or *I*s, who tell different stories from different perspectives about their respective *Me*s, has become popular. Thus, the "modern" dialogical approach on the self was born (e.g., Hermans & Kempen, 1993; Wertsch, 1991), in which the *I* moves, as in a space, and endows each position with a voice, so that dialogical relations can be established between the positions as between interacting characters in a story, resulting in a complex, narratively structured self (Hermans, 1995).

### The Legacy of George Herbert Mead

This modern dialogical approach is built upon the theoretical heritage of scholars like Martin Buber (1923/1994) and George Herbert Mead (e.g., 1913). The dialogue as a form is central to Mead's thought, as he believed that it is through the reflexivity of the dialogue that the self arises. The self is an organization of internalized perspectives of others. Thinking for Mead involved the ability to both assume one's own perspective and to take the attitude of the group on it, being able to shift between these with ease, in Mead's words: "the mechanisms of thought, in so far as thought uses symbols which are used in social intercourse, is but an inner conversation" (1913, p. 377).

Similar to Vygotsky's theorizing, development is assumed to shift from the intermental to the intramental plane: The internalized dialogues of the mind have their origin in real interactions, for example, between child and parent. "Thus the child can think about his conduct as good or bad only as he reacts to his own acts in the remembered words of his parents" (p. 377).

Mead compared our modern mind with a novel (versus drama in earlier times), which means that roles are most often not acted out dramatically (Mead, 1913)—although they can be immediately "personalized" if necessary.

> Later, the inner stage changes into the forum and workshop of thought. The features and intonations of the *dramatis personae* fade out and the emphasis falls upon the meaning of the inner speech, the imagery becomes merely the barely necessary cues. But the mechanism remains social, and at any moment the process may become personal. (pp. 377–378)

## OVERCOMING MENTALISM: THE RELATION BETWEEN COLLECTIVE AND PERSONAL STORIES

The dialogical self-narratives are not reducible to the person's private, individual mental constructions. They are deeply rooted in and constrained by the specific collective cultural stories we are constantly confronted with, like stories about power and gender, about individuality and identity, and so forth.

Boesch (1991), a pioneer in cultural psychology, made an important analytic, nondualistic distinction between cultural stories—*myths* in his terms—and the person's *I*–world relationships or *I*–world views—the *fantasms*. Myths and fantasms are related through dynamic processes that can be described in terms of assimilation and accommodation, and subjectivation and objectivation. For Boesch the crucial question was not how the person "uses" or "refuses" cultural stories (e.g., stories of national identity, see, e.g., Wertsch, 1996). He faced the much more challenging and genuinely developmental question of how people create new stories by actively transforming the cultural ones. Through this, novelty emerges on both the personal and cultural side.

## CONSTRUCTING THE SELF THROUGH THE DIALOGUE WITH THE DEAD

An understanding of the self as a multivoiced system that is co-constructed by multiple external and internalized voices makes it necessary to think about ways how to describe and analyze these voices and the structure of their talking. One specific question that can be asked here is how the dialogue continues after a close person's death.

### An Example From Anthropology: The Dead as "Generalized Other"

The meaning of the dead for the living is a neglected topic in contemporary psychology. In anthropology, however, this topic has been studied in-depth (see, e.g., Lévi-Strauss's [1974] analysis of the relation between the living and the dead, especially in myths and rituals). Kopytoff (1971) analyzed the concrete dialogical exchange between the living and the dead in an African community among the Suku. For the Suku, ancestors are nothing but dead elders who are consulted in difficult or otherwise important situations.

> The manner of addressing the living elder is the same as the one used in addressing the dead. .... Everyone goes to his elder. If I am young, I go to my elders who happen to be alive. The old people go to their elders; but since these are dead, they are to be found at the grave or at the cross-roads at night. Given the continuum of eldership, the use of any grave, as long as the dead is older than the petitioner, is understandable. (p. 133)

> Communication with the dead takes the form of a conversational monologue, patterned but not stereotyped, and devoid of repetitive formulae. One speaks the way one speaks to living people: "You, [such and such], your junior is ill. We do not know why, we do not know who is responsible. If it is you, if you are angry, we ask your forgiveness. If we have done wrong, pardon us. Do not let him die. Other lineages are prospering and our people are dying. Why are you doing this? Why do you not look after us properly?" The words typically combine complaints, scolding, sometimes even anger, and at the same time appeals for forgiveness. (p. 130)

Thus, African lineages are communities of both the living and the dead. It is interesting that the specific dead person is not important, but rather the dead as general elder person—the group of elders, as in Mead's concept of the generalized other.

## An Example From Psychology: The Dead as Particularized Other

In our Western world with its emphasis on individualism, one can ask how the internal dialogue with a specific dead person instead of the generalized dead other looks like. With a semistructured interview, my students and I interviewed adults who had lost a close person in the recent past. In the tradition of William James's (1890) self theory, we specifically assessed personal narratives about the transformation of the grave—as a collective cultural symbol—into a part of the living person's "material self." We assumed that the grave is used as a vehicle (like other memories of the dead person, such as photographs) in reorganizing one's self-system. The following extract comes from a 66-year-old woman who has lost her husband (X) 1 year ago.

> When I enter the cemetery, then I first say: Lord, let all souls find eternal peace—that is one thing. And the second is, this comes now automatically to my mind, that some day I will also lie there. That's why I also include myself in the prayer.
> First, I go to the grave and say "hello, here am I"—as if he were still alive. (Interviewer: Aloud or internally?) Internally. But when I am alone, then also aloud from time to time. But then I first make sure, that really nobody is there. Otherwise they think: Well, what is going on with her? And then I do my rounds, I go through the whole quarter and say hello to the others whom I knew, whom I got to know and whom I knew, and then I go back to X. Well, this is a visit, yes, I visit him.
> When others are on the cemetery next to the grave, I feel disturbed, then I cannot talk with X. If from the right and from the left side they ask you "how are you", then I cannot come into contact with him. I need the silence. I need his grave and nobody around it. If they are quiet, OK—but mostly one talks then, and then I try to escape, I do again my rounds, and then I try again to get into contact with him.
> When I look at the grave, then I say: "If you saw that now, X, then you would be very happy with it". He would like it. The gravestone is the non plus ultra. That is X.
> Well, at the grave I imagine him alive. And when something good has happened, when I was successful, then I say: "something very good happened to me. I have to tell you". Or on my mind ... , mostly I have that on my mind when I enter the cemetery, that I think you would say now: "You have done that very well". Or when I had bad luck, that I say, "O boy, that went completely wrong, I spoiled everything". And then he is in front of me. And not dead. He is alive in front of me and I can see, in his face I see that he thinks: "Don't worry". That is, ... I also get answers to my questions. I don't

*know. Maybe I only construct them. But I mean when he says: "Don't take it so seriously, it is not such a catastrophe". It's more like remembering. Well, I do not get answers, but the memory of similar situations, that is the answer. That I spontaneously remember how he reacted when the chaos happened with the car. That somebody had crashed right into my car which I had parked in front of the house. And it was the day we came from the celebration of the final school exams of my daughter. And then the smashed car in front of the house. That he said: "We wanted to drink coffee now, and so we will do it". And we did exactly that. This calmness, this only comes when I am in panic, when I am standing on the cemetery and say "well, I have lived through something very bad", and then I hear that. And then I get also quieter.*

This extract gives a good illustration of the process of dialogical self-formation: Supported by the symbolic power of the grave, the person constructs the reaction of a specific dead person's voice—and that is why I speak of the "particularized other" here, a term borrowed from Watkins (1990, p. 56)—towards her own narrated life events. The voice does not come from outside, it is internalized and has become part of the self. The living person can regulate her feelings through the interaction with the dead person's voice. The question whether the dead person "really" answers or not—that is, the question for the limits of the construction—is not relevant in this process. As long as it works, it can be as it may. Furthermore, the relation between the symbol, here the grave, and the person's dialogical reflexivity, facilitates the experience of continuity between past, present, and future, which is an important aspect for the formation and reorganization of the self (see also Boesch, 1991).

The dialogical analysis of this extract, which cannot be described here completely, is intriguing: The living person does not only pray to somebody (God) *for* the dead one, but is at the same time talking *with* the dead one, who in that moment seems to belong to the living. Thus, the boundary between life and dead is a fuzzy one.

## CONCLUSION

Our story started with Labov and Waletzky's paper in 1967, from which we moved quite a bit on our voyage to explore the role of narrative, and more specifically, of dialogue for the construction of the self. Thus, instead of celebrating the narrative approach as a goal in itself, it is used here as a means for the analysis of fundamental self-formative processes, whose study is theoretically grounded in the respective theories. In other words, the narrative—however fascinating and colorful it might be—can never "speak" for itself. Thus, we have to think about explicit ways of data construction, data analysis, and interpretation—processes which themselves cannot be separated from the underlying theory. Though this is an artistic and creative process, it is certainly not a process in which "everything goes," without boundaries (e.g., Eco, 1990/1995). Without these explicit and theoretically grounded considerations, we might easily run the risk of being either lost in the trap of implicit and far-reaching generalizations that are based on nothing but anecdotal evidence, or of stopping the analysis altogether while praising colorful multiplicity and refusing any attempts of generalization. To my understanding both ways are counter-productive for psychology. However, this is—to use the words of the novelist Michael Ende (1979)—already "another story, which shall be told at another time ... " (p. 428, my translation).

## ACKNOWLEDGMENT

I am grateful to Sabine Gartz and Irmgard Koops for their help in conducting this study.

## REFERENCES

Bakhtin, M. M. (1981). *The dialogical imagination: Four essays*. Austin: University of Texas Press.
Bartlett, F. C. (1995). *Remembering. A study in experimental and social psychology*. Cambridge, England: Cambridge University Press. (Original work published 1932)
Boesch, E. E. (1991). *Symbolic action theory and cultural psychology*. Berlin, Germany: Springer.
Bruner, J. (1990). *Acts of meaning*. Cambridge, MA: Harvard University Press
Buber, M. (1994). Ich und Du [I and Thou]. In M. Buber (Ed.), *Das dialogische Prinzip* (pp. 7–136). Gerlingen, Germany: Verlag Lambert Schneider. (Original work published in 1923)
Eco, U. (1995). *Die Grenzen der Interpretation* [The boundaries of interpretation]. München, Germany: Deutscher Taschenbuch Verlag. (Original work published in 1990)
Ende, M. (1979). *Die unendliche Geschichte* [The never ending story]. Stuttgart, Germany: K. Thienemanns Verlag.
Frisch, M. (1964). *Mein Name sei Gantenbein* [My name be Gantenbein]. Frankfurt, Germany: Suhrkamp.
Frisch, M. (1983). Geschichten [Stories]. In M. Frisch (Ed.), *Ausgewählte Prosa*. Frankfurt, Germany: Suhrkamp. (Originally published in 1960 in *Das kleine Buch der 100 Bücher*)
Frisch, M. (1995). Biografie: Ein Spiel [Biography: A game]. In M. Frisch, *Sämtliche Stücke* (pp. 625–724). Frankfurt, Germany: Suhrkamp. (Original work published in 1967)
Hermans, H. J. M. (1996). Opposites in a dialogical self: Constructs as characters. *Journal of Constructivist Psychology, 9*, 1–26.
Hermans, H. J. M., & Kempen, H. J. G. (1993). *The dialogical self*. San Diego, CA: Academic.
James, W. (1890). *The principles of psychology*. New York: Henry Holt.
Kopytoff, I. (1971). Ancestors as elders in Africa. *Africa, 41*, 129–142.
Labov, W., & Waletzky, J. (this issue). Narrative analysis: Oral versions of personal experience. In J. Helm (Ed.), *Essays on the verbal and visual arts: Proceedings of the 1966 Annual Spring Meeting of the American Ethnological Society* (pp. 12–44). Seattle: University of Washington Press. (Original work published 1967)

Lévi-Strauss, C. (1974). *Tristes tropiques.* New York: Penguin.
Mead, G. H. (1913). The social self. *The Journal of Philosophy, 10,* 374–380.
Polkinghorne, D. E. (1988). *Narrative knowing and the human sciences.* Albany: State University of New York Press.
Sarbin, T. R. (1986). The narrative as a root metaphor for psychology. In T. R. Sarbin (Ed.), *Narrative psychology: The storied nature of human conduct* (pp. 3–21). New York: Praeger.
Watkins, M. (1990). *Invisible guests.* Boston: Sigo.
Wertsch, J. (1991). *Voices of the mind.* Cambridge, MA: Harvard University Press.
Wertsch, J. V. (1996, September, 11–15). *The production and consumption of historical narratives.* Paper presented at the Second Conference for Socio-Cultural Research, Geneva, Switzerland.

# Labov's Legacy for Narrative Research—And Its Ironies

## Ageliki Nicolopoulou
*Department of Psychology, Lehigh University*

It has seemed to me for some time that Labov's long-term impact on narrative research has some curious, even ironic, aspects that deserve more consideration than they have received. My primary focus here is his influence on the study of children's narratives in the overlapping disciplines of psychology and linguistics, but the issues involved also have wider implications. To offer a preliminary formulation of the central puzzle: In terms of the overall thrust of his work, Labov has correctly been regarded as a committed and pioneering *socio*linguist. He has insisted, above all, on the need to study both the uses of language and linguistic change in social context—which includes, for Labov, not only the immediate microsocial arenas of face-to-face interaction, but also the larger frameworks of communities, institutions, social structure, and social stratification. Labov has consistently emphasized the ways that linguistic phenomena are inextricably bound up with issues of individual and group identity and with the social dynamics of intergroup relationships. On the other hand, the tendencies in developmental research that have drawn on Labov's analysis of narrative have done so in largely formalist and decontextualized ways. What follows is a set of reflections on this paradoxical outcome.

The disparity between Labov's own orienting concerns and those of the main tendencies he has influenced in the field of children and narratives testifies, in part, to the predominantly formalist agenda that has shaped the reception and (selective) appropriation of his work. However, it is also due, I would suggest, to some intrinsic limitations of the Labovian model of narrative analysis itself from the standpoint of a more fully sociocultural approach—and even from the perspective of Labov's own general approach to the analysis of language and discourse. To explore these questions, we must first situate the model of narrative analysis introduced by Labov

---

Requests for reprints should be sent to Ageliki Nicolopoulou, Department of Psychology, Lehigh University, 17 Memorial Drive East, Bethlehem, PA 18015–3068. E-mail: agn3@lehigh.edu

and Waletzky (1967/this issue, henceforth L&W) in their brilliant and seminal paper in two broader contexts: the field of research on children's narratives since 1967 and the overall framework of Labov's own work, within which his treatment of narrative has in some respects been anomalous.

## CHILDREN AND NARRATIVES: THE TURN TO FORMALISM

Despite the complicated variety of research programs in the field of children and narratives, the striking fact is that since the 1970s the great bulk of this work has been dominated by various strategies of what I have termed *formalist* analysis (Nicolopoulou, 1997a). That is, they tend to focus more or less exclusively on the formal structure of narratives and to neglect both their symbolic content and the ways that children *use* narrative for diverse modes of symbolic action, from making sense of the world and conferring meaning on experience to building up group life and forming identity. One result is that these approaches rarely seek to integrate their analysis of linguistic or plot structure with the interpretive reconstruction of structures of meaning—indeed, they largely bypass the significance of narrative as a vehicle of meaning. Furthermore, they rarely attempt to situate children's narrative activities systematically in the sociocultural context of their everyday interactions, their group life, and their cultural world.

There are often well-considered methodological reasons for these choices, but one-sidedly formalist analysis also carries unavoidable costs. The contributions of the approaches that now dominate the field are unquestionable. Taken by themselves, however, they are not adequate to address key dimensions of children's narrative activity that ought to concern developmental research; in particular, they leave important gaps in our understanding of the role that narrative plays in children's construction of reality and of individual and collective identity. Part of the solution lies in building upon emerging tendencies toward a more interpretive and sociocultural approach to the study of narrative and its role in development. (For the larger arguments behind these remarks, see Nicolopoulou, 1996a, 1996b, 1997a, 1997b. Others have argued along similar lines, notably Bruner, 1990.)

This formalist turn has been so pervasive, and is now so taken for granted, that it is rarely discussed explicitly. However, the overwhelming hegemony of (more or less) formalist approaches in the field of children and narratives actually goes back only to the 1970s. For several decades leading up to the 1960s, for example, there was an active research tradition, exemplified by Pitcher and Prelinger (1963), that analyzed the thematic content of children's stories from a psychoanalytic perspective to bring out underlying patterns of symbolism associated with psychosexual and personality development. Applebee's (1978) reanalysis of the corpus of stories assembled by Pitcher and Prelinger, which focused on narrative structure rather than symbolic content, was one of the most important studies marking the transition to formalism. Other milestones in this process included the early work on narrative by Sutton-Smith and his associates (e.g., Sutton-Smith, Botvin, & Mahoney, 1976) and the beginnings of what proved to be the massive research enterprise of story grammar analysis. (See, for example, Stein & Glenn, 1979. Unlike the other pivotal figures in this process, Sutton-Smith has not remained within an exclusively formalist perspective.) Although these lines of research differed in various ways, they shared a commitment to tracing the development of children's narrative competence by analyzing the structure of narratives—usually understood as linguistic or plot structure—in abstraction from their content.

In retrospect, it is clear that the analytical framework presented by L&W also made a significant contribution to the formalist turn in narrative analysis. In some ways, this is not entirely surprising: L&W noted explicitly that their analysis was "*formal*" (their italics), with the aim of "isolating the invariant structural units" that underlie the "superficial" variety of actual narratives (1967/this issue, p. 4). However, in itself what the paper offered was a set of valuable and suggestive analytical tools whose ultimate import would depend very much on the overall research strategies within which they were employed. To appreciate what is puzzling about the long-term impact of this paper, we first need to step back from it and consider the larger picture of Labov's work taken as a whole.

## LABOV'S PROJECT: THE "SOCIALLY REALISTIC" STUDY OF LANGUAGE

My focus here is not on the specific empirical topics Labov has addressed but on his theoretical and methodological approach, and especially on some of the orienting themes and concerns that have informed and unified his work. In this respect, three features of Labov's overall agenda stand out as critical: It has been sociocultural, comparative, and concerned both theoretically and methodologically with studying the naturally occurring patterns of language use in everyday social life.

First, Labov's orientation has been—with one important qualification to be mentioned in a moment—consistently and polemically sociocultural. From the beginning of his career, he has insisted that language is a fundamentally social phenomenon that cannot properly be studied as an isolated system or as a set of purely individual capacities or characteristics, but that must be situated within a broader social context. This social context, as noted earlier, comprises more than a sum of interactions; it is above all structured by larger sociocultural frameworks that need to be grasped as genuinely collective realities. Labov argued, for example, that the coherence of a mode of speech can never really be captured at the level of the individual speaker, but only at the level of the speech community—remembering, of course, that this coherence includes systematic patterns of linguistic variation structured by such factors as social class, cultural prestige, institutional location, and so on (these are central messages of Labov, 1966, to which he returns repeatedly in later works). The complexities and apparent inconsistencies in the idiolects of individuals, which might be taken as inexplicable "free variation," make sense if we can locate the individual at the intersection of several influential social contexts, and if we take account of the patterned variations in the larger framework of the relevant speech community.

The major qualification that must be noted is that Labov has largely focused on the form of speech or discourse as distinct from the interpretation of its content. On the other hand, one of his central themes has been that linguistic forms themselves have social meanings and are the objects of social evaluation and that these social meanings and evaluations are critical in explaining linguistic usage, diversity, and change. This is especially true because modes of speech are crucial markers and expressions of social identity and group membership. For example, one of the long-term lines of research that has brought Labov the greatest attention—and which has again become very timely—has been his analysis of what he terms the Black English Vernacular (e.g., Labov, 1972, 1982); he was among the first to argue that it forms a distinct and coherent dialect. This work was in part motivated by an effort to understand the troubling levels of reading failure among Black (and Puerto Rican) students in New York City public schools, which he linked to differences between the students' nonstandard dialect and the Standard English of the school curriculum. But one of his most striking conclusions—whose significance is not always fully recognized in discussions of his work—was that the central problems were *not* fundamentally linguistic, but were rooted in systematic tensions between the "vernacular culture" of the streets and the culture of the school. The greater the extent to which inner-city Black students were socially "well adjusted" in the sense of being securely integrated into the peer culture of their neighborhood communities, the worse they usually did in school—and this included being less likely to learn to read and to master Standard English, even when the individuals involved seemed to have exceptional cognitive and verbal skills. On the other hand, Black students from these neighborhoods who did well in school often tended to be "lames"—that is, relatively marginalized and socially isolated individuals—on whom the school had a greater impact. In this respect, in short, the sociocultural significance of the Black English Vernacular dialect was more important than its strictly linguistic differences from Standard English. As Labov (1972) put it: "One major conclusion of our work ... is that the major causes of reading failure are political and cultural conflicts in the classroom, and dialect differences are important because they are symbols of this conflict" (p. xiv; see also Labov, 1982).

A second key feature of Labov's approach has already been suggested by the previous discussion: A commitment to a comparative perspective has been integral to his work. One reason is that the characteristics of linguistic systems can adequately be brought out only by comparing them with other systems and tracing their changes over time. In addition, Labov insisted that the socially recognized *contrasts* between different dialects and modes of speech are often an essential part of their sociocultural significance. Particular speech modes function not only to assert the identity of social groups and to maintain their cohesion, but also to demarcate them from other groups. Thus, "for a working class New Yorker, the social significance of the speech forms that he uses, in so far as they contain the variables in question, is that they are *not* the forms used by middle class speakers, and *not* the forms used by upper middle class speakers" (Labov, 1966, p. 8; italics added). Similarly, the intensification of the distinctive features of White working-class dialects in Philadelphia (pushing "the local vowel system even further along its traditional path, diverging even more from the dialects of other cities") is linked to increasing tensions between White and Black ethnic communities in the city (Labov, 1980, p. 263).

Finally, Labov has always been concerned to capture the actual modes of language use as they are embedded in the practices of everyday social life. For example, this concern is expressed in Labov's (1972) insistence that "the logic of nonstandard English" (pp. 201–240) needs to be reconstructed and analyzed in its own terms, rather than being treated as simply a series of deviations from the norms of Standard English. Methodologically, this commitment to the "socially realistic" study of language (to borrow a phrase from Labov, 1966, p. 9) has also involved a continuing preoccupation with finding ways to overcome the limitations and distortions of data derived from formal interviews and other artificial situations. As one extreme illustration of this problem, Labov (1972) observed that studies of Black children based on interviews with adult researchers yielded the widespread conclusion that these children had limited verbal skills and were, in the jargon of the time, "verbally deprived." This belief, Labov argued, was actually absurd, given the remarkably talented, sophisticated, and imaginatively rich ways that these children displayed their verbal skills in the context of everyday family and peer-group interactions. Findings of verbal deprivation had less to do with the children's cognitive and verbal deficiencies than with the methodological deficiencies of the research techniques (Labov, 1972, particularly pp. 201–222). Well before this, Labov had already emphasized that "we must somehow become witnesses to the every-day speech which the informant will use as soon as the door closes behind us" (Labov, 1966, p. 99). Labov has thus been inventive in developing techniques within the interview framework to minimize or evade its inherent limitations; and, beginning with his Harlem studies, he has also sought to draw on participant observation conducted in peer-group contexts.

Indeed, it is worth noting that Labov's study of narrative appears to have begun as a methodological by-product, so to speak, of his injunction that "within the interview, we must go beyond the interview situation" (Labov, 1966, p. 99). Labov discovered that if interviewees were asked to recount an experience in which they felt in danger of being killed, they often became sufficiently emotionally involved in telling the story that they shifted from the "careful speech" encouraged by the interview context to more casual and spontaneous speech. This broke the spell of the interview situation (however temporarily) and offered a chance to "observe how people speak when they are not being observed" (1966, p. xvii)—a window into the world of everyday discourse.

## LABOV ON NARRATIVE: THE IRONIES OF INFLUENCE

How far have these orienting concerns been reflected in Labov's influence on developmental research on narrative? There is no question that the analytical framework introduced in L&W has had a valuable and stimulating impact in many ways. One of its contributions was to help open up a wider field for narrative research by offering both encouragement and analytical tools for the examination of children's narratives of personal experience. In the process, it has also encouraged researchers to attend to children's own narratives, in contrast to the concentration on children's comprehension and recall of narratives presented to them that has marked other lines of research. A characteristic focus has been on children's narratives embedded in their conversations with others—usually with adults, either interviewers or caretakers, but sometimes with other children as well (influential examples include Peterson & McCabe, 1983; Umiker-Sebeok, 1979).

However, there are also ways in which the Labovian strain in narrative research has had a problematic relation to the larger thrust of his work. This research has generally taken as its conceptual starting point Labov's model of a fully formed oral narrative (more or less modified). In studies of children's narratives, this approach generally tends to generate findings that young children are unable to produce stories that match the canonical Labovian model and then gradually acquire the competence to do so. In effect, the prime focus (shared by other tendencies in research on narrative development) is on the elements that characterize the narratives of older children and adults and on the achievement of those elements. This orientation, unobjectionable in itself, has the ironic consequence that the stories of younger children are often not really analyzed for their own sake, but instead are treated as a primitive or inchoate starting point on the road to later competence. To capture the distinctive logic of the stories of preschool children in their own terms—which would accord with the spirit of Labov's approach—requires that we go beyond the specific model of narrative offered in L&W and develop new conceptual tools better adapted to the task. As it is, these stories tend to be viewed primarily in negative terms—in terms of the characteristics they do *not* (yet) possess.

Second, given the crucial role of a comparative perspective in Labov's work, it is also ironic that the work influenced by his model of narrative analysis has, on the whole, not been comparative—in terms of examining sociocultural differences in narrative modes, the influence of different social contexts within which narrative activities occur, and so on. On the other hand, the most significant lines of research on children's narratives that have attempted systematically comparative analyses—for example, the work of Michaels (e.g., 1981) or Heath (e.g., 1983)—have generally not drawn on Labov's framework.

What is even more striking is that Labov's own studies of narrative—as distinct from the larger pattern of his work as a whole—do not actually have a significant comparative dimension either. This is surprising in light of the fact that L&W (this issue) includes several promissory notes indicating that the general model of narrative presented there should, in time, be integrated into a systematically comparative framework. "The ultimate aims of our work, require close correlations of the narrators' social characteristics with the structure of their narratives, since we are concerned with problems of effective communication and class and ethnic differences in verbal behavior. ... This view of narrative structure will achieve greater significance when materials from radically different cultures are studied in the same way" (pp. 5, 38). Labov (1972) did include some attempts to compare aspects of the narrative modes used by speakers from different ethnic communities, but the results are fairly skimpy, especially by the usual standards of Labov's analyses. Labov has done little to develop this kind of comparative analysis further in his subsequent work.

Why has this been so? A full consideration of this puzzle would require a longer discussion than the available space permits. However, I would (briefly) venture the suggestion that at least part of the problem lies in the limitations of a purely formalist conception of narrative for pursuing an effective and illuminating comparative analysis. Thus, Labovian narrative analysis has in some ways been boxed in by the lack of a genuine interpretive dimension in its theoretical starting point. The way out of this box, I would argue, lies in developing conceptual tools more along the lines of Bakhtin's (1986) conception of narrative genres—which involve characteristic modes of interrelating form and content—than the specifically formal model offered in L&W.

Several lines of current research provide evidence that a more fully sociocultural and interpretive approach to the study of children's narratives has the potential to address some of the larger orienting concerns of Labov's work more effectively than research that remains tied to Labov's own explicit model of narrative analysis. I offer one example from my own work: In a long-term study based on the analysis of a spontaneous storytelling and story-acting practice carried out by 3- to 5-year-old children in a number of preschool classrooms, I found that the boys and girls involved develop two highly distinctive gender-related narrative styles that differ systematically, and increasingly over time, in both form and content. These narrative styles embody different modes of ordering and interpreting experience and express different underlying images of the social world and of the self. It is also clear that they are developed, to a considerable degree, in dialectical contrast with each other. Furthermore, this narrative polarization is one aspect of a larger process by which two distinct gendered subcultures are actively built up and maintained by the children themselves within the classroom miniculture, and these serve in turn as contexts for the further appropriation and assertion of crucial dimensions of personal identity as defined by the larger society, including gender. Thus, children's narrative activity should be seen as a form of socioculturally situated symbolic action that links the construction of reality with the formation of identity (Nicolopoulou, 1997b; Nicolopoulou, Scales, & Weintraub, 1994). Approaches to narrative research that lack this kind of sociocultural dimension can be systematically misleading even for tracing the development of young children's narrative competence (Nicolopoulou, 1996a, 1996b).

In short, the effort to develop an effective sociocultural approach to the study of children and narratives can draw considerable inspiration from Labov—though in some respects, ironically, more from the larger thrust of his sociolinguistic project than from his own explicit analysis of narrative. Or, to put it the other way, fulfilling the spirit of Labov's work in our analysis of narrative will require going beyond the letter of his 1967 model, by integrating the analytical resources it offers into a more comprehensive and genuinely sociocultural framework.

## REFERENCES

Applebee, A. N. (1978). *The child's concept of story: Ages two to seventeen.* Chicago: University of Chicago Press.
Bakhtin, M. M. (1986). *Speech genres and other late essays.* Austin: University of Texas Press.
Bruner, J. S. (1990). *Acts of meaning.* Cambridge, MA: Harvard University Press.
Heath, S. B. (1983). *Ways with words: Language, life, and work in communities and classrooms.* Cambridge, England: Cambridge University Press.
Labov, W. (1966). *The social stratification of English in New York City.* Washington, DC: Center for Applied Linguistics.
Labov, W. (1972). *Language in the inner city: Studies in the Black English vernacular.* Philadelphia: University of Pennsylvania Press.
Labov, W. (1980). The social origins of sound change. In W. Labov (Ed.), *Locating language in time and space* (pp. 251–265). New York: Academic.
Labov, W. (1982). Competing value systems in the inner-city schools. In P. Gilmore & A. A. Glatthorn (Eds.), *Children in and out of school: Ethnography and education* (pp. 148–171). Washington, DC: Center for Applied Linguistics.
Labov, W., & Waletzky, J. (this issue). Narrative analysis: Oral versions of personal experience. In J. Helm (Ed.), *Essays on the verbal and visual arts: Proceedings of the 1966 Annual Spring Meeting of the American Ethnological Society* (pp. 12–44). Seattle: University of Washington Press. (Original work published 1967)
Michaels, S. (1981). "Sharing time": Children's narrative styles and differential access to literacy. *Language in Society, 10,* 423–442.
Nicolopoulou, A. (1996a). Narrative development in social context. In D. I. Slobin, J. Gerhardt, A. Kyratzis, & J. Guo (Eds.), *Social interaction, social context, and language: Essays in honor of Susan Ervin-Tripp* (pp. 369–390). Mahwah, NJ: Lawrence Erlbaum Associates, Inc.

Nicolopoulou, A. (1996b, July). *Problems, strategies, and intentions in young children's narrative genres*. Paper presented at the annual meeting of the International Congress for the Study of Child Language, Istanbul, Turkey.

Nicolopoulou, A. (1997a). Children and narratives: Toward an interpretive and sociocultural approach. In M. Bamberg (Ed.), *Narrative development: Six approaches* (pp. 179–215). Mahwah, NJ: Lawrence Erlbaum Associates, Inc.

Nicolopoulou, A. (1997b). Worldmaking and identity formation in children's narrative play-acting. In B. Cox & C. Lightfoot (Eds.), *Sociogenetic perspectives on internalization* (pp. 157–187). Mahwah, NJ: Lawrence Erlbaum Associates, Inc.

Nicolopoulou, A., Scales, B., & Weintraub, J. (1994). Gender differences and symbolic imagination in the stories of four-year-olds. In A. H. Dyson & C. Genishi (Eds.), *The need for story: Cultural diversity in classroom and community* (pp. 102–123). Urbana, IL: National Council of Teachers of English.

Peterson, C., & McCabe, A. (1983). *Developmental psycholinguistics: Three ways of looking at a child's narrative*. New York: Plenum.

Pitcher, E. G., & Prelinger, E. (1963). *Children tell stories: An analysis of fantasy*. New York: International Universities Press.

Stein, N. L., & Glenn, C. G. (1979). An analysis of story comprehension in elementary school children. In R. Freedle (Ed.), *New directions in discourse processing* (Vol. 2, pp. 53–120). Norwood, NJ: Ablex.

Sutton-Smith, B., Botvin, G., & Mahoney, D. (1976). Developmental structures in fantasy narratives. *Human Development, 19*, 1–13.

Umiker-Sebeok, D. J. (1979). Preschool children's intraconversational narratives. *Journal of Child Language, 6*, 91–109.

# Analyzing Stories of Moral Experience: Narrative, Voice, and the Dialogical Self

## Mark B. Tappan
*Education and Human Development, Colby College*

Asked whether she has ever been in a situation in which she experienced a moral conflict and had to make a difficult choice or decision, 18-year-old Harriet, a first-year college student, tells the following story:

> One time last spring my mother found a marijuana pipe of my brother's in front of the driveway, and she's kind of naive about drugs and stuff like that, and she was like ... she always asks me, when it comes to something like that ... she would never ask my brother, 'cause she just figured it must have been his ... she was like ... "Is this some kind of drug paraphernalia?" And I didn't know what to say, because I didn't want to, like ... on the one hand, I felt really bad because she was naive and I just felt like explaining what it was, just so she would know ... like I thought everyone should kind of know ... but on the other hand, I didn't want to get my brother in trouble, and I didn't want ... I knew that it would turn into the biggest issue if she had any clue that my brother would ever smoke pot or something like that ... I didn't know what to do. Finally, I just said ... I just acted like I was naive too, because I didn't know what to do ... I didn't think either decision was a good one, so I just said, "Yeah, it is. I don't know where it came from," or something like that. I was like, "Yeah, I think it is ... "
>
> SO WHAT WAS THE CONFLICT IN THIS SITUATION FOR YOU?
>
> I guess the conflict was whether I was going to get my brother in trouble ... not that he would have really gotten in trouble ... but whether I would just come out and say "Yeah, that's my brother's pipe; he does drugs, you didn't know that." You know, that would have been a pretty big thing. I mean, it would have hit her really hard, too, and I didn't want to really do anything to

---

Requests for reprints should be sent to Mark B. Tappan, Colby College, 4426 Mayflower Hill, Waterville, ME 04901.

upset her that much, or upset him, or ... I guess the other side of it was that I really felt like she had a right to know, for some reason.
IN THINKING ABOUT WHAT TO DO, WHAT DID YOU CONSIDER?
I considered just telling her, but then after I thought about it, I was like "Well, no, she'll probably get upset and it will turn into, like, a big thing between her and my brother ... it would, like, effect their relationship." And then I considered just not saying anything at all, but I knew she would know I was lying because that's pretty obvious. Then I considered the point in between, which was what I decided on.

I begin with this brief interview excerpt because it highlights well the relation between Labov and Waletzky's (1967/this issue; henceforth L&W) ground-breaking contribution to the field of narrative analysis and recent attempts to articulate and explore a narrative approach to the study of moral experience and moral development (see Day & Tappan, 1996; Tappan, 1991a, 1991b, 1992; Tappan & Brown, 1989). Specifically, I would argue that although this narrative can be analyzed in useful and interesting ways by employing the structural dimensions and categories introduced by L&W, ultimately such an analysis misses a number of important aspects of this narrative that are key to understanding Harriet's moral life—aspects that are better illuminated by a focus on the *dialogical* nature of the moral self. Thus, in the end, my contribution to this special issue honoring the legacy of L&W's work will seek to build on and extend their perspective in order to articulate a more complete approach to the narrative study of moral experience.

## THE STRUCTURAL PERSPECTIVE

L&W's approach to narrative analysis offered two central insights to those interested in exploring a narrative approach to the study of moral experience and moral functioning. First, as Harriet's interview excerpt illustrates, there is much to be gained by employing L&W's strategy of simply asking participants in research interviews to talk about their own real life moral experiences. When they are asked about moral problems, conflicts, and dilemmas they have faced in their lives, persons inevitably tell stories, construct narratives, present "oral versions of personal experience" that recount the actions and events of interest in some kind of temporal sequence. These narratives, moreover, reveal much more about human moral experience and moral functioning than do answers to hypothetical moral dilemmas, the method typically used to study moral development (see Kohlberg, 1981, 1984). Within the field of moral psychology, Carol Gilligan (1978, 1982) was the first to invite research participants to tell stories about their real-life moral conflicts; many others have subsequently followed Gilligan's lead, exploring, in so doing, the variety of ways persons rely on narrative and storytelling to chart, carry out, evaluate, and justify the actions they take when confronted with such dilemmas (see Day, 1991a, 1991b; see also, Attanucci, 1991; Johnston, 1991; Lyons, 1983; Tappan, 1989; 1991a, 1991b; Tappan & Brown, 1989; Ward, 1991; Witherell & Edwards, 1991).

Second, L&W's conception of the universal structure common to all narratives, and their method for analyzing narratives of personal experience to reveal this structure, has interesting implications for the study of moral experience and moral functioning. Specifically, as Attanucci (1991) argued, the structural elements that Labov and Waletzky argued are to be found in all narratives—orientation, complication, evaluation, resolution, and coda—mirror the structure of the "real-life moral conflict and choice interview protocol" introduced by Gilligan (1982), revised and refined by her colleagues and collaborators (see Brown, Debold, Tappan, & Gilligan, 1992; Brown & Gilligan, 1991; Brown, Tappan, Gilligan, Miller, & Argyris, 1989; Gilligan, Ward, & Taylor, 1988; Tappan & Brown, 1989) and widely used by those interested in eliciting narratives of lived moral experience. Thus, for example, even Harriet's brief interview excerpt can easily be analyzed using L&W's structural categories—it contains, that is to say, an orientation ("one time last spring my mother found a marijuana pipe of my brother's in front of the driveway"), a complication ("she was like ... 'Is this some kind of drug paraphernalia?'"), an evaluation ("I didn't think either decision was a good one"), and a resolution ("so I just said, 'Yeah, it is. I don't know where it came from,' or something like that. I was like, 'Yeah, I think it is ... '"). Although such an analysis obviously does not do justice to the complexity and detail of L&W's analytic framework and method, it does illustrate what can be gained by utilizing such an approach to identify structures, elements, and themes that are central to understanding the meaning that persons, like Harriet, make of their lived moral experience (see Attanucci, 1991).

There is, indeed, obvious value in L&W's effort to identify structures and elements that are universally found in all narratives of personal experience—including narratives of moral experience—just as there is value in the cognitive-developmental effort to identify universal structures of reasoning about justice and fairness (see Kohlberg, 1981, 1984). Yet, in the final analysis, I would argue that what is lost in these efforts is an adequate and compelling account of *the self*. Simply put, there is no place for a self—an entity that thinks and feels, acts and interacts, reflects on and evaluates its actions and interactions—in the kind of strictly structural approach to narrative analysis that L&W offered.[1] Because, however, an

---

[1] As such, I would argue that Labov and Waletzky's approach suffers from the same limitations facing the cognitive-developmental approach to moral development—the cognitive-developmental conception of a disembodied, transcendental, *epistemic subject* (see Kohlberg, 1984) is not a true self, but a hypothetical construct devised to explain the existence of a universal developmental sequence of structures and stages of moral reasoning.

adequate and compelling account of the self is absolutely critical in the domain of moral psychology (see Noam & Wren, 1993), a narrative approach to moral experience must ultimately move beyond the structural perspective, toward a perspective that rests on an embodied, relational, fundamentally dialogical conception of the moral self.

## THE DIALOGICAL PERSPECTIVE

In seeking to articulate a different approach to narrative analysis vis-à-vis the study of moral experience and moral functioning, I have turned to the work of Mikhail Bakhtin (1981, 1984, 1986). Bakhtin's literary approach to narrative, grounded in a conception of the dialogical nature of both language and the self, is anchored by his claim that "authorship"—in literature and in real life—is a function of both self and other. The utterances that self-as-author produces thus do not arise ex nihilo from a single, solitary mind, spoken by a single, monotonic voice. Instead such utterances emerge from a *dialogical relation* that must be the primary unit of analysis (see Wertsch, 1991). This is, in fact, the essence of self, for Bakhtin: self is dialogical, it is a "relation of simultaneity" between self and other (Holquist, 1990, p. 19), and it speaks in a voice that is fundamentally polyphonic (see also Day & Tappan, 1996; Hermans & Kempen, 1993; Hermans, Kempen, & van Loon, 1992; Sampson, 1993a, 1993b). The "living language," Bakhtin (1981) wrote, lies on the "borderline" between self and other; "the word in language is half someone else's" (p. 293). As such, the authorship of any text, whether it is a novel or a narrative of personal experience, is necessarily "shared" between self and other.

Yet, in spite of the fundamentally dialogic nature of authorship, we are ultimately asked to assume responsibility and accountability for our thoughts, feelings, and actions. In the end, therefore, it is necessary to understand how one comes to make the word (language) of others "one's own." On Bakhtin's view this process occurs as one selectively "appropriates" and "assimilates" the words of others—allowing and enabling, that is, the voices of others to enter into an ongoing inner dialogue with one's own voice. This is what Bakhtin calls the process of "ideological becoming," and it is key to understanding the development of the dialogical self:

> The importance of struggling with another's discourse, its influence in the history of an individual's coming to ideological consciousness, is enormous. One's own discourse and one's own voice, although born of another or dynamically stimulated by another, will sooner or later begin to liberate themselves from the authority of the other's discourse. This problem is made more complex by the fact that a variety of alien voices enter into the struggle for influence within an individual's consciousness (just as they struggle with one another in surrounding social reality). (p. 348)

In extending Bakhtin's (1981) dialogic view of the self and its development to the domain of moral psychology, I would argue that any narrative of moral experience will necessarily be "populated"—perhaps even "overpopulated" (p. 294)—by many different voices, voices struggling for hegemony within the narrative, just as they struggle for hegemony within the self. Moreover, if Bakhtin is correct, we should be able not only to hear and identify these different voices, but also to make some determination about which of these voices are more "externally authoritative" and which are more "internally persuasive," vis-à-vis the self's own process of moral decision making (see Tappan, 1991a). For example, in Harriet's narrative excerpt, not only can we identify several of the different voices speaking in her text—including her mother ("Is this some kind of drug paraphernalia?"), a "truth-telling voice" ("Yeah, that's my brother's pipe; he does drugs, you didn't know that"), a "justice voice" ("I really felt like she had a right to know, for some reason"), and a "care voice" ("it would have hit her really hard, too, and I didn't want to really do anything to upset her that much, or upset him")—but we can also get a sense of which voice ultimately prevails in Harriet's own inner moral dialogue—"I considered the point in between, which was what I decided on."

Identifying such voices, and making such judgments about interview texts, calls for a method for interpreting and analyzing narratives that does not ask researchers to look for typical narrative structures, or to match key words, phrases, or target sentences to a predetermined set of categories. Rather, it requires a method that is sensitive to voice, and open to the fundamentally polyphonic nature of discourse; a method that honors the complexity of persons' narratives of lived moral experience; a method that thus captures, fully, the personal, relational, and cultural dimensions of psychic life. Lyn Brown and her colleagues have developed just such a method for reading narratives of lived experience for the ways in which self represents and orchestrates different moral voices, moral languages, and forms of moral discourse (see Brown, Debold, Tappan, & Gilligan, 1992; Brown & Gilligan, 1991, 1992; Brown et al., 1989); it is a method I commend to anyone interested in exploring more fully this dialogical approach to narrative analysis.

## CONCLUSION

I would argue that the kind of dialogical, voice-centered approach to the analysis of narratives of moral experience that I have presented here, in contrast to the kind of structural, "monological" analysis suggested by L&W's work, highlights, in a very helpful way, the ultimate "unfinalizability" (Morson & Emerson, 1990) of the moral self and moral experience. Paraphrasing Dostoevsky, Bakhtin (1984) argued that "nothing conclusive has yet taken place in the world, the ultimate word of the world and about the world has not yet been spoken, the world is open and free, everything is still in the future and will always be in the future" (p. 166). This is particularly true for moral experience, wherein different moral voices, from different moral perspectives, must be kept alive, and treated with respect, so they can partake in the ongoing dialogue that is the self. No voice is always right or always wrong; an authentic moral self must remain open to new perspectives, new interpretations, new experiences (see Sidorkin, 1996).

Simply put, this kind of openness and unfinalizability is not well-captured by monological, structural perspectives:

> With a monologic approach (in its extreme or pure form) *another person* remains wholly and merely an *object* of consciousness, and not another consciousness. No response is expected from it that could change everything in the world of my consciousness. Monologue is finalized and deaf to the other's response, does not expect it and does not acknowledge in it any *decisive* force. Monologue manages without the other ... [it] pretends to be the *ultimate word.* It closes down the represented word and represented persons. (Bakhtin, 1984, p. 293; emphasis in original)

A dialogic approach, in contrast, is quite amenable to the ongoing, unfinalizable dialogue that is the essence not only of moral experience, but of life itself:

> The single adequate form for *verbally expressing* authentic human life is the *open-ended dialogue.* Life by its very nature is dialogic. To live means to participate in dialogue: to ask questions, to heed, to respond, to agree, and so forth. In this dialogue a person participates wholly and throughout his [sic] whole life: with his eyes, lips, hands, soul, spirit, and with his whole body and deeds. He invests his entire self in discourse, and this discourse enters into the dialogic fabric of human life, into the world symposium (p. 293; emphasis in original).

L&W's (this issue) emphasis on the importance of inviting persons to tell their own stories about their own lived experience was critical to the emergence of a narrative approach to the study of moral experience, moral functioning, and moral development. In the end, however, I believe that it is Bakhtin's emphasis on the dialogic nature of self, and his focus on the parallels that exist between the ways in which a novelist creates her narrative and the ways in which a person lives and tells her own (moral) stories, that provides the most fruitful source of insight and inspiration for further theoretical and empirical work in the field of narrative moral psychology.

## ACKNOWLEDGMENT

Preparation of this article was supported in part by a Small Grant from the Spencer Foundation.

# REFERENCES

Attanucci, J. (1991). Changing subjects: Growing up and growing older. *Journal of Moral Education, 20*, 317–128.
Bakhtin, M. (1981). *The dialogic imagination* (M. Holquist, Ed., C. Emerson & M. Holquist, Trans.). Austin: University of Texas Press.
Bakhtin, M. (1984). *Problems of Dostoevsky's poetics* (C. Emerson, Ed. & Trans.). Minneapolis: University of Minnesota Press.
Bakhtin, M. (1986). *Speech genres and other late essays* (C. Emerson & M. Holquist, Eds., V. McGee, Trans.). Austin: University of Texas Press.
Brown, L., Debold, E., Tappan, M., & Gilligan, C. (1992). Reading narratives of conflict and choice for self and moral voice: A relational method. In W. Kurtines & J. Gewirtz (Eds.), *Handbook of moral behavior and development: Theory, research, and application* (pp. 25–62). Hillsdale, NJ: Lawrence Erlbaum Associates, Inc.
Brown, L., & Gilligan, C. (1991). Listening for voice in narratives of relationship. In M. Tappan & M. Packer (Eds.), *Narrative and storytelling: Implications for understanding moral development* (pp. 43–61). San Francisco: Jossey-Bass.
Brown, L., & Gilligan, C. (1992). *Meeting at the crossroads: Women's psychology and girls' development.* Cambridge, MA: Harvard University Press.
Brown, L., Tappan, M., Gilligan, C., Miller, B., & Argyris, D. (1989). Reading for self and moral voice: A method for interpreting narratives of real-life moral conflict and choice. In M. Packer & R. Addison (Eds.), *Entering the circle: Hermeneutic investigation in psychology* (pp. 141–164). Albany: State University of New York Press.
Day, J. (1991a). The moral audience: On the narrative mediation of moral "judgment" and moral "action." In M. Tappan & M. Packer (Eds.), *Narrative and storytelling: Implications for understanding moral development* (pp. 27–42). San Francisco: Jossey-Bass.
Day, J. (1991b). Role-taking reconsidered: Narrative and cognitive-developmental interpretations of moral growth. *The Journal of Moral Education, 20*, 305–317.
Day, J., & Tappan, M. (1996). The narrative approach to moral development: From the epistemic subject to dialogical selves. *Human Development, 39*, 67–82.
Gilligan, C. (1977). In a different voice: Women's conceptions of self and morality. *Harvard Educational Review, 47*, 481–517.
Gilligan, C. (1982). *In a different voice: Psychological theory and women's development.* Cambridge, MA: Harvard University Press.
Gilligan, C., Ward, J., & Taylor, J. (Eds.). (1988). *Mapping the moral domain: A contribution of women's thinking to psychological theory and education.* Cambridge, MA: Harvard University Press.
Hermans, H., & Kempen, H. (1993). *The dialogical self: Meaning as movement.* New York: Academic.
Hermans, H., Kempen, H., & van Loon, R. (1992). The dialogical self: Beyond individualism and rationalism. *American Psychologist, 47*, 23–33.
Holquist, M. (1990). *Dialogism: Bakhtin and his world.* London: Routledge.
Johnston, D. K. (1991). Cheating: Reflections on a moral dilemma. *Journal of Moral Education, 20*, 283–292.
Kohlberg, L. (1981). *Essays on moral development, Vol. I: The philosophy of moral development.* San Francisco: Harper & Row.
Kohlberg, L. (1984). *Essays on moral development, Vol. II: The psychology of moral development.* San Francisco: Harper & Row.
Labov, W., & Waletzky, J. (this issue). Narrative analysis: Oral versions of personal experience. In J. Helm (Ed.), *Essays on the verbal and visual arts: Proceedings of the 1966 Annual Spring Meeting*

*of the American Ethnological Society* (pp. 12–44). Seattle: University of Washington Press. (Original work published 1967)
Lyons, N. (1983). Two perspectives: On self, relationships, and morality. *Harvard Educational Review, 53,* 125–145.
Morson, G., & Emerson, C. (1990). *Mikhail Bakhtin: Creation of a prosaics.* Stanford, CA: Stanford University Press.
Noam, G., & Wren, T. (Eds.). (1993). *The moral self.* Cambridge, MA: The MIT Press.
Sampson, E. (1993a). *Celebrating the other: A dialogic account of human nature.* Boulder, CO: Westview.
Sampson, E. (1993b). Identity politics: Challenges to psychology's understanding. *American Psychologist, 48,* 1219–1230.
Sidorkin, A. (1996, November). *Integrity, authenticity, and other over-advertised commodities: Towards the dialogical concept of the self.* Paper presented at the Annual Meeting of the Association for Moral Education, Ottawa, Ontario.
Tappan, M. (1989). Stories lived and stories told: The narrative structure of late adolescent moral development. *Human Development, 32,* 300–315.
Tappan, M. (1991a). Narrative, authorship, and the development of moral authority. In M. Tappan & M. Packer (Eds.), *Narrative and storytelling: Implications for understanding moral development* (pp. 5–25). San Francisco: Jossey-Bass.
Tappan, M. (1991b). Narrative, language, and moral experience. *Journal of Moral Education, 20,* 243–256.
Tappan, M. (1992). Texts and contexts: Language, culture, and the development of moral functioning. In L. T. Winegar & J. Valsiner (Eds.), *Children's development within social contexts: Metatheoretical, theoretical, and methodological issues* (pp. 93–117). Hillsdale, NJ: Lawrence Erlbaum Associates, Inc.
Tappan, M., & Brown, L. (1989). Stories told and lessons learned: Toward a narrative approach to moral development and moral education. *Harvard Educational Review, 59,* 182–205.
Ward, J. (1991). "Eyes in the back of your head": Moral themes in African-American narratives of racial conflict. *Journal of Moral Education, 20,* 267–282.
Wertsch, J. (1991). *Voices of the mind: A sociocultural approach to mediated action.* Cambridge, MA: Harvard University Press.
Witherell, C., & Edwards, C. P. (1991). Moral versus social-conventional reasoning: A narrative and cultural critique. *Journal of Moral Education, 20,* 293–304.

# Dialogue Shakes Narrative: From Temporal Storyline to Spatial Juxtaposition

## Hubert J. M. Hermans
*Department of Clinical Psychology and Personality*
*University of Nijmegen*

In agreement with prevailing notions, Labov and Waletzky (1967/this issue), and other theoreticians after them, conceptualized narrative in temporal terms, with the implication that spatial characteristics are rather neglected. Sarbin (1990), for example, held:

> The temporal context of experience and action is what makes the narrative a congenial organizing principle. Action, and the silent preparation for action, because extended in time, is storied. We live in a story-shaped world. Action takes on the narrative quality, the familiar beginning, middle, and ending. (pp. 61–62)

Similarly, Gergen and Gergen (1988) saw time as the defining characteristic of narrative: "We shall employ the term self-narrative ... to refer to the individual's account of the relationship among self-relevant events across time" (p. 19). For Bruner (1986) the term *then* functions differently in the logical proposition "if x, then y" than in the narrative: "The king died, and then the queen." As this sentence suggests, Bruner also emphasized the temporal dimension of narrative. McAdams (1993), another advocate of a narrative approach, saw narratives as a build-up of a series of coherently organized episodes, each characterized by a sequence of events, again stressing the relevance of the temporal dimension.

Drawing on Bakhtin (1929/1973) I want to emphasize time and space as the two basic notions that are of equal importance in the organization of narrative. This results in a conception of story that recognizes not only *continuity* but also

---

Requests for reprints should be sent to Hubert J. M. Hermans, P.O. Box 9104, 6500 HE Nijmegen, The Netherlands. E-mail: hhermans@psych.kun.nl

*discontinuity* and not only *coherence* but also *separateness* of different story parts as intrinsic features of the narrative mode. My proposal is to approach the self as composed of a multiplicity of positions that are located at different places in an imaginal landscape. At the same time, the self is multivoiced so that the different voices, located at different positions, can enter into dialogical relationships with one another. The different positions cohere as far as they are dialogically related; at the same time, they are separate as far as one and the same person is like "different characters," each with their own story to tell.

## THE MULTIVOICEDNESS OF THE SELF

In line with Bakhtin (1929/1973) my basic supposition is that a story always implies a storyteller and, by implication, an actual or imaginal listener. When an adult tells about a particular event, it makes a difference if he or she addresses a child or another adult. Or, to take another example, when a surgeon talks about a planned operation, he or she tells it to a patient in a different way than to a colleague. By his actual or imaginal presence, the listener codetermines, during the act of talking, the story both in its form and content (Hilton, 1990). As Bakhtin's colleague Voloshinov (1929) explained: "... *word is a two-sided act.* It is determined equally by whose word it is and for whom it is meant. As word, it is precisely the product of the reciprocal relationship between speaker and listener, addresser and addressee" (p. 58).

### Bakhtin's Polyphonic Novel: Position and Opposition

The spatial nature of narrative is basic to Bakhtin's metaphor of the polyphonic novel. The principle feature of the novel is that it is composed of a number of independent and mutually opposing viewpoints embodied by characters involved in dialogical relationships. As playing their part in the novel, each character is "ideologically authoritative and independent," that is, each character is perceived as the author of his or her own view of the world, not as an object of Dostoyevsky's all-encompassing artistic vision. The author Dostoyevsky is only one of many, with the implication that the characters are not "obedient slaves," in the service of Dostoyevsky's intentions, but are capable of standing beside their creator, disagreeing with the author, even rebelling against him. The characters are not subordinated to Dostoyevsky's individual vision but have their own voice and tell their own story. As "a plurality of consciousnesses," the different characters express their own ideas. As in a polyphonic composition, the several voices have different spatial positions and accompany and oppose each other in a dialogical fashion.

The notion of dialogue, as expressed in questioning and answering and in agreement or disagreement, opens for Bakhtin the possibility to differentiate the inner world of one and the same individual in the form of an interpersonal relationship. When an "inner" thought of a particular character is transformed into an utterance, dialogical relations spontaneously occur between this utterance and the utterance of imaginal others. In Dostoyevsky's novel *The Double,* for example, the second hero (the double) serves as a personification of the interior voice of the first hero (Golyadkin). By the externalization of the interior thought of the first hero in two spatially separated positions, a full-fledged dialogue between two independent parties develops. In this way Bakhtin (1929/1973) is able to transform temporal relations into spatial structures:

> This persistent urge to see all things as being coexistent and to perceive and depict all things side by side and simultaneously, *as if in space rather than time,* leads him [Dostoyevsky] to dramatize in space even the inner contradictions and stages of development of a single person ... (p. 23, emphasis added)

As a result of this narrative spatialization, Dostoyevsky constructs a plurality of voices representing a plurality of worlds that are discontinuous and even opposed.

## THE DIALOGICAL SELF: THE PLAY OF POSITIONS

Drawing on Bakhtin's metaphor of the polyphonic novel, Hermans, Kempen, and Van Loon (1992) conceptualized the self in terms of a dynamic multiplicity of relatively autonomous *I*-positions in an imaginal landscape. In its most concise form this conception can be formulated as follows:

> The *I* has the possibility to move, as in a space, from one position to the other in accordance with changes in situation and time. The *I* fluctuates among different and even opposed positions. The *I* has the capacity to imaginatively endow each position with a voice so that dialogical relations between positions can be established. The voices function like interacting characters in a story. Once a character is set in motion in a story, the character takes on a life of its own and thus assumes a certain narrative necessity. Each character has a story to tell about experiences from its own stance. As different voices, these characters exchange information about their respective *Me*(s) and their worlds, resulting in a complex, narratively structured self. (Hermans, Kempen, & Van Loon, 1992, pp. 28–29)

Imaginal others may exemplify the workings of the dialogical self. As Watkins (1986) described, we may find ourselves speaking to the photograph of someone we miss, to an internal advisor, to a deceased parent or grandparent, to a figure in a movie or dream, to our cat or dog, or to our reflection in the mirror. Even when we appear to be outwardly silent, we may talk with our mothers or fathers, oppose our critics, converse with our gods, or ask for the opinion of some personification of our conscience. The question is here: Do these imaginal figures belong to the self or not? Given the previously mentioned definition of the dialogical self, the answer is affirmative: The imaginal figures belong to the self as relatively autonomous *I*-positions that are able to enter into dialogue with the person himself and with each other (e.g., I imagine my mother and father talking with each other about me). The assumption of multivoicedness extends the self beyond the traditional split between self and other. Other people are not simply "outside" but "in" the self and continuously play their roles as voiced characters in a multifaceted mind.

### The Innovative Quality of the Dialogical Self

A specific feature of the dialogical self is its innovative potential. In order to clarify this thesis, let us discuss an example presented by Baldwin (1992) and analyzed by Hermans (1996b). A teenage boy wants to borrow the keys to his mother's car. He expects that the goal of his mother is to make sure that he and the car are returned safely. If she is reluctant, he knows that the required behavior is to reassure his mother that he will act in a responsible way. So he verbalizes phrases that have been successful in the past, for example: "I'll drive carefully" and "I'll be home before 1!" If he proceeds this way, he expects that his mother will give him the keys. If not, he may engage different routines, such as expressing his urgent need for transport or complaining about the unfairness of her behavior. Along these lines "multiple if–then sequences" (Baldwin, 1992) are organized into a complete production system for guiding behavior. As a result of these sequences, the mother finally gives the keys.

What happens in the mind of the mother before she decides to do so? Concerned with the welfare of her son, she is hesitant and perhaps fearful to give the keys. At the same time she is sympathetic with her son, who wants to enjoy a fine day. So she vacillates between two positions, the fearful mother and the helpful mother. From the first position she would say: "I am afraid that ... ," from the second: "I can imagine that ... ." After moving to and fro between the two positions, and after a process of negotiation between them, she finally decides to give the keys. During the process of self-negotiation, the mother's self is, to borrow a term from Bruner (1990), "distributed" between two positions and her decision is preceded by dialogical movements between them. Although the example illustrates the multivoiced nature of the self, it reflects a strongly stereotypical sequence of events. That is, prior interactions are patterned in repetitive ways on the basis of expected sequences. Such stereotypical interactions, which Baldwin (1992) described in terms of "relational schemas," can certainly be understood as dialogical, as the earlier analysis shows, but they lack a central ingredient that is crucial to the understanding of the dialogical self, the element of novelty. Let us, therefore, present a second example, which leads us to the heart of the dialogical self.

An author submits a manuscript to a scientific journal and, after some time, receives three helpful but critical comments, with the encouraging advice to resubmit. As a result, the author is challenged by entirely new information and new problems to resolve. This can only be done by taking the positions of the reviewers into account in relation to the author's own position. In order to achieve this, the author has to move to and fro between the several reviewers to check them on consistencies and inconsistencies. Moreover, the author has to move between the reviewers' points of view and his or her original position as represented by the original manuscript. At first, all these positions may sound like a "cacophony of voices," but after several rounds of intensive dialogical interchange, a new structure may emerge. The author arrives at a point of juxtaposition of the several views that are simultaneously present, so that new, sometimes suddenly emerging, relations between the diversity of insights arise. The final result may be a thoroughly revised manuscript, in which the original position of the author, as materialized in the first manuscript, may be significantly altered. The new manuscript can be seen as the sediment of a process, in which the opposing positions of the author and the reviewers, and the repositioning of the author, are part of a highly open, dynamic, multivoiced self. This highly complex process is potentially innovative as a result of the introduction of new voices and new information.

## Empirical Approaches

Drawing on Marková's (1987) dialogical model, Hermans and Kempen (1993) invited participants to enter in an imaginal dialogue with a person depicted on a painting, *Mercedes de Barcelona* (1930), made by the Dutch artist Pyke Koch (1901–1992). Participants were invited to select one of their previously formulated valuations (narrative units of meaning referring to important experiences in the participant's past, present, or future). After concentrating on the picture, they were asked to imagine that the woman would respond to their personal valuation. After the woman's imaginal response, participants were invited to respond to the woman from the perspective of the original valuation. This is the example of Frank, a 48-year-old man, who referred to his work as manager in a company:

Step 1: Frank: I trust most people in advance; however, when this trust is violated, I start to think in a negative way; this can have harmful consequences.
Step 2: Woman: You should keep your openness; however, your trust should become somewhat more reserved and take into account the topic involved.

Step 3: Frank: You are right; I must pay attention to this; reservations in this will also help me to control my negative feelings.

In this example, the woman, in the role of a wise advisor, presents a new viewpoint (Step 2), that is incorporated in Frank's final reaction (Step 3) in such a way that the original formulation (Step 1) has been further developed. Step 3 involves not only a main element of the woman's response (reservation), but also a central element of the original valuation (negative thinking). In Step 3, elements from Steps 1 and 2 are incorporated, and thus a valuation with a considerable innovative and synthesizing quality emerges.

In another research project participants were invited to mention two opposite sides in their own personality (e.g., open vs. closed, active vs. passive, rational vs. emotional) and to conceive them as *I*-positions. The participants were instructed to tell two self-narratives, and, correspondingly, formulate two valuation systems, one from the dominant position (e.g., I as an active person) and another from the opposite, less dominant position (e.g., I as a passive person). In one of the studies (Hermans, 1996a), a participant, Nicole, explained that she saw herself mainly as an "self-assertive" person, but that she had, less dominant, an "anxious–uncertain" side as well. Although responding to the same set of open questions, the participant formulated, from the two positions, two very different sets of valuations referring to different memories of the past, different concerns in the present, and different expectations of the future. The valuations from the self-assertive position mainly represent a fairly optimistic outlook on the world, whereas the valuations from the uncertain–anxious position refer to more negative experiences. At the same time, the valuations are not simply "different" as the valuation systems of two unrelated people may be different. Rather, the two "characters" oppose one another in a dialogical way, sometimes even disagreeing with each other. For example, as a self-assertive position she said about her future: "Although my boyfriend also has a relationship with another woman, I expect that he will eventually choose me, so that we will have a future together." From her uncertain–anxious position, however, she said: "If my friend does not choose me, this relationship will break me so that my trust in relationships will be gone, and also the basic trust in myself."

Moreover, participants were followed over time in order to investigate the relative dominance of the valuations from the two positions. The results showed that at the onset of a 3-week period of investigation, the valuations associated with Nicole's self-assertive position were rated as more dominant and more meaningful than the valuations from her (suppressed) uncertain–anxious position. In the course of the following weeks, however, in which she broke off the relationship with her friend, the valuations from the uncertain–anxious position became not only more dominant, but also more meaningful, despite their negative character. This phenomenon, called "dominance reversal," suggests that a hidden or suppressed position can become, quite suddenly, more dominant than the position that corresponds with the trait the person considers as a prevalent and stable part of her personality. Such changes illustrate the highly dynamic nature of the multivoiced self.

A person who tells his or her self-narrative does not follow a linear storyline with a beginning, a middle, and an ending. Rather, the continuity of the storyline is shaken by the discontinuous process of positioning and repositioning, so typical of a self which is populated by voices engaged in a process of self-negotiations, self-oppositions, and self-integrations.

Inspired by Bakhtin's metaphor of the polyphonic novel, I have emphasized the theoretical and methodological relevance of the spatial nature of the self, representing a neglected area in the psychology of the self. The focus was on the multivoicedness of the self, reflecting a view that, in Heraclitean terms, can be summarized as "unity-in-multiplicity" or as "multiplicity in unity." Whereas the multiplicity of the self is reflected in the multitude of separate positions, its unity is guaranteed by the integrative workings of dialogue.

## REFERENCES

Bakhtin, M. (1973). *Problems of Dostoevsky's poetics* (2nd ed.; R. W. Rotsel, Trans.). Ann Arbor, MI: Ardis. (Originally published in 1929 under the title *Problemy tvorchestva Dostoevskogo* [Problems of Dostoevsky's Art])

Baldwin, M. W. (1992). Relational schemas and the processing of social information. *Psychological Bullletin, 112,* 461–484.

Bruner, J. S. (1986). *Actual minds, possible worlds.* Cambridge, MA: Harvard University Press.

Bruner, J. S. (1990). *Acts of meaning.* Cambridge, MA: Harvard University Press.

Gergen, K. J., & Gergen, M. M. (1988). Narrative and the self as relationship. *Advances in Experimental Social Psychology, 21,* 17–56.

Hermans, H. J. M. (1996a). Opposites in a dialogical self: Constructs as characters. *The Journal of Constructivist Psychology, 9,* 1–26.

Hermans, H. J. M. (1996b). Voicing the self: From information processing to dialogical interchange. *Psychological Bulletin, 119,* 31–50.

Hermans, H. J. M., & Kempen, H. J. G. (1993). *The dialogical self: Meaning as movement.* San Diego, CA: Academic.

Hermans, H. J. M., Kempen, H. J. G., & Van Loon, R. J. P. (1992). The dialogical self: Beyond individualism and rationalism. *American Psychologist, 47,* 23–33.

Hilton, D. J. (1990). Conversational processes and causal explanation. *Psychological Bulletin, 107,* 65–81.

Labov, W., & Waletzky, J. (this issue). Narrative analysis: Oral versions of personal experience. In J. Helm (Ed.), *Essays on the verbal and visual arts: Proceedings of the 1966 Annual Spring Meeting of the American Ethnological Society* (pp. 12–44). Seattle: University of Washington Press. (Original work published 1967)

Marková, I. (1987). On the interaction of opposites in psychological processes. *Journal for the Theory of Social Behavior, 17,* 279–299.

McAdams, D. P. (1993). *The stories we live by: Personal myths and the making of the self.* New York: William Morrow.
Sarbin, Th. R. (1990). The narrative quality of action. *Theoretical and Philosophical Psychology, 10,* 49–65.
Voloshinov, V. N. (1929). Marxism and the philosophy of language. In P. Morris, *The Bakhtin reader: Selected writings of Bakhtin, Medvedev, Voloshinov* (pp. 50–61). London: Edward Arnold.
Watkins, M. (1986). *Invisible guests: The development of imaginal dialogues.* Hillsdale, NJ: Lawrence Erlbaum Associates, Inc.

# Some Further Steps in Narrative Analysis

## William Labov
### Department of Linguistics, University of Pennsylvania

The first steps in narrative analysis taken by Joshua Waletzky and myself were a by-product of the sociolinguistic field methods that had been developed in the survey of the Lower East Side of New York City (Labov, 1966) and in the work that engaged us at the time—the study of African American Vernacular English in South Harlem (Labov, Cohen, Robins, & Lewis, 1968). We defined the vernacular as the form of language first acquired, perfectly learned, and used only among speakers of the same vernacular. The effort to observe how speakers talked when they were not being observed created the Observer's Paradox. Among the partial solutions to that paradox within the face-to-face interview, the elicitation of narratives of personal experience proved to be the most effective. We were therefore driven to understand as much as we could about the structure of these narratives and how they were introduced into the everyday conversation that our interviews simulated. Labov and Waletzky (1967/this issue; henceforth L&W) laid out a framework that proved useful for narrative in general, as this volume demonstrates.

Since that time I have published only a few studies of narrative (Labov, 1972, 1981; Labov & Fanshel, 1977). This is not because I have lost interest in the subject, for I have written and delivered a great many unpublished papers in the area.[1] I may not have pursued these papers into the domain of publication because the analysis of narrative was competing with quantitative studies of language variation and change, in which cumulative theories can be built upon decisive answers to

---

Requests for reprints should be sent to William Labov, Linguistics Laboratory, University of Pennsylvania, 1106 Blockley Hall, 418 Guardian Drive, Philadelphia, PA 19104.

[1]Particularly, *The Reorganization of Reality,* a series on narrative given at the University of Rochester, October, 1977; *The Vernacular Origins of Epic Style,* the W. P. Ker Lecture at the University of Glasgow, May 4, 1983; *On Not Putting Two and Two Together: The Shallow Interpretation of Narrative,* Pitzer College, March 10, 1986; and a number of presentations under the title of "*Great Speakers of the Western World.*"

successively more general questions. The discussion of narrative and other speech events at the discourse level rarely allows us to prove anything. It is essentially a hermeneutic study, in which continual engagement with the discourse as it was delivered gains entrance to the perspective of the speaker and the audience, tracing the transfer of information and experience in a way that deepens our own understandings of what language and social life are all about. The most important data that I have gathered on narrative is not drawn from the observation of speech production or controlled experiments, but from the reactions of audiences to the narratives as I have retold them. In a regular and predictable fashion, certain narratives produce in the audience a profound concentration of attention that creates uninterrupted silence and immobility, an effect that continues long after the ending is reached. It is the effort to understand the compelling power of such narratives that brings me to this essay, an abstract of a more extended treatment of narratives of personal experience to follow.[2]

L&W demonstrated that the effort to understand narrative is amenable to a formal framework, particularly in the basic definition of narrative as the choice of a specific linguistic technique to report past events. The L&W framework developed for oral narratives of personal experience proved to be useful in approaching a wide variety of narrative situations and types, including oral memoirs, traditional folk tales, avant garde novels, therapeutic interviews, and, most importantly, the banal narratives of everyday life. It allowed us to understand pseudonarratives like recipes, apartment-house layouts, and other types of experience remodeled into narrative form. It gradually appeared that narratives are privileged forms of discourse that play a central role in almost every conversation.[3] Our efforts to define other speech events with comparable precision have shown us that narrative is the prototype, perhaps the only example of a well-formed speech event with a beginning, a middle, and an end.

Narrative and the broader field of storytelling has become a keen focus of attention in many academic and literary disciplines. Here the traditional trajectory of the storyteller runs athwart the main focus of this article. The classic image of the storyteller is someone who can make something out of nothing, who can engage our attention with a fascinating elaboration of detail that is entertaining, amusing, and emotionally rewarding. From the first lines of such a narrative, we know that we are in the presence of a gifted user of the language. *Credibility* is rarely an issue

---

[2]The most recent form of the approach to narrative presented here is the product of a class on Narrative Analysis that I taught at Penn in the fall of 1996 and is much indebted to the contributions of members of the class. I thank in particular Trevor Stack, Matt Rissanen, Kirstin Smith, Pierette Thibault, and Dr. Herbert Adler.

[3]In fact, one approach to the definition of conversation is to see it as a way of instancing general principles by means of narrative.

here. Tall tales, myths, and outright lies carry the day, and we normally do not know or care whether the events as told were the personal experience of the storyteller or anyone else. The narratives that are the central focus of my current work are altogether different. The tellers were not known as gifted storytellers; people did not gather to hear them speak. They were ordinary people in the deepest sense of the word. They did not manufacture events or elaborate the experience of others. Their narratives were an attempt to convey simply and seriously the most important experiences of their own lives. Sometimes the stories had been told many times, but very often they had not been, or were perhaps told for the very first time. They deal with the major events of life and death, including the sudden outbreak of violence; the near approach of death and the witness of it; premonitions of the future, often through communication with the dead; courage in the face of adversity and the struggle against overwhelming odds; and cowardice and the betrayal of trust. I don't believe that this focus on serious and momentous issues limits the scope of the analysis. Rather, the use of narrative to deal with issues of life and death highlights the abilities displayed in more casual, humorous, or even trivial accounts. In the less serious and more frequent deployment of narrative, techniques are practiced to perfection; in the more serious domain, they are put to the test.

The narratives that form the focus of this work were normally told in the course of a sociolinguistic interview, in which the interviewer formed an ideal audience: attentive, interested, and responsive. Though they are fitted to some extent to the situation and often to a question posed by the interviewer, they are essentially monologues and show a degree of decontextualization. They exhibit a generality that is not to be expected from narratives that subserve an argumentative point in a highly interactive and competitive conversation. Such narratives are often highly fragmented and may require a different approach. Yet studies of spontaneous conversation also show a high frequency of monologic narratives that command the attention of the audience as fully as the narratives of the interview. The principles developed in this article are exemplified most clearly in narratives of this type.

The issues that are raised here go beyond the analysis of L&W, which dealt with temporal organization and evaluation. The framework I present here begins with these aspects of narrative and then goes on to consider the further issues of reportability, credibility, objectivity, causality, and the assignment of praise and blame.

In this skeletal presentation, I use one narrative to illustrate the principles involved:[4]

---

[4] This narrative is one of those discussed in detail in the exploration of the relation of speech to violence in Labov, 1981.

Narrative 1
(1) Harold Shambaugh, Tape A-304, Columbus, Ohio, 7/28/70
(What happened in South America?)
  a  Oh I w's settin' at a table drinkin'
  b  And—this Norwegian sailor come over
  c  an' kep' givin' me a bunch o' junk
      about I was sittin' with his woman.
  d  An' everybody sittin' at the table with me were my shipmates.
  e  So I jus' turn aroun'
  f  an' shoved 'im,
  g  an' told 'im, I said,
      "Go away,
  h    I don't even wanna fool with ya."
  i  An' nex' thing I know I 'm layin' on the floor, blood all over me,
  j  An' a guy told me, says,
      "Don't move your head.
  k    Your throat's cut."

This brief narrative has been proven to be paradigmatic in its ability to transfer experience from narrator to the audience. The reader is invited to commit these 12 lines to memory and retell the story to an individual or group of others. Many listeners report the experience of viewing in the scene in a smoke-filled room in lines a–h; that with lines i–k there is a sudden change of perspective, looking up from below; and after k, about one third of the people in any audience make a sudden intake of breath, as if it were in fact their throat that was cut.

Over the course of some 20 years, I have dealt with the question of how this brief narrative commands attention and conveys experience as effectively as it does. The following pages are an outline of my attempt to provide an answer. The presentation is in the form of definitions; implications from those definitions; empirical findings from the study of a larger body of narrative; and theorems, which propose relations with empirical content that are more problematic. The reader is asked to accept the validity of those findings provisionally until a larger body of material can be presented.

## 0. NARRATIVES OF PERSONAL EXPERIENCE

0.1. Definition: A narrative of personal experience is a report of a sequence of events that have entered into the biography of the speaker by a sequence of clauses that correspond to the order of the original events.

This definition is based on the initial conception of L&W; a definition that separates narrative in this sense from other means of telling a story or recounting the past. It is an arbitrary segregation of one sense of narrative for technical purposes, but it proves to be a useful one. By here specifying that the experience must have "entered into the biography" of the speaker, I distinguish narrative from simple recounting of observations such as the events of a parade by a witness leaning out a window. It will turn out that events that have entered into the speaker's biography are emotionally and socially evaluated and so transformed from raw experience.

## 1. THE TEMPORAL ORGANIZATION OF NARRATIVE

This discussion of temporal organization includes a new piece of terminology not present in L&W, a sequential clause.

> 1.1. Definition: Two clauses are separated by a *temporal juncture* if a reversal of their order results in a change in the listener's interpretation of the order of the events described.

Thus all the clauses in Narrative 1 are separated by temporal juncture with the following exceptions: a and b overlap so there is no juncture between them, and i overlaps j and k, so there is no juncture between i and j.[5]

> 1.1.1. Implication (and definition) of a *minimal narrative:* A narrative must contain at least one temporal juncture. As L&W pointed out, stories can be told without any temporal juncture by syntactic embedding, the use of the past perfect, and other grammatical devices. Temporal juncture is the simplest, most favored or unmarked way of recounting the past.

> 1.2. Definition: A sequential clause is a clause that can be an element of a temporal juncture.

Any temporal relation of a subordinate clause to its matrix clause will be indicated by its subordinate conjunction, such as *before, after*. Other subordinate conjunctions like *about* in c can only indicate simultaneity. Subordinate (i.e., dependent) clauses cannot therefore enter into temporal juncture.

---

[5]The question of ordering events within quotations is a difficult one; my best judgment is that the utterances of g and h could have been uttered in either order without change in their logical or interactive force, and so for j and k. However, for the moment, I take the narrative literally, saying that the two sets of utterances were so ordered. The question as to whether e,f,g are well ordered within themselves is also open.

1.2.1. Implication: All sequential clauses are independent clauses (but not all independent clauses are sequential clauses).

For an independent clause to be a sequential clause, its head must include a tense that is not only deictic, indicating a specific time domain, but it must identify sequential time relations. The English past progressive designates a time before the time of speaking but does not focus on the beginning or end points of that time. Can the progressive function as the head of a sequential clause? A number of cases like i indicate that this is a possibility. The progressive in i is simultaneous with j,k but appears to be sequenced after h.[6]

1.2.2. Implication: In English, sequential clauses are headed by verbs in the preterit tense, past progressive, or the present tense with the semantic interpretation of a preterit (historical present).

Both the general definition of narrative and the definition of temporal juncture demand that the reports be reports of real events. It follows that modals, futures, and negatives cannot serve as the heads of verb phrases that enter into temporal juncture. In English, this function is reserved for the indicative mood, which is our only *realis* mood.

1.2.3. Implication: All Sequential Clauses Are in the Realis Mood

1.3. Definition: A *narrative clause* consists of a sequential clause (the head) with all subordinate clauses that are dependent upon it.

## 2. TEMPORAL TYPES OF NARRATIVE CLAUSES

We can now employ these definitions to give a simpler and clearer picture of temporal ranges than L&W provided. With the narrative clause defined on the basis of sequential clauses—clauses that *can* have temporal juncture—it is possible to focus only upon temporal relations of the narrative clauses and exclude others.[7]

2.1. Definition: The *range* of a narrative clause is the set of narrative clauses between the first preceding and next following temporal juncture.

---

[6] If we interpret the grammatical construction as derived from "The next thing I know *is* ... " then the verb *to be* would be a sequential clause, which is not likely. "The next thing I know" must then be interpreted as equivalent to *next*.

[7] Thus, it is no longer necessary to engage in a lengthy tabulation of the range of free clauses, including all preceding and all following clauses, numbers which may change each time we revise the transcription.

In the transcription conventions followed here, the narrative range is indicated by a left subscript indicating the number of preceding narrative clauses the particular clause is simultaneous with and the right subscript the number of following clauses. The range is then the sum of the two.

2.2. Definition: A *free clause* is a clause that refers to a condition that holds true during the entire narrative.

A free clause is not then defined syntactically, but semantically. A past progressive that serves as a restricted clause in one narrative may be a free clause in another.

2.2.1. Implication: A free clause cannot serve as a sequential clause in that narrative in which it is free.

2.3. Definition: A (temporally) *bound clause* is an independent clause with a range of zero.

2.3.1. Implication: All bound clauses are sequential clauses.

2.4. Definition: A narrative clause with a range greater than 0 is a *restricted clause*.

2.4.1. Implication: Narratives are sets of bound, restricted, and free clauses.

We can then rewrite Narrative 1 with temporal ranges and classes of narrative clauses indicated. Quotations with multiple clauses are resolved into individual sequential actions. In narrative, an important distinction between actions and quotations is that the actions frequently overlap, whereas quotations rarely do so. The rule that one person talks at a time is never flouted in personal narrative.

(1')

| | | |
|---|---|---|
| $_0a_2$ | restricted | Oh I w's settin' at a table drinkin' |
| $_1b_0$ | restricted | And—this Norwegian sailor come over |
| $_0c_0$ | bound | an' kep' givin' me a bunch o' junk about I was sittin' with his woman. |
| d | free | An' everybody sittin' at the table with me were my shipmates. |
| $_0e_0$ | bound | So I jus' turn aroun' |
| $_0f_0$ | bound | an' shoved 'im, |
| $_0g_0$ | bound | an' told 'im, I said, "Go away." |
| $_0h_0$ | bound | [and I said] "I don't even wanna fool with ya." |

|  |  |  |
|---|---|---|
| $_0i_2$ |  | An' nex' thing I know |
|  | restricted | I 'm layin' on the floor, blood all over me, |
| $_1j_0$ | restricted | An' a guy told me, says, "Don't move your head." |
| $_0k_0$ | bound | [And he said,] "Your throat's cut." |

Here the subscripts for Clause a indicate that a is not simultaneous with any preceding events, but does overlap with the two following (and with the free clause d, which is not counted). However, it is not simultaneous with e, because at that point Shambaugh is no longer simply sitting at the table drinking.

## 3. STRUCTURAL TYPES OF NARRATIVE CLAUSES

We now consider the structural types of narrative clauses introduced by L&W. The chief addition to this part of the framework is that *complicating action clauses* are necessarily sequential clauses, that is, they can participate in temporal junctures; this is not true of abstracts, orientations, and codas.

3.1. Definition: An *abstract* is an initial clause in a narrative that reports the entire sequence of events of the narrative.

3.2. Definition: An *orientation clause* gives information on the time, place of the events of a narrative, the identities of the participants, and their initial behavior.

3.3. Definition: A clause of *complicating action* is a sequential clause that reports a next event in response to a potential question: "And what happened [then]?"

3.3.1. Implication: All sequential clauses are clauses of complicating action, and all clauses of complicating action are sequential clauses.

3.4. Definition: A coda is a final clause that returns the narrative to the time of speaking, precluding a potential question: "And what happened then?"

These are all self-explanatory, but also quite incomplete. Missing as yet is the notion of a conclusion or *resolution,* which cannot be defined until the concept of *most reportable event* is introduced. More important is the fact that many clauses in narratives do none of these things. The major thrust of the L&W analysis is to raise the question: "If a narrative is a report of events that occurred, why do we find sentences headed by negatives, futures, and modals in narratives?" Or to put it another way, under what conditions is it relevant to talk about what did not, but might have occurred? The primary contribution of that paper was to link this structural question with the socioemotional concept of evaluation.

## 4. EVALUATION

I begin here with a nonlinguistic definition of this basic concept.

> 4.1. Definition: *Evaluation* of a narrative event is information on the consequences of the event for human needs and desires.

> 4.2. Definition: An *evaluative clause* provides evaluation of a narrative event.

Though this is quite straightforward, it does not by itself relate to the structural features of narrative in Section 2. L&W and Labov (1972) discussed many types of linguistic structures that served the function of evaluating narrative events, including emphasis, parallel structures and comparatives. By far the most important of these were the modals, negatives, and futures that were questioned earlier. Our proposal that these references to events that did not occur, might have occurred, or would occur, served an evaluative purpose was the main theoretical thrust of earlier work and might be described as the:

> 4.3. Hypothesis: A narrative clause in an irrealis mood is an evaluative clause

More generally, looking at comparatives as well, we can advance this proposal to the level of a theorem:

> 4.4. Theorem: A narrator evaluates events by comparing them with events in an alternative reality that was not in fact realized.

From work that followed immediately after L&W, we know that the frequency of *irrealis clauses* in narrative increases rapidly with age, as speakers gain the ability to evaluate their experience (Labov, 1972).

Finally, we have to distinguish between an evaluative clause and an *evaluation section*. Evaluative material is frequently spread throughout a narrative, but more frequently it is concentrated in a way that suspends the forward movement of the action. More generally, we define such sections:

> 4.5. Definition: A *section* of a narrative is a group of clauses of a common functional type.

and by this means restate a second L&W Theorem:

4.6. Theorem: Evaluation is characteristically concentrated in an evaluation section, placed just before the most highly evaluated action or "point" of the narrative.

The application of this conception of evaluation to Narrative 1 is straightforward except for the problem of quotations. On the one hand, (1)g can be viewed as a simple action which is a bound event: Shambaugh said something to the Norwegian sailor. On the other hand, what was said represents two distinct speech actions: a bare imperative which represents an unmitigated command and a negative scalar ("if I don't want to do a minimal action like fooling with you, it follows that I don't want to do any more important action.") From everything we know about the connectivity of speech acts, the analysis must ultimately rise to this more abstract level of action. Yet it is at the level of sentence grammar that we find our most direct clues to evaluation. When an actor in the narrative is animated to speak directly, no matter what the topic or the addressee, the current situation is open to evaluation. The use of negatives, comparatives, modals, or futures is therefore to be read as a form of evaluation. In this sense, h evaluates the narrative situation by comparing it with one in which Shambaugh would want to fool with the other, and in j the other evaluates the situation in comparison with one in which it would be safe for Shambaugh to move his head. The assignment of structural categories to the 12 clauses can be assigned as OR(ientation), EV(aluation), and CA (complicating action).

(1″)

| | | |
|---|---|---|
| OR $_0a_2$ | restricted | Oh I w's settin' at a table drinkin' |
| CA $_1b_0$ | restricted | And—this Norwegian sailor come over |
| CA $_0c_0$ | bound | an' kep' givin' me a bunch o' junk about I was sittin' with his woman. |
| OR d | free | An' everybody sittin' at the table with me were my shipmates. |
| CA $_0e_0$ | bound | So I jus' turn aroun' |
| CA $_0f_0$ | bound | an' shoved 'im, |
| CA $_0g_0$ | bound | an' told 'im, I said, "Go away," |
| EV $_0h_0$ | bound | [and I said,] "I don't even wanna fool with ya." An' nex' thing I know |
| CA $_0i_2$ | restricted | I 'm layin' on the floor, blood all over me, |
| EV $_1j_0$ | restricted | An' a guy told me, says, "Don't move your head." |
| CA $_0k_0$ | bound | [and he said], "Your throat's cut." |

## 5. REPORTABILITY

One of the most difficult, yet essential, concepts in narrative analysis is *reportability*. The original concept is that the telling a narrative requires a person to occupy more social space than in other conversational exchanges—to hold the floor longer—and the narrative must carry enough interest for the audience to justify this action. Otherwise, an implicit or explicit "So what?" is in order, with the implication that the speaker has violated social norms by making this unjustified claim. The difficulty is that there is no absolute standard of inherent interest, and it has been proposed that in some relaxed circumstances with no competing topics, a narrative can be told that is thoroughly banal and ordinary. Given the difficulty of measuring the interest of the narrative or the competing claims, this approach to reportability is itself of limited interest. Yet the concept of the most reportable event is central to the organizational structure of the narrative, as we see later.

One approach to this problem is to turn to a more objective aspect of the narrator's social situation, as developed in Sacks's approach to the insertion of narrative into conversation (1992, Vol. 2, pp. 3–5). In Sacks's approach, the problem is not seen as one of "holding the floor," but rather of controlling the assignment of speaker. For Sacks, a narrative is rarely told as a single turn of talk, because the frequent back channel signals of the addressee are themselves taken as turns of talk. I summarize his discussion as:

> 5.1. Sacks Assignment Theorem: In free conversation, speakers have no control over the assignment of speaker in the second or third turn following their turns, but the performance of the narrative is effectively a claim to return the assignment of speakership to the narrator until the narrative is completed.

This Sacks principle has four implications that lead to a new definition of reportability.

> 5.1.1. Implication 1: Because a narrative requires a series of narrative units longer than the normal turn allows, the successful completion of the narrative requires automatic reassignment of speaker role to the narrator after the following turn of talk if the narrative is not completed in that turn.

> 5.1.2. Implication 2: A narrative must be introduced by a speech act that informs listener that automatic reassignment to the narrator will be required if the narrative is not completed within that stream of speech.

> 5.1.3. Implication 3. Listeners have a reliable means of recognizing the ends of narratives.

> 5.1.4. Implication 4: To be an acceptable social act, a narrative must be accepted as justifying the automatic reassignment of turns to the narrator.

We can now reintroduce a definition of reportability in terms not of the general concept, but of a reportable event in the narrative.

> 5.2. Definition: A *reportable event* is one that justifies the automatic reassignment of speaker role to the narrator.
>
>> 5.2.1. Implication: To be an acceptable social act, a narrative of personal experience must contain at least one reportable event.

It is clear that the reportability of the same event will vary widely depending on the age, experience, cultural patterns of the speakers, and, even more importantly, the immediate social context with its competing claims for reassignment of speakership. The universal principles of interest that underlie this approach to narrative dictate that certain events will almost always carry a high degree of reportability: those dealing with death, sex, and moral indignation. Yet one step outside of these parameters leads us to such a high degree of contextualization of reportability that only a person intimately acquainted with the audience and the recent history of the social situation can be sure of not making a misstep in introducing a narrative. This relativization of reportability does not, however, prevent us from recognizing within a narrative degrees of reportability with some confidence. In fact, the creation of a narrative, and the ensuing narrative structures, are dependent upon the recognition of a unique event that is the most reportable.

> 5.3. Definition: A *most reportable event* is the event that is less common than any other in the narrative and has the greatest effect upon the needs and desires of the participants in the narrative (is evaluated most strongly).

A narrative of personal experience is essentially a narrative of the most reportable event in it. This is normally reflected in the abstract, if there is one. As we will see, the construction of narrative must logically and existentially begin with the decision to report the most reportable event. Narrative 1 is introduced as a narrative about a situation in which Shambaugh was close to dying. The most reportable event in it is that the Norwegian sailor cut Shambaugh's throat. The problem of narrative construction is how to construct a series of events that include in a logical and meaningful way this most reportable event. However, before considering how this is done, we must recognize another dimension, orthogonal to that of reportability. Given the constraints of social situations and the pressure to assert claims to speakership, it is normal for speakers to put forward narratives of the most reportable event in their immediately relevant biography. It follows that:

>> 5.3.1. Implication. The more reportable the most reportable event of a narrative, the greater justification for the automatic reassignment of speaker role to the narrator. This creates the paradox of the next section.

## 6. CREDIBILITY

At the outset, it was pointed out that this approach to narrative is based upon serious and straightforward accounts of events that are asserted to have actually taken place, rather than jokes, tall tales, dreams, or other genres of a less serious nature.[8] The narrative is then heard as an assertion that the events narrated did take place, in roughly a form corresponding to the verbal account. This immediately involves the concept of the credibility of the narrative.

> 6.1. Definition: The *credibility* of a narrative is the extent to which listeners believe that the events described actually occurred in the form described by the narrator.

Remembering that the reportability of an event is related to its frequency, as well as its effects upon the needs and desires of the actors, it follows almost automatically that as reportability increases, credibility decreases. This in fact may be termed the *Reportability Paradox,* which may be stated as a theorem.

> 6.2. Theorem: Reportability is inversely correlated with credibility.

The further understanding of how narrators create narratives, and what structures they erect as they produce them, depends upon an understanding of this paradoxical relation. The next proposition is not an obvious implication, but one that proceeds from the observation of social life. It is limited to "serious" narratives in the sense stated at the beginning of this section and may be relative to various social contexts.

> 6.3. Theorem: A serious narrative that fails to achieve credibility is considered to have failed, and the narrator's claim to reassignment of speakership will then be seen as invalid.

An "invalid claim to reassignment" is a technical way of stating that the narrator has suffered a loss of status, which will affect future claims of this sort as well as other social prerogatives. It is an outcome normally to be avoided.

> 6.3.1. Implication: The more reportable the events of a narrative, the more effort the narrator must devote to establishing credibility.

The nature of that effort must now command our attention.

---

[8]This does not preclude the presence of humorous elements in a narrative that is fundamentally serious: All that counts here is that the narrative is understood as asserting that the events actually took place in roughly the form reported.

## 7. CAUSALITY

Given the fact that the narrator has decided to produce a narrative about the most reportable event, considerations of credibility lead logically and inevitably to the following mechanism of narrative construction:

### 7.1. Theorem: Narrative construction requires a personal theory of causality.

1. The narrator first selects a most reportable event, $e_0$, which the narrative is going to be about.
2. The narrator then selects a prior event, $e_{-1}$, that is the efficient cause of $e_0$, which answers the question about $e_0$: "How did that happen?"
3. The narrator continues the process of Step 2, recursively, until an event $e_{-n}$ is reached for which the question of Step 2 is not appropriate.

The question: "How did that happen?" is not appropriate when the answer is: "Because you should know that that is the kind of thing we always (usually) do." Event $e_{-n}$ is the Orientation or the narrative, more specifically, the behavioral context of the Orientation. In Narrative 1, such orientation is provided by Clause a. Shambaugh need not explain why it came about that he and his shipmates were sitting around a bar drinking: this is the kind of thing that they always do in port, and the listener is assumed to know this.

We have no direct evidence of the actual sequence of Steps 1 through 3; the view of narrative as a folk theory of causality does not rest upon observation. It is a necessary implication of all the definitions and implications of Sections 5 and 6. There are many intricacies and complications in the full description of the options open to the narrator in constructing this causal theory. In the case of Narrative 1, the causal sequence of events reconstructable from the form of Shambaugh's account may be given as follows:

(7.2)
- $e_4$ Orientation: Shambaugh and his shipmates were sitting at a table drinking.
- $e_3$ [For no known reason,] a Norwegian sailor came to complain to Shambaugh about a nonexistent condition.
- $e_2$ [Because there was no basis for the complaint,] Shambaugh rejected the complaint.
- $e_1$ [Because there was nothing further to be said,] Shambaugh turned his back on the sailor.
- $e_0$ [Because Shambaugh had turned his back to the sailor,] the sailor was able to cut Shambaugh's throat.

The causal relations are not given as explicitly in the narrative as in Section 7.2. The causal basis of $e_2$ is given in the word *junk* of (1)c and d; $e_1$ is implied but not stated. The causal link between $e_1$ and $e_0$ is actually given by Shambaugh in a discussion that followed the narrative. The moral he drew from the story is that the next time he shoves someone he will stand up and hit him. Shambaugh's theory of the events is that he got his throat cut because he turned his back on someone who was behaving in an incomprehensible way.

There are many intricate and difficult issues in the reduction of a narrative statement to a causal one, and undoubtedly there will be wide variations in such acts of interpretation. The essential construction is that there is a proposed chain of events linking the orientation to the most reportable event. It will turn out eventually that the selection of the Orientation is a crucial act of interpretation of the stream of events and a necessary step in the next aspect of narrative, the assignment of praise and blame.

## 8. THE ASSIGNMENT OF PRAISE AND BLAME

In Section 7, narrative construction is equivalent to assigning a theory of causality. In accounts of conflict between human actors, or the struggle of human actors against natural forces, the narrator and the audience inevitably assign praise and blame to the actors for the actions involved. The ways in which this is done are too varied to be reduced to a simple set of propositions. They include the use of linguistic devices of mood, factivity and causativity, evaluative lexicon, the insertion of "pseudoevents,"[9] and the wholesale omission of events. Narratives may be *polarizing,* in that the antagonist is viewed as maximally violating social norms and the protagonist maximally conforming to them, or they may be *integrating,* in that blame is set aside or passed over by a variety of devices. The study of how narrators assign praise and blame is a major aspect of narrative analysis that lies beyond the scope of this article.

It may be sufficient at the moment to see that in Narrative 1 the antagonist is assigned to a social type conventionally associated with Scandinavian sailors in port: a large, violent, drunken, and irrational person (see O'Neill, 1956). Shambaugh views himself as a rational being who made a mistake in underestimating the extent of the irrationality of the other.

An understanding of how the underlying events are presented can be obtained from a broader view of the most likely cause of the events involved. The scene in the bar in Buenos Aires reflects a common source of violence in working class society, as reflected in many narratives that I have gathered over the years. The

---

[9]The use of *turn around* in (1)e is one of the many verbs of motion that are used to amplify the degree of activity of a narrator, which do not necessarily involve an observable action.

situation is most clearly analyzed in the following extract from an interview with Joe Dignall, 20, of Liverpool:

> A lot of fellas, if they're with a gang, they let their birds sit with their mates, while he stands at the bar with his mates, talkin' about things. And you could go up, start chattin' this bird up, an' next thing—y'know, you're none the wiser. An' she's edgin' yer on, on, you're a nice fella, you've got a few bob. Great! And—you're chattin' it up there, you're buyin' her a few shorts ... Nex' thing, eh, a fella comin' there over there, "Eh ay lads ... what are ya doin'?" Well *you* don't know he's goin' with her, so you tell *him* to push off. Nex' thing he's got his friends—his mates on to you, an' uh ... you're in lumber! You've either got to run, or fight!

Thus one can see behind these events the possibility that there *was* in fact a woman sitting at the table who had originally come with or been with the Norwegian sailor; that she had joined Shambaugh's group, or that his group had joined her, seeing no connection between her and the Norwegian sailor; that she had stayed to pick up a few drinks or customers; and that the Norwegian sailor had, in his own eyes, a legitimate complaint. The sequence of causal factors from the point of view of the Norwegian sailor would be quite different, and the motivation for his behavior might be less incomprehensible. This is not our problem here, however. It is sufficient to see that Shambaugh has presented a causal sequence beginning with the Orientation (1)a that implements his own causal theory. It is equally clear that if the story had been presented from the *viewpoint* of the Norwegian sailor, a different orientation would have been selected, one considerably earlier in the sequence of events.

The assignment of praise or blame certainly reflects the point of view of the narrator. However, it is not usually a conscious part of the information conveyed by the narrator to the audience; it is rather the ideological framework within which events are viewed. By making that ideology overt, we are departing from the dramatic mechanism that is the essence of the narrative speech event: the transfer of experience from the narrator to the audience. That experience is certainly colored by the moral stance taken by the narrator. One might think that those who take the same moral stance will be more impressed by the narrative than those who do not and therefore find it more credible as well as more interesting and engaging. So far, it appears that this is true only to a limited extent. Shambaugh's narrative appears to have an equal impact on those who accept his point of view and those who find him insensitive to the social reality around him. The effect of the narrative in transferring experience is relatively independent of the narrator's assignment of praise and blame. Through one means or another, the narrator induces the audience to see the world through the narrator's eyes.

## 9. VIEWPOINT

In trying to understand how experience is transferred from the narrator to the audience, we encounter the most characteristic feature of narratives of personal experience, the particular point of view or viewpoint from which the action is seen.

> 9.1. Definition: The *viewpoint* of a narrative clause is the spatio–temporal domain from which the information conveyed by the clause could be obtained by an observer.

One feature of oral narratives of personal experience that distinguishes them most sharply from literary narrative is that in literature one can switch viewpoints, take an impersonal viewpoint, and enter into the consciousness of any or all of the actors. In oral narratives of personal experience there is only one option. The events are seen through the eyes of the narrator.

> 9.2. Finding: The viewpoint in oral narratives of personal experience is that of the narrator at the time of the events referred to.

This finding applies consistently to all the narrative and free clauses in the narrative. It applies to all of the clauses of Narrative 1, which are consistently an account of events as they become known to Shambaugh.

> 9.2.1. Implication: The temporal sequence of events in oral narratives of personal experience follows the order in which the events became known to the narrator.

In literary narrative, it is not uncommon for the viewpoint to shift to give information about events that occurred at an earlier point in time. Classically, this is expressed as a *flashback:* "Meanwhile, back at the farm ... ." It is an empirical finding of some weight that flashbacks are not used in the type of narrative that we are dealing with here.

> 9.2.2. Finding: There are no flashbacks in oral narratives of personal experience.

The *no flashback condition* holds for a very large number of narratives of personal experience that have been collected and studied over the years. In Narrative 1, Shambaugh's throat is cut without him realizing it. We do not learn that this has happened until Shambaugh learns of it. One can easily construct a plausible narrative in which the opposite technique is used. For example: "The next thing I know I'm lying on the floor, blood all over me. He had pulled a knife and cut me before I knew what happened. A guy told me, says ... ." Yet no such examples have been found. The past perfect is used, but only to report events that the narrator knew at the time they are reported. Perhaps examples will be found if the search continues long enough, but at this time it seems to be an empirical fact that the no flashback condition is binding on oral narratives of personal experience.

## 10. OBJECTIVITY

Among the thousands of personal narratives that have been recorded and studied over the past few decades, we find a great deal of variability in the degree of objectivity. L&W presented a scale of the objectivity of evaluative statements that ranged from reports of internal emotions to observations of material objects and events.

In general, we find that narratives of upper-middle-class, university-educated speakers tend to report on the narrators' emotions. In contrast, many working-class narrators are sparing in their reporting of subjective feelings. It was somewhat surprising to me to find that the "subjectivity" characteristic of middle-class speakers is considered a positive quality by therapeutically oriented writers, and people who do not report their emotions in narratives of bereavement, for example, are considered to be suffering from an impairment of normal and desirable abilities. My own experience in retelling narratives of various experiences indicates a somewhat different scale of values. Those narratives that have the greatest impact upon audiences in the sense outlined previously—that seize the attention of listeners and allow them to share the experience of the narrator—are those that use the most objective means of expression. To follow this argument more exactly, some definitions are required.

> 10.1. Definition: An *objective event* is one that became known to the narrator through sense experience. A *subjective event* is one that the narrator became aware of through memory, emotional reaction, or internal sensation.

The general observation that narratives that report experience objectively are more effective than those that report subjectively is not a strongly evidentiary statement; no hard data supports it. Nevertheless, some experimental evidence supports the belief that objectivity increases credibility.

> 10.2. Theorem: Because it is generally agreed that the narrators' observations can be affected by their internal states, reports of objective events are more credible than reports of subjective events.

To explore the many ways in which objective and subjective approaches to narrative differ would go beyond the scope of this brief summary. The clauses of Narrative

1 are entirely objective. At no point are there any statements that describe how the actors felt. We are told what they said and what they did. The concluding statements of (1)j,k are those of a third-person witness to the events, more objective than any statements of the main actors. It is proposed here that this objectivity is a necessary condition for the capacity of narratives like this to transmit experience to the audience. To develop this point clearly, a further implication may be drawn from the finding in Section 9.2:

> 10.3. Theorem: The transfer of experience of an event to listeners occurs to the extent that they become aware of it "as if" it were their own experience.

The *as-if condition* may be expanded to mean that listeners achieve awareness of the event in the same way that the narrator became aware of it. The essential no flashback condition follows immediately from this condition. If Theorem 10.3 holds, two consequences immediately follow to mark the limits of the transfer of experience in personal narrative:

> 10.3.1. Implication: The transfer of experience from narrator to audience is limited, because the verbal account gives only a small fraction of the information that the narrator received through sight, sound, and other senses.[10]

> 10.3.2. Implication: To the extent that narrators add subjective reports of their emotions to the description of an objective event, listeners become aware of that event as if it were the narrator's experience and not their own.

These two implications lead to a further proposition that is more than an implication. It combines the experience derived from retelling stories and observations of social class differences in narrative structure with the logic of 10.3.1–2 to derive the following theorem:

> 10.3.3. Theorem: The objectivity of the description of an event is a necessary condition for the transfer of experience in personal narrative.

There is more than a hint of a paradox here. The transfer of experience is a subjective phenomenon, which is not easy to observe or measure. The theorem argues that this

---

[10] In Sacks's (1992) view, listeners are not in fact entitled to the experience of the narrator; it cannot become "their" experience (Vol. II, pp. 242–248). Although no one can doubt Sacks's fundamental insight that experience cannot be transferred as easily as information, this article's take is based on the empirical finding that some degree of experience is in fact transferred.

subjective experience is obtainable only through the objective presentation of events.

## 11. RESOLUTION

In the L&W treatment, the resolution of a narrative was simply the ending or outcome; there was no very precise way of distinguishing it from the last complicating action. However, this situation is sharply altered with the introduction of the most reportable action as a structural unit in Section 5. The resolution can be seen to be logically the series of complicating actions that follow rather than precede $e_0$.

11.1. Definition: The resolution of a personal narrative is the set of complicating actions that follow the most reportable event.

In Narrative 1, there appears to be no distinct resolution section. At first glance, the narrative ends with the most reportable event, so that the resolution coincides with the $e_0$. Yet closer examination shows that (1)j,k is not the most reportable event, but a report of the most reportable event, which itself is implied rather than reported. Is it then a resolution?

L&W defined the coda as the clause or clauses that bring the narrative back to the time of telling, so that the question: "What happened then?" is no longer appropriate. This does not mean that the listener is automatically satisfied with all of the information given on the outcome of the most reportable event. If a resolution is not satisfactory in this respect, the listener will have the impression that the narrative is incomplete. I have probed a number of audiences for their reaction to Narrative 1 on this point, and the consensus seems to be that the narrative does come to an end. Shambaugh stopped talking. I then asked a question, and in a series of exchanges I learned that the Norwegian sailor's knife had cut his throat but missed the jugular vein; that Shambaugh, in fact, had the knife upstairs in his room; that one of his friends had hit the Norwegian sailor with a chair; and that the blow had killed him. These facts are interesting, and their absence from the narrative throws light on Shambaugh's approach to the matter. However, they do not form part of the narrative as it is now constituted, and we must infer that (1)j,k is indeed its resolution.

## 12. CONCLUSION

The L&W analysis introduced the definition of narrative as a technique of reporting past events through temporal juncture and established a basis for the understanding of the temporal organization and evaluation of narrative. This article explores further the concept of reportability, arguing that the most reportable event is the semantic and structural pivot on which the narrative is organized. Given an initial inverse relation between credibility and reportability, it follows that narrators who command the attention and interest of their audience will normally maximize credibility by the objective reporting of events.

The second half of this contribution focuses upon the capacity of a narrative to transfer the experience of the narrator to the audience. This capacity is seen to depend upon the unique and defining property of personal narrative that events are experienced as they first became known to the narrator. It is proposed that the transfer of experience of an event to listeners occurs to the extent that they become aware of it as if it were their own experience. It follows that this is only possible if the narrator reports events as objective experience without reference to the narrator's emotional reactions.

It is also proposed that a narrative can be viewed as a theory of the causes of the most reportable event, so that the crucial interpretive act is the location of the orientation as the situation that does not require an explicit cause. The chain of causal events selected in the narrative is intimately linked with the assignment of praise and blame for the actions reported. This view of narrative as a theory of moral behavior and the narrator as an exponent of cultural norms will be pursued in later publications.

## REFERENCES

Labov, W. (1966). *The social stratification of English in New York City.* Washington, DC: Center for Applied Linguistics.

Labov, W. (1972). *Language in the inner city.* Philadelphia: University of Pennsylvania Press.

Labov, W. (1981). Speech actions and reactions in personal narrative. In D. Tannen (Ed.), *Analyzing discourse: Text and talk. Georgetown University Round Table* (pp. 217–247). Washington, DC: Georgetown University Press.

Labov, W., Cohen, P., Robins, C., & Lewis, J. (1968). *A study of the non-standard English of Negro and Puerto Rican speakers in New York City* (Cooperative Research Rep. 3288, Vols. I & II). Philadelphia: University of Pennsylvania, Linguistics Laboratory, U.S. Regional Survey.

Labov, W., & Fanshel, D. (1977). *Therapeutic discourse: Psychotherapy as conversation.* New York: Academic.

Labov, W., & Waletzky, J. (this issue). Narrative analysis: Oral versions of personal experience. In J. Helm (Ed.), *Essays on the verbal and visual arts: Proceedings of the 1966 Annual Spring Meeting of the American Ethnological Society* (pp. 12–44). Seattle: University of Washington Press. (Original work published 1967)

O'Neill, E. (1956). *Long day's journey into night.* New Haven, CT: Yale University Press.

Sacks, H. (1992). *Lectures on conversation* (Vols. I & II). Cambridge, England: Blackwell.

# DYNAMICS AND INDETERMINISM IN DEVELOPMENTAL AND SOCIAL PROCESSES

edited by
**Alan Fogel**
*University of Utah*
**Maria C.D.P. Lyra**
*Federal University of Pernambuco, Brazil*
**Jaan Valsiner**
*University of North Carolina, Chapel Hill*

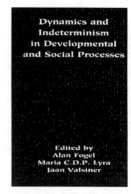

One of the most profound insights of the dynamic systems perspective is that new structures resulting from the developmental process do not need to be planned in advance, nor is it necessary to have these structures represented in genetic or neurological templates prior to their emergence. Rather, new structures can emerge as components of the individual and the environment self-organize; that is, as they mutually constrain each other's actions, new patterns and structures may arise. This theoretical possibility brings into developmental theory the important concept of indeterminism — the possibility that developmental outcomes may not be predictable in any simple linear causal way from their antecedents.

This is the first book to take a critical and serious look at the role of indeterminism in psychological and behavioral development.
- What is the source of this indeterminism?
- What is its role in developmental change?
- Is it merely the result of incomplete observational data or error in measurement?

As such, it reviews the concepts of indeterminism and determinism in their historical, philosophical, and theoretical perspectives — particularly in relation to dynamic systems thinking — and applies these general ideas to systems of non-verbal communication. Stressing the indeterminacy inherent to symbols and meaning making in social systems, several chapters address the issue of indeterminism from metaphorical, modeling, and narrative perspectives. Others discuss those indeterministic processes within the individual related to emotional, social, and cognitive development.

**Contents:** Editor's Introduction. **Part I:** *Determinacy and Indeterminacy: Theoretical and Philosophical Perspectives.* **B. Hopkins, P. Beek,** Determinism and Development: An Historical Overview. **P. van Geert,** Que Sera, Sera: Determinism and Non-linear Dynamic Model Building in Development. **A. Gulerce,** Change in the Process of Change: Coping with Indeterminism. **A. Fogel, A. Branco,** Meta-communication as a Source of Indeterminism in Relationships. **M.C.D.P. Lyra, T. Winegar,** Proccesual Dynamics of Interaction Through Time: Adult-Child Interactions and the Process of Development. **G. Butterworth,** Commentary on Part I. **Part II:** *Theoretical Approaches to Peer Interaction Processes.* **Z.M.R. de Oliveira, J. Valsiner,** Play and Imagination: The Psychological Construction of Novelty. **M.I.P.C. Pedrosa, A.M.A. Carvalho, A.I. Hamburger,** From Disordered to Ordered Movement: Attractor Configuration and Development. **A.L. Smolka, M.C. Goes, A. Pino,** (In)determinacy and Semiotic Constitution of Subjectivity. **C. Lightfoot, G. Litvinovic,** Commentaries on Part II. **Part III:** *Theoretical Approaches to Individual Developmental Processes.* **M. Lewis,** Personality Self-Organization: Cascading Constraints on Cognition-Emotion Interaction. **A. Roazzi, B. Souza,** Determinism and Indeterminism: Science and Cognitive Science. **M. Legerstee,** Changes in Social-conceptual Development: Domain Specific Structures, Self-organization and Indeterminism. **H. Hurme, H. Kojima,** Commentaries on Part III.
0-8058-1805-7 [cloth] / 1997 / 304pp. / $59.95
0-8058-1806-5 [paper] / 1997 / 304pp. / $29.95

Prices subject to
change without notice.

**Lawrence Erlbaum Associates, Inc.**
10 Industrial Avenue, Mahwah, NJ 07430
201/236-9500   FAX 201/236-0072

**Call toll-free to order: 1-800-9-BOOKS-9**...9am to 5pm EST only.
e-mail to: orders@erlbaum.com
visit LEA's web site at http://www.erlbaum.com

# NUIT BLANCHE ÉDITEUR
## PRESENTS
### « LANGUE ET PRATIQUES DISCURSIVES »

A NEW COLLECTION IN LINGUISTICS AND DISCOURSE

*Autour de la narration.*
*Les abords du récit conversationnel*
directed by Marty LAFOREST
with contributions of : Antoine Auchlin,
Ulrich Dausendschön-Gay, Martina Drescher,
Ulrich Krafft, Marty Laforest, Jacques Moeschler
and Diane Vincent

176 p.              23,95 $ CDN

*Le discours rapporté*
*au quotidien*
by Diane VINCENT
and Sylvie DUBOIS

150 p.              23,95 $ CDN

Please send me :

\_\_\_\_\_ *Autour de la narration*
\_\_\_\_\_ *Le discours rapporté au quotidien*

Name ........................................................................................................
Address ........................................................................................................
........................................................................................................

Mail coupon and check\money order to :
Nuit blanche éditeur, 1026, St-Jean Street, room 403, Quebec, Canada, G1R 1R7

VISA accepted
Card number ........................................................................................................
Expiration date ........................................................................................................
Signature ........................................................................................................

E-mail orders are accepted at this address : guy.champagne@creliq.ulaval.ca

# THE FRAGILE COMMUNITY
## Living Together with AIDS
**Mara B. Adelman**
*Seattle University*
**Lawrence R. Frey**
*Loyola University*
A VOLUME IN THE EVERYDAY COMMUNICATION SERIES

This book examines the concept of "community," focusing on how communication practices help manage the tensions of creating and sustaining everyday communal life amidst the crisis of human loss. While acknowledging how the contradictory and inconsistent nature of human relationships inevitably affects community, this intimate and compelling text shows how community is created and sustained in concrete communication practices.

The authors explore these ideas at Bonaventure House, an award-winning residential facility for people with AIDS, where the web of social relationships and the demands of a life-threatening illness intersect in complex ways. Facing a life-threatening illness can defy meaningful social connections, but it can also inspire such ties, sometimes in ways that elude us in the course of daily life. By understanding how collective communication practices help residents forge a sense of community out of the fragility and chaos of living together with AIDS, we are able to better understand how communication is inexorably intertwined with the formation of community in other environments.

Based on seven years of ethnographic research including participant-observation, in-depth interviews, and questionnaires, this book weaves together narratives and visual images with conceptual analysis to uncover the ongoing oppositional forces of community life, and to show how both mundane and profound communication processes ameliorate these tensions, and thereby sustain this fragile community. Because the average length of stay for a resident is seven months — in which time he or she moves from being a newcomer to a community member to someone the community remembers — the text reflects this short, but crystallized life, starting with the day a new resident opens the door to the day he or she passes away.

The writing is very rich — intimate, engaging, personal, compelling, and vivid. The stories told discuss such deeply personal topics as the dilemmas of romantic relationships in a context fraught with many perils; issues of power, authority, and control that enable and constrain social life; and communicative practices that help residents cope with bereavement over the loss of others as well as their own impending deaths. The text concludes by examining the lessons learned from Bonaventure House about creating and sustaining a health community, and serves as an inspiration for strengthening interpersonal relationships and communities in other environments.

**Contents:** Editors' Preface. Acknowledgments. The Search for Community. The Fragility of Place: The Entry Experience. The Fragility of Relationship: The Social Dynamics of Everyday Life. The Fragility of Loss: Coping With Death and Bereavement. Epilogue: Stability Amidst the Fragility.
0-8058-1843-X [cloth] / 1996 / 136pp. / $32.50
**0-8058-1844-8 [paper] / 1996 / 136pp. / $16.50**

Prices subject to
change without notice.

**Lawrence Erlbaum Associates, Inc.**
10 Industrial Avenue, Mahwah, NJ 07430
201/236-9500   FAX 201/236-0072

**Call toll-free to order: 1-800-9-BOOKS-9**...9am to 5pm EST only.
e-mail to: orders@erlbaum.com
visit LEA's web site at http://www.erlbaum.com

# PRETEND PLAY AS IMPROVISATION
## Conversation in the Preschool Classroom
### R. Keith Sawyer
#### University of California, Santa Cruz

Everyday conversations including gossip, boasting, flirting, teasing, and informative discussions are highly creative, improvised interactions. Children's play is also an important, often improvisational activity. One of the most improvisational games among three- to five-year-old children is social pretend play — also called fantasy play, sociodramatic play, or role play. Children's imaginations have free reign during pretend play. Conversations in these play episodes are far more improvisational than the average adult conversation. Because pretend play occurs in a dramatized, fantasy world, it is less constrained by social and physical reality.

This book adds to our understanding of preschoolers' pretend play by examining it in the context of a theory of improvisational performance genres. This theory, derived from in-depth analyses of the implicit and explicit rules of theatrical improvisation, proves to generalize to pretend play as well. The two genres share several characteristics:

- There is no script; they are created in the moment.
- There are loose outlines of structure which guide the performance.
- They are collective; no one person decides what will happen. Because group improvisational genres are collective and unscripted, improvisational creativity is a collective social process.

The pretend play literature states that this improvisational behavior is most prevalent during the same years that many other social and cognitive skills are developing. Children between the ages of three and five begin to develop representations of their own and others' mental states as well as learn to represent and construct narratives. Freudian psychologists and other personality theorists have identified these years as critical in the development of the personality. The author believes that if we can demonstrate that children's improvisational abilities develop during these years — and that their fantasy improvisations become more complex and creative — it might suggest that these social skills are linked to the child's developing ability to improvise with other creative performers.

**Contents:** Introduction: Play as Improvisational Performance. Play and Conversation. An Improvisational Theory of Children's Play. Studying Pretend Play in the Preschool Classroom. Performance Style and Performances. Joining the Performance: The Metapragmatics of Play Entry. The Improvisational Exchange: Using Metapragmatic Strategies to Negotiate the Play Frame. The Performance of Play: Children's Group Improvisations. Improvisation and Development.
0-8058-2119-8 [cloth] / 1997 / 232pp. / $39.95
**Special Prepaid Offer! $22.50
No further discounts apply.**
Prices subject to change without notice.

### Lawrence Erlbaum Associates, Inc.
10 Industrial Avenue, Mahwah, NJ 07430
201/236-9500   FAX 201/236-0072

Call toll-free to order: 1-800-9-BOOKS-9...9am to 5pm EST only.
e-mail to: orders@erlbaum.com
visit LEA's web site at http://www.erlbaum.com

# NARRATIVE DEVELOPMENT
## Six Approaches
edited by
**Michael Bamberg**
*Clark University*

Based on a recent symposium sponsored by the International Society of the Study of Behavioral Development (ISSBD), this book discusses the basic assumptions that led the contributors to conduct research in the field of narrative development. This collection gathers their research reflections and varying approaches to narrative and its development. It illustrates each type of approach and highlights their respective motives. The book presents some of the basic motivating assumptions of each approach and provides insight into what holds each set of assumptions together, potentially transforming them into actions.

The editor has organized this volume in accordance with the six main points of the symposium:

- **Specification of the Domain** — how narratives are defined in terms of textual structures, knowledge thereof, interactive moves, sociocultural conventions, and the like.
- **The Individual's Involvement in the Developmental Process** — the relationship between some internal or external forces and the organism's own active participation in the developmental process.
- **The Course of Development** — if it is continuous or discontinuous; whether it proceeds in an additive fashion or whether regressive phases occur; and what changes at different points in the developmental process signify.
- **The Goal of Development** — the implicit notion of a telos, a target or endpoint that needs to occur in the developmental process.
- **Mechanisms of Development** — the forces and/or conditions that both instigate the developmental process and keep it moving toward its telos.
- **Methodology** — where and how to look in the establishment of a developmental framework.

The contributors approach narrative development from six different angles — cognitive, interactionist, linguistic/constructivist, crosslinguistic, sociocultural/interpretive, and life-span. Their work samples the research traditions widely and extracts individual aspects that are claimed to be central to the topics of "narrative" and "development." An indispensable text in the fields of narrative and/or discourse, linguistics, language studies, psychology, and education in general, this book will be useful for students and teachers alike.

0-8058-2057-4 [cloth] / 1997 / 288pp. / $59.95
**0-8058-2058-2 [paper] / 1997 / 288pp. / $29.95**

Lawrence Erlbaum Associates, Inc.
10 Industrial Avenue, Mahwah, NJ 07430
201/236-9500   FAX 201/236-0072

Prices subject to change without notice.

**Call toll-free to order: 1-800-9-BOOKS-9**...9am to 5pm EST only.
e-mail to: orders@erlbaum.com
visit LEA's web site at http://www.erlbaum.com